Better Homes and Gardens®

BIGGEST BOOK OF EASY CANNED SOUP RECIPES

Meredith® Books
Des Moines, Iowa

BIGGEST BOOK OF EASY CANNED SOUP RECIPES

Editor: Carrie E. Holcomb
Contributing Designer: Joyce DeWitt
Cover Designer: Daniel Pelavin
Contributing Editors: Tricia Laning, Winifred Moranville, Spectrum
  Communication Services, Inc.
Copy Chief: Terri Fredrickson
Copy and Production Editor: Victoria Forlini
Editorial Operations Manager: Karen Schirm
Managers, Book Production: Pam Kvitne, Marjorie J. Schenkelberg, Rick von Holdt,
  Mark Weaver
Recipe Developers: Tami Leonard, Shelli McConnell, Marcia Stanley
Contributing Copy Editor: Susan Fagan
Contributing Proofreaders: Gretchen Kauffman, Susan J. Kling, Donna Segal
Indexer: Elizabeth Parson
Editorial Assistant: Cheryl Eckert
Test Kitchen Director: Lynn Blanchard
Test Kitchen Product Supervisor: Marilyn Cornelius
Test Kitchen Home Economists: Juliana Hale; Laura Harms, R.D.;
  Jennifer Kalinowski, R.D.; Maryellyn Krantz; Jill Moberly;
  Colleen Weeden; Lori Wilson

Meredith® Books
Editor in Chief: Linda Raglan Cunningham
Design Director: Matt Strelecki
Managing Editor: Gregory H. Kayko
Executive Editor: Jennifer Dorland Darling

Publisher: James D. Blume
Executive Director, Marketing: Jeffrey Meyers
Executive Director, New Business Development: Todd M. Davis
Executive Director, Sales: Ken Zagor
Director, Operations: George A. Susral
Director, Production: Douglas M. Johnston
Business Director: Jim Leonard

Vice President and General Manager: Douglas J. Guendel

Better Homes and Gardens® Magazine
Editor in Chief: Karol DeWulf Nickell
Deputy Editor, Food and Entertaining: Nancy Hopkins

Meredith Publishing Group
President, Publishing Group: Stephen M. Lacy
Vice President-Publishing Director: Bob Mate

Meredith Corporation
Chairman and Chief Executive Officer: William T. Kerr

In Memoriam: E. T. Meredith III (1933-2003)

Our Better Homes and Gardens®
Test Kitchen seal on the back cover
of this book assures you that every
recipe in *Biggest Book of Easy Canned
Soup Recipes* has been tested in the
Better Homes and Gardens® Test
Kitchen. This means that each recipe
is practical and reliable, and meets our
high standards of taste appeal. We
guarantee your satisfaction with this
book for as long as you own it.

All of us at Meredith® Books are dedicated to providing you with the information and ideas
you need to create delicious foods. We welcome your comments and suggestions. Write
to us at: Meredith Books, Cookbook Editorial Department, 1716 Locust St., Des Moines, IA
50309-3023.

If you would like to purchase any of our cooking, crafts, gardening, home improvement,
or home decorating and design books, check wherever quality books are sold.
Or visit us at: **bhgbooks.com**

TABLE OF CONTENTS

INTRODUCTION

In the 1950s edition of the *Better Homes and Gardens New Cook Book*, our editors enthused, "There's many a trick between the can opener and dinner that can make a hurry-up meal a really good meal." Since then, canned soup has emerged as top shortcut strategy for bringing delicious, satisfying meals to the family table in a hurry.

Nowadays, cooking with canned soup is not only easy—it's exciting. With so many different kinds of canned soups available today, plus our ever-growing craving for more dynamic and worldly flavors, it's no wonder we've come up with so many terrific recipes—nearly 400, in fact—that can be jump-started by pulling out the can opener.

Go ahead—dig into your old-time favorites, including casseroles, soups, stews, potpies, noodle bakes, oven meals, skillet suppers, side dishes, and more. Your family will love the simple, home-style appeal of these sure-to-please meals.

But don't stop there! When you're in the mood for something new, you'll find plenty of surprises, including Mexican, Thai, Chinese, Hungarian, and Italian specialties too. We've also included a bonus chapter of recipes that call on other convenience products—from frozen meatballs to sauce mixes and refrigerated breads—to help you get a head start on all kinds of foods for all sorts of occasions.

Enjoy our all-time biggest book of canned soup recipes—and enjoy the extra time these shortcut strategies will save you each day.

The Editors

APPETIZERS & SNACKS

1

You just can't go wrong with this tried-and-true crowd-pleasing dip. It's simple to make and sure to satisfy.

QUICK CHILE CON QUESO DIP

START TO FINISH:

10 minutes

MAKES:

*3 cups dip
(12 appetizer servings)*

1   16-ounce jar salsa (1¾ cups)

1   11-ounce can condensed nacho cheese soup

½   cup chopped green sweet pepper

     Tortilla chips

     Milk (optional)

1 Place salsa in a medium microwave-safe bowl; cover with vented plastic wrap. Cook on 100% power (high) 1 to 3 minutes or until salsa is hot, stirring once.

2 Stir in nacho cheese soup. Cover with vented plastic wrap. Microwave on high for 1 to 2 minutes more or until soup is combined with the salsa and mixture is heated through, stirring once. Stir in sweet pepper.

3 Serve with tortilla chips. (If mixture becomes too thick upon standing, stir in a small amount of milk.)

Nutrition Facts per ¼ cup dip: 42 cal., 2 g total fat (1 g sat. fat), 3 mg chol., 336 mg sodium, 5 g carbo., 1 g fiber, 2 g pro.

SAUCEPAN METHOD: In a medium saucepan heat salsa until hot. Reduce heat to low. Add nacho cheese soup. Cook and stir until mixture is smooth. Stir in sweet pepper. Serve as directed in step 3.

If you're looking for variety when hosting a party, consider this dip. Its spright, fresh flavors will complement heavier, more cheesy options.

BLACK BEAN SALSA DIP

1	15-ounce can black beans, rinsed and drained
1	11-ounce can condensed black bean soup
¾	cup bottled salsa
½	cup chopped red or yellow sweet pepper
½	teaspoon ground cumin
2	medium tomatoes, seeded and chopped
1	medium avocado, halved, seeded, peeled, and chopped
2	tablespoons snipped fresh cilantro (optional)
	Tortilla chips

1 In a medium bowl stir together black beans, black bean soup, salsa, sweet pepper, and cumin. Spread in the bottom of a 9-inch pie plate. Cover and chill for at least 2 hours or up to 24 hours.

2 Before serving, sprinkle with tomatoes. Top with avocado and, if desired, cilantro. Serve with tortilla chips.

Nutrition Facts per ¼ cup dip: 74 cal., 2 g total fat (0 g sat. fat), 0 mg chol., 378 mg sodium, 12 g carbo., 5 g fiber, 4 g pro.

PREP:
15 minutes

CHILL:
2 to 24 hours

MAKES:
*3 cups dip
(12 appetizer servings)*

Few hot party dips are easier—and few will disappear more quickly—than this fantastic, four-ingredient crowd-pleaser.

SUPER SIMPLE BEAN DIP

PREP:

10 minutes

COOK:

*3$^1/_2$ to 4 hours
(low-heat setting)*

MAKES:

*about 5$^1/_2$ cups
(about 22 appetizer servings)*

2   16-ounce cans refried beans

1   11-ounce can condensed nacho cheese soup

$^1/_2$ cup bottled salsa

$^1/_4$ cup sliced green onions

Tortilla chips

1 In a 1$^1/_2$-quart slow cooker combine refried beans, nacho cheese soup, and salsa. Cover and cook for 3$^1/_2$ to 4 hours.

2 Sprinkle with green onions. Serve dip with tortilla chips.

*NOTE: Some 1$^1/_2$-quart slow cookers include variable heat setting; others offer only one standard (low) setting. The 1$^1/_2$-quart slow cooker recipes in this book were only tested on the low-heat setting, if one was present.

Nutrition Facts per $^1/_4$ cup dip: 53 cal., 1 g total fat (0 g sat. fat), 2 mg chol., 330 mg sodium, 8 g carbo., 2 g fiber, 3 g pro.

*

Fresh, sweet onions caramelized to a mellow golden brown give this gourmet version of onion dip the edge!

FRENCH ONION DIP

2	tablespoons butter or margarine
1½	cups chopped sweet onions (such as Vidalia, Maui, or Walla Walla)
1	10¾-ounce can condensed cream of onion soup
¼	teaspoon coarsely ground black pepper
⅛	teaspoon cayenne pepper
4	teaspoons snipped fresh chives
	Potato or tortilla chips, and/or baby carrots

1 In a large skillet melt butter over medium heat. Add onions; cook for 10 to 15 minutes or until tender and golden, stirring occasionally. Cool.

2 In a blender container or food processor bowl combine cooked onions, cream of onion soup, black pepper, and cayenne pepper. Cover and blend or process until nearly smooth.

3 Transfer to a small bowl. Stir in chives. Cover and chill for at least 1 hour or up to 24 hours. Serve with potato chips.

Nutrition Facts per ¼ cup dip: 96 cal., 6 g total fat (3 g sat. fat), 17 mg chol., 429 mg sodium, 9 g carbo., 1 g fiber, 2 g pro.

PREP:
25 minutes

CHILL:
1 to 24 hours

MAKES:
*about 1½ cups dip
(about 6 appetizer servings)*

Big game on tonight? Get the drinks chilling in the fridge and have these ingredients ready to go for a sports bar-style dip that can be ready in less time than it takes to drive to a sports bar.

ITALIAN ARTICHOKE DIP

START TO FINISH:

15 minutes

MAKES:

*3 cups dip
(12 appetizer servings)*

2   14-ounce cans artichoke hearts, drained
     and coarsely chopped

1   10¾-ounce can condensed cream of chicken
     or cream of mushroom soup

1   teaspoon dried Italian seasoning, crushed

¼   cup grated Parmesan cheese (1 ounce)

2   green onions, sliced

¼   teaspoon crushed red pepper

     Red sweet pepper wedges or crackers

1 In a medium saucepan combine artichoke hearts, cream of chicken soup, and Italian seasoning. Cook and stir over medium heat until heated through. Remove from heat.

2 Stir in Parmesan cheese, green onions, and crushed red pepper. Serve warm or at room temperature with sweet pepper wedges.

Nutrition Facts per ¼ cup dip: 54 cal., 2 g total fat (1 g sat. fat), 3 mg chol., 430 mg sodium, 6 g carbo., 2 g fiber, 2 g pro.

A duo of colorful veggies replaces the spinach in typical artichoke dip, and a can of soup makes this party favorite easier than ever. Enjoy!

VEGGIE ARTICHOKE DIP

2   14-ounce cans artichoke hearts, drained
    and coarsely chopped

1   10¾-ounce can condensed cream of chicken soup

1   cup coarsely shredded carrots

¾   cup finely shredded Parmesan cheese (3 ounces)

½   cup small broccoli florets

1   tablespoon Dijon-style mustard

    Assorted crackers or bagel chips

PREP:

15 minutes

BAKE:

25 minutes

MAKES:

*about 4 cups dip
(about 8 servings)*

1 In a large bowl combine artichoke hearts, cream of chicken soup, carrots, ½ cup of the Parmesan cheese, broccoli, and mustard; mix well. Transfer to a 9-inch pie plate; sprinkle with remaining ¼ cup cheese.

2 Bake, uncovered, in a 350°F oven about 25 minutes or until heated through. Serve with crackers.

Nutrition Facts per ½ cup dip: 113 cal., 5 g total fat (2 g sat. fat), 9 mg chol., 770 mg sodium, 10 g carbo., 4 g fiber, 6 g pro.

Here's a creamy, colorful dip that few people can resist. If you like, you can serve it with assorted cut-up vegetables too.

CONFETTI SPINACH DIP

START TO FINISH:

20 minutes

MAKES:

*3¹/₂ cups dip
(14 appetizer servings)*

2   10-ounce packages frozen chopped spinach, thawed and well drained

1   10³/₄-ounce can condensed cream of onion soup

1   3-ounce package cream cheese, cut up

1   clove garlic, minced

¹/₄   teaspoon salt

¹/₈   teaspoon cayenne pepper

¹/₂   cup chopped red sweet pepper

1   8-ounce can sliced water chestnuts, drained and chopped

Flatbread, crackers, or toasted baguette slices

1 In a medium saucepan combine spinach, cream of onion soup, cream cheese, garlic, salt, and cayenne pepper. Cook over medium heat about 5 minutes or until cream cheese is melted and mixture is heated through, stirring frequently. Stir in sweet pepper and water chestnuts.

2 Serve warm with flatbread.

Nutrition Facts per ¹/₄ cup dip: 61 cal., 3 g total fat (2 g sat. fat), 10 mg chol., 256 mg sodium, 7 g carbo., 2 g fiber, 2 g pro.

The inspiration for this recipe is a famous Greek dip called skordalia. For a Mediterranean-themed appetizer spread, serve this with a variety of imported olives, salamis, and cheeses.

WHITE BEAN & DRIED TOMATO DIP

1	15-ounce can white kidney beans (cannellini beans), rinsed and drained
1	10¾-ounce can condensed cream of potato soup
1½	teaspoons finely shredded lemon peel
1	cup sliced green onions
2	cloves garlic, minced
1	tablespoon olive oil
¼	cup oil-packed dried tomatoes, drained and finely snipped
½	teaspoon dried oregano, crushed
1	recipe Toasted Pita Wedges (recipe on page 14)

1 In a food processor bowl or blender container combine beans, cream of potato soup, and lemon peel. Cover and process or blend until nearly smooth; set aside.

2 In a large skillet cook green onions and garlic in hot oil until tender. Remove from heat. Stir in bean mixture, dried tomatoes, and oregano. Serve with Toasted Pita Wedges.

MAKE-AHEAD DIRECTIONS: Prepare dip and Toasted Pita Wedges as directed. Cover and chill dip for up to 24 hours. Store pita wedges in an airtight container for up to 5 days. Let dip stand at room temperature for 30 minutes before serving.

Nutrition Facts per ¼ cup dip and 6 pita wedges: 181 cal., 4 g total fat (1 g sat. fat), 3 mg chol., 569 mg sodium, 31 g carbo., 4 g fiber, 6 g pro.

START TO FINISH:

20 minutes

MAKES:

*about 2 cups dip
(about 8 appetizer servings)*

Flag the Toasted Pita Wedges recipe below! Those little bites are great to serve with all kinds of dips, as well as with soups and salads.

GARLIC & SPINACH DIP WITH TOASTED PITA WEDGES

START TO FINISH:

20 minutes

MAKES:

*about 2 cups dip
(about 8 appetizer servings)*

1	10¾-ounce can condensed cream of mushroom soup with roasted garlic
1	10-ounce package frozen chopped spinach, thawed and well drained
½	cup shredded carrot
⅛	teaspoon cayenne pepper
¼	cup milk (optional)
1	recipe Toasted Pita Wedges or tortilla chips

1 In a medium saucepan stir together cream of mushroom soup with roasted garlic, spinach, carrot, and cayenne pepper. Cook and stir over medium heat until heated through. If necessary, stir in milk to make dipping consistency.

2 Transfer to a serving dish. Serve with Toasted Pita Wedges.

TOASTED PITA WEDGES: Split 4 pita bread rounds in half horizontally; cut each half into 6 wedges. Place wedges, cut sides up, in a single layer on 2 ungreased baking sheets. Bake in a 375°F oven for 7 to 9 minutes or until light brown. Store in an airtight container for up to 5 days.

Nutrition Facts per ¼ cup dip and 6 pita wedges: 134 cal., 3 g total fat (1 g sat. fat), 0 mg chol., 476 mg sodium, 21 g carbo., 2 g fiber, 4 g pro.

Your guests will feel truly treated to something special when they taste this spicy and warm chock-full-of-shrimp dip.

CAJUN SPINACH-SHRIMP DIP

1   10¾-ounce can condensed cream of shrimp or cream of chicken soup

1   10-ounce package frozen chopped spinach, thawed and well drained

1   8-ounce package cream cheese, cubed

1   4-ounce can tiny shrimp, drained

¼   cup finely chopped onion

¼   to ½ teaspoon Cajun seasoning

2   cloves garlic, minced

      Celery sticks, sweet pepper strips, and/or crackers

1 In a 1½-quart slow cooker combine cream of shrimp soup, spinach, cream cheese, shrimp, onion, Cajun seasoning, and garlic. Cover and cook, on low-heat setting if available,* for 2 to 3 hours.

2 Stir before serving. Serve dip with celery sticks.

*NOTE: Some 1½-quart slow cookers include variable heat setting; others offer only one standard (low) setting. The 1½-quart slow cooker recipes in this book were only tested on the low-heat setting, if one was present.

Nutrition Facts per ¼ cup dip: 103 cal., 8 g total fat (5 g sat. fat), 40 mg chol., 290 mg sodium, 4 g carbo., 1 g fiber, 5 g pro.

PREP:
15 minutes

COOK:
2 to 3 hours

MAKES:
*3 cups dip
(12 appetizer servings)*

Many variations of hot spinach dips have appeared at parties over the years, but it's not likely your guests have seen this one! Coconut milk, soy sauce, crushed red pepper, and peanuts give it the Thai treatment.

SPICY THAI SPINACH DIP

PREP:

10 minutes

BAKE:

20 minutes

MAKES:

*about 2 cups dip
(about 8 appetizer servings)*

1	10¾-ounce can condensed cream of celery or cream of broccoli soup
1	10-ounce package frozen chopped spinach, thawed and drained
¼	cup unsweetened coconut milk
1	tablespoon soy sauce
¼	to ½ teaspoon crushed red pepper
⅓	cup finely chopped peanuts
1	recipe Toasted Pita Wedges (recipe on page 14)

1 In a medium bowl combine cream of celery soup, spinach, coconut milk, soy sauce, and crushed red pepper. Transfer to an ungreased 9-inch pie plate. Sprinkle with peanuts.

2 Bake in a 350°F oven about 20 minutes or until heated through. Serve with Toasted Pita Wedges.

Nutrition Facts per ¼ cup dip and 6 pita wedges: 172 cal., 7 g total fat (2 g sat. fat), 4 mg chol., 654 mg sodium, 23 g carbo., 2 g fiber, 6 g pro.

Be prepared for spur-of-the-moment parties. Stock your pantry with the soup, olives, and crackers and keep a package of shredded cheddar in the fridge. That way, you can make this super simple dip anytime you want.

CHEDDAR CHEESE & OLIVE DIP

2 cups finely shredded cheddar cheese (8 ounces)

1 10¾-ounce can condensed cream of celery soup

¾ cup chopped pitted ripe olives

Assorted crackers, sliced vegetables, and/or chips

1 In a medium saucepan combine cheddar cheese, cream of celery soup, and olives. Cook and stir over medium-low heat until cheese is melted.

2 Serve dip with crackers.

Nutrition Facts per 2 tablespoons dip: 65 cal., 5 g total fat (3 g sat. fat), 12 mg chol., 229 mg sodium, 2 g carbo., 0 g fiber, 3 g pro.

START TO FINISH:

15 minutes

MAKES:

*about 2½ cups dip
(about 20 appetizer servings)*

To bring a little style to an appetizer buffet, prepare this in a mold. For more casual occasions, try the quick stir-together version.

CREAM CHEESE CRAB SPREAD

PREP:

20 minutes

CHILL:

4 hours

MAKES:

*about 5 cups spread
(about 80 appetizer servings)*

Nonstick cooking spray

1   10¾-ounce can condensed cream of mushroom soup

1   envelope unflavored gelatin

1   8-ounce package cream cheese, softened

1   cup mayonnaise or salad dressing

½   teaspoon lemon juice

Several dashes bottled hot pepper sauce

1   6- or 8-ounce package flake- or chunk-style imitation crabmeat, finely chopped, or one 6-ounce can crabmeat, drained and flaked

1   cup finely chopped celery

½   cup finely chopped green onions

Assorted crackers

1   Lightly coat a 4½- to 5-cup mold with nonstick cooking spray; set aside.

2   In a medium saucepan stir together cream of mushroom soup and gelatin; let stand for 5 minutes. Cook and stir over medium heat until bubbly. Add cream cheese; stir until melted. Remove from heat. Stir in mayonnaise, lemon juice, and hot pepper sauce. Fold in imitation crabmeat, celery, and green onions.

3   Spoon gelatin mixture into prepared mold. Cover and chill about 4 hours or until firm. Unmold. Serve with crackers.

SPEEDY CRAB DIP: Assemble ingredients for Cream Cheese Crab Spread, except omit nonstick cooking spray and unflavored gelatin. In a medium mixing bowl combine cream of mushroom soup and cream cheese. Beat with an electric mixer on low speed until combined. Stir in mayonnaise, lemon juice, and hot pepper sauce. Fold in imitation crabmeat, celery, and green onions. Cover; chill for at least 1 hour or up to 24 hours. Serve with assorted crackers and/or vegetable dippers. Makes about 5 cups dip (about 80 [1-tablespoon] servings).

Nutrition Facts per 1 tablespoon spread: 37 cal., 4 g total fat (1 g sat. fat), 5 mg chol., 69 mg sodium, 1 g carbo., 0 g fiber, 1 g pro.

For a chicken version, use condensed cream of chicken soup in place of the shrimp soup and canned chicken in place of the salmon.

SEAFOOD PESTO SPREAD

1	8-ounce package cream cheese, softened
1	10¾-ounce can condensed cream of shrimp soup
¼	cup purchased basil pesto
2	tablespoons sliced green onion
¼	teaspoon coarsely ground black pepper
1	14¾- to 15½-ounce can red salmon, drained, flaked, and skin and bones removed
	Assorted crackers or bread

PREP:
20 minutes
CHILL:
6 to 24 hours
MAKES:
about 3½ cups spread (about 14 appetizer servings)

1 Line the bottom and sides of a 7½×3½×2-inch loaf pan or 3-cup mold with plastic wrap; set aside.

2 In a medium mixing bowl beat the cream cheese with an electric mixer on medium speed about 30 seconds to soften. Add cream of shrimp soup, pesto, green onion, and pepper; beat until combined. Fold in salmon. Spread evenly in the prepared pan or mold. Cover and chill for at least 6 hours or up to 24 hours.

3 To serve, invert pan or mold onto a serving platter; remove pan or mold. Remove plastic wrap. Serve with crackers.

Nutrition Facts per ¼ cup spread: 170 cal., 13 g total fat (6 g sat. fat), 40 mg chol., 472 mg sodium, 3 g carbo., 0 g fiber, 10 g pro.

Imitation lobster and crabmeat may not be real lobster and seafood, but they are real fish. They're often made from pollock and whiting, and are an inexpensive substitute for their high-end counterparts.

OVEN-ROASTED CORN & SEAFOOD SPREAD

PREP:
15 minutes

ROAST:
15 minutes

BAKE:
20 minutes

MAKES:
*about 1³/₄ cups spread
(about 14 appetizer servings)*

1   cup frozen loose-pack whole kernel corn

¹/₃   cup chopped red and/or green sweet pepper

6   ounces Monterey Jack cheese with jalapeño peppers, shredded (1¹/₂ cups)

1   10³/₄-ounce can condensed cream of shrimp soup

1   3-ounce package cream cheese, softened

2   teaspoons lemon juice

1   6- or 8-ounce package flake-style imitation lobster or crabmeat

     Sweet pepper wedges or crackers

1 In a greased shallow baking pan combine corn and chopped sweet pepper. Roast in a 425°F oven about 15 minutes or until vegetables begin to brown, stirring occasionally. Reduce oven temperature to 350°F.

2 Meanwhile, in a medium bowl stir together Monterey Jack cheese, cream of shrimp soup, cream cheese, and lemon juice. Stir in roasted vegetables and imitation lobster. Spread evenly in an 8-inch quiche dish or shallow casserole.

3 Bake, uncovered, in 350°F oven for 20 to 25 minutes or until heated through. Before serving, stir to blend cream cheese. Serve with sweet pepper wedges.

Nutrition Facts per 2 tablespoons spread: 109 cal., 7 g total fat (4 g sat. fat), 27 mg chol., 273 mg sodium, 5 g carbo., 1 g fiber, 6 g pro.

A cinch to make, this eye-catching, crowd-pleasing nibble will disappear quickly from an appetizer buffet.

CHEESY VEGETABLE BITES

1	10¾-ounce can condensed cream of mushroom or cream of onion soup
1	8-ounce package cream cheese, softened
2	teaspoons dried Italian seasoning, crushed
¼	teaspoon black pepper
1	16-ounce loaf unsliced French bread
½	cup shredded carrot
½	cup chopped zucchini
½	cup chopped red sweet pepper
½	cup finely shredded Parmesan cheese (2 ounces)

PREP:
10 minutes
BAKE:
15 minutes
STAND:
5 minutes
MAKES:
24 appetizer servings

1 In a medium mixing bowl combine cream of mushroom soup, cream cheese, Italian seasoning, and black pepper; beat with an electric mixer on medium speed until smooth. Set aside.

2 Cut French bread in half horizontally. Place French bread, cut sides up, on an ungreased baking sheet. Spread soup mixture evenly on cut sides of bread. Sprinkle with carrot, zucchini, and sweet pepper. Sprinkle with Parmesan cheese.

3 Bake in a 450°F oven about 15 minutes or until topping is heated through and cheese is melted. Let stand for 5 minutes. Cut into 1-inch slices. Serve warm.

Nutrition Facts per serving: 147 cal., 8 g total fat (4 g sat. fat), 19 mg chol., 420 mg sodium, 12 g carbo., 1 g fiber, 7 g pro.

Process Swiss cheese is part of what makes this a "no-fail" fondue, because it doesn't form clumps as it melts. Canned soup is the other part of the "no-fail" equation.

NO-FAIL SWISS FONDUE

START TO FINISH:

25 minutes

MAKES:

*3¹/₂ cups fondue
(14 appetizer servings)*

1   10³/₄-ounce can condensed cream of onion soup

¹/₄   cup dry white wine

¹/₄   cup milk

3   cups shredded process Swiss cheese (12 ounces)

¹/₈   teaspoon ground nutmeg

¹/₈   teaspoon white pepper

6   to 8 cups toasted French bread cubes, precooked broccoli, cauliflower florets, and/or sweet pepper pieces

1 In a large saucepan combine cream of onion soup, wine, and milk; cook and stir over medium heat until bubbly. Add the cheese, a little at a time, stirring constantly and making sure cheese is melted before adding more. Stir until cheese is melted.

2 Stir in nutmeg and white pepper. Transfer cheese mixture to a fondue pot. Keep warm over a fondue burner. (If mixture becomes too thick, stir in a little more milk.) Serve with toasted French bread cubes.

Nutrition Facts per ¹/₄ cup serving with French bread cubes: 135 cal., 9 g total fat (5 g sat. fat), 29 mg chol., 609 mg sodium, 6 g carbo., 0 g fiber, 8 g pro.

Just about anyone who loves pizza (and who doesn't) will like this, but kids especially will get a kick out of the "dig in" fondue-style presentation.

SIMPLE PIZZA FONDUE

4   ounces bulk Italian or pork sausage
1   small onion, finely chopped
1   clove garlic, minced
1   14½-ounce can diced tomatoes, undrained
1   11-ounce can condensed tomato bisque soup
1   4-ounce can (drained weight) sliced mushrooms, drained
⅔   cup chopped pepperoni or Canadian-style bacon
¼   cup chopped green sweet pepper
1   teaspoon dried basil or oregano, crushed
     Italian bread cubes or cooked tortellini or ravioli

PREP:
20 minutes

COOK:
10 minutes

MAKES:
*about 4 cups fondue
(about 8 to 10 servings)*

1 In a large saucepan cook the sausage, onion, and garlic until meat is brown. Drain off fat. Stir in tomatoes, tomato bisque soup, mushrooms, pepperoni, sweet pepper, and basil. Bring to boiling; reduce heat. Simmer, uncovered, for 10 minutes, stirring occasionally.

2 Transfer mixture to a fondue pot. Keep mixture warm over a fondue burner. Serve with Italian bread cubes.

Nutrition Facts per ½ cup serving: 173 cal., 11 g total fat (4 g sat. fat), 21 mg chol., 787 mg sodium, 12 g carbo., 2 g fiber, 6 g pro.

For eye-catching color, use a combination of red and green sweet pepper.

SOUTHWEST CHEESE FONDUE

START TO FINISH:

15 minutes

MAKES:

*about 2⅔ cup fondue
(about 14 servings)*

2 10¾-ounce cans condensed cream of potato soup

8 ounces process American cheese, shredded (2 cups)

½ cup finely chopped red and/or green sweet pepper

⅓ cup milk

½ teaspoon ground cumin

   Crusty bread cubes, corn chips, and/or sliced vegetables

   Milk (optional)

1 Place cream of potato soup in a medium saucepan. Mash any pieces of potato. Stir in cheese, sweet pepper, the ⅓ cup milk, and the cumin. Cook over medium heat until cheese is melted and mixture is heated through, stirring occasionally. Stir until smooth.

2 Transfer to fondue pot. Keep mixture warm over a fondue burner. Serve with crusty bread cubes. If mixture becomes too thick, stir in additional milk.

Nutrition Facts per ⅓ cup serving: 98 cal., 6 g total fat (4 g sat. fat), 19 mg chol., 558 mg sodium, 6 g carbo., 0 g fiber, 5 g pro.

Because this highly flavorful cheesecake is made with many ingredients that are preseasoned with salt—Parmesan, pesto, bread crumbs, and canned soup, choose crackers with less salt.

PESTO PARMESAN CHEESECAKE

- ⅓ cup fine dry bread crumbs
- ⅓ cup grated Parmesan cheese
- 2 tablespoons butter or margarine, melted
- 2 8-ounce packages cream cheese, softened
- 1 10¾-ounce can condensed cream of onion soup
- ½ cup purchased basil pesto
- 1 cup grated Parmesan cheese (4 ounces)
- 4 beaten eggs
- ½ cup chopped almonds, toasted

  Assorted crackers

PREP:
30 minutes
BAKE:
35 minutes
COOL:
1¾ hours
CHILL:
4 to 24 hours
STAND:
30 minutes
MAKES:
16 to 20 servings

1 For crust, in a small bowl combine bread crumbs, the ⅓ cup Parmesan cheese, and the melted butter. Press mixture evenly onto the bottom of an ungreased 9-inch springform pan; set aside.

2 For filling, in a large mixing bowl combine cream cheese, cream of onion soup, and pesto. Beat with an electric mixer on medium speed until combined. Stir in the 1 cup Parmesan cheese and the eggs until combined.

3 Pour into crust-lined springform pan. Place the springform pan in a shallow baking pan on the oven rack. Bake in a 325°F oven for 35 to 40 minutes or until center appears nearly set when shaken.

4 Cool in pan on a wire rack for 15 minutes. Using a narrow metal spatula, loosen crust from side of pan; cool for 30 minutes more. Remove side of pan; cool cheesecake for at least 1 hour or until completely cooled. Cover and chill for at least 4 hours or up to 24 hours.

5 Let cheesecake stand at room temperature for 30 minutes before serving. Just before serving, sprinkle cheesecake with almonds, pressing down lightly. Serve with crackers.

Nutrition Facts per serving: 265 cal., 23 g total fat (9 g sat. fat), 97 mg chol., 461 mg sodium, 7 g carbo., 1 g fiber, 9 g pro.

Savory cheesecakes, such as this one studded with roasted red sweet peppers, are particularly well suited to an appetizer buffet.

ROASTED RED PEPPER & MUSHROOM CHEESECAKE

PREP:

30 minutes

BAKE:

25 minutes

COOL:

1³⁄₄ hours

CHILL:

3 to 24 hours

STAND:

30 minutes

MAKES:

16 to 20 appetizer servings

1   cup seasoned fine dry bread crumbs

¼   cup butter or margarine, melted

1   12-ounce jar roasted red sweet peppers, well drained

2   8-ounce packages cream cheese, softened

1   10³⁄₄-ounce can condensed cream of mushroom soup

¼   cup finely shredded Parmesan cheese (1 ounce)

2   eggs

1   teaspoon bottled minced garlic (2 cloves)

½   teaspoon dried basil, crushed

½   teaspoon dried thyme, crushed

     Assorted crackers

① For crust, in a medium bowl combine bread crumbs and melted butter. Press mixture evenly onto the bottom of a greased 9-inch springform pan; set aside.

② For filling, chop ½ cup of the drained sweet peppers; set aside. In a food processor bowl combine the remaining drained sweet peppers, cream cheese, cream of mushroom soup, and Parmesan cheese. Cover and process for 1 to 1½ minutes or until smooth. Add eggs, garlic, basil, and thyme. Cover and process with several on/off turns until smooth. Stir in reserved chopped sweet peppers.

③ Pour filling into crust-lined springform pan. Place the springform pan on a shallow baking pan on the oven rack. Bake in a 350°F oven for 25 to 30 minutes or until center appears nearly set when shaken.

④ Remove springform pan from baking pan. Cool on a wire rack for 15 minutes. Using a narrow metal spatula, loosen cheesecake from side of pan. Cool for 30 minutes more. Remove side of pan. Cool about 1 hour or until completely cooled. Cover and chill for at least 3 hours or up to 24 hours.

⑤ Let cheesecake stand at room temperature for 30 minutes before serving. Serve with crackers.

Nutrition Facts per serving: 220 cal., 18 g total fat (10 g sat. fat), 72 mg chol., 582 mg sodium, 8 g carbo., 0 g fiber, 8 g pro.

Here's a great way to transform a can of smoked salmon into an opulent appetizer for a crowd!

SMOKED SALMON CHEESECAKE

1½ cups finely crushed sesame or butter-flavored crackers

6 tablespoons butter or margarine, melted

2 tablespoons grated Parmesan cheese

2 8-ounce packages cream cheese, softened

1 10¾-ounce can condensed cream of shrimp soup

½ cup dairy sour cream

1 tablespoon lemon juice

½ teaspoon dried dill

3 beaten eggs

1 4-ounce piece smoked salmon, flaked,
with skin and bones removed

Assorted crackers or toasted baguette slices

1 For crust, in a medium bowl combine crushed crackers, melted butter, and Parmesan cheese. Press mixture evenly onto the bottom and about 1 inch up the side of an ungreased 9-inch springform pan; set aside.

2 For filling, in a large mixing bowl beat cream cheese with an electric mixer on medium speed until smooth. Add cream of shrimp soup, sour cream, lemon juice, and dill; beat until combined. Stir in eggs and salmon.

3 Pour into crust-lined springform pan. Place the springform pan in a shallow baking pan on the oven rack. Bake in a 350°F oven for 45 to 50 minutes or until center appears nearly set when shaken.

4 Remove springform pan from baking pan. Cool in pan on a wire rack for 15 minutes. Using a narrow metal spatula, loosen crust from side of pan. Cool for 30 minutes more. Remove side of pan. Cool about 1 hour more or until completely cooled. Cover and chill for at least 4 hours or up to 24 hours.

5 Let cheesecake stand at room temperature for 30 minutes before serving. Serve with crackers.

Nutrition Facts per serving: 236 cal., 19 g total fat (11 g sat. fat), 91 mg chol., 421 mg sodium, 11 g carbo., 2 g fiber, 7 g pro.

PREP:

30 minutes

BAKE:

45 minutes

COOL:

1¾ hours

CHILL:

4 to 24 hours

STAND:

30 minutes

MAKES:

16 to 20 appetizer servings

Hint: For easier unmolding, dip the mold in warm water before inverting it onto the tray.

SALMON MOUSSE

PREP:

30 minutes

CHILL:

30 minutes + 4 hours

MAKES:

16 servings

1   14¾- to 15½-ounce can red salmon

2   envelopes unflavored gelatin

1   teaspoon sugar

1   10¾-ounce can condensed tomato soup

½   cup mayonnaise or salad dressing

2   tablespoons lemon juice

2   teaspoons Worcestershire sauce

½   cup finely chopped celery

2   hard-cooked eggs, chopped

2   tablespoons snipped fresh chives

¼   teaspoon black pepper

½   cup whipping cream

Lettuce (optional)

Thin cucumber slices (optional)

Fresh dill (optional)

Assorted crackers

1 Drain salmon, reserving liquid. Bone and flake salmon; set aside. Add enough water to reserved salmon liquid to equal 1 cup; pour into a small saucepan. Sprinkle unflavored gelatin and sugar over the salmon liquid mixture; let stand for 3 minutes to soften gelatin. Heat and stir over medium-low heat until gelatin is dissolved. Remove from heat.

2 In a large bowl whisk together the tomato soup, mayonnaise, lemon juice, and Worcestershire sauce until smooth; stir in gelatin mixture. Chill about 30 minutes or until partially set (mixture should have the consistency of unbeaten egg whites). Fold in salmon, celery, chopped hard-cooked eggs, chives, and pepper.

3 In a small mixing bowl beat whipping cream with an electric mixer on medium speed until soft peaks form. Fold whipped cream into gelatin mixture. Pour into a 6-cup ring mold. Cover and chill about 4 hours or until firm.

4 If desired, line a tray or serving plate with lettuce. Unmold mousse onto tray. If desired, garnish with cucumber slices and fresh dill. Serve with crackers.

Nutrition Facts per serving: 145 cal., 11 g total fat (3 g sat. fat), 49 mg chol., 314 mg sodium, 4 g carbo., 0 g fiber, 7 g pro.

For an easy appetizer, prepare and chill the spread portion ahead of time. Then just toast and top the bread slices when you're ready to serve.

MUSHROOM VEGGIE CHEDDAR BRUSCHETTA

1   16-ounce loaf baguette-style French bread
    (16 to 18 inches long)

1   10¾-ounce can condensed cream of mushroom soup

1   cup shredded cheddar or Monterey Jack cheese (4 ounces)

¼   cup chopped red or green sweet pepper

2   green onions, sliced

1   medium carrot, shredded

½   teaspoon dried oregano or basil, crushed

¼   teaspoon garlic powder

2   to 3 tablespoons grated Parmesan cheese

1 Cut bread into 24 slices. Arrange bread on an ungreased baking sheet. Broil 4 to 5 inches from the heat for 2 to 4 minutes or until lightly toasted, turning once.

2 In a medium bowl stir together cream of mushroom soup, cheddar cheese, sweet pepper, green onions, carrot, oregano, and garlic powder. Spread soup mixture over toasted bread slices. Sprinkle with Parmesan cheese.

3 Broil for 2 to 4 minutes more or until mixture is heated through and shredded cheese begins to melt.

Nutrition Facts per serving: 88 cal., 3 g total fat (1 g sat. fat), 5 mg chol., 241 mg sodium, 11 g carbo., 1 g fiber, 3 g pro.

PREP:
25 minutes

BROIL:
2 minutes + 2 minutes

MAKES:
24 appetizer servings

When stuffing mix is unavailable, use croutons and lightly crush them with a rolling pin or the bottom of a mixing bowl. For even quicker preparation, use 2 pounds frozen cooked appetizer-size meatballs, thawed, rather than the homemade version.

ZESTY COCKTAIL MEATBALLS

PREP:

30 minutes

BAKE:

15 minutes

COOK:

2 hours (high-heat setting)

MAKES:

about 16 appetizer servings

1	egg
1	10½-ounce can condensed French onion soup
2	cups herb-seasoned stuffing mix
2	pounds ground beef
1	15-ounce can tomato sauce
⅓	cup packed brown sugar
2	tablespoons Worcestershire sauce
2	tablespoons vinegar

1 In a large bowl whisk egg; whisk in French onion soup. Stir in stuffing mix. Add ground beef; mix well. Shape into 1-inch meatballs (about 50 total). Place meatballs in an ungreased 15×10×1-inch baking pan.

2 Bake meatballs in a 350°F oven for 15 to 18 minutes or until done in center (an instant-read meat thermometer inserted in center of a meatball registers 160°F). Drain off fat. Place meatballs in a 3½- to 5-quart slow cooker.

3 In a medium bowl combine tomato sauce, brown sugar, Worcestershire sauce, and vinegar. Pour over meatballs; stir gently to coat.

4 Cover; cook on high-heat setting for 2 hours. Serve immediately or keep warm on low-heat setting for up to 2 hours. Use toothpicks to serve.

Nutrition Facts per serving: 178 cal., 8 g total fat (3 g sat. fat), 49 mg chol., 430 mg sodium, 13 g carbo., 1 g fiber, 13 g pro.

Everyone loves Buffalo wings. Make them extra-irresistible by serving a warm, bacon-studded blue cheese dip alongside.

BUFFALO WINGS WITH WARM BLUE CHEESE DIP

18   chicken wings (about 3 pounds)

¼   cup bottled hot pepper sauce

3   tablespoons butter or margarine, melted

2   teaspoons paprika

¼   teaspoon salt

¼   teaspoon cayenne pepper

1   recipe Warm Blue Cheese Dip

      Celery sticks (optional)

PREP:
20 minutes

MARINATE:
30 minutes

BROIL:
10 minutes + 10 minutes

MAKES:
18 appetizer servings

1 Cut off and discard tips of chicken wings. Cut wings at joints to form 36 pieces. Place chicken wing pieces in a resealable plastic bag set in a shallow dish.

2 For marinade, stir together bottled hot pepper sauce, melted butter, paprika, salt, and cayenne pepper. Pour over chicken wings. Seal bag; turn to coat wings. Marinate in refrigerator for 30 minutes.

3 Place chicken wing pieces on unheated rack of a broiler pan (if necessary, broil half at a time). Broil 4 to 5 inches from heat about 10 minutes or until lightly browned. Turn chicken wing pieces. Broil for 10 to 15 minutes more or until chicken is tender and no longer pink. Serve with Warm Blue Cheese Dip and, if desired, celery sticks.

WARM BLUE CHEESE DIP: In small saucepan stir together one 10¾-ounce can condensed cream of chicken soup, ¼ cup dairy sour cream, and ¼ cup milk. Cook and stir over low heat until heated through. Remove from heat. Stir in ¼ cup crumbled blue cheese (1 ounce); transfer to serving bowl. Top with ¼ cup crumbled blue cheese (1 ounce) and ¼ cup crumbled crisp-cooked bacon (3 to 4 slices). Serve with wings.

Nutrition Facts per serving: 184 cal., 15 g total fat (5 g sat. fat), 70 mg chol., 334 mg sodium, 2 g carbo., 0 g fiber, 11 g pro.

If you're one of those cooks who turns the page when you spot a recipe with more than just a few ingredients, give this one a chance anyway! The ingredients are easy to find and they come together quickly for an unbelievably rich, velvety soup.

CREAMY CRAB & CORN CHOWDER

START TO FINISH:

35 minutes

MAKES:

10 appetizer servings

$\frac{1}{2}$	cup chopped celery
$\frac{1}{2}$	cup chopped green onions
$\frac{1}{4}$	cup chopped green sweet pepper
$\frac{1}{4}$	cup butter or margarine
2	$10\frac{3}{4}$-ounce cans condensed cream of potato soup
1	$14\frac{3}{4}$-ounce can cream-style corn
$1\frac{1}{2}$	cups half-and-half or light cream
$1\frac{1}{2}$	cups milk
2	bay leaves
1	teaspoon dried thyme, crushed
$\frac{1}{2}$	teaspoon garlic powder
$\frac{1}{4}$	teaspoon white pepper
	Several dashes bottled hot pepper sauce
1	pound cooked lump crabmeat, cartilage removed
	Snipped fresh parsley (optional)
	Lemon slices (optional)

1 In a large saucepan or Dutch oven cook celery, green onions, and sweet pepper in hot butter until tender.

2 Stir in cream of potato soup, corn, half-and-half, milk, bay leaves, thyme, garlic powder, white pepper, and hot pepper sauce. Heat through, stirring occasionally. Discard bay leaves. Stir in crabmeat. Heat through. If desired, garnish with parsley and lemon slices.

Nutrition Facts per serving: 236 cal., 12 g total fat (7 g sat. fat), 80 mg chol., 787 mg sodium, 19 g carbo., 1 g fiber, 13 g pro.

Traditionally stewed for hours in an open cauldron, seafood chowders gave hungry fishermen warm, stick-to-your-ribs sustenance. This fast fix-up chowder is ready in minutes and every bit as inviting as its ancestor.

EASY SHRIMP CHOWDER

8	ounces fresh or frozen small shrimp
1	10¾-ounce can condensed cream of shrimp soup
1	cup milk, half-and-half, or light cream
¼	cup dry sherry, milk, half-and-half, or light cream
	Snipped fresh parsley (optional)

START TO FINISH:

20 minutes

MAKES:

4 to 6 appetizer servings

1 Thaw shrimp, if frozen. Peel and devein shrimp. Rinse shrimp; pat dry with paper towels. If desired, chop shrimp. Set shrimp aside.

2 In a 2-quart saucepan combine cream of shrimp soup, the 1 cup milk, and sherry. Bring to boiling; reduce heat. Simmer, uncovered, for 5 minutes, stirring often.

3 Add shrimp to soup. Return to boiling; reduce heat. Simmer, uncovered, for 1 to 2 minutes more or until shrimp turn opaque. If desired, garnish servings with parsley.

Nutrition Facts per serving: 186 cal., 8 g total fat (2 g sat. fat), 116 mg chol., 687 mg sodium, 10 g carbo., 0 g fiber, 15 g pro.

When the garden and farm stands are brimming with fresh, homegrown tomatoes, that's the time to indulge in this colorful cold soup. Serve it with a lemony Caesar salad for a refreshing summer supper on the deck.

GARDEN GAZPACHO

PREP:

20 minutes

CHILL:

4 to 24 hours

MAKES:

8 appetizer servings

3 medium tomatoes, peeled and chopped (about 2¼ cups)

1 medium yellow or green sweet pepper, chopped

1 small zucchini, chopped (about 1 cup)

2 green onions, thinly sliced

½ teaspoon dried basil, crushed, or 1 tablespoon snipped fresh basil

1 clove garlic, minced

1 10¾-ounce can condensed tomato soup

1 tablespoon lemon juice

1 tablespoon cider vinegar

⅛ teaspoon salt

Dash freshly ground black pepper

Several dashes bottled hot pepper sauce

1 In a large bowl combine tomatoes, sweet pepper, zucchini, green onions, basil, and garlic. Stir in tomato soup, lemon juice, vinegar, salt, black pepper, and hot pepper sauce. Cover and chill for at least 4 hours or up to 24 hours.

2 To serve, ladle soup into chilled soup bowls.

Nutrition Facts per serving: 46 cal., 0 g total fat (0 g sat. fat), 0 mg chol., 274 mg sodium, 10 g carbo., 2 g fiber, 2 g pro.

MEATY MAIN DISHES

2

This is the best kind of comfort food—simple, hearty, and warming. Carrots and parsnips add variety and color to the casserole.

BEEF STEW BAKE

PREP:

30 minutes

BAKE:

2 hours

MAKES:

6 servings

1½   pounds beef chuck roast

¼   cup all-purpose flour

2   tablespoons cooking oil

1   10½-ounce can condensed French onion soup

1   cup water

½   teaspoon dried thyme, crushed

¼   teaspoon black pepper

4   medium potatoes, peeled and quartered (1¼ pounds)

1   pound parsnips and/or carrots, cut into 1-inch pieces

1 Trim fat from meat. Cut meat into 1-inch cubes. In a large plastic bag combine meat and flour. Close bag and shake to coat meat with flour. In a large skillet brown meat, half at a time, in hot oil. Drain off fat. Return all meat to skillet. Stir in French onion soup, water, thyme, and pepper.

2 In an ungreased 3-quart casserole combine potatoes and parsnips. Top with meat mixture. Bake, covered, in a 350°F oven about 2 hours or until meat and vegetables are tender, stirring once or twice during baking.

Nutrition Facts per serving: 351 cal., 10 g total fat (2 g sat. fat), 68 mg chol., 494 mg sodium, 36 g carbo., 5 g fiber, 28 g pro.

Liven up your chili routine with this unusual version! Hominy and pinto beans add pleasant surprises, while nacho cheese soup makes it irresistibly cheesy.

MEXICAN BEEF CHILI

1   pound ground beef

1   15-ounce can pinto beans, rinsed and drained

1   15-ounce can golden hominy, rinsed and drained

1   15-ounce can chopped tomatoes and
     green chile peppers, undrained

1   11-ounce can condensed nacho cheese soup

1   cup water

1   1¼-ounce envelope taco seasoning mix

     Corn chips (optional)

     Dairy sour cream (optional)

     Sliced pitted ripe olives (optional)

PREP:
20 minutes
COOK:
20 minutes
MAKES:
6 servings

1 In a large saucepan cook ground beef until brown. Drain off fat. Stir pinto beans, hominy, undrained tomatoes, nacho cheese soup, water, and taco seasoning mix into beef in saucepan.

2 Bring to boiling, stirring often; reduce heat. Simmer, covered, for 20 minutes, stirring occasionally. If desired, serve with corn chips, sour cream, and olives.

Nutrition Facts per serving: 331 cal., 15 g total fat (6 g sat. fat), 54 mg chol., 1,581 mg sodium, 27 g carbo., 6 g fiber, 23 g pro.

This casserole is a hit at family tables—especially when there are teenagers involved.
(It's easy enough for teenagers to make, so hand this recipe over to them and take the night off.)

NACHO CASSEROLE

PREP:

20 minutes

BAKE:

40 minutes + 5 minutes

MAKES:

6 servings

1 pound lean ground beef

½ cup chopped onion

1 15-ounce can pork and beans in tomato sauce

1 11-ounce can whole kernel corn with sweet peppers, drained

1 10¾-ounce can condensed tomato soup

1 4-ounce can diced green chile peppers

2 teaspoons chili powder

2 cups shredded Monterey Jack cheese or Monterey Jack cheese with jalapeño peppers (8 ounces)

2 cups coarsely crushed tortilla chips

1 In a large skillet cook ground beef and onion until beef is brown and onion is tender. Drain off fat. Stir pork and beans, corn, tomato soup, chile peppers, and chili powder into beef mixture in skillet. Transfer to an ungreased 2-quart rectangular baking dish.

2 Bake, covered, in a 350°F oven about 40 minutes or until heated through. Remove from oven. Sprinkle with shredded cheese; top with tortilla chips. Bake, uncovered, for 5 minutes more. Serve immediately.

Nutrition Facts per serving: 555 cal., 32 g total fat (14 g sat. fat), 94 mg chol., 1,194 mg sodium, 42 g carbo., 7 g fiber, 30 g pro.

Soup up refrigerated precooked roast beef—found in the meat department—with just a few common ingredients for uncommonly delicious results.

MEXICAN-STYLE HASH

1	17-ounce package refrigerated cooked beef roast au jus
1½	cups finely chopped potato
1	11-ounce can whole kernel corn, drained
1	10¾-ounce can condensed tomato soup
⅓	cup chopped onion
1½	teaspoons chili powder
¼	teaspoon black pepper

PREP:
20 minutes
COOK:
15 minutes
MAKES:
4 servings

1 Drain meat, reserving juices. Chop meat.

2 In a 10-inch skillet combine chopped meat, reserved meat juices, potato, corn, tomato soup, onion, chili powder, and pepper. Bring to boiling; reduce heat. Simmer, covered, for 15 to 20 minutes or until potatoes are tender, stirring occasionally to prevent sticking.

Nutrition Facts per serving: 334 cal., 10 g total fat (4 g sat. fat), 64 mg chol., 1,069 mg sodium, 40 g carbo., 4 g fiber, 27 g pro.

Classic shepherd's pie, an English favorite, is known for its great flavor but not for speedy preparation. This quick, streamlined version also sports a Latin flavor twist.

FAST FIESTA SHEPHERD'S PIE

START TO FINISH:

25 minutes

MAKES:

4 servings

1	pound ground beef
1	8-ounce can tomato sauce
1	cup frozen loose-pack whole kernel corn
¾	cup bottled picante sauce
1	teaspoon ground cumin
¼	teaspoon sugar
1	11-ounce can condensed nacho cheese soup
1	cup milk
2	tablespoons butter or margarine
1⅔	cups packaged instant mashed potato flakes
	Snipped fresh cilantro or parsley

1 In a large skillet cook ground beef until brown. Drain off fat. Stir in tomato sauce, corn, picante sauce, cumin, and sugar. Bring to boiling; reduce heat. Simmer, covered, for 5 minutes.

2 Meanwhile, in a medium saucepan combine nacho cheese soup, milk, and butter; bring to boiling, stirring frequently. Remove from heat; stir in potato flakes. Let stand for several minutes. Stir with a fork. Spoon potato mixture into mounds onto hot meat mixture. Sprinkle with cilantro.

Nutrition Facts per serving: 561 cal., 27 g total fat (13 g sat. fat), 102 mg chol., 1,333 mg sodium, 46 g carbo., 5 g fiber, 32 g pro.

Shepherd's pie is a classic mashed potato-topped casserole from England. Refrigerated mashed potatoes, frozen vegetables, and a can of soup make it all come together more quickly than ever.

EASY SHEPHERD'S PIE

1	pound lean ground beef, ground turkey, or ground chicken
2	cups frozen loose-pack mixed vegetables
¼	cup water
1	teaspoon dried minced onion
1	10¾-ounce can condensed tomato soup
1	tablespoon Worcestershire sauce
½	teaspoon dried thyme, crushed
¼	teaspoon salt
⅛	teaspoon black pepper
1	20-ounce package refrigerated mashed potatoes
½	cup shredded cheddar cheese (2 ounces)

PREP:

25 minutes

COOK:

5 minutes + 5 minutes

STAND:

10 minutes

MAKES:

6 servings

1 In a large skillet cook ground beef until brown. Drain off fat. Stir mixed vegetables, water, and dried minced onion into meat in skillet.

2 Bring to boiling; reduce heat. Simmer, covered, for 5 to 10 minutes or until vegetables are tender. Stir in tomato soup, Worcestershire sauce, thyme, salt, and pepper. Return to boiling.

3 Stir potatoes in container or a medium bowl until smooth. Drop potatoes in 6 mounds on top of hot meat mixture. Sprinkle with cheese; reduce heat. Simmer, covered, about 5 minutes or until heated through. Remove from heat. Let stand, covered, for 10 minutes before serving.

Nutrition Facts per serving: 372 cal., 20 g total fat (8 g sat. fat), 65 mg chol., 686 mg sodium, 27 g carbo., 3 g fiber, 20 g pro.

Cooking for kids? You just can't go wrong with anything that's as filled with cheeseburger flavors as this bake. P.S.: Adults love it too!

CHEESE-BURGER CASSEROLE

PREP:

25 minutes

BAKE:

30 minutes

STAND:

10 minutes

MAKES:

6 servings

2	cups dried penne pasta
1	pound ground beef or ground pork
½	cup chopped onion
1	clove garlic, minced
2	10¾-ounce cans condensed cheddar cheese soup
½	cup milk
1	teaspoon dried basil, crushed
⅛	teaspoon black pepper
1½	cups shredded Swiss or American cheese (6 ounces)
2	medium tomatoes, chopped

1 Cook pasta according to package directions; drain and set aside. Meanwhile, in a large skillet cook ground beef, onion, and garlic until meat is brown. Drain off fat. Stir in cheddar cheese soup, milk, basil, and pepper. Stir in cooked pasta and 1 cup of the shredded cheese. Spoon mixture into an ungreased 2-quart rectangular baking dish.

2 Bake, covered, in a 375°F oven for 30 to 35 minutes or until heated through. Uncover; sprinkle with remaining ½ cup cheese and tomatoes. Let stand for 10 minutes before serving.

Nutrition Facts per serving: 519 cal., 34 g total fat (15 g sat. fat), 103 mg chol., 944 mg sodium, 32 g carbo., 2 g fiber, 28 g pro.

Yes, this casserole is as all-out kid-pleasing as it sounds, especially when you serve it with the optional toppings and let everyone garnish his or her plate with "the works."

CHEESEBURGER & FRIES CASSEROLE

2   pounds lean ground beef

1   10¾-ounce can condensed golden mushroom soup

1   10¾-ounce can condensed cheddar cheese soup

1   20-ounce package frozen, french-fried crinkle-cut shoestring potatoes

Catsup, pickles, mustard, chopped tomato (optional)

PREP:
15 minutes
BAKE:
45 minutes
MAKES:
8 to 10 servings

1 In a large skillet cook ground beef, half at a time, until brown. Drain off fat. Place cooked beef in an ungreased 3-quart rectangular baking dish. In a bowl stir together golden mushroom soup and cheddar cheese soup. Spread over meat in baking dish. Sprinkle potatoes over soup.

2 Bake, uncovered, in a 350°F oven for 45 to 55 minutes or until potatoes are golden. If desired, serve with catsup, pickles, mustard, and chopped tomato.

Nutrition Facts per serving: 348 cal., 18 g total fat (6 g sat. fat), 78 mg chol., 654 mg sodium, 24 g carbo., 2 g fiber, 24 g pro.

A side dish of fresh, in-season fruit would make a beautiful accompaniment to this rich pie. Serve it as a brunch or luncheon dish.

CHEESY HAM-SPINACH PIE

PREP:
25 minutes
BAKE:
1 hour
STAND:
5 minutes
MAKES:
6 servings

1 9-inch frozen unbaked pastry shell

2 eggs

1 10¾-ounce can condensed cream of mushroom or cream of celery soup

¼ cup all-purpose flour

1 tablespoon prepared horseradish

1 tablespoon Dijon-style mustard

1 10-ounce package frozen chopped spinach, thawed and well drained

1 cup cubed deli ham

1 cup refrigerated diced potatoes with onion

1 cup shredded Gruyère or Swiss cheese (4 ounces)

1 Prick bottom and side of pastry shell with fork. Bake in a 450°F oven for 10 to 12 minutes or until golden. Remove from oven; reduce oven temperature to 350°F.

2 Meanwhile, in a medium bowl whisk together eggs, cream of mushroom soup, flour, horseradish, and mustard; stir in spinach.

3 Sprinkle ham and potatoes in baked pastry shell; spoon spinach mixture over potato mixture. Bake, uncovered, in the 350°F oven for 60 to 65 minutes or until a knife inserted near center comes out clean, covering edge of pie with foil the last 15 minutes to prevent overbrowning. Sprinkle cheese over pie. Let stand for 5 minutes before serving.

Nutrition Facts per serving: 358 cal., 21 g total fat (7 g sat. fat), 105 mg chol., 1,007 mg sodium, 25 g carbo., 2 g fiber, 16 g pro.

This potato-topped casserole first graced the pages of Better Homes and Gardens magazine in the 1940s. Wholesome, satisfying, and easy to prepare, it's a classic winter warmer—just the sort of weeknight fare that has brought families together over nourishing meals for decades.

HAMBURGER PIE

1	recipe Mashed Potatoes
1	pound ground beef
½	cup chopped onion
½	teaspoon salt
	Dash black pepper
2	cups frozen loose-pack green beans, thawed
1	10¾-ounce can condensed tomato soup
½	cup shredded process American cheese (2 ounces) (optional)

PREP:
30 minutes
BAKE:
25 minutes
MAKES:
4 to 6 servings

1 Prepare Mashed Potatoes; set aside. In a large skillet cook ground beef and onion until meat is brown and onion is tender. Drain off fat. Add salt and pepper to meat mixture in skillet. Stir in green beans and tomato soup. Pour into a greased 1½-quart baking dish.

2 Spoon Mashed Potatoes in mounds on bean mixture (or, if desired, pipe Mashed Potatoes using a pastry bag and a large star tip). If desired, sprinkle cheese on the potatoes.

3 Bake, uncovered, in a 350°F oven for 25 to 30 minutes or until mixture is bubbly and potatoes are golden.

MASHED POTATOES: Peel and quarter 1½ pounds baking potatoes. Place potatoes and ½ teaspoon salt in a medium saucepan. Add enough water to cover. Bring to boiling; reduce heat. Cover and cook potatoes for 20 to 25 minutes or until tender. Drain. Mash cooked potatoes with a potato masher or beat with an electric mixer on low speed. Add 2 tablespoons butter or margarine. Season to taste with salt and black pepper. Gradually beat in enough milk (2 to 4 tablespoons) to make mixture light and fluffy.

Nutrition Facts per serving: 508 cal., 23 g total fat (10 g sat. fat), 112 mg chol., 1,104 mg sodium, 40 g carbo., 5 g fiber, 35 g pro.

Portions of mashed potatoes are stuffed with a cube of cheese, then rolled in cornflakes to top a creamy ground-beef stew. Sound tasty? You better believe it! When Midwest Living *magazine held a Hot-Dish Cook-Off, the recipe won first place.*

PRAIRIE POTATO BAKE

PREP:

45 minutes

BAKE:

40 minutes

COOL:

1 hour

MAKES:

6 servings

1	recipe Mashed Potatoes
1½	pounds ground beef
½	cup chopped onion
¾	cup beef broth
¼	cup all-purpose flour
¼	teaspoon salt
⅛	teaspoon black pepper
1	10¾-ounce can condensed cream of mushroom soup
1	8-ounce carton dairy sour cream
6	ounces process cheese food, cut into six 1½-inch cubes
2	cups cornflakes, crushed

1 Prepare Mashed Potatoes; set aside to cool about 1 hour or until cool enough to handle.

2 In a large skillet cook beef and onion until beef is brown and onion is tender. Drain off fat. In a small bowl stir together beef broth, flour, salt, and pepper until well mixed. Stir broth mixture into meat mixture in skillet. Cook and stir over medium heat until thickened. Remove from heat. Stir in cream of mushroom soup and sour cream. Transfer meat mixture to an ungreased 3-quart casserole; set aside.

3 For potato topping, shape about ⅔ cup of the Mashed Potatoes into a ball. Make a hole in the center of the ball and insert a cube of cheese in the hole; reshape into a ball, enclosing the cheese. Repeat with remaining mashed potatoes and cheese cubes. Roll each ball in crushed cornflakes. Arrange potato balls on top of meat mixture.

4 Bake, uncovered, in a 350°F oven about 40 minutes or until mixture is bubbly and potatoes are heated through.

MASHED POTATOES: Peel and quarter 2 pounds (about 6 medium) potatoes. In a covered large saucepan cook potatoes in a small amount of boiling lightly salted water for 20 to 25 minutes or until tender. Drain. Mash cooked potatoes with a potato masher or beat with an electric mixer on low speed. Add ¼ cup butter or margarine. Season to taste with salt and black pepper. Gradually beat in enough milk (⅓ to ½ cup) to make potato mixture light and fluffy.

Nutrition Facts per serving: 685 cal., 41 g total fat (21 g sat. fat), 130 mg chol., 1,157 mg sodium, 44 g carbo., 2 g fiber, 34 g pro.

Your grandmother may have made Hot Tamale Pie—the recipe dates from the November 1941 issue of Better Homes and Gardens *magazine and has rated high with families ever since. Tip: Freshen it with a little sour cream and fresh tomatoes spooned on top.*

HOT TAMALE PIE

1½	pounds lean ground beef
1	cup chopped onion
1	10¾-ounce can condensed tomato soup
1	8-ounce can tomato sauce
¾	cup frozen loose-pack whole kernel corn
½	cup chopped pitted ripe olives
2	tablespoons chili powder
½	teaspoon black pepper
¾	cup cornmeal
½	cup all-purpose flour
1	teaspoon baking powder
½	teaspoon baking soda
½	teaspoon salt
1	egg
1	cup buttermilk
2	tablespoons cooking oil
½	cup shredded cheddar cheese (2 ounces) (optional)

PREP:
30 minutes
BAKE:
20 minutes
MAKES:
6 to 8 servings

1 In a large skillet cook ground beef and onion until meat is brown and onion is tender. Drain off fat. Stir tomato soup, tomato sauce, corn, olives, chili powder, and pepper into meat mixture in skillet. Bring to boiling over medium heat. Pour into an ungreased 2-quart square baking dish; set aside.

2 In a medium bowl stir together cornmeal, flour, baking powder, baking soda, and salt. In a small bowl beat egg with a fork; stir in buttermilk and oil. Add to flour mixture; stir until batter is smooth. If desired, fold in cheese. Pour over hot meat mixture, spreading evenly.

3 Bake in a 425°F oven for 20 to 25 minutes or until golden.

Nutrition Facts per serving: 534 cal., 30 g total fat (10 g sat. fat), 119 mg chol., 1,138 mg sodium, 40 g carbo., 4 g fiber, 27 g pro.

Thrifty grandmothers of yesteryear called on casseroles like this one as a way to stretch one-half pound of ground beef into a dinner for four. You can call on it as an easy, inexpensive way to satisfy a hungry family.

GRANDMA'S SPAGHETTI CASSEROLE

PREP:

30 minutes

BAKE:

40 minutes

STAND:

5 minutes

MAKES:

4 to 6 servings

8   ounces dried spaghetti

8   ounces ground beef

½   cup chopped onion

½   cup chopped green sweet pepper

1   14½-ounce can diced tomatoes, undrained

1   10¾-ounce can condensed tomato soup

½   teaspoon black pepper

2   cups shredded cheddar cheese (8 ounces)

4   slices bacon, crisp-cooked, drained, and crumbled

1 Cook spaghetti according to package directions; drain and set aside.

2 In a large skillet cook and stir ground beef, onion, and sweet pepper until beef is brown. Drain off fat. Stir tomatoes, tomato soup, and black pepper into beef mixture in skillet. Bring to boiling. Add 1½ cups of the shredded cheese; stir until melted.

3 Add cooked spaghetti and bacon to the beef mixture, tossing to combine. Transfer mixture to a greased 2-quart casserole.

4 Bake, covered, in a 350°F oven about 40 minutes or until bubbly and heated through. Uncover; sprinkle with remaining ½ cup cheese. Let stand for 5 to 10 minutes or until cheese is melted.

Nutrition Facts per serving: 675 cal., 31 g total fat (16 g sat. fat), 100 mg chol., 1,007 mg sodium, 61 g carbo., 3 g fiber, 35 g pro.

Sixty-some years after this recipe first appeared in Better Homes and Gardens magazine, the Test Kitchen still get requests for the comfort-food classic. It's easy, it's tasty, and people can't seem to get enough of it.

IRISH-ITALIAN SPAGHETTI

- 1 pound ground beef
- ½ cup chopped onion
- 1 10¾-ounce can condensed cream of mushroom soup
- 1 10¾-ounce can condensed tomato soup
- ½ teaspoon chili powder
- ½ teaspoon bottled hot pepper sauce
- ¼ teaspoon black pepper
  Dash cayenne pepper
- 1 pound dried spaghetti
- ½ cup finely shredded Parmesan cheese (2 ounces)

PREP:
20 minutes
COOK:
45 minutes
MAKES:
4 servings

1 In a large saucepan cook ground beef and onion until meat is brown and onion is tender. Drain off fat. Stir cream of mushroom soup, tomato soup, chili powder, hot pepper sauce, black pepper, and cayenne pepper into meat mixture in saucepan. Bring to boiling, stirring often; reduce heat. Simmer, covered, for 45 minutes, stirring often.

2 Meanwhile, cook spaghetti according to package directions. Serve sauce over hot cooked spaghetti. Sprinkle with Parmesan cheese.

Nutrition Facts per serving: 869 cal., 26 g total fat (10 g sat. fat), 104 mg chol., 1,305 mg sodium, 104 g carbo., 5 g fiber, 51 g pro.

There is more to this casserole than old-fashioned beef and noodles. Corn, sweet pepper, pimiento, onion, and mushrooms add plenty of zip to the saucy dish.

BEEFY VEGETABLES & NOODLES

PREP:

35 minutes

BAKE:

30 minutes

MAKES:

6 servings

1	8-ounce package dried extra-wide noodles
1	pound lean ground beef or ground turkey
¾	cup coarsely chopped green sweet pepper
½	cup chopped onion
1	10¾-ounce can condensed golden mushroom soup
1	10-ounce package frozen whole kernel corn
1	cup chopped fresh mushrooms
½	of an 8-ounce package cream cheese, cut up
⅓	cup milk
1	2-ounce jar diced pimiento, drained
½	teaspoon salt
½	teaspoon dried marjoram, crushed
¼	teaspoon black pepper

1 Cook noodles according to package directions. Drain; rinse and drain well.

2 Meanwhile, in a 4-quart Dutch oven cook ground beef, sweet pepper, and onion until meat is brown and vegetables are tender. Drain off fat. Stir in golden mushroom soup, corn, mushrooms, cream cheese, milk, pimiento, salt, marjoram, and black pepper. Heat and stir until cream cheese melts. Gently stir in cooked noodles.

3 Spoon ground beef mixture into an ungreased 2-quart rectangular baking dish. Bake, covered, in a 350°F oven for 30 to 35 minutes or until heated through.

Nutrition Facts per serving: 416 cal., 18 g total fat (8 g sat. fat), 107 mg chol., 688 mg sodium, 41 g carbo., 3 g fiber, 23 g pro.

This recipe is a more creamy take on the classic French beef stew.

BRIEF BEEF BURGUNDY

1½ pounds beef stew meat, trimmed and cut into 1-inch pieces

2 tablespoons cooking oil

1 10¾-ounce can condensed cream of celery soup or reduced-fat and reduced-sodium condensed cream of celery soup

1 10¾-ounce can condensed cream of mushroom soup or reduced-fat and reduced-sodium condensed cream of mushroom soup

¾ cup Burgundy wine

1 envelope (½ of a 2-ounce package) dry onion soup mix

8 ounces fresh mushrooms, sliced (3 cups)

Hot cooked noodles or rice

1 In a large skillet brown meat, half at a time, in hot oil. Drain off fat. Return all meat to skillet.

2 Stir in cream of celery soup, cream of mushroom soup, Burgundy, and onion soup mix. Bring to boiling; reduce heat. Simmer, covered, for 1½ hours.

3 Stir in mushrooms; cook for 30 minutes more. Serve over hot cooked noodles.

Nutrition Facts per serving: 451 cal., 19 g total fat (5 g sat. fat), 82 mg chol., 1,247 mg sodium, 32 g carbo., 2 g fiber, 32 g pro.

PREP:
20 minutes
COOK:
1½ hours + 30 minutes
MAKES:
6 servings

Here's a great recipe to serve when you have houseguests. Just put the ingredients in a pan, pop it in the oven, and you're free to kick back and relax with everyone.

BEEFY MUSHROOM OVEN STEW

PREP:

25 minutes

BAKE:

2 hours

MAKES:

8 to 10 servings

2	pounds beef stew meat, trimmed and cut into 1-inch cubes
1/2	teaspoon salt
1/2	teaspoon black pepper
1 1/2	pounds medium potatoes, peeled and quartered
1	pound carrots, peeled and cut into 1 1/2-inch pieces
4	stalks celery, cut into 1 1/2-inch pieces
1	medium rutabaga, peeled and cut into 1-inch chunks
1	large onion, cut into wedges
1	4 1/2-ounce jar (drained weight) whole mushrooms, drained
1	10 3/4-ounce can condensed cream of celery soup
1	10 3/4-ounce can condensed beefy mushroom or cream of mushroom soup
1 1/4	cups water
1/2	cup dry sherry (optional)

1 Place meat in a roasting pan. Sprinkle with salt and pepper. Add potatoes, carrots, celery, rutabaga, onion, and mushrooms. In a large bowl combine cream of celery soup, beefy mushroom soup, water, and, if desired, sherry; pour over mixture in roasting pan. Stir.

2 Bake, covered, in a 350°F oven for 2 to 2 1/2 hours or until meat and vegetables are tender. Skim off fat; stir meat and vegetables before serving.

Nutrition Facts per serving: 368 cal., 16 g total fat (6 g sat. fat), 68 mg chol., 917 mg sodium, 32 g carbo., 5 g fiber, 23 g pro.

Served with sides, ready-made refrigerated meat entrées can make for quick, satisfying suppers in themselves. A little doctoring up—as in this recipe—adds a homespun quality to the meal.

SPEEDY BEEF STEW

1	17-ounce package refrigerated cooked beef roast au jus
2	10¾-ounce cans condensed beefy mushroom soup
1	16-ounce package frozen mixed vegetables (any combination)
4	teaspoons snipped fresh basil or 1½ teaspoons dried basil, crushed
1½	cups milk

① Cut beef into bite-size pieces. In a 4-quart Dutch oven combine beef and au jus, beefy mushroom soup, vegetables, and, if using, dried basil.

② Bring to boiling; reduce heat. Simmer, covered, for 10 minutes. Stir in milk and, if using, fresh basil. Heat through.

Nutrition Facts per serving: 386 cal., 15 g total fat (7 g sat. fat), 80 mg chol., 1,688 mg sodium, 33 g carbo., 5 g fiber, 33 g pro.

PREP:
15 minutes

COOK:
10 minutes

MAKES:
4 servings

Real Burgundy wine, from the Burgundy region of France, is usually a pricey item, but you don't have to splurge for this stew. Cook with wines that you wouldn't mind drinking, and fortunately, you can find many good, drinkable wines that are also affordable.

BURGUNDY BEEF STEW

PREP:

25 minutes

COOK:

1 hour + 30 minutes

MAKES:

4 servings

1½ pounds beef chuck roast, trimmed and cut into 1-inch cubes

2 tablespoons cooking oil

3 tablespoons all-purpose flour

½ teaspoon dried basil, crushed

¼ teaspoon black pepper

1 10¾-ounce can condensed tomato soup

1 10½-ounce can condensed beef broth

½ cup Burgundy wine

4 medium potatoes, peeled and halved

4 medium carrots, quartered

1 large onion, sliced

1 In a 4-quart Dutch oven brown meat, half at a time, in hot oil. Return all meat to Dutch oven. Stir in flour, basil, and pepper. Stir in tomato soup, beef broth, and wine. Bring to boiling; reduce heat. Simmer, covered, for 1 hour, stirring occasionally.

2 Add potatoes, carrots, and onion. Simmer, covered, about 30 minutes more or until meat and vegetables are tender, stirring occasionally.

Nutrition Facts per serving: 503 cal., 14 g total fat (3 g sat. fat), 101 mg chol., 1,188 mg sodium, 45 g carbo., 6 g fiber, 44 g pro.

Biscuit-topped stews keep getting easier and are just as satisfying! First came the condensed soup, then refrigerated biscuits. Frozen meatballs mean you don't even have meat to brown. Now that's progress!

BISCUIT-TOPPED OVEN MEATBALL STEW

2	10¾-ounce cans condensed cream of onion soup
¾	cup water
1	tablespoon bottled steak sauce
1	teaspoon dried basil, crushed
1	16- or 18-ounce package frozen Italian-style meatballs
1	16-ounce package frozen California vegetable blend (broccoli, cauliflower, and carrots), thawed
1	7½-ounce package (10) refrigerated biscuits
1	tablespoon butter or margarine, melted
2	tablespoons grated Parmesan cheese

PREP:

15 minutes

BAKE:

40 minutes

MAKES:

6 servings

1 In an ungreased 2½-quart casserole combine cream of onion soup, water, steak sauce, and basil. Stir in meatballs and vegetables. Bake, covered, in a 400°F oven for 40 to 45 minutes or until heated through, stirring once.

2 Meanwhile, place biscuits on an ungreased baking sheet. Brush tops with melted butter; sprinkle with Parmesan cheese. If space allows, bake during the last 8 to 10 minutes of casserole baking time. If there is not enough room in the oven, let stew stand, covered, while biscuits bake. Serve biscuits with stew.

Nutrition Facts per serving: 474 cal., 29 g total fat (12 g sat. fat), 68 mg chol., 1,837 mg sodium, 36 g carbo., 6 g fiber, 19 g pro.

Cream of onion soup really bumps up the satisfaction factor in this less-than-30-minute soup. If you like, substitute fresh parsley for the dried parsley, but use 6 tablespoons and stir it in toward the end of cooking time.

EASY BEEF & NOODLE SOUP

START TO FINISH:

25 minutes

MAKES:

4 servings

1	pound lean ground beef
2½	cups water
1	10¾-ounce can condensed cream of onion soup
1	10½-ounce can condensed beef broth
1½	cups dry medium noodles
2	tablespoons dried parsley flakes
	Parmesan cheese (optional)

1 In a large saucepan or skillet cook meat until brown. Drain off fat. Stir in water, cream of onion soup, beef broth, noodles, and parsley flakes.

2 Bring to boiling; reduce heat. Simmer, covered, 5 minutes or until noodles are tender, stirring occasionally. If desired, sprinkle with Parmesan cheese.

Nutrition Facts per serving: 357 cal., 19 g total fat (7 g sat. fat), 98 mg chol., 1,218 mg sodium, 19 g carbo., 1 g fiber, 27 g pro.

During cooking, the bean with bacon soup flavors the roast. In turn, juices from the meat flavor the soup, which ends up making a dynamite sauce for this one-dish meal.

VEGETABLE-TOPPED RUMP ROAST

2	tablespoons all-purpose flour
¼	teaspoon salt
¼	teaspoon paprika
	Dash black pepper
1	2- to 2½-pound boneless beef round rump roast (rolled and tied)
2	tablespoons cooking oil
1	11½-ounce can condensed bean with bacon soup
½	cup water
1	teaspoon dried basil, crushed
1	pound boiling onions, peeled
6	medium carrots, halved (1 pound)
1	medium green sweet pepper, cut into 1-inch pieces

PREP:
30 minutes
BAKE:
1½ hours + 1 hour
MAKES:
6 servings

❶ In a small bowl combine flour, salt, paprika, and pepper; coat roast with flour mixture. In a 4- to 5-quart Dutch oven brown the roast on all sides in hot oil. Remove from heat. Drain off fat. In another small bowl combine bean with bacon soup, water, and basil; pour over roast.

❷ Bake roast, covered, in a 325°F oven for 1½ hours. Add boiling onions, carrots, and sweet pepper. Bake, covered, about 1 hour more or until meat and vegetables are tender.

❸ To serve, remove strings from meat. Arrange meat and vegetables on platter. Spoon some of the soup mixture over meat and vegetables; pass remaining soup mixture.

Nutrition Facts per serving: 374 cal., 12 g total fat (3 g sat. fat), 81 mg chol., 622 mg sodium, 26 g carbo., 6 g fiber, 40 g pro.

Tomato-basil soup stands in as a convenient sauce for this family-friendly steak-and-noodle dish.

TOMATO-SAUCED STEAK

PREP:

20 minutes

BAKE:

30 minutes + 1 hour

MAKES:

8 servings

2   tablespoons all-purpose flour

1   teaspoon dry mustard

¼   teaspoon salt

Dash black pepper

2   pounds boneless beef round steak, cut ¾ inch thick

2   tablespoons cooking oil

1   19-ounce can ready-to-serve tomato-basil soup

1   medium onion, chopped

1   tablespoon Worcestershire sauce

Hot cooked noodles or spaetzle

1 In a small bowl combine flour, mustard, salt, and pepper. Trim fat from meat. Cut meat into 8 serving-size pieces. On a cutting board or work surface, lightly pound flour mixture into meat with the ridged side of a meat mallet. In a 10-inch ovenproof skillet brown meat, half at a time, in hot oil, turning once. Drain off fat. Return all meat to skillet.

2 In a medium bowl stir together tomato-basil soup, onion, and Worcestershire sauce; pour over meat.

3 Bake, covered, in a 325°F oven for 30 minutes. Uncover; bake about 1 hour more or until meat is tender. Serve over hot cooked noodles.

Nutrition Facts per serving: 309 cal., 7 g total fat (1 g sat. fat), 75 mg chol., 370 mg sodium, 28 g carbo., 1 g fiber, 31 g pro.

The triangle-shape tri-tip roast is ideal for grilling. If you are unable to find a beef roast labeled "tri-tip," look for a boneless beef sirloin roast or sirloin steak that is cut 1½ to 2 inches thick.

TRI-TIP WITH JAMBALAYA RICE

¼ cup soy sauce

2 tablespoons granulated sugar

2 tablespoons packed brown sugar

2 tablespoons finely chopped onion

2 tablespoons lemon juice

1 tablespoon vinegar

½ teaspoon chili powder

1 1½- to 2-pound beef bottom sirloin roast (tri-tip) or boneless beef sirloin steak, cut 1½ to 2 inches thick

4 ounces bulk hot Italian sausage

2 stalks celery, chopped

1 small red sweet pepper, chopped

1 small yellow sweet pepper, chopped

⅓ cup chopped onion

1 clove garlic, minced

¾ cup uncooked long grain rice

¼ teaspoon cayenne pepper

¼ teaspoon paprika

1 10¾-ounce can condensed cream of mushroom or cream of chicken soup

PREP:
25 minutes
GRILL:
35 minutes
STAND:
10 minutes
MAKES:
6 servings

① For basting sauce, stir together soy sauce, granulated sugar, brown sugar, the 2 tablespoons onion, the lemon juice, vinegar, and chili powder; set aside. Trim fat from meat.

② For charcoal grill, arrange medium-hot coals around a drip pan. Test for medium heat above pan. Place meat on grill rack over drip pan. Cover and grill until desired doneness. Allow 35 to 40 minutes for medium-rare doneness (145°F) or 40 to 45 minutes for medium doneness (160°F). Brush meat often with basting sauce during the last 10 minutes of grilling. Cover meat with foil; let stand for 10 minutes before slicing.

③ Meanwhile, in a large saucepan cook Italian sausage until meat is lightly browned. Add celery, sweet pepper, the ⅓ cup onion, and the garlic. Cook and stir for 5 minutes. Add rice, cayenne pepper, and paprika; cook and stir for 2 minutes more. Add cream of mushroom soup and 1¼ cups water.

④ Bring to boiling; reduce heat. Simmer, covered, for 15 to 20 minutes or until rice is tender, stirring occasionally. Serve rice mixture with sliced meat.

Nutrition Facts per serving: 387 cal., 14 g total fat (5 g sat. fat), 80 mg chol., 1,204 mg sodium, 34 g carbo., 2 g fiber, 30 g pro.

Cracked black pepper adds a wonderfully sharp flavor to the rich meat.

DIJON-PEPPER STEAK

START TO FINISH:
30 minutes

MAKES:

4 servings

4   beef sirloin steaks (1¼ pounds), cut ¾ inch thick

1   teaspoon cracked black pepper

2   tablespoons butter or margarine

1   10½-ounce can condensed French onion soup

¼   cup water

2   tablespoons Dijon-style mustard

1   tablespoon all-purpose flour

1   4-ounce can (drained weight) sliced mushrooms, drained

    Hot cooked noodles

1 Trim fat from steaks. Press pepper into both sides of each steak. In a large skillet cook steaks in hot butter over medium heat for 8 to 10 minutes for medium-rare to medium doneness, turning once.

2 Transfer steaks to a serving platter, reserving drippings in skillet. Cover steaks; keep warm. Remove skillet from heat and allow to stand for 1 minute.

3 For sauce, in a medium bowl combine French onion soup, water, mustard, and flour; stir into skillet. Add mushrooms. Cook and stir until slightly thickened and bubbly. Cook and stir for 1 minute more. Serve sauce with steaks and noodles.

Nutrition Facts per serving: 451 cal., 14 g total fat (6 g sat. fat), 144 mg chol., 1,041 mg sodium, 39 g carbo., 3 g fiber, 38 g pro.

It's hard to say what you'll love more about this recipe—the mere 10 minutes of hands-on prep time or the wonderful boost of flavor that the packet of onion soup mix adds to the succulent cooking juices.

EASY POT ROAST

1	2- to 3-pound beef chuck pot roast
2	tablespoons cooking oil
¼	cup water
1	10¾-ounce can condensed cream of mushroom soup
1	envelope (½ of a 2-ounce package) dry onion soup mix
¼	teaspoon black pepper
3	medium potatoes (about 1 pound), peeled and quartered
3	medium carrots, quartered
2	small onions, cut into wedges
2	stalks celery, cut into 1-inch pieces

1 In a 5- to 6-quart Dutch oven brown roast on both sides in hot oil. Drain off fat. Add water. In a small bowl combine cream of mushroom soup, onion soup mix, and pepper; spread over roast.

2 Bake, covered, in a 325°F oven for 1½ hours. Arrange potatoes, carrots, onions, and celery around the roast, pushing vegetables down into the liquid. Bake, covered, for 1 to 1¼ hours more or until meat and vegetables are tender.

Nutrition Facts per serving: 331 cal., 12 g total fat (3 g sat. fat), 90 mg chol., 640 mg sodium, 21 g carbo., 2 g fiber, 35 g pro.

PREP:
20 minutes

BAKE:
1½ hours + 1 hour

MAKES:
6 to 8 servings

Let's hear it for frozen meatballs—and let's hear it for another way to serve these all-time-great shoo-ins for terrific meals.

CREAMY MEATBALL CASSEROLE

PREP:

15 minutes

BAKE:

1 hour

MAKES:

6 servings

1 10¾-ounce can condensed cream of mushroom or cream of onion soup

1 cup milk

½ cup dairy sour cream

½ teaspoon salt

⅛ teaspoon black pepper

32 frozen cooked meatballs (½ ounce each)

1 20-ounce package refrigerated red-skinned potato wedges

1 16-ounce package frozen loose-pack stir-fry vegetables (any combination)

1 In a large bowl stir together cream of mushroom soup, milk, sour cream, salt, and pepper. Stir in meatballs, potato wedges, and vegetables. Transfer to an ungreased 3-quart rectangular baking dish.

2 Bake, covered, in a 350°F oven about 1 hour or until heated through.

Nutrition Facts per serving: 423 cal., 28 g total fat (12 g sat. fat), 37 mg chol., 1,291 mg sodium, 28 g carbo., 6 g fiber, 17 g pro.

Frozen meatballs are readily available, easy to use, and sure to please. Here's an off-the-beaten-path way to make the most of these gems of the freezer.

SAUCY STROGANOFF-STYLE MEATBALLS

1	10¾-ounce can condensed golden mushroom soup
½	cup dairy sour cream
½	cup milk
¼	cup dry white wine or beef broth
2	tablespoons all-purpose flour
32	to 36 frozen cooked meatballs (½ ounce each)
1	4-ounce can (drained weight) sliced mushrooms, drained
	Hot cooked noodles

START TO FINISH:

35 minutes

MAKES:

6 servings

1 In a large saucepan combine golden mushroom soup, sour cream, milk, white wine, and flour. Add meatballs and mushrooms.

2 Bring to boiling; reduce heat. Simmer, covered, about 20 minutes or until meatballs are heated through, stirring occasionally. Serve with noodles.

Nutrition Facts per serving: 436 cal., 26 g total fat (11 g sat. fat), 64 mg chol., 1,094 mg sodium, 34 g carbo., 4 g fiber, 16 g pro.

This recipe tastes like a cross between luscious Swedish meatballs and ever-favorite stuffed cabbage rolls. Tip: If the cabbage leaves adhere tightly to the head of the cabbage, immerse the entire head in boiling water for 1 minute to loosen the leaves.

SWEDISH CABBAGE ROLLS

PREP:

35 minutes

BAKE:

65 minutes

MAKES:

6 servings

1	egg
½	cup milk
¼	cup finely chopped onion
1	teaspoon dried basil, crushed
¼	teaspoon salt
	Dash black pepper
8	ounces ground beef
8	ounces ground pork
¾	cup cooked rice
6	large or 12 medium cabbage leaves
1	10¾-ounce can condensed cream of onion soup
¼	cup water

1 In a medium bowl beat egg with a whisk; stir in milk, onion, basil, salt, and pepper. Add ground meats and rice; mix well.

2 Remove center veins from cabbage leaves, keeping each leaf in one piece. Immerse leaves in boiling water about 3 minutes or until limp; drain. Place ½ cup of the meat mixture on each large leaf or ¼ cup of the meat mixture on each medium leaf; fold in sides. Starting at unfolded edge, roll up each leaf, making sure folded sides are included in roll. Arrange in an ungreased 2-quart rectangular baking dish.

3 In a small bowl stir together cream of onion soup and water; pour over cabbage rolls.

4 Bake, uncovered, in a 350°F oven for 65 to 70 minutes or until an instant-read thermometer inserted into the center of a cabbage roll reads 160°F, basting once or twice with sauce.

Nutrition Facts per serving: 298 cal., 18 g total fat (7 g sat. fat), 98 mg chol., 556 mg sodium, 15 g carbo., 1 g fiber, 17 g pro.

Round steak draped in rich brown sauce—it's a simple dish, but oh-so-satisfying!

WINE-SAUCED BEEF OVER NOODLES

1	tablespoon all-purpose flour
1/8	teaspoon black pepper
1	pound beef top round steak, cut 1 inch thick
1	tablespoon cooking oil
1	10¾-ounce can condensed beefy mushroom soup
1/3	cup dry red wine
1/2	teaspoon dried basil, crushed
	Hot cooked noodles

PREP:

20 minutes

COOK:

1 hour

MAKES:

4 servings

1 In a shallow dish combine flour and pepper. Trim fat from meat. Cut meat into 4 serving-size pieces. Coat both sides of meat with flour mixture. In a large skillet brown meat in hot oil. Add beefy mushroom soup, wine, and basil.

2 Bring to boiling; reduce heat. Simmer, covered, about 1 hour or until meat is tender. Serve meat and soup mixture over hot cooked noodles.

Nutrition Facts per serving: 322 cal., 9 g total fat (2 g sat. fat), 77 mg chol., 699 mg sodium, 26 g carbo., 2 g fiber, 31 g pro.

When wintertime comes and the outdoor grill is covered up, you can still enjoy the flavors of barbecue beef sandwiches. This slow-stewing oven version makes it easy.

SHREDDED BEEF SANDWICHES

PREP:

15 minutes

BAKE:

3¹/₂ hours

MAKES:

12 to 16 servings

1   5- to 6-pound boneless beef chuck roast

1   10³/₄-ounce can condensed cream of onion or cream of mushroom soup

³/₄ cup bottled barbecue sauce

¹/₄ cup water

12 to 16 onion buns or kaiser rolls, split and toasted

1 Trim fat from meat. Place meat in a roasting pan. In a small bowl combine cream of onion soup, barbecue sauce, and water; pour over roast.

2 Bake, covered, in a 350°F oven for 3¹/₂ to 4 hours or until meat is very tender.

3 Remove meat from pan. When meat is cool enough to handle, use two forks to shred, pulling meat in opposite directions. Skim fat from sauce in roasting pan. Stir enough sauce into shredded beef to coat. If necessary, transfer meat mixture to a large saucepan and reheat over medium heat, stirring frequently. Serve meat on buns. Pass remaining sauce with sandwiches.

Nutrition Facts per serving: 401 cal., 12 g total fat (4 g sat. fat), 115 mg chol., 688 mg sodium, 26 g carbo., 1 g fiber, 45 g pro.

It's the soup that makes these loose-meat burgers so good and saucy. Add dill pickles and buns, and dinner is ready in less than half an hour.

SLOPPY BEEF BURGERS

- 1½   pounds lean ground beef
- ½   cup chopped onion
- ⅓   cup chopped green sweet pepper
- 1   10¾-ounce can reduced-fat and reduced-sodium condensed tomato soup
- 1   tablespoon Worcestershire sauce
- 1   tablespoon yellow mustard
- 8   whole wheat or white hamburger buns, split and toasted

     Dill pickle slices (optional)

START TO FINISH:
25 minutes
MAKES:
8 servings

1 In a large skillet cook ground beef, onion, and sweet pepper until beef is brown and vegetables are tender. Drain off fat. Stir in tomato soup, Worcestershire sauce, and mustard. Bring to boiling; reduce heat. Simmer, covered, for 5 minutes.

2 Spoon beef mixture into buns. If desired, serve with pickles.

Nutrition Facts per serving: 289 cal., 11 g total fat (4 g sat. fat), 54 mg chol., 417 mg sodium, 27 g carbo., 2 g fiber, 20 g pro.

Ever hear of Cincinnati chili? It's a spicy chili that's often served over spaghetti and topped with cheese—and sometimes onions and more beans. This fun version of burgers is patterned after that classic.

CHILI-SAUCED BURGERS & SPAGHETTI

PREP:

20 minutes

COOK:

15 minutes

MAKES:

6 servings

¼ cup milk

¾ cup soft bread crumbs

½ teaspoon salt

Dash black pepper

1 pound lean ground beef

¼ cup chopped onion

1 clove garlic, minced

1 11¼-ounce can condensed chili beef soup

⅔ cup water

12 ounces dried spaghetti, cooked according to package directions

⅓ cup shredded cheddar cheese

1 In a medium bowl combine milk, bread crumbs, salt, and pepper. Add ground beef; mix well. Shape into six ¾-inch-thick oblong patties. In a large skillet cook patties over medium heat until brown. Remove from skillet.

2 Cook onion and garlic in drippings in skillet until tender. Stir in chili beef soup and the water. Return patties to skillet. Bring mixture to boiling; reduce heat. Simmer, covered, for 15 minutes.

3 To serve, place patties on top of hot cooked spaghetti. Top with soup mixture and sprinkle with cheddar cheese.

Nutrition Facts per serving: 461 cal., 13 g total fat (6 g sat. fat), 63 mg chol., 707 mg sodium, 57 g carbo., 3 g fiber, 27 g pro.

A juicy burger, slathered with chili and topped with melted cheese, is an ever-popular sports-bar favorite. It's also the inspiration behind this easy skillet dish.

CHILI-BURGER SUPPER

1	cup dried elbow macaroni or penne pasta
1	pound ground beef
½	teaspoon chili powder
1	11¼-ounce can condensed chili beef soup
1	14½-ounce can diced tomatoes, undrained
½	cup shredded cheddar cheese (2 ounces)
	Dairy sour cream (optional)
	Sliced green onions (optional)

START TO FINISH:

20 minutes

MAKES:

4 servings

1 Cook pasta according to package directions; drain well.

2 Meanwhile, in a large skillet cook ground beef until meat is brown. Drain off fat. Add chili powder to beef in skillet; cook and stir for 1 minute.

3 Add chili beef soup, tomatoes, and cooked pasta to beef mixture in skillet. Cook and stir over medium heat until mixture is bubbly. Sprinkle with cheese. If desired, serve with sour cream and green onions.

Nutrition Facts per serving: 501 cal., 23 g total fat (11 g sat. fat), 94 mg chol., 948 mg sodium, 38 g carbo., 7 g fiber, 33 g pro.

Mounds of golden potatoes top this easy casserole. Serve it with some steamed green beans or glazed carrots and crusty bread.

POTATO-PAN BURGER

PREP:

30 minutes

BAKE:

25 minutes

MAKES:

8 servings

2   pounds ground beef

¼   cup all-purpose flour

1   envelope (½ of a 2-ounce package) dry onion soup mix

1   10¾-ounce can condensed cream of mushroom soup

1   8-ounce carton dairy sour cream

¾   cup water

1   tablespoon catsup

1½   cups water

¼   cup butter or margarine

½   teaspoon salt

2   cups packaged instant mashed potato flakes

½   cup milk

2   beaten eggs

1   cup all-purpose flour

2   teaspoons baking powder

1 In an extra-large skillet cook ground beef until brown. Drain off fat. Stir in the ¼ cup flour and the onion soup mix. Stir in cream of mushroom soup, sour cream, the ¾ cup water, and catsup. Cook until heated through, stirring occasionally.

2 Meanwhile, in a medium saucepan combine the 1½ cups water, butter, and salt; bring to boiling. Remove from heat. Add potato flakes and milk, stirring until combined. Stir in eggs, the 1 cup flour, and the baking powder.

3 Transfer beef mixture to an ungreased 3-quart rectangular baking dish; spoon potato mixture in mounds on top of beef mixture. Bake in a 425°F oven about 25 minutes or until potatoes are golden on top.

Nutrition Facts per serving: 558 cal., 36 g total fat (16 g sat. fat), 831 mg chol., 831 mg sodium, 30 g carbo., 1 g fiber, 27 g pro.

This recipe comes straight from the pages of the first edition of the Better Homes and Gardens Junior Cook Book, *which appeared in 1955. Generation of kids have grown up cooking—and loving—these simple sloppy-joe-style sandwiches. Why not let your kids join in the tradition?*

BAR-B-Q-BURGERS

PREP:
15 minutes
COOK:
30 minutes
MAKES:
8 servings

1   pound ground beef
⅔   cup chopped onion
1   10¾-ounce can condensed chicken gumbo soup
¼   cup water
1   tablespoon catsup
1   tablespoon yellow mustard
    Dash black pepper
8   hamburger buns, split
    Sliced dill pickles (optional)
    Yellow mustard (optional)

1 In a large skillet cook ground beef and onion until beef is brown. Drain off fat. Stir in chicken gumbo soup, water, catsup, mustard, and the pepper.

2 Bring to boiling; reduce heat. Simmer, covered, over low heat for 30 minutes, stirring occasionally. Spoon into buns. If desired, serve with dill pickle slices and additional mustard.

Nutrition Facts per serving: 286 cal., 11 g total fat (4 g sat. fat), 51 mg chol., 642 mg sodium, 26 g carbo., 2 g fiber, 19 g pro.

You can use cooking sherry for this, but remember that cooking wines usually include salt as an ingredient. Be sure to taste the dish before you add salt at the table.

SHERRIED BEEF STROGANOFF

PREP:

30 minutes

BAKE:

1½ hours

MAKES:

6 to 8 servings

2	pounds beef stew meat, cut into 1-inch cubes
¼	cup all-purpose flour
2	tablespoons cooking oil
1	10¾-ounce can condensed cream of mushroom soup
¾	cup water
½	cup dry sherry
1	1½-ounce envelope dry stroganoff sauce mix
1	tablespoon dried minced onion
1	4-ounce can (drained weight) sliced mushrooms, drained
½	cup dairy sour cream
	Hot cooked rice (optional)
	Snipped fresh parsley (optional)

1 In a plastic bag toss beef cubes with flour to coat. In a large skillet brown meat, half at a time, in hot oil. Drain off fat.

2 In a medium bowl combine cream of mushroom soup, water, sherry, stroganoff sauce mix, and minced onion; stir into meat with mushrooms. Turn mixture into an ungreased 2-quart casserole.

3 Bake, covered, in a 350°F oven about 1½ hours or until meat is tender. Stir in sour cream. If desired, serve over hot cooked rice and sprinkle with parsley.

Nutrition Facts per serving: 422 cal., 20 g total fat (7 g sat. fat), 79 mg chol., 1,029 mg sodium, 16 g carbo., 1 g fiber, 37 g pro.

The great thing about making mini meat loaves is that they cook much more quickly than one large loaf, bringing dinner to the table sooner.

MINI LOAVES WITH BEER-CHEESE SAUCE

PREP:
35 minutes
BAKE:
30 minutes
MAKES:
6 servings

²/₃	cup water
¹/₃	cup uncooked long grain rice
1	teaspoon dried parsley flakes, crushed
¹/₂	teaspoon instant beef bouillon granules
¹/₂	teaspoon dried minced onion
¹/₈	teaspoon garlic powder
1	egg
1	10³/₄-ounce can condensed cheddar cheese soup
1	pound lean ground beef
¹/₃	cup beer
	Snipped fresh parsley (optional)

1 In a small saucepan stir together water, rice, parsley flakes, bouillon granules, minced onion, and garlic powder. Bring to boiling; reduce heat. Simmer, covered, for 15 minutes. Remove from the heat. Let stand, covered, for 10 minutes. Fluff rice mixture with a fork. Cool slightly.

2 In a large bowl combine egg and ¹/₄ cup of the cheddar cheese soup. Stir in cooked rice mixture. Add beef; mix well. Shape into six 4×2-inch loaves. Place in an ungreased 8×8×2-inch baking pan.

3 Bake in a 350°F oven for 30 to 35 minutes or until done (160°F).*

4 Meanwhile, for sauce, in a small saucepan combine the remaining cheddar cheese soup and the beer. Cook and stir until smooth and heated through. Arrange the meat loaves on a serving platter. Spoon some of the sauce over meat loaves. If desired, sprinkle with fresh parsley. Pass remaining sauce.

*NOTE: **The internal color of a meat loaf is not a reliable doneness indicator. A beef meat loaf cooked to 160°F is safe, regardless of color. To measure the doneness of this mini meat loaf, insert an instant-read thermometer through the side of the loaf.**

Nutrition Facts per serving: 216 cal., 11 g total fat (4 g sat. fat), 89 mg chol., 505 mg sodium, 13 g carbo., 1 g fiber, 17 g pro.

Torn fresh spinach—added just at the end so it doesn't overcook—really helps brighten this tasty dish.

ASIAN BEEF SKILLET

1	pound boneless beef round steak, cut ½ inch thick*
2	tablespoons cooking oil
1	cup bias-sliced celery
½	cup coarsely chopped onion
1	10¾-ounce can condensed cream of mushroom soup
1	cup fresh bean sprouts
⅔	cup water
2	tablespoons soy sauce
3	cups torn fresh spinach
	Hot cooked rice
	Soy sauce (optional)

1 Trim fat from beef. Slice beef into thin, bite-size strips. In a large skillet brown beef, half at a time, in hot oil. Remove beef; add celery and onion to skillet. Cook and stir until crisp-tender.

2 Stir in cream of mushroom soup, bean sprouts, water, and the 2 tablespoons soy sauce; bring to boiling. Stir in beef and spinach; heat through. Serve over hot cooked rice. If desired, pass additional soy sauce.

*TEST KITCHEN TIP: **Partially freeze the beef round steak to make slicing easier.**

Nutrition Facts per serving: 451 cal., 15 g total fat (3 g sat. fat), 50 mg chol., 1,100 mg sodium, 43 g carbo., 4 g fiber, 34 g pro.

Two cans of soup give you a head start on an incredibly beefy, flavorful chili. Serve with sliced apple wedges, chunks of cheddar cheese, and crackers.

BEER CHILI

1	pound lean ground beef
½	cup chopped onion
1	15½-ounce can red kidney beans, rinsed and drained
1	12-ounce can (1½ cups) beer
1	11¼-ounce can condensed chili beef soup
1	10¾-ounce can condensed tomato soup
½	cup water
½	cup chopped green sweet pepper
2	teaspoons chili powder
1	teaspoon Worcestershire sauce
½	teaspoon garlic powder
	Shredded cheddar cheese (optional)
	Dairy sour cream (optional)

PREP:

25 minutes

COOK:

30 minutes

MAKES:

4 or 5 servings

1 In a 4-quart Dutch oven cook ground beef and onion until beef is brown. Drain off fat. Stir in kidney beans, beer, chili beef soup, tomato soup, water, sweet pepper, chili powder, Worcestershire sauce, and garlic powder.

2 Bring to boiling; reduce heat. Simmer, covered, for 30 minutes. If desired, sprinkle servings with cheddar cheese and top with sour cream.

Nutrition Facts per serving: 472 cal., 15 g total fat (6 g sat. fat), 79 mg chol., 1,341 mg sodium, 49 g carbo., 14 g fiber, 34 g pro.

Here's an easy oven meal that serves six. It's homey enough for every night, but the rich, zucchini-studded stuffing makes it interesting enough to serve at an informal dinner with friends or neighbors.

ZUCCHINI PORK CHOP SUPPER

PREP:
30 minutes

BAKE:
50 minutes

MAKES:
6 servings

1   14-ounce package herb-seasoned stuffing croutons (about 9½ cups)

¼   cup butter or margarine, melted

4   cups coarsely chopped zucchini

1   10¾-ounce can condensed cream of celery soup

1   8-ounce carton light dairy sour cream

¾   cup milk

½   cup shredded carrot

1   tablespoon snipped fresh parsley or 1 teaspoon dried parsley, crushed

¼   to ½ teaspoon black pepper

6   pork loin chops, cut ¾ inch thick (about 2¼ pounds)

1 In a large bowl stir together 7½ cups of the croutons and the melted butter. Place half of the buttered croutons in a greased 3-quart rectangular baking dish.

2 In another large bowl stir together zucchini, cream of celery soup, light sour cream, ½ cup of the milk, the carrot, parsley, and pepper. Spoon over buttered croutons in baking dish. Sprinkle remaining buttered croutons on top of zucchini mixture.

3 Coarsely crush remaining stuffing croutons; place in a shallow dish. Place remaining ¼ cup milk in another shallow dish. Trim fat from chops. Dip chops into milk, then into crushed croutons to coat.

4 Place chops on top of croutons in baking dish. Sprinkle with any remaining crushed croutons.

5 Bake, uncovered, in a 350°F oven for 50 to 60 minutes or until chops are done and juices run clear (160°F).

Nutrition Facts per serving: 639 cal., 24 g total fat (10 g sat. fat), 130 mg chol., 1,417 mg sodium, 57 g carbo., 4 g fiber, 46 g pro.

Yum! Pork chops in creamy mushroom gravy have been a comfort-food classic for years. The vegetable stir-ins add a fresh update.

PORK CHOPS IN CREAMY VEGETABLE SAUCE

6 pork rib chops, cut ½ inch thick (about 1¾ pounds)

Salt

Black pepper

Nonstick cooking spray

1½ cups sliced fresh mushrooms

1 medium green or red sweet pepper, cut into thin strips

1 10¾-ounce can reduced-fat and reduced-sodium condensed cream of mushroom soup

½ cup dairy sour cream

¼ cup milk

1 teaspoon paprika

1 medium tomato, seeded and chopped

Hot cooked noodles or rice

START TO FINISH:
35 minutes
MAKES:
6 servings

1 Trim fat from chops. Season chops with salt and black pepper. Lightly coat an unheated 12-inch skillet with nonstick cooking spray. Preheat over medium heat. Brown chops, half at a time, in hot skillet. Return all chops to skillet. Add mushrooms and sweet pepper. Cover and cook about 6 minutes more or until chops are tender and juices run clear (160°F).

2 For sauce, in a small bowl stir together cream of mushroom soup, sour cream, milk, and paprika. Spoon soup mixture over pork chop mixture. Cover and cook for 5 minutes more.

3 Add the tomato. Cook for 1 to 2 minutes more or until heated through. Remove chops to a serving platter. Stir sauce and spoon over chops. Serve with hot cooked noodles.

Nutrition Facts per serving: 302 cal., 10 g total fat (4 g sat. fat), 79 mg chol., 353 mg sodium, 28 g carbo., 2 g fiber, 23 g pro.

Anyone who grew up in mid-20th century America will likely have fond memories of the good ol' potato-and-pork-chop oven meal! This version simplifies the classic dish even more with refrigerated diced potatoes.

PORK CHOPS WITH SCALLOPED POTATOES

PREP:

20 minutes

BAKE:

40 minutes

MAKES:

4 servings

1   10¾-ounce can condensed cream of celery soup

1   cup milk

3   green onions, sliced

4   slices American cheese (4 ounces), torn

1   20-ounce package refrigerated diced potatoes with onions

4   cooked smoked pork chops (1½ to 2 pounds)

⅛   teaspoon black pepper

2   tablespoons snipped fresh chives

1 In a medium saucepan combine cream of celery soup, milk, and green onions. Heat through over medium heat. Stir in cheese; cook and stir until cheese is melted. Remove from heat; set aside.

2 In an ungreased 3-quart rectangular baking dish arrange potatoes in a single layer. Place pork chops on top of potatoes. Sprinkle chops with pepper. Pour soup mixture over chops and potatoes.

3 Bake, covered, in a 350°F oven about 40 minutes or until heated through. Sprinkle with chives just before serving.

Nutrition Facts per serving: 541 cal., 23 g total fat (11 g sat. fat), 123 mg chol., 3,226 mg sodium, 39 g carbo., 4 g fiber, 43 g pro.

Why reserve those handy canned onions exclusively for the classic green bean casserole? Pop open a can to sprinkle on this meaty casserole.

PORK CHOP CASSEROLE

PREP:
25 minutes
BAKE:
25 minutes + 5 minutes
MAKES:
8 servings

8   boneless pork loin chops, cut about ¾ inch thick (about 2 pounds)

⅓   cup all-purpose flour

¼   teaspoon salt

¼   teaspoon black pepper

2   tablespoons cooking oil

1   10¾-ounce can condensed cream of mushroom soup

⅔   cup chicken broth

½   cup dairy sour cream

½   teaspoon ground ginger

½   teaspoon dried rosemary, crushed

1   2.8-ounce can french-fried onions

Hot cooked noodles

1 Trim fat from chops. In a shallow dish combine flour, salt, and pepper. Coat chops with flour mixture.

2 In a large skillet cook chops, half at a time, in hot oil until brown on both sides (about 8 to 10 minutes). Remove from heat.

3 In a medium bowl stir together cream of mushroom soup, chicken broth, sour cream, ginger, and rosemary. Stir in half of the french-fried onions. Pour into an ungreased 3-quart rectangular baking dish. Top with brown chops.

4 Bake, covered, in a 350°F oven for 25 minutes. Uncover; sprinkle with remaining french-fried onions. Bake, uncovered, for 5 to 10 minutes more or until pork chops are tender and juices run clear (160°F). Serve with hot cooked noodles.

LOWER-FAT PORK CHOP CASSEROLE: **Prepare as directed, except substitute reduced-fat and reduced-sodium condensed cream of mushroom soup, reduced-sodium chicken broth, and light dairy sour cream for the regular soup, broth, and sour cream. Nutrition Facts per serving: 387 cal., 16 g total fat (4 g sat. fat), 99 mg chol., 393 mg sodium, 32 g carbo., 1 g fiber, 27 g pro.**

Nutrition Facts per serving: 411 cal., 19 g total fat (5 g sat. fat), 95 mg chol., 536 mg sodium, 31 g carbo., 1 g fiber, 28 g pro.

Here the old-fashioned pork chop and rice bake gets an update with a new style of cream of mushroom soup—one that's been infused with roasted garlic. Serve with buttered green beans, upscaled with chopped, toasted cashews if you're feeling splashy!

PORK CHOP & RICE BAKE

PREP:

25 minutes

BAKE:

35 minutes

STAND:

10 minutes

MAKES:

4 servings

4	pork rib chops, cut ½ inch thick (about 2 pounds total)
1	tablespoon cooking oil
	Black pepper
1	small onion, thinly sliced and separated into rings
1	10¾-ounce can condensed cream of mushroom with roasted garlic soup
¾	cup water
½	cup dry white wine
¾	cup uncooked long grain rice
1	4-ounce can (drained weight) sliced mushrooms, drained
1	teaspoon Worcestershire sauce
¼	teaspoon dried thyme, crushed
2	tablespoons snipped fresh parsley

1 In a 12-inch skillet cook chops in hot oil until brown on both sides. Remove chops from skillet, reserving drippings. Season chops with pepper; set aside.

2 In the same skillet cook onion in the drippings until tender; set aside. In a large bowl combine mushroom with roasted garlic soup, water, and wine; stir in rice, mushrooms, Worcestershire sauce, and thyme. Spoon into an ungreased 3-quart rectangular baking dish. Top with pork chops and cooked onions.

3 Bake, covered, in a 375°F oven for 35 to 40 minutes or until rice is done and chops are tender and juices run clear (160°F). Let stand, covered, for 10 minutes before serving. Sprinkle with parsley before serving.

Nutrition Facts per serving: 602 cal., 22 g total fat (7 g sat. fat), 124 mg chol., 735 mg sodium, 36 g carbo., 2 g fiber, 55 g pro.

You can certainly use pork or ham leftover from the Sunday roast for this rich dish—but whatever you do, don't call it "leftovers," as it's a luscious and lovely creation in itself.

PORK & SPINACH BAKE

1	10¾-ounce can condensed cream of chicken soup
¼	cup shredded Swiss cheese (1 ounce)
2	tablespoons mayonnaise or salad dressing
1	teaspoon lemon juice
½	teaspoon Worcestershire sauce
2	10-ounce packages frozen chopped spinach, thawed and well drained
1½	cups chopped cooked pork or ham
1½	cups soft bread crumbs (2 slices)
2	tablespoons butter or margarine, melted

PREP:
20 minutes
BAKE:
35 minutes
MAKES:
6 servings

1 In a small saucepan stir together cream of chicken soup, Swiss cheese, mayonnaise, lemon juice, and Worcestershire sauce. Bring to boiling, stirring occasionally; remove from heat.

2 In a large bowl stir ¾ cup of the soup mixture into drained spinach. Spread spinach mixture in an ungreased 2-quart square baking dish. Sprinkle pork over spinach mixture. Spoon remaining soup mixture over all. In a small bowl toss together bread crumbs and melted butter; sprinkle over casserole.

3 Bake, uncovered, in a 350°F oven about 35 minutes or until heated through.

Nutrition Facts per serving: 254 cal., 16 g total fat (6 g sat. fat), 52 mg chol., 680 mg sodium, 11 g carbo., 3 g fiber, 16 g pro.

With stir-fry vegetables, soy sauce, and Oriental noodles, this casserole definitely has some Asian inspiration. But its wonderful creaminess has that rich, unmistakably American comfort-food angle.

CREAMY PORK-NOODLE BAKE

PREP:

30 minutes

FREEZE:

1 hour

BAKE:

35 minutes

MAKES:

4 to 6 servings

1	pound boneless pork loin
$\frac{1}{4}$	cup all-purpose flour
$\frac{1}{4}$	teaspoon black pepper
2	tablespoons cooking oil
1	16-ounce package frozen pepper stir-fry vegetables (yellow, green, and red peppers and onion), thawed
1	$10\frac{3}{4}$-ounce can condensed cream of mushroom soup
1	4-ounce can (drained weight) sliced mushrooms, drained
2	tablespoons soy sauce
$\frac{1}{4}$	teaspoon ground ginger
1	3-ounce package Oriental noodles with mushroom seasoning
$\frac{1}{4}$	cup slivered almonds

1 Freeze pork about 1 hour or until partially frozen; thinly slice pork across the grain into bite-size strips. In a medium bowl combine flour and pepper. Add pork strips, half at a time, and toss to coat. In a large skillet cook pork, half at a time, in hot oil until brown (use additional oil, if necessary). Return all meat to skillet. Stir in stir-fry vegetables, cream of mushroom soup, mushrooms, soy sauce, and ginger. Set aside.

2 Meanwhile, cook the noodles in boiling water about 3 minutes or until tender; drain. Stir cooked noodles into pork mixture; stir in the seasoning mix from noodles. Spoon mixture into a greased 2-quart casserole. Sprinkle with almonds.

3 Bake, uncovered, in a 350°F oven about 35 minutes or until heated through.

Nutrition Facts per serving: 530 cal., 28 g total fat (7 g sat. fat), 63 mg chol., 1,592 mg sodium, 34 g carbo., 5 g fiber, 35 g pro.

Precooked dinner entrées, available in the meat section, make fuss-free, simple meals. With just a few more ingredients, and not a lot of time, you can have an entrée worthy of a Sunday dinner.

PORK STUFFING CASSEROLE

2	eggs
1	10¾-ounce can condensed cream of mushroom with roasted garlic soup
1	6-ounce package chicken-flavor stuffing mix
1	cup water
¼	cup butter or margarine
1	17-ounce package refrigerated cooked pork au jus
¼	cup milk

PREP:
15 minutes
BAKE:
45 minutes
MAKES:
6 servings

1 In a large bowl whisk together eggs and half of the mushroom with roasted garlic soup (about ⅔ cup); stir in stuffing mix to moisten. In a small saucepan combine water and butter; bring to boiling. Stir into stuffing mixture; mix well. Set aside.

2 Chop pork, reserving juices. In a medium bowl combine remaining mushroom with roasted garlic soup, milk, and reserved meat juices; stir in chopped meat. Spread into an ungreased 2-quart square baking dish. Spoon stuffing mixture evenly over meat mixture.

3 Bake, uncovered, in a 350°F oven about 45 minutes or until an instant-read thermometer inserted in center registers 160°F.

Nutrition Facts per serving: 367 cal., 19 g total fat (8 g sat. fat), 142 mg chol., 1,229 mg sodium, 25 g carbo., 1 g fiber, 24 g pro.

Pork shoulder is a good cut of meat for "walk away" cooking; its succulence comes through a long simmering time. So go ahead—mix up this dish, put it in the oven, and forget about it until mealtime.

FORGOTTEN PORK STEW

PREP:

25 minutes

BAKE:

2 hours

MAKES:

6 servings

1½ pounds boneless pork shoulder

1 tablespoon cooking oil

3 medium potatoes (1 pound), peeled and quartered

3 medium carrots, coarsely chopped

2 stalks celery, sliced

1 medium onion, chopped

1 10-ounce package frozen lima beans

1 10¾-ounce can condensed tomato soup

½ cup water

2 tablespoons quick-cooking tapioca

1 teaspoon dried basil, crushed

½ teaspoon salt

¼ teaspoon garlic powder

¼ teaspoon cayenne pepper

Snipped fresh basil (optional)

1 Trim fat from meat. Cut meat into 1-inch cubes.

2 In a 4-quart Dutch oven brown meat, half at a time, in hot oil. Drain off fat. Return all meat to Dutch oven; add potatoes, carrots, celery, onion, and lima beans. In a medium bowl combine tomato soup, water, tapioca, dried basil, salt, garlic powder, and cayenne pepper. Add to Dutch oven; stir to combine.

3 Bake, covered, in a 325°F oven for 2 to 2¼ hours or until meat and vegetables are tender. If desired, sprinkle with fresh basil before serving.

Nutrition Facts per serving: 350 cal., 10 g total fat (3 g sat. fat), 73 mg chol., 621 mg sodium, 36 g carbo., 6 g fiber, 29 g pro.

Crusty rolls and creamy coleslaw are good complements for this quick, meaty soup.

QUICK PORK-BEAN SOUP

12	ounces lean boneless pork
1	large onion, chopped
2	tablespoons cooking oil
2	cups water
1	11½-ounce can condensed bean with bacon soup
3	medium carrots, sliced
1	teaspoon Worcestershire sauce
¼	teaspoon dry mustard

PREP:
15 minutes
COOK:
15 minutes
MAKES:
4 servings

1 Cut pork into thin bite-size strips. In a large skillet cook pork and onion in hot oil for 3 to 4 minutes or until meat is brown. Stir in water, bean with bacon soup, carrots, Worcestershire sauce, and dry mustard.

2 Bring to boiling; reduce heat. Simmer, covered, for 15 minutes.

Nutrition Facts per serving: 312 cal., 13 g total fat (3 g sat. fat), 52 mg chol., 678 mg sodium, 23 g carbo., 6 g fiber, 24 g pro.

For this one-pot casserole, don't precook the macaroni. It cooks perfectly in the oven with the rest of the ingredients.

STIR-AND-BAKE HAM CASSEROLE

PREP:

10 minutes

BAKE:

30 minutes + 20 minutes + 5 minutes

MAKES:

4 servings

Nonstick cooking spray

1   $10^3/_4$-ounce can condensed cream of celery soup

$1^1/_4$ cups milk

1   $4^1/_2$-ounce jar (drained weight) sliced mushrooms, drained

1   tablespoon dried minced onion

2   cups chopped cooked ham

1   cup dried elbow macaroni

Dash black pepper

$^1/_2$ cup shredded American or cheddar cheese (2 ounces)

1 Lightly coat a $1^1/_2$-quart casserole with nonstick cooking spray. In the prepared casserole combine cream of celery soup, milk, mushrooms, and minced onion. Add ham, macaroni, and pepper. Mix well.

2 Bake, covered, in a 375°F oven for 30 minutes. Stir well (mixture may appear curdled). Bake, covered, for 20 to 30 minutes more or until macaroni is tender. Uncover; sprinkle with cheese. Bake, uncovered, for 5 minutes more.

Nutrition Facts per serving: 393 cal., 18 g total fat (8 g sat. fat), 59 mg chol., 1,837 mg sodium, 34 g carbo., 2 g fiber, 23 g pro.

If you like "ham-and-Swiss on rye" at the deli, bring the idea home and make it even better by baking those flavors into a creamy, warming casserole.

HAM-SAUERKRAUT CASSEROLE

2   cups diced cooked ham

1   14-ounce can Bavarian-style sauerkraut, rinsed, drained, and snipped*

1   10¾-ounce can condensed cream of potato soup

1   cup shredded Swiss cheese (4 ounces)

½   cup milk

1   tablespoon yellow mustard

¾   cup rye bread crumbs

1   tablespoon butter or margarine, melted

PREP:
15 minutes
BAKE:
25 minutes
MAKES:
6 servings

1 In a large bowl combine ham, sauerkraut, cream of potato soup, cheese, milk, and mustard. Turn mixture into an ungreased 1½-quart casserole. In a small bowl stir together bread crumbs and melted butter; sprinkle over ham mixture.

2 Bake, uncovered, in a 375°F oven about 25 minutes or until heated through.

*NOTE: **If Bavarian-style sauerkraut is not available, substitute one 14½-ounce can sauerkraut plus 2 tablespoons brown sugar and ½ teaspoon caraway seeds.**

Nutrition Facts per serving: 236 cal., 13 g total fat (7 g sat. fat), 53 mg chol., 1,611 mg sodium, 13 g carbo., 2 g fiber, 17 g pro.

Panko—Japanese-style bread crumbs—are more coarse than American bread crumbs. They bring an invitingly crunchy, golden brown topping to this casserole.

ASPARAGUS-HAM BAKE

PREP:
25 minutes
BAKE:
40 minutes
STAND:
10 minutes
MAKES:
6 servings

1	10¾-ounce can condensed cream of asparagus soup
¾	cup milk
2	cups cubed cooked ham (about 10 ounces)
2	cups cooked rice*
1	9-ounce package frozen cut asparagus, thawed
½	cup shredded Swiss cheese (2 ounces)
¼	cup finely chopped onion
½	cup panko (Japanese-style) bread crumbs
2	tablespoons butter or margarine, melted

1 In a large bowl combine cream of asparagus soup and milk. Add ham, rice, asparagus, cheese, and onion. Spoon ham mixture into an ungreased 2-quart square baking dish.

2 In a small bowl combine bread crumbs and butter; sprinkle evenly over asparagus mixture. Bake, uncovered, in a 375°F oven for 40 to 45 minutes or until heated through and lightly browned. Let stand for 10 minutes before serving.

*TEST KITCHEN TIP: **For 2 cups cooked rice, in a medium saucepan combine ⅔ cup uncooked long grain rice and 1⅓ cups water. Bring to boiling; reduce heat. Simmer, covered, for 15 to 18 minutes or until rice is tender.**

Nutrition Facts per serving: 306 cal., 14 g total fat (7 g sat. fat), 50 mg chol., 1,056 mg sodium, 28 g carbo., 2 g fiber, 16 g pro.

At its heart, this is that ever-favorite cheesy hash brown casserole that has starred on potluck tables for years. Ham transforms it into a crowd-pleasing breakfast dish.

HASH BROWN CASSEROLE

1	16-ounce carton dairy sour cream
1	10¾-ounce can condensed cream of chicken soup
1	32-ounce package frozen loose-pack diced hash brown potatoes
2	cups diced cooked ham (about 10 ounces)
2	cups cubed American cheese (8 ounces)
½	cup chopped onion
¼	teaspoon black pepper
2	cups crushed cornflakes
⅓	cup butter or margarine, melted

PREP:
20 minutes
CHILL:
8 to 24 hours
BAKE:
50 minutes
MAKES:
12 servings

1 In a very large bowl combine sour cream and cream of chicken soup. Stir in frozen potatoes, ham, cheese, onion, and pepper. Evenly spread the mixture into an ungreased 3-quart rectangular baking dish. Cover and chill for at least 8 hours or up to 24 hours.

2 In a small bowl combine cornflakes and melted butter. Sprinkle over potato mixture. Bake, uncovered, in a 350°F oven for 50 to 55 minutes or until hot in center and bubbly around edges.

Nutrition Facts per serving: 388 cal., 24 g total fat (14 g sat. fat), 64 mg chol., 968 mg sodium, 31 g carbo., 1 g fiber, 13 g pro.

This satisfying stew stars the delicious duo of ham and broccoli—with their contrasting salty/smoky and sweet flavors. The instant mashed potatoes help thicken the mix.

CREAMY HAM WITH BROCCOLI

START TO FINISH:

25 minutes

MAKES:

4 servings

3½   cups milk

1   10¾-ounce can condensed golden mushroom or cream of mushroom soup

¼   teaspoon dried thyme, crushed

⅛   teaspoon black pepper

2   cups frozen loose-pack cut broccoli or peas

½   cup packaged instant mashed potatoes

1   5-ounce can chunk-style ham, drained and broken into pieces

1 In a large saucepan combine milk, golden mushroom soup, thyme, and pepper. Bring to boiling. Add broccoli; cover and cook about 5 minutes or until vegetables are tender.

2 Stir potatoes into soup mixture. Stir in ham. Heat through.

Nutrition Facts per serving: 349 cal., 13 g total fat (5 g sat. fat), 38 mg chol., 1,208 mg sodium, 40 g carbo., 3 g fiber, 17 g pro.

If you enjoy poached eggs but find poaching them a little tricky, try this bake. The eggs pretty much poach themselves as they bake into the casserole.

HAM & EGG BAKE

1	10¾-ounce can condensed cream of chicken soup
¼	cup milk
1	teaspoon dried basil, crushed
⅛	teaspoon black pepper
1	cup shredded Swiss cheese (4 ounces)
1½	cups diced cooked ham (about 8 ounces)
4	eggs
	Toast points or toasted English muffin halves

PREP:
20 minutes

BAKE:
25 minutes

STAND:
10 minutes

MAKES:
4 servings

1 In a medium saucepan combine cream of chicken soup, milk, basil, and pepper. Bring to boiling over medium heat, stirring frequently. Add Swiss cheese; stir until cheese is melted. Remove from heat. Stir in ham.

2 Pour the soup mixture into a greased 1½-quart casserole. Break 1 egg into a measuring cup or custard cup. Carefully slide egg on top of soup mixture. Repeat with remaining eggs, spacing evenly.

3 Bake, uncovered, in a 350°F oven for 25 to 30 minutes or until eggs are set. Let stand for 10 minutes before serving. Serve over toast points.

Nutrition Facts per serving: 423 cal., 24 g total fat (10 g sat. fat), 274 mg chol., 1,547 mg sodium, 22 g carbo., 1 g fiber, 28 g pro.

Just whisk in cheese dip toward the end of cooking time to make this stew extra easy, extra cheesy—and extra delicious.

CREAMY HAM & VEGETABLE STEW

START TO FINISH:

35 minutes

MAKES:

4 servings

1½ cups water

2 medium carrots, cut into 1-inch pieces

1 medium potato, peeled and chopped

1 medium onion, cut into chunks

1 cup frozen loose-pack peas

1 cup cubed cooked ham

1 10¾-ounce can condensed reduced-fat and reduced-sodium cream of celery soup

½ of an 8-ounce jar process cheese dip (½ cup)

1 In a large saucepan combine water, carrots, potato, and onion. Bring to boiling; reduce heat. Simmer, covered, for 10 minutes. Stir in peas and ham. Return to boiling; reduce heat. Cover and cook for 5 minutes more.

2 Whisk in cream of celery soup and cheese dip. Cook and stir until heated through.

Nutrition Facts per serving: 260 cal., 11 g total fat (6 g sat. fat), 40 mg chol., 1,269 mg sodium, 27 g carbo., 4 g fiber, 14 g pro.

Bread pudding is typically a dessert but don't let that stop you from trying this savory version. Basil pesto gives it terrific flavor.

SAUSAGE BREAD PUDDING

1	pound sweet Italian sausage (remove casings, if present)
1	medium onion, chopped
2	cloves garlic, minced
$^1/_3$	cup purchased basil pesto sauce
6	cups dried white or wheat bread cubes*
1	cup provolone or cheddar cheese, shredded (4 ounces)
4	eggs
$2^1/_2$	cups milk
1	$10^3/_4$-ounce can condensed cream of mushroom soup
$^1/_4$	teaspoon salt
$^1/_8$	teaspoon black pepper

PREP:
40 minutes
BAKE:
40 minutes
STAND:
10 minutes
MAKES:
8 servings

1 In a large skillet cook sausage, onion, and garlic until meat is brown and onion is tender, stirring to break up sausage. Drain off fat. Stir in pesto; set aside.

2 Meanwhile, lightly coat a 3-quart rectangular baking dish with nonstick cooking spray. Spread half of the bread cubes in bottom of prepared dish. Top evenly with meat mixture and cheese. Top with remaining bread cubes.

3 In a large bowl beat eggs with a fork; stir in the milk, soup, salt, and pepper. Pour evenly over casserole. Use the back of a large spoon or rubber spatula to lightly press bread down into egg mixture.

4 Bake, uncovered, in a 350°F oven for 40 minutes until set or until a knife inserted near the center comes out clean. Let stand for 10 minutes before serving.

*NOTE: **For 6 cups of bread cubes, use about 9 slices of bread. To dry, spread evenly in a shallow baking pan. Bake in a 300°F oven for 10 to 15 minutes or until dry, stirring twice; cool. (Or let bread stand, loosely covered, at room temperature for 8 to 12 hours.**

Nutrition Facts per serving: 507 cal., 35 g total fat (11 g sat. fat), 168 mg chol., 1184 mg sodium, 24 g carbo., 1 g fiber, 22 g pro.

A corn muffin mix provides a super-simple topper for this wholesome sausage-bean bake.

CORN BREAD-TOPPED SAUSAGE BAKE

PREP:

25 minutes

BAKE:

20 minutes

MAKES:

6 servings

1	8½-ounce package corn muffin mix
½	cup chopped carrot
¼	cup chopped onion
¼	cup chopped green sweet pepper
¼	cup chopped celery
2	tablespoons cooking oil
1	11½-ounce can condensed bean with bacon soup
¾	cup milk
2	teaspoons yellow mustard
1	pound cooked smoked Polish sausage, sliced

1 Prepare muffin mix according to package directions; set aside.

2 In a medium saucepan cook carrot, onion, sweet pepper, and celery in hot oil until tender. Stir in bean with bacon soup, milk, and mustard; stir in sausage. Heat and stir until bubbly. Transfer sausage mixture to an ungreased 2-quart rectangular baking dish. Spoon muffin batter over hot mixture.

3 Bake, uncovered, in a 425°F oven for 20 to 25 minutes or until a wooden toothpick inserted into muffin mixture comes out clean.

Nutrition Facts per serving: 562 cal., 34 g total fat (11 g sat. fat), 94 mg chol., 1,566 mg sodium, 43 g carbo., 6 g fiber, 20 g pro.

Crisp rice cereal in a casserole? Yes—it adds surprising flavor and texture to this bold, flavorful bake.

CHEESY SAUSAGE & RICE BAKE

1	pound mild and/or hot bulk pork sausage
1/4	cup chopped onion
3	cups crisp rice cereal
3/4	cup cooked rice
1	cup shredded cheddar cheese (4 ounces)
3	eggs
1	10 3/4-ounce can reduced-fat and reduced-sodium condensed cream of celery soup
1/4	cup milk
1 1/2	teaspoons butter or margarine, melted

PREP:
25 minutes

BAKE:
45 minutes

STAND:
10 minutes

MAKES:
6 servings

1 In a large skillet cook sausage and onion until sausage is brown and onion is tender. Drain off fat. Set sausage mixture aside.

2 Meanwhile, in a large bowl combine 2 1/2 cups of the cereal and rice. Spread rice mixture evenly in the bottom of a greased 2-quart square baking dish. Spoon sausage mixture over rice layer. Sprinkle with cheddar cheese.

3 In a medium bowl whisk together eggs, cream of celery soup, and milk; carefully pour over layers in baking dish. Press down lightly with the back of a spoon. Toss the remaining 1/2 cup cereal with the melted butter; sprinkle over the top.

4 Bake, uncovered, in a 325°F oven for 45 to 50 minutes or until bubbly and golden brown. Let stand for 10 minutes before serving.

Nutrition Facts per serving: 493 cal., 33 g total fat (15 g sat. fat), 175 mg chol., 874 mg sodium, 24 g carbo., 1 g fiber, 19 g pro.

This casserole is similar to a strata but calls on seasoned croutons as a shortcut. That means the bread has already been cubed for you!

SAUSAGE BREAKFAST CASSEROLE

PREP:

25 minutes

CHILL:

2 to 24 hours

BAKE:

45 minutes + 5 minutes

STAND:

10 minutes

MAKES:

10 servings

1½   pounds bulk pork sausage or Italian sausage

Nonstick cooking spray

2½   cups seasoned croutons

2   cups shredded cheddar cheese (8 ounces)

4   eggs

2½   cups milk

¾   teaspoon dry mustard

1   10¾-ounce can condensed cream of mushroom soup

½   cup milk

1 In a large skillet cook sausage over medium heat until brown. Drain off fat.

2 Meanwhile, lightly coat a 3-quart rectangular baking dish with nonstick cooking spray. Spread croutons evenly in bottom of prepared baking dish. Sprinkle 1 cup of the cheese over croutons. Top with sausage.

3 In a large bowl beat eggs with a fork; stir in the 2½ cups milk and the dry mustard. Pour over layers in baking dish. In a small bowl stir together cream of mushroom soup and the ½ cup milk. Spoon soup mixture evenly over mixture in baking dish. Cover and chill for at least 2 hours or up to 24 hours.

4 Bake, uncovered, in a 325°F oven for 45 minutes. Sprinkle with remaining 1 cup cheese. Bake for 5 to 10 minutes more or until a knife inserted near the center comes out clean. Let stand for 10 minutes before serving.

Nutrition Facts per serving: 472 cal., 35 g total fat (15 g sat. fat), 154 mg chol., 883 mg sodium, 14 g carbo., 1 g fiber, 20 g pro.

This one's perfect for a holiday or bridal-shower brunch. Serve with a salad of the freshest, most colorful in-season fruits you can find.

SPINACH BREAKFAST CASSEROLE

4 cups seasoned croutons

1 pound bulk pork sausage, cooked and drained

1 10-ounce package frozen chopped spinach, thawed and well drained

½ cup coarsely shredded carrot

4 eggs

2 cups milk

1 10¾-ounce can condensed cream of mushroom soup

1 4-ounce can (drained weight) sliced mushrooms, drained

1 cup shredded cheddar cheese (4 ounces)

1 cup shredded Monterey Jack cheese (4 ounces)

¼ teaspoon dry mustard

Shredded cheddar and/or Monterey Jack cheese (optional)

PREP:
30 minutes

CHILL:
8 to 24 hours

BAKE:
45 minutes + 10 minutes

STAND:
10 minutes

MAKES:
12 servings

1 Spread croutons in an even layer in an ungreased 3-quart rectangular baking dish. Spread sausage evenly over croutons. Sprinkle spinach and carrot evenly over sausage.

2 In a medium bowl beat eggs with a whisk; stir in milk, cream of mushroom soup, mushrooms, the 1 cup cheddar cheese, the 1 cup Monterey Jack cheese, and the dry mustard until well mixed. Pour over layers in dish. Cover and chill for at least 8 hours or up to 24 hours.

3 Uncover and bake in a 325°F oven for 45 minutes. If desired, sprinkle with additional cheese. Bake about 10 minutes more or until edges are bubbly and center is heated through. Let stand for 10 minutes before serving.

Nutrition Facts per serving: 346 cal., 24 g total fat (10 g sat. fat), 115 mg chol., 754 mg sodium, 15 g carbo., 2 g fiber, 15 g pro.

A stuffing mixture creates a bottom layer and topper for this tasty dish. It's a delicious way to use your summer crop of zucchini.

ZUCCHINI-SAUSAGE CASSEROLE

PREP:

25 minutes

BAKE:

30 minutes

MAKES:

8 servings

1	pound bulk pork sausage
4	medium zucchini
1	10¾-ounce can condensed cream of chicken soup
1	8-ounce carton dairy sour cream
4	cups packaged chicken-flavor stuffing mix
⅓	cup butter or margarine, melted
	Nonstick cooking spray

1 In a 12-inch skillet cook sausage until brown. Drain off fat. Return sausage to skillet.

2 Meanwhile, quarter zucchini lengthwise; cut each quarter crosswise into ½-inch slices. Stir zucchini slices into sausage in skillet.

3 In a small bowl combine cream of chicken soup and sour cream; stir into sausage-zucchini mixture. Set aside. In a large bowl combine stuffing mix and melted butter.

4 Lightly coat a 3-quart rectangular baking dish with nonstick cooking spray. Spoon half of the stuffing mixture into prepared baking dish. Spread sausage-zucchini mixture over stuffing mixture in baking dish. Spoon remaining stuffing mixture evenly over the top.

5 Bake, covered, in a 350°F oven about 30 minutes or until heated through.

Nutrition Facts per serving: 487 cal., 34 g total fat (16 g sat. fat), 70 mg chol., 1,128 mg sodium, 28 g carbo., 2 g fiber, 14 g pro.

Tailor this recipe to your heat tolerance. If spicy food is your style, use more hot Italian sausage and less sweet. Or use all of one or the other.

SAUSAGE-RICE CASSEROLE

1	pound uncooked sweet (mild) and/or hot Italian sausage links (remove casings, if present)
½	cup chopped onion
2½	cups cooked rice
1	4-ounce can diced green chile peppers, drained
1	4-ounce can (drained weight) mushroom stems and pieces, drained
1	10¾-ounce can condensed cream of chicken soup
1	cup milk
¾	cup shredded cheddar cheese (3 ounces)

PREP:
20 minutes
BAKE:
50 minutes
MAKES:
6 servings

1 In a large skillet cook sausage and onion until sausage is brown, stirring to break up sausage; drain off fat.

2 Meanwhile, in a large bowl stir together rice, chile peppers, and mushrooms. Stir in cream of chicken soup, milk, and cheddar cheese. Stir in sausage mixture. Spoon mixture into an ungreased 2-quart rectangular baking dish.

3 Bake, covered, in a 350°F oven about 50 minutes or until heated through.

MAKE-AHEAD DIRECTIONS: Prepare as directed. Cover and chill for up to 24 hours. Bake, covered, in a 350°F oven for 65 to 70 minutes or until heated through.

Nutrition Facts per serving: 442 cal., 26 g total fat (11 g sat. fat), 73 mg chol., 1,056 mg sodium, 28 g carbo., 1 g fiber, 20 g pro.

If you love the flavor of Reuben sandwiches, you'll simply love this chowder. Be sure to use process Swiss cheese—it melts more smoothly than natural Swiss.

REUBEN CHOWDER

START TO FINISH:

30 minutes

MAKES:

4 servings

1 tablespoon butter, softened

4 slices rye bread

½ teaspoon caraway seeds

3 cups milk

1 10¾-ounce can condensed cream of celery soup

2 ounces process Swiss cheese slices, torn

1 14- or 16-ounce can sauerkraut, rinsed, drained, and snipped

2 5-ounce packages sliced corned beef, chopped or torn

1 Butter both sides of each bread slice; sprinkle with caraway seeds. Cut into triangles; place on a baking sheet. Bake in a 325°F oven about 15 minutes or until toasted.

2 Meanwhile, in a large saucepan combine milk, cream of celery soup, and cheese. Cook and stir until bubbly. Stir in sauerkraut and corned beef; heat through. Serve soup with toasted bread.

Nutrition Facts per serving: 456 cal., 23 g total fat (11 g sat. fat), 77 mg chol., 2,696 mg sodium, 35 g carbo., 5 g fiber, 27 g pro.

Next time you make corned beef, be sure to set some aside for this heavenly hash. Serve with poached eggs and English muffins for a fabulous weekend brunch.

CORNED BEEF BREAKFAST HASH

5	cups frozen loose-pack hash brown potatoes, thawed
1	10¾-ounce can condensed cream of chicken soup
½	cup dairy sour cream
1	cup finely chopped cooked corned beef
⅓	cup finely chopped onion
⅓	cup finely chopped green sweet pepper
1	cup shredded sharp cheddar cheese (4 ounces)
	Paprika

1 Spread potatoes over the bottom of a greased 2-quart square baking dish. In a medium bowl combine cream of chicken soup and sour cream; stir in corned beef, onion, and sweet pepper. Spread corned beef mixture over potatoes.

2 Bake, uncovered, in a 350°F oven for 40 to 45 minutes or until bubbly and top begins to brown. Sprinkle with cheese and paprika just before serving.

Nutrition Facts per serving: 551 cal., 27 g total fat (13 g sat. fat), 81 mg chol., 1,248 mg sodium, 56 g carbo., 4 g fiber, 22 g pro.

PREP:
15 minutes

BAKE:
40 minutes

MAKES:
4 servings

This warming, sausage-filled casserole will taste great as the cold weather starts to hit. A Waldorf salad makes a terrific serve-along, as autumn's apples will complement the heavenly hot dish.

CHEESY BRAT CASSEROLE

PREP:
20 minutes

BAKE:
45 minutes

MAKES:
6 servings

6   cooked bratwurst or Polish sausage, cut into ½-inch-thick slices (1 pound)

4   medium potatoes (about 1¼ pounds), cooked, peeled, and cubed

1   10-ounce package frozen cut green beans, thawed

1   10¾-ounce can reduced-fat and reduced-sodium condensed cream of mushroom soup

1   cup shredded cheddar cheese (4 ounces)

⅓   cup finely chopped onion

1 In a large bowl stir together bratwurst, potatoes, green beans, cream of mushroom soup, cheddar cheese, and onion. Transfer to an ungreased 2-quart rectangular baking dish.

2 Bake, covered, in a 350°F oven about 45 minutes or until heated through.

Nutrition Facts per serving: 408 cal., 27 g total fat (11 g sat. fat), 69 mg chol., 747 mg sodium, 23 g carbo., 3 g fiber, 18 g pro.

If your family enjoys Reubens, take note! Now you can enjoy all of those wonderful flavors in a casserole without having to make individual sandwiches.

INSTANT REUBEN CASSEROLE

6   slices rye bread, toasted

2   5- to 6-ounce packages sliced corned beef, chopped

1   14- to 16-ounce can sauerkraut, rinsed, drained, and snipped

1   10¾-ounce can condensed cream of celery soup

1   cup shredded Swiss cheese (4 ounces)

3   tablespoons bottled Thousand Island salad dressing

2   tablespoons water

1   tablespoon butter or margarine, melted

1 Cut 4 slices of the toasted bread into cubes. Toss bread cubes with corned beef; place in the bottom of a greased 2-quart square baking dish.

2 In a medium bowl stir together sauerkraut, cream of celery soup, ½ cup of the Swiss cheese, the Thousand Island dressing, and water; spoon over corned beef mixture. Tear remaining 2 slices bread; place in a food processor bowl or blender container. Cover and process or blend until coarse bread crumbs form. Toss crumbs with melted butter; sprinkle on top of sauerkraut mixture.

3 Bake, uncovered, in a 375°F oven about 30 minutes or until heated through. Sprinkle with remaining ½ cup cheese; bake about 5 minutes more or until cheese is melted.

Nutrition Facts per serving: 301 cal., 15 g total fat (6 g sat. fat), 46 mg chol., 1,643 mg sodium, 24 g carbo., 4 g fiber, 19 g pro.

PREP:
25 minutes

BAKE:
30 minutes + 5 minutes

MAKES:
6 servings

When you bring it to the table, this may look like Swedish meatballs, but the lamb—infused with orange and cinnamon—makes this a whole new (meat)ball game!

SAUCY LAMB MEATBALLS

PREP:
35 minutes
COOK:
15 minutes
MAKES:
4 or 5 servings

1   beaten egg

¼   cup orange juice

¾   cup soft bread crumbs (1 slice white bread)

¾   teaspoon salt

⅛   teaspoon ground cinnamon

⅛   teaspoon black pepper

1   pound ground lamb

1   10¾-ounce can condensed cream of mushroom soup

1   4-ounce can (drained weight) sliced mushrooms, drained

½   cup orange juice

¼   cup water

  Dash black pepper

½   cup dairy sour cream

1   tablespoon all-purpose flour

  Hot cooked noodles

1 In a large bowl combine egg, the ¼ cup orange juice, the bread crumbs, salt, cinnamon, and the ⅛ teaspoon pepper. Add lamb; mix well. Shape into 1½-inch meatballs. In a large skillet brown meatballs, turning occasionally to brown evenly. Drain off fat.

2 In a medium bowl combine cream of mushroom soup, mushrooms, the ½ cup orange juice, water, and dash pepper; pour over meatballs. Bring to boiling; reduce heat. Simmer, covered, for 15 to 20 minutes or until done (160°F).

3 In a small bowl stir together sour cream and flour; add to meatball mixture. Cook and stir until thickened and bubbly. Cook and stir for 1 minute more. Serve over hot cooked noodles.

Nutrition Facts per serving: 592 cal., 26 g total fat (9 g sat. fat), 183 mg chol., 1,221 mg sodium, 58 g carbo., 3 g fiber, 32 g pro.

POULTRY ENTRÉES

3

What to serve with this luscious and lemony chicken bake? Steamed fresh broccoli would add great crunch and color to the meal.

CREAMY BAKED CHICKEN

PREP:

15 minutes

BAKE:

25 minutes

MAKES:

6 servings

1	tablespoon cooking oil
6	skinless, boneless chicken breast halves (about 2 pounds)
1	10¾-ounce can condensed cream of chicken soup
¾	cup mayonnaise or salad dressing
½	teaspoon finely shredded lemon peel
1	cup soft bread crumbs
1	tablespoon butter or margarine, melted
½	cup shredded sharp cheddar cheese (2 ounces)

1 In a 12-inch skillet heat oil over medium-high heat. Add chicken; cook for about 5 minutes or until brown, turning once. Transfer chicken to a lightly greased 2-quart rectangular baking dish.

2 In a medium bowl combine cream of chicken soup, mayonnaise, and lemon peel; spoon over chicken. In a small bowl combine bread crumbs and melted butter. Stir in cheddar cheese. Sprinkle crumb mixture over soup mixture.

3 Bake, uncovered, in a 350°F oven for 25 to 30 minutes or until chicken is no longer pink (170°F) and sauce is bubbly.

Nutrition Facts per serving: 511 cal., 35 g total fat (8 g sat. fat), 117 mg chol., 714 mg sodium, 8 g carbo., 1 g fiber, 39 g pro.

Long grain and wild rice mix gives you a head start on this casserole.
The wine helps intensify the flavors.

CHICKEN & WILD RICE CASSEROLE

1	6-ounce package uncooked long grain and wild rice mix
½	cup chopped onion
½	cup chopped celery
2	tablespoons butter or margarine
1	10¾-ounce can condensed chicken white and wild rice soup or cream of chicken soup
½	cup dairy sour cream
⅓	cup dry white wine or chicken broth
½	teaspoon dried basil, crushed
2	cups cubed cooked chicken or turkey (about 10 ounces)
⅓	cup finely shredded Parmesan cheese

PREP:
30 minutes
BAKE:
25 minutes + 5 minutes
MAKES:
4 servings

1 Prepare rice mix according to package directions. Meanwhile, in a large skillet cook onion and celery in hot butter until tender. Stir in chicken white and wild rice soup, sour cream, dry white wine, and basil. Stir in cooked rice mix and chicken. Spoon mixture into an ungreased 2-quart rectangular baking dish.

2 Bake, uncovered, in a 350°F oven for 25 to 30 minutes or until heated through. Sprinkle with Parmesan cheese. Bake about 5 minutes more or until cheese is melted.

Nutrition Facts per serving: 479 cal., 20 g total fat (10 g sat. fat), 101 mg chol., 1,559 mg sodium, 42 g carbo., 2 g fiber, 30 g pro.

Next Sunday noon, gather everyone—in the dining room no less—around this wholesome, family-friendly bake.

SUNDAY CHICKEN-RICE BAKE

PREP:

20 minutes

BAKE:

55 minutes

MAKES:

4 to 6 servings

1	10¾-ounce can condensed cream of chicken soup
1	cup milk
½	cup water
1	4-ounce can (drained weight) sliced mushrooms, drained
1	10-ounce package frozen peas and carrots, thawed
1	6.2-ounce package lemon and herb flavored rice
	Nonstick cooking spray
2½	pounds meaty chicken pieces (breast halves, thighs, and drumsticks), skinned

1 In a large bowl stir together cream of chicken soup, milk, water, and mushrooms. Remove ½ cup of the soup mixture; set aside. Stir vegetables and rice into remaining soup mixture.

2 Coat a 3-quart rectangular baking dish with nonstick cooking spray. Spoon rice mixture into prepared dish; top with chicken pieces. Pour reserved soup mixture over chicken. Cover tightly with foil.

3 Bake in a 375°F oven for 55 to 60 minutes or until chicken is no longer pink (170°F for breasts; 180°F for thighs and drumsticks) and rice is tender.

Nutrition Facts per serving: 545 cal., 16 g total fat (5 g sat. fat), 126 mg chol., 1,178 mg sodium, 52 g carbo., 4 g fiber, 47 g pro.

Patterned after a popular Texas recipe, this irresistible main dish includes seasoned chicken layered with chile peppers, tortillas, a sour cream sauce, and cheese.

LAYERED CHICKEN & CHILE CASSEROLE

1	tomatillo
1	tablespoon cooking oil
½	cup chopped onion
2	teaspoons chili powder
1	clove garlic, minced
1	10¾-ounce can condensed cream of chicken soup
1	4-ounce can diced green chile peppers, drained
1	4-ounce jar diced pimiento, drained
¼	cup dairy sour cream
6	6-inch corn tortillas, torn
1½	cups cubed cooked chicken (about 8 ounces)
1	cup shredded Monterey Jack cheese (4 ounces)
	Bottled green salsa (optional)

PREP:
25 minutes
BAKE:
35 minutes
STAND:
10 minutes
MAKES:
6 servings

1 For sauce, remove and discard the thin, brown, papery husks from the tomatillo. Rinse tomatillo; finely chop (you should have about ¼ cup).

2 In a medium saucepan heat oil over medium heat. Add chopped tomatillo, onion, chili powder, and garlic; cook until vegetables are tender. Remove from heat; stir in cream of chicken soup, chile peppers, pimiento, and sour cream.

3 Spread ½ cup of the sauce in the bottom of an ungreased 2-quart square baking dish. Arrange half of the torn corn tortillas over the sauce. Layer with half of the chicken, half of the remaining sauce, and half of the Monterey Jack cheese. Repeat layers.

4 Bake, covered, in a 350°F oven for 35 to 40 minutes or until heated through. Let stand for 10 minutes before serving. If desired, serve with green salsa.

Nutrition Facts per serving: 297 cal., 16 g total fat (7 g sat. fat), 55 mg chol., 663 mg sodium, 20 g carbo., 3 g fiber, 19 g pro.

To young cooks, it may seem strange to put mayonnaise in a casserole, but many traditional American casseroles call on this ingredient. You'll find it adds a little richness and a mild tang to the finished dish.

CURRIED CHICKEN & BROCCOLI

PREP:
25 minutes

BAKE:
20 minutes

MAKES:
4 servings

1   10-ounce package frozen cut broccoli

1   10¾-ounce can condensed cheddar cheese soup

⅓   cup mayonnaise or salad dressing

2   tablespoons milk

1½   to 2 teaspoons curry powder

1½   cups cubed cooked chicken (about 8 ounces)

½   of an 8-ounce can sliced water chestnuts (½ cup), drained

¼   cup chopped cashews or peanuts

1   Cook broccoli according to package directions; drain.

2   Meanwhile, for cheese sauce, in a medium bowl stir together cheddar cheese soup, mayonnaise, milk, and curry powder.

3   Divide broccoli evenly among 4 ungreased 10- to 12-ounce au gratin dishes. Top with chicken and water chestnuts. Spoon cheese sauce over chicken mixture. Sprinkle with cashews.

4   Bake, uncovered, in a 375°F oven about 20 minutes or until heated through.

Nutrition Facts per serving: 366 cal., 28 g total fat (6 g sat. fat), 63 mg chol., 795 mg sodium, 14 g carbo., 3 g fiber, 22 g pro.

Cacciatore means "hunter" in Italian. Some say this dish was devised by clever cooks when their husbands came home from the hunt empty-handed.

BAKED CHICKEN CACCIATORE

8   skinless, boneless chicken thighs (about 2 pounds total)
1   tablespoon olive oil
1   teaspoon dried oregano, crushed
¼   teaspoon black pepper
3   cups sliced fresh mushrooms
1   large green sweet pepper, cut into ½-inch-wide strips
1   medium onion, chopped
1   10¾-ounce can condensed tomato soup
1   tablespoon snipped fresh parsley
     Hot cooked mashed potatoes (optional)

PREP:
20 minutes
BAKE:
20 minutes + 10 minutes
MAKES:
4 servings

1 In a very large ovenproof skillet brown chicken in hot oil, turning to brown evenly. Drain off fat. Sprinkle chicken with oregano and black pepper. Add mushrooms, sweet pepper, and onion to skillet.

2 Cover and bake in a 375°F oven for 20 minutes.

3 Stir in tomato soup. Bake, uncovered, about 10 minutes more or until chicken is no longer pink (180°F) and vegetables are crisp-tender. Sprinkle with parsley. If desired, serve with mashed potatoes.

Nutrition Facts per serving: 285 cal., 10 g total fat (2 g sat. fat), 115 mg chol., 587 mg sodium, 18 g carbo., 3 g fiber, 31 g pro.

Serve this easy-to-make casserole with buttered peas, crusty breadsticks, and a quick fruit salad.

CHEESY CHICKEN CASSEROLE

PREP:

20 minutes

BAKE:

45 minutes

STAND:

5 minutes

MAKES:

4 to 6 servings

8 ounces dried curly noodles (about 4 cups)

1 10¾-ounce can condensed cream of broccoli or cream of celery soup

1 cup milk

1½ cups cream-style cottage cheese (one 12-ounce carton)

2 cups chopped cooked chicken or turkey (about 10 ounces)

1 4-ounce can (drained weight) sliced mushrooms, drained

¾ cup shredded American or cheddar cheese (3 ounces)

1 teaspoon dried basil or thyme, crushed

1 Cook noodles according to package directions; drain and set aside. In a large bowl combine cream of broccoli soup and milk. Stir in cooked noodles, cottage cheese, chicken, mushrooms, half of the American cheese, and basil. Turn chicken-noodle mixture into an ungreased 1½-quart casserole.

2 Bake, covered, in a 350°F oven for 45 to 50 minutes or until heated through. Uncover and sprinkle with remaining American cheese. Let stand about 5 minutes or until cheese is melted.

Nutrition Facts per serving: 613 cal., 23 g total fat (11 g sat. fat), 155 mg chol., 1,329 mg sodium, 53 g carbo., 3 g fiber, 47 g pro.

Sometimes all you're looking for is a satisfying, uncomplicated dish to warm and nourish the family after a busy day. This is that kind of recipe.

SAUCY CHICKEN DELIGHT

2½ to 3 pounds meaty chicken pieces
(breast halves, thighs, and drumsticks)

1 teaspoon paprika

½ teaspoon salt

Dash black pepper

2 tablespoons cooking oil

1 14-ounce jar pasta sauce (1½ cups)

1 10¾-ounce can condensed cream of chicken soup

1 4-ounce can (drained weight) sliced mushrooms, drained

Hot cooked noodles

PREP:
20 minutes
BAKE:
45 minutes
MAKES:
4 to 6 servings

1 If desired, skin chicken. In a small bowl combine paprika, salt, and pepper. Sprinkle mixture evenly over chicken pieces.

2 In a 12-inch skillet brown chicken in hot oil, turning to brown evenly. Place chicken in an ungreased 3-quart rectangular baking dish. In a medium bowl combine spaghetti sauce, cream of chicken soup, and mushrooms. Pour soup mixture over chicken.

3 Bake, covered, in a 350°F oven for 45 to 55 minutes or until chicken is no longer pink (170°F for breasts; 180°F for thighs and drumsticks). Serve chicken and soup mixture over hot cooked noodles.

Nutrition Facts per serving: 679 cal., 31 g total fat (8 g sat. fat), 175 mg chol., 1,551 mg sodium, 50 g carbo., 5 g fiber, 52 g pro.

Here's a quintessential one-dish meal. The chicken, rice, broccoli, and a savory soup-based sauce bake together for a true fix-and-forget favorite.

CHICKEN, BROCCOLI & RICE BAKE

PREP:

20 minutes

BAKE:

1 hour

STAND:

5 minutes

MAKES:

4 servings

1 10¾-ounce can condensed cream of broccoli or cream of chicken soup

½ cup dairy sour cream

½ cup milk

1 teaspoon dried basil, crushed

1 cup uncooked instant white rice

4 skinless, boneless chicken breast halves (about 1¼ pounds)

Salt

Black pepper

1 10-ounce package frozen broccoli spears, thawed

½ cup shredded Swiss cheese (2 ounces)

1 In a medium bowl combine cream of broccoli soup, sour cream, milk, and basil. Set aside ½ cup of the soup mixture. Add rice to remaining soup mixture. Spoon into an ungreased 2-quart rectangular baking dish.

2 Sprinkle chicken lightly with salt and pepper. Arrange chicken and broccoli spears over rice mixture. Spoon reserved soup mixture over all.

3 Bake, covered, in a 350°F oven for 60 to 70 minutes or until chicken is no longer pink (170°F) and broccoli is tender. Sprinkle with Swiss cheese. Let stand, uncovered, for 5 minutes before serving.

Nutrition Facts per serving: 452 cal., 16 g total fat (8 g sat. fat), 110 mg chol., 684 mg sodium, 32 g carbo., 3 g fiber, 44 g pro.

When was the last time you had a wonderfully comforting meal of chicken and dumplings? Try this up-to-date version with shortcuts that include condensed soup and ready-to-bake buttermilk biscuits.

CREAMY CHICKEN & DUMPLINGS

1	tablespoon all-purpose flour
12	ounces skinless, boneless chicken breast halves or thighs, cut into 1-inch pieces
2	tablespoons butter or margarine
1	stalk celery, sliced
1	medium carrot, chopped
1	onion, cut into wedges
1	10¾-ounce can condensed cream of chicken and herbs soup
1¼	cups chicken broth
⅛	teaspoon black pepper
1	4.5-ounce package (5 or 6) refrigerated buttermilk biscuits*
1	cup frozen loose-pack peas

PREP:
20 minutes
COOK:
20 minutes + 10 minutes
MAKES:
4 servings

1 Place flour in a plastic bag. Add chicken pieces; shake until coated. In a large saucepan melt butter over medium heat. Add chicken, celery, carrot, and onion; cook for 2 to 3 minutes or until chicken is brown. Stir in cream of chicken and herbs soup, chicken broth, and pepper.

2 Bring to boiling; reduce heat. Simmer, covered, about 20 minutes or until chicken and vegetables are tender.

3 Meanwhile, separate biscuits. Cut each biscuit into quarters. Stir peas into chicken mixture; return to boiling. Place biscuit pieces on top of chicken mixture.

4 Cover and cook over medium-low heat for 10 to 15 minutes or until a toothpick inserted into center of a biscuit comes out clean. Serve in bowls.

*NOTE: **If you prefer, substitute drop biscuits for refrigerated biscuits. To prepare biscuits, in a medium bowl combine 1 cup packaged biscuit mix and ⅓ cup milk. Drop mixture into 8 dumplings on hot chicken mixture. Cover and cook as directed in step 4.**

Nutrition Facts per serving: 338 cal., 11 g total fat (4 g sat. fat), 71 mg chol., 1,194 mg sodium, 31 g carbo., 4 g fiber, 28 g pro.

This classic dish is usually made with beef, but this version, made with chicken, has all the mushroom-sauced appeal of the original.

CHICKEN STROGANOFF

START TO FINISH:

25 minutes

MAKES:

4 servings

4   skinless, boneless chicken breast halves
    (about 1¼ pounds)

1   teaspoon bottled minced garlic (2 cloves)

1   tablespoon cooking oil

2   cups sliced fresh mushrooms

1   10¾-ounce can condensed cream of chicken soup

¼   cup dry white wine

1   teaspoon dried basil, crushed, or 1 tablespoon
    snipped fresh basil

1   8-ounce carton dairy sour cream

1   tablespoon all-purpose flour

    Hot cooked noodles

    Snipped fresh parsley (optional)

1 Cut chicken breast pieces into bite-size strips. In a 12-inch skillet cook and stir chicken and garlic in hot oil about 5 minutes or until chicken is no longer pink. Add mushrooms, cream of chicken soup, dry white wine, and, if using, dried basil. Heat through.

2 In a small bowl stir together sour cream and flour; stir into chicken mixture. Cook and stir until thickened and bubbly. Cook and stir for 1 minute more. If using, stir in fresh basil. Serve over hot cooked noodles. If desired, sprinkle with parsley.

Nutrition Facts per serving: 632 cal., 26 g total fat (10 g sat. fat), 165 mg chol., 722 mg sodium, 51 g carbo., 2 g fiber, 46 g pro.

Crisp, bright Asian-style vegetables add color to this easy chicken-rice medley, while ginger and dry mustard add intriguing flavor.

CHICKEN & RICE WITH VEGETABLES

$2/3$	cup uncooked long grain rice
$1 1/3$	cups water
$1/2$	cup chopped onion
2	tablespoons cooking oil
1	$10^3/4$-ounce can condensed cream of chicken soup
$1/4$	cup reduced-sodium soy sauce
1	teaspoon sugar
3	cups cubed cooked chicken or turkey (about 1 pound)
2	cups cubed zucchini
1	16-ounce package frozen broccoli stir-fry vegetables (broccoli, carrots, onions, red peppers, celery, water chestnuts, and mushrooms), thawed
$1/2$	teaspoon ground ginger
$1/2$	teaspoon dry mustard

START TO FINISH:
35 minutes
MAKES:
6 servings

1 In a small saucepan cook rice in water according to package directions; drain rice, if necessary.

2 Meanwhile, in a 12-inch skillet cook onion in hot oil until crisp-tender. Add cream of chicken soup, soy sauce, and sugar. Bring to boiling. Stir in cooked rice, chicken, zucchini, stir-fry vegetables, ginger, and dry mustard. Cook and stir until heated through.

Nutrition Facts per serving: 348 cal., 13 g total fat (3 g sat. fat), 66 mg chol., 848 mg sodium, 29 g carbo., 3 g fiber, 26 g pro.

Chicken with noodles—a classic comfort dish—gets a colorful, confetti-like update with olives, red sweet pepper, and peas.

CHICKEN WITH NOODLES

8   ounces dried egg noodles (4 cups)

1   10¾-ounce can condensed cream of chicken soup

½   cup milk

1   2¼-ounce can sliced pitted ripe olives, drained

2   tablespoons chopped roasted red sweet pepper

¼   teaspoon dried marjoram, crushed

⅛   teaspoon black pepper

2   cups chopped cooked chicken (about 10 ounces)

1   cup frozen loose-pack peas

¼   cup dry white wine or chicken broth

1 Cook noodles according to package directions. Drain and keep warm.

2 Meanwhile, in a large saucepan combine cream of chicken soup and milk. Stir in olives, roasted sweet red pepper, marjoram, and black pepper; bring to boiling, stirring occasionally. Stir in chicken, peas, and wine; heat through. Stir in drained noodles.

Nutrition Facts per serving: 506 cal., 15 g total fat (4 g sat. fat), 125 mg chol., 827 mg sodium, 55 g carbo., 5 g fiber, 33 g pro.

Dijon-style mustard, which contains white wine and seasonings, adds a sharp flavor and a little French refinement to cooking.

DIJON CHICKEN & MUSHROOMS

3	tablespoons butter or margarine
2	cups sliced fresh mushrooms
4	skinless, boneless chicken breast halves (about 1¼ pounds)
1	10¾-ounce can condensed cream of chicken soup
¼	cup dry white wine
¼	cup water
2	tablespoons Dijon-style mustard
½	teaspoon dried thyme or tarragon, crushed
	Hot cooked pasta

START TO FINISH:
30 minutes
MAKES:
4 servings

1 In a large skillet melt 1 tablespoon of the butter over medium-high heat. Add mushrooms; cook for 3 to 4 minutes or until tender. Remove mushrooms from skillet. In same skillet cook chicken in remaining 2 tablespoons butter for 8 to 10 minutes or until tender and no longer pink (170°F), turning to brown evenly.

2 Meanwhile, in a small bowl stir together cream of chicken soup, wine, the water, mustard, and thyme.

3 Return mushrooms to skillet; add soup mixture. Bring to boiling; reduce heat. Simmer, uncovered, for 2 minutes. Serve chicken and soup mixture over hot cooked pasta.

Nutrition Facts per serving: 498 cal., 18 g total fat (8 g sat. fat), 112 mg chol., 947 mg sodium, 37 g carbo., 2 g fiber, 41 g pro.

You'll love the make-ahead angle to this super-satisfying recipe. Put it together in the morning (or the night before). Then when you get home after a day of work, holiday shopping, or running errands, pop it into the oven...and relax!

SAUCY CHICKEN CASSEROLE

PREP:

20 minutes

CHILL:

3 to 24 hours

BAKE:

1 hour

MAKES:

6 servings

1	10¾-ounce can condensed cream of chicken soup
½	cup milk
1	tablespoon dried minced onion
¼	teaspoon dried basil or sage, crushed
⅛	teaspoon black pepper
4	1-ounce slices American cheese, torn into small pieces
1	9¾- or 10-ounce can chunk-style chicken, undrained
1	cup dried elbow macaroni
¼	cup chopped red sweet pepper or one 2-ounce jar sliced pimiento, drained

1 In an ungreased 1½-quart casserole stir together cream of chicken soup, milk, dried minced onion, basil, and black pepper.

2 Add cheese, chicken, macaroni, and sweet pepper to soup mixture; mix well. Cover and chill for at least 3 hours or up to 24 hours.

3 Bake, covered, in a 375°F oven about 1 hour or until macaroni is tender, stirring once.

Nutrition Facts per serving: 265 cal., 12 g total fat (5 g sat. fat), 46 mg chol., 815 mg sodium, 22 g carbo., 1 g fiber, 19 g pro.

Chicken and noodles—ready in less than 30 minutes, and with just one pan? This recipe is delicious proof it can be done.

CREAMY CHICKEN & NOODLES

2	cups frozen stir-fry vegetables (such as broccoli, carrots, onion, red peppers, celery, water chestnuts, and mushrooms)
1	$10^3/_4$-ounce can condensed cheddar cheese soup
$^3/_4$	cup milk
$^1/_2$	teaspoon dried thyme, crushed
	Several dashes bottled hot pepper sauce
2	cups cubed cooked chicken (about 10 ounces)
	Hot cooked noodles

START TO FINISH:
25 minutes
MAKES:
4 servings

1 In a large skillet or saucepan cook frozen vegetables according to package directions. Drain, if necessary; set aside.

2 In same skillet or saucepan stir together cheddar cheese soup, milk, thyme, and hot pepper sauce. Add chicken and cooked vegetables. Cook and stir over medium heat about 10 minutes or until heated through. Serve over hot cooked noodles.

Nutrition Facts per serving: 352 cal., 12 g total fat (4 g sat. fat), 102 mg chol., 702 mg sodium, 35 g carbo., 2 g fiber, 29 g pro.

This take on chicken and noodles has the comfort-food classic in a casserole with cheese and sour cream for extra flavor and richness.

CHICKEN-NOODLE CASSEROLE

PREP:

30 minutes

BAKE:

30 minutes

MAKES:

4 to 6 servings

4	ounces dried medium noodles (2 cups)
1	cup sliced fresh mushrooms
½	cup chopped green or red sweet pepper
3	tablespoons sliced green onions
2	tablespoons butter or margarine
2	cups chopped cooked chicken (about 10 ounces)
1	10¾-ounce can condensed cream of chicken or cream of broccoli soup
1	cup frozen loose-pack peas and carrots
1	cup shredded cheddar cheese (4 ounces)
½	cup dairy sour cream
⅛	teaspoon black pepper
⅓	cup fine dry bread crumbs
2	tablespoons grated Parmesan cheese
2	tablespoons butter or margarine, melted

1 Cook noodles according to package directions; drain. Set aside.

2 Meanwhile, in a large saucepan cook mushrooms, sweet pepper, and green onions in the 2 tablespoons hot butter until tender. Stir in chicken, cream of chicken soup, peas and carrots, cheddar cheese, sour cream, and black pepper. Bring to boiling over medium heat, stirring frequently. Gently fold in cooked noodles. Spoon into an ungreased 2-quart casserole.

3 In a small bowl combine bread crumbs, Parmesan cheese, and the 2 tablespoons melted butter. Sprinkle the crumb mixture over the chicken mixture.

4 Bake, uncovered, in a 350°F oven for 30 to 35 minutes or until heated through and top is golden.

Nutrition Facts per serving: 659 cal., 40 g total fat (20 g sat. fat), 170 mg chol., 1,229 mg sodium, 38 g carbo., 3 g fiber, 38 g pro.

Chicken potpie is one of the world's greatest comfort foods. And since refrigerated piecrusts came on the scene, it's never been easier.

SHORTCUT CHICKEN POTPIE

½	of a 15-ounce package folded refrigerated unbaked piecrust (1 crust)
1	10¾-ounce can condensed cream of chicken soup
⅓	cup milk
1	16-ounce package frozen mixed vegetables
1	cup chopped cooked chicken breast (about 5 ounces)
1	4-ounce can (drained weight) sliced mushrooms, drained
¼	teaspoon black pepper

PREP:
20 minutes
BAKE:
1 hour
STAND:
10 minutes
MAKES:
4 servings

1 Let piecrust stand at room temperature and unfold according to package directions.

2 Meanwhile, for the filling, in a medium bowl stir together cream of chicken soup and milk. Stir in vegetables, chicken, mushrooms, and pepper. Transfer filling to an ungreased 1½-quart casserole.

3 Cut shapes or slits in the piecrust to allow steam to escape. Center crust on top of the filling; fold excess crust under edge of casserole. Crimp edge as desired.

4 Bake in a 350°F oven for 60 to 65 minutes or until top is golden and filling is bubbly. If necessary to prevent overbrowning, cover edge of piecrust with foil for the last 10 to 15 minutes of baking. Let stand for 10 minutes before serving.

Nutrition Facts per serving: 357 cal., 16 g total fat (3 g sat. fat), 25 mg chol., 1,064 mg sodium, 39 g carbo., 6 g fiber, 16 g pro.

This version of shepherd's pie gets a colorful and tasty new twist with mashed sweet potatoes instead of regular mashed potatoes.

SWEET POTATO-TOPPED CHICKEN STEW

PREP:

25 minutes

COOK:

10 minutes

MAKES:

4 servings

1   17-ounce can sweet potatoes, drained

1   tablespoon butter or margarine, melted

½   cup chopped onion

2   tablespoons butter or margarine

1   10¾-ounce can condensed cream of mushroom soup

2   cups chopped cooked chicken (about 10 ounces)

1   10-ounce package frozen peas and carrots

½   teaspoon dried sage, crushed

1   In a medium bowl mash sweet potatoes with an electric mixer on low to medium speed; beat in the 1 tablespoon melted butter. Set aside.

2   In a large skillet cook onion in the 2 tablespoons hot butter until tender. Stir in cream of mushroom soup, chicken, peas and carrots, and sage. Cook and stir until bubbly.

3   Spoon the sweet potato mixture into 6 mounds on top of chicken mixture. Simmer, covered, about 10 minutes more or until heated through.

Nutrition Facts per serving: 436 cal., 19 g total fat (9 g sat. fat), 88 mg chol., 815 mg sodium, 41 g carbo., 6 g fiber, 25 g pro.

Thanks to roasted deli chickens as well as convenient packages of frozen, cooked chicken strips, it's now easier than ever to get cooked chicken needed for casseroles. Of course, chicken leftover from Sunday's roasted bird always works too.

CHEESY CHICKEN & MACARONI

1	medium onion, chopped
1	tablespoon cooking oil
8	ounces dried elbow macaroni (2 cups)
1	14½-ounce can diced tomatoes with basil, garlic, and oregano, undrained
1	10¾-ounce can condensed tomato soup
1	cup milk
1	cup shredded mozzarella cheese (4 ounces)
⅛	teaspoon black pepper
2	cups chopped cooked chicken (about 10 ounces)
¼	cup finely shredded Parmesan cheese (1 ounce)

PREP:
20 minutes
BAKE:
30 minutes + 10 minutes
STAND:
10 minutes
MAKES:
4 to 6 servings

1 In a small skillet cook onion in hot oil until tender. In a large saucepan cook elbow macaroni in a large amount of boiling salted water for 4 minutes. Drain macaroni well. Transfer cooked macaroni to an ungreased 2-quart casserole. Add cooked onion, diced tomatoes, tomato soup, milk, ½ cup of the mozzarella cheese, and the pepper. Mix well. Add chicken; stir to combine.

2 Bake, uncovered, in a 350°F oven for 30 minutes. Stir gently. Top with the remaining ½ cup mozzarella cheese and the Parmesan cheese. Bake about 10 minutes more or until heated through and cheese is melted. Let stand for 10 minutes before serving.

Nutrition Facts per serving: 712 cal., 24 g total fat (11 g sat. fat), 107 mg chol., 1,782 mg sodium, 69 g carbo., 4 g fiber, 52 g pro.

Oozing out of the pastry crust is a creamy and luscious cheese, chicken, and corn filling.
Serve a crisp vinaigrette-tossed salad for a terrific contrast.

CHEESY CORN & CHICKEN TURNOVERS

PREP:

25 minutes

BAKE:

15 minutes

MAKES:

4 servings

1 15-ounce package folded refrigerated unbaked piecrust (2 crusts)

2 cups chopped cooked chicken (about 10 ounces)

1 11-ounce can whole kernel corn with sweet peppers, drained

1 10¾-ounce can condensed cream of chicken and herbs or cream of mushroom soup

1 cup shredded cheddar cheese (4 ounces)

1 Let piecrusts stand and unfold according to package directions. On a lightly floured surface or pastry cloth, roll each piecrust into a 13-inch circle. Cut each piecrust into quarters.

2 In a medium bowl combine chicken, corn, cream of chicken and herbs soup, and cheese. Spoon about ½ cup of the chicken mixture along 1 straight side of each piecrust triangle, about ¾ inch from edge. Brush edges of each triangle with a little water. Fold other straight side of each triangle over the filling. Seal edges with a fork. Prick the top of each turnover several times with a fork. Place turnovers on a greased large baking sheet.

3 Bake in a 400°F oven about 15 minutes or until wedges are golden. Serve hot.

Nutrition Facts per serving: 862 cal., 47 g total fat (21 g sat. fat), 118 mg chol., 1,625 mg sodium, 73 g carbo., 3 g fiber, 33 g pro.

This super-easy version of chicken pie is a little different than most—it calls for minestrone soup and cream cheese. Combined, they bring a delightful tomato-cream flavor to the dish.

GOLDEN-CRUSTED CHICKEN PIES

¾	cup milk
4	teaspoons all-purpose flour
¼	teaspoon black pepper
1	10¾-ounce can condensed minestrone soup
2	cups cubed cooked chicken or turkey (about 10 ounces)
1	3-ounce package cream cheese, cubed
1	4.5 ounce package (5 or 6) refrigerated buttermilk or country-style biscuits

PREP:
15 minutes
BAKE:
12 minutes
MAKES:
4 servings

1 In a screw-top jar combine milk, flour, and pepper. Cover and shake well. In a medium saucepan stir milk mixture into minestrone soup. Cook and stir over medium heat until thickened and bubbly. Stir in chicken and cream cheese. Heat through, stirring to melt cream cheese.

2 Pour hot chicken mixture into 4 ungreased 10-ounce custard cups. Separate the biscuits; cut biscuits into quarters. Arrange 5 biscuit quarters on top of each custard cup.

3 Bake, uncovered, in a 375°F oven for 12 to 15 minutes or until biscuits are golden.

Nutrition Facts per serving: 415 cal., 20 g total fat (8 g sat. fat), 92 mg chol., 1,139 mg sodium, 31 g carbo., 3 g fiber, 28 g pro.

You'll love the way stirring in just a little sour cream adds so much richness.

CHICKEN BREASTS IN HERBED TOMATO SAUCE

START TO FINISH:
40 minutes

MAKES:

4 servings

4 skinless, boneless chicken breast halves (about 1¼ pounds)

2 tablespoons olive oil or cooking oil

1 10¾-ounce can condensed tomato soup

¼ cup water

1 teaspoon dried minced onion

1 teaspoon dried basil, crushed

½ teaspoon dried oregano, crushed

Dash black pepper

½ cup dairy sour cream

Hot cooked noodles

1 In a 10-inch skillet cook chicken in hot oil about 5 minutes or until brown, turning once. In a medium bowl stir together tomato soup, water, dried minced onion, basil, oregano, and pepper; pour over chicken. Bring to boiling; reduce heat. Simmer, covered, about 15 minutes or until chicken is tender and no longer pink (170°F). Remove chicken to platter; keep warm.

2 For sauce, spoon sour cream into a small bowl; gradually whisk about ½ cup of the pan juices into sour cream. Return sour cream mixture to skillet. Cook and stir until heated through (do not boil).

3 Arrange chicken on noodles. Spoon some of the sauce over chicken; pass remaining sauce.

Nutrition Facts per serving: 431 cal., 15 g total fat (5 g sat. fat), 119 mg chol., 560 mg sodium, 33 g carbo., 2 g fiber, 39 g pro.

Coq au Vin is a classic dish of chicken baked in wine. This recipe wraps up those irresistible flavors in a lusciously rich dish that's worthy of a special occasion.

COQ AU VIN ROSETTES

1½	cups sliced fresh mushrooms
⅓	cup chopped onion
1	tablespoon butter or margarine
1¼	pounds skinless, boneless chicken breast halves, cut into 1-inch pieces
⅓	cup dry white wine
½	teaspoon dried tarragon, crushed
¼	teaspoon white pepper
⅛	teaspoon salt
4	dried lasagna noodles
1	10¾-ounce can condensed cream of chicken or cream of mushroom soup
½	cup dairy sour cream
1	cup shredded Swiss cheese (4 ounces)
2	tablespoons slivered almonds, toasted (optional)

PREP:
30 minutes
BAKE:
35 minutes
MAKES:
4 servings

1 In a large skillet cook mushrooms and onion in hot butter until tender. Add chicken, wine, tarragon, white pepper, and salt. Bring to boiling; reduce heat. Simmer, covered, about 5 minutes or until chicken is no longer pink. Remove from heat.

2 Meanwhile, cook lasagna noodles according to package directions; drain. Halve each noodle lengthwise. Curl each lasagna noodle half into a 2½-inch-diameter ring and place, cut side down, in an ungreased 2-quart rectangular baking dish. Using a slotted spoon, spoon chicken mixture into center of the lasagna noodle rings, reserving the liquid in skillet (should have ½ cup liquid).

3 In a medium bowl stir together cream of chicken soup and sour cream; stir in ½ cup of the reserved cooking liquid and the Swiss cheese. Spoon soup mixture over lasagna noodle rings. If desired, sprinkle with slivered almonds.

4 Bake, covered, in a 325°F oven about 35 minutes or until heated through.

TEST KITCHEN TIP: **Lay the cooked, drained lasagna noodles on a sheet of waxed paper. That way, they won't stick to your work surface or each other while you work with them.**

Nutrition Facts per serving: 536 cal., 24 g total fat (13 g sat. fat), 133 mg chol., 860 mg sodium, 27 g carbo., 2 g fiber, 48 g pro.

Round out the meal with hot cooked fettuccine sprinkled with snipped fresh parsley, buttered broccoli spears, and fresh fruit.

CHICKEN WITH MARSALA SAUCE

START TO FINISH:

35 minutes

MAKES:

4 servings

4   skinless, boneless chicken breast halves (about 1¼ pounds)

½   teaspoon salt

⅛   teaspoon black pepper

3   tablespoons butter

1   8-ounce package sliced fresh mushrooms (3 cups)

1   10¾-ounce can condensed cream of mushroom or golden mushroom soup

¼   cup dry Marsala

½   teaspoon dried thyme, crushed

1 Place a chicken breast half between 2 pieces of plastic wrap. Using the flat side of a meat mallet, pound chicken lightly to about ¼-inch thickness. Remove plastic wrap. Repeat with remaining chicken breast halves. Sprinkle chicken pieces with salt and pepper.

2 In a 12-inch skillet melt 2 tablespoons of the butter over medium heat. Add chicken; cook about 8 minutes or until chicken is no longer pink (170°F), turning once. Transfer chicken to a serving platter; cover and keep warm.

3 Add remaining 1 tablespoon butter to the skillet. Add mushrooms; cook and stir about 5 minutes or until mushrooms are tender.

4 Stir in cream of mushroom soup, Marsala, and thyme. Cook and stir until heated through. Spoon mushroom mixture over chicken.

Nutrition Facts per serving: 351 cal., 18 g total fat (8 g sat. fat), 107 mg chol., 992 mg sodium, 8 g carbo., 1 g fiber, 37 g pro.

To add even more interest to this dish, choose one of the many varieties of flavored couscous mixes available now. Simply cook according to package directions and serve in place of the regular couscous.

GREEK-STYLE CHICKEN SKILLET

4	skinless, boneless chicken breast halves (about 1¼ pounds)
	Salt
	Black pepper
1	tablespoon olive oil or cooking oil
1	medium zucchini, sliced (about 1½ cups)
1	medium green sweet pepper, chopped
1	medium onion, sliced and separated into rings
2	cloves garlic, minced
⅛	teaspoon black pepper
¼	cup water
1	10¾-ounce can condensed tomato soup
2	cups hot cooked couscous*
½	cup crumbled feta cheese (2 ounces)
	Lemon wedges

START TO FINISH:
40 minutes
MAKES:
4 servings

1 Season chicken with salt and black pepper. In a large skillet heat oil over medium heat. Add chicken; cook for 12 to 15 minutes or until no longer pink (170°F), turning once. Remove chicken from skillet; keep warm.

2 Add zucchini, sweet pepper, onion, garlic, and the ⅛ teaspoon black pepper to skillet. Add water; reduce heat. Cover and cook for 5 minutes, stirring once or twice. Stir in tomato soup. Bring to boiling; reduce heat. Simmer, covered, for 5 minutes, stirring once.

3 To serve, divide couscous among 4 dinner plates. Place chicken on couscous. Spoon vegetable mixture over chicken and couscous. Sprinkle servings with feta cheese. Serve with lemon wedges.

*NOTE: For 2 cups cooked couscous, in a small saucepan bring 1 cup water and dash salt to boiling. Stir in ⅔ cup quick-cooking couscous. Remove from heat. Cover and let stand for 5 minutes. Fluff with a fork before serving.

Nutrition Facts per serving: 401 cal., 10 g total fat (4 g sat. fat), 99 mg chol., 827 mg sodium, 36 g carbo., 4 g fiber, 41 g pro.

This makes a big batch, but that's good news! The Test Kitchen tried leftovers the next day and found they tasted great cold—as a pasta salad.

HERBED CHICKEN PASTA PRIMAVERA

START TO FINISH:

40 minutes

MAKES:

8 servings

8 ounces dried mostaccioli pasta

Nonstick cooking spray

8 ounces packaged peeled baby carrots, cut in half lengthwise

1½ cups fresh green beans, bias-sliced into 2-inch pieces

2 green onions, sliced

1 clove garlic, minced

1 small zucchini, sliced

2 tablespoons water

2 cups chopped cooked chicken (about 10 ounces)

1 10¾-ounce can condensed cream of chicken soup

½ cup milk

1 teaspoon dried basil, crushed

1 teaspoon dried oregano, crushed

¼ cup pine nuts, toasted

Cracked black pepper

1 Cook mostaccioli according to package directions; drain and return mostaccioli to saucepan.

2 Meanwhile, lightly coat a large skillet with nonstick cooking spray. Preheat skillet over medium-high heat. Stir-fry carrots in hot skillet for 5 minutes. Add green beans, green onions, and garlic. Stir-fry for 2 minutes more. Stir in zucchini and the water. Reduce heat. Cover and cook for 4 to 5 minutes or until vegetables are crisp-tender.

3 Stir chicken, cream of chicken soup, milk, basil, oregano, and vegetables into pasta. Heat through. Sprinkle with pine nuts and cracked pepper. Serve immediately.

Nutrition Facts per serving: 269 cal., 9 g total fat (2 g sat. fat), 36 mg chol., 333 mg sodium, 31 g carbo., 3 g fiber, 17 g pro.

To streamline the preparation of this popular pasta casserole, omit cooking the manicotti shells in boiling water. Instead spoon the filling into uncooked shells—they'll cook as they bake.

SHORTCUT CHICKEN MANICOTTI

1	egg
1	10-ounce package frozen chopped spinach, thawed and well drained
1	cup finely chopped cooked chicken or turkey (about 5 ounces)
½	cup ricotta cheese or cream-style cottage cheese, drained
½	cup grated Parmesan cheese (2 ounces)
12	dried manicotti shells
1	10¾-ounce can condensed cream of chicken soup
1	8-ounce carton dairy sour cream
1	cup milk
½	teaspoon dried Italian seasoning, crushed
1	cup boiling water
1	cup shredded mozzarella cheese (4 ounces)
2	tablespoons snipped fresh parsley (optional)

PREP:
25 minutes
BAKE:
1 hour
STAND:
10 minutes
MAKES:
6 servings

❶ For filling, in a medium bowl beat egg with a fork; stir in spinach, chicken, ricotta cheese, and Parmesan cheese. Spoon about ¼ cup of the filling into each uncooked manicotti shell. Arrange filled shells in an ungreased 3-quart rectangular baking dish, making sure shells do not touch each other.

❷ For sauce, in another medium bowl combine cream of chicken soup, sour cream, milk, and Italian seasoning. Pour over manicotti shells, spreading to cover shells. Slowly pour boiling water around edge of baking dish. Cover baking dish tightly with foil.

❸ Bake in a 350°F oven for 60 to 65 minutes or until manicotti shells are tender. Sprinkle with mozzarella cheese and, if desired, parsley. Let stand for 10 minutes before serving.

Nutrition Facts per serving: 463 cal., 23 g total fat (13 g sat. fat), 106 mg chol., 758 mg sodium, 35 g carbo., 3 g fiber, 27 g pro.

Remember this recipe when asparagus season rolls around. The vegetable is usually at its freshest, in-season best from February to June.

LEMON CHICKEN WITH ASPARAGUS

START TO FINISH:

30 minutes

MAKES:

4 servings

Nonstick cooking spray

4   skinless, boneless chicken breast halves (about 1¼ pounds)

1   pound fresh asparagus spears, trimmed

1   cup water

1   10¾-ounce can condensed cream of chicken or cream of asparagus soup

¾   cup chicken broth

1   tablespoon lemon juice

Hot cooked couscous

1 Lightly coat a large nonstick skillet with nonstick cooking spray. Preheat skillet over medium heat. Cook chicken in hot skillet for 8 to 10 minutes or until tender and no longer pink (170°F), turning once. Remove chicken from skillet; cover and keep warm.

2 In the same skillet combine asparagus and water. Bring to boiling; reduce heat. Simmer, covered, for 3 to 5 minutes or until asparagus is crisp-tender. Drain.

3 Meanwhile, in a small saucepan combine cream of chicken soup, chicken broth, and lemon juice. Cook and stir until heated through. Serve sauce with chicken, asparagus, and hot cooked couscous.

Nutrition Facts per serving: 354 cal., 8 g total fat (3 g sat. fat), 88 mg chol., 844 mg sodium, 27 g carbo., 3 g fiber, 40 g pro.

Thai seasoning varies from brand to brand, but most include a great variety of herbs and spices, such as coriander, ginger, lemon peel, and chile peppers. The product makes it easy to bring a windfall of flavor to a recipe—without a lengthy ingredient list!

QUICK THAI CHICKEN PASTA

8	ounces dried angel hair pasta
1	cup sliced carrots
1	cup fresh pea pods, trimmed and cut in half
12	ounces skinless, boneless chicken thighs, cut into strips
1	tablespoon cooking oil
1	13½-ounce can unsweetened coconut milk
1	10¾-ounce can condensed cream of chicken soup
1½	to 2 teaspoons Thai seasoning
½	cup chopped peanuts

START TO FINISH:
20 minutes
MAKES:
4 servings

1 Cook pasta and carrots according to pasta package directions, adding pea pods for the last 1 minute of cooking. Drain well. Return pasta mixture to saucepan; cover and keep warm.

2 Meanwhile, in a large skillet cook chicken in hot oil until no longer pink; drain off fat. Add coconut milk, cream of chicken soup, and Thai seasoning. Cook over medium heat until heated through, stirring frequently.

3 Pour hot chicken mixture over cooked pasta; toss gently to coat. Transfer to a serving platter or bowl. Sprinkle with peanuts. Serve immediately.

Nutrition Facts per serving: 727 cal., 39 g total fat (21 g sat. fat), 74 mg chol., 858 mg sodium, 60 g carbo., 5 g fiber, 33 g pro.

For variety use chipotle- or lime-flavored salsa in this family-friendly dish.

CHICKEN FAJITAS

PREP:

20 minutes

BAKE:

10 minutes

MAKES:

4 servings

8   7- to 8-inch flour tortillas

2   tablespoons cooking oil

1   medium onion, cut into thin wedges

2   cloves garlic, minced

2   medium red and/or green sweet peppers, cut into thin bite-size strips

12   ounces skinless, boneless chicken breast halves, cut into bite-size strips

1   10¾-ounce can condensed cream of chicken soup

⅓   cup bottled salsa

2   cups shredded lettuce

Dairy sour cream, shredded cheddar cheese, and/or thinly sliced green onion (optional)

1 Wrap tortillas tightly in foil. Heat in a 350°F oven for 10 minutes to soften.

2 Meanwhile, in a large skillet heat 1 tablespoon of the oil over medium-high heat. Add onion and garlic; cook and stir for 2 minutes. Add sweet peppers; cook and stir for 1 to 2 minutes more or until vegetables are crisp-tender. Remove from skillet.

3 Add remaining 1 tablespoon oil to skillet. Add chicken; cook and stir for 3 to 4 minutes or until chicken is no longer pink. Return vegetables to skillet. Add cream of chicken soup and salsa; cook and stir until heated through.

4 To serve, divide chicken mixture evenly among warmed tortillas. Top with lettuce. If desired, top with sour cream, cheese, and/or green onion. Roll up tortillas.

Nutrition Facts per serving: 491 cal., 13 g total fat (3 g sat. fat), 56 mg chol., 1,342 mg sodium, 62 g carbo., 5 g fiber, 27 g pro.

Skip a step! Some supermarkets now offer pre-pounded chicken breasts. They'll make a speedy recipe even more so.

GOLDEN SKILLET CHICKEN

START TO FINISH:
20 minutes

MAKES:
4 servings

4 skinless, boneless chicken breast halves
   (about 1¼ pounds)

1 10¾-ounce can condensed golden mushroom soup

¾ cup reduced-sodium chicken broth

½ of an 8-ounce tub cream cheese with chives and onion

   Hot cooked angel hair pasta or thin spaghetti

1 Place each chicken breast half, boned side up, between 2 pieces of plastic wrap. Using the flat side of a meat mallet, pound lightly to ¼-inch thickness. Discard plastic wrap.

2 Heat a large nonstick skillet over medium-high heat for 1 minute. Add chicken; cook for 4 to 5 minutes or until tender and no longer pink, turning once. (If necessary, cook half of the chicken at a time.) Remove chicken from skillet; keep warm.

3 For sauce, add golden mushroom soup, chicken broth, and cream cheese to hot skillet. Cook and stir over medium heat until combined and mixture is heated through. Serve chicken and sauce over hot cooked pasta.

Nutrition Facts per serving: 520 cal., 14 g total fat (8 g sat. fat), 113 mg chol., 906 mg sodium, 51 g carbo., 2 g fiber, 43 g pro.

This chicken-rice bake is as versatile as they come. Serve it with your favorite vegetable or salad— it goes with just about anything!

CHICKEN PILAF

PREP:

20 minutes

BAKE:

55 minutes + 10 minutes

STAND:

10 minutes

MAKES:

4 servings

3¼   cups water

1   10¾-ounce can condensed cream of broccoli soup

1¼   cups uncooked long grain rice

¼   teaspoon salt

¼   teaspoon black pepper

2   cups chopped cooked chicken (about 10 ounces)

1   medium red or green sweet pepper, coarsely chopped

½   cup shredded carrot

½   cup grated Parmesan cheese (2 ounces)

1 In a large bowl stir together water, cream of broccoli soup, rice, salt, and black pepper. Transfer to an ungreased 2-quart casserole.

2 Bake, covered, in a 375°F oven for 55 to 60 minutes or until rice is tender, stirring twice during baking. Stir in chicken, sweet pepper, and carrot. Bake, covered, about 10 minutes more or until heated through.

3 Remove casserole from oven; gently stir in Parmesan cheese. Let stand for 10 minutes before serving.

Nutrition Facts per serving: 467 cal., 12 g total fat (5 g sat. fat), 72 mg chol., 895 mg sodium, 56 g carbo., 2 g fiber, 30 g pro.

Corn bread stuffing mix brings extra crunch to oven-fried chicken. For a real down-home supper, serve with refrigerated mashed potatoes, a jar of gravy, and a side of cooked frozen corn.

CORN BREAD-COATED CHICKEN

3	cups corn bread stuffing mix
¼	cup butter or margarine, melted
1	10¾-ounce can condensed cream of chicken soup
⅓	cup milk
2½	pounds meaty chicken pieces (breast halves, thighs, and drumsticks), skinned

PREP:
20 minutes
BAKE:
45 minutes
MAKES:
6 servings

❶ In a large bowl combine dry corn bread stuffing mix and melted butter; toss to coat. In a medium bowl stir together cream of chicken soup and milk. Dip chicken into soup mixture, coating well; dip into stuffing mixture, pressing with hands to coat chicken pieces. Place coated chicken pieces in an ungreased 15×10×1-inch baking pan.

❷ Bake, uncovered, in a 375°F oven for 45 to 55 minutes or until chicken is no longer pink (170°F for breast halves; 180°F for thighs and drumsticks).

Nutrition Facts per serving: 407 cal., 19 g total fat (8 g sat. fat), 104 mg chol., 855 mg sodium, 27 g carbo., 2 g fiber, 29 g pro.

Some cooks use paprika mostly as a garnish—its deep, bright color can liven up the look of a dish. Hungarian cooks, however, use the spice to add full flavor to their cooking.

HUNGARIAN-STYLE CHICKEN

START TO FINISH:

30 minutes

MAKES:

6 servings

6   skinless, boneless chicken breast halves (about 2 pounds total)

2   teaspoons Hungarian paprika

3   tablespoons cooking oil

1   cup chopped onion

1   10¾-ounce can condensed cream of chicken soup

1   8-ounce carton dairy sour cream

¼   cup milk

     Hot cooked noodles

1 Sprinkle chicken with 1 teaspoon of the paprika. In a large skillet heat 2 tablespoons of the oil over medium heat. Add chicken; cook for 8 to 10 minutes or until chicken is tender and no longer pink (170°F), turning once. Remove chicken from skillet; cover and keep warm.

2 In the same skillet heat remaining 1 tablespoon oil over medium heat. Add onion; cook for 5 to 6 minutes or until tender.

3 Meanwhile, in a small bowl combine cream of chicken soup, sour cream, milk, and remaining 1 teaspoon paprika. Add to cooked onion; cook and stir until heated through. Serve soup mixture over chicken. Serve with hot cooked noodles.

Nutrition Facts per serving: 485 cal., 22 g total fat (8 g sat. fat), 136 mg chol., 487 mg sodium, 29 g carbo., 2 g fiber, 42 g pro.

Cream of chicken soup might be one of the all-time best starters for hearty, homemade-tasting soups—it's creamy and chickeny, and combines well with so many flavors. Here it takes on an especially intriguing flair, thanks to a touch of curry powder.

CURRIED CHICKEN & CORN CHOWDER

1	17-ounce can cream-style corn, undrained
2	cups milk
1	10¾-ounce can condensed cream of chicken soup
¾	cup chopped green or red sweet pepper
1	tablespoon dried minced onion
2	to 3 teaspoons curry powder
1	9¾- or 10-ounce can chunk-style chicken, undrained, or 1½ cups frozen diced cooked chicken
	Coarsely chopped peanuts (optional)

START TO FINISH:
20 minutes
MAKES:
4 servings

1 In a large saucepan stir together corn, milk, cream of chicken soup, sweet pepper, dried minced onion, and curry powder. Bring to boiling, stirring frequently.

2 Stir in canned chicken; cook about 2 minutes or until heated through. If desired, sprinkle with peanuts.

Nutrition Facts per serving: 324 cal., 11 g total fat (4 g sat. fat), 49 mg chol., 1,201 mg sodium, 39 g carbo., 3 g fiber, 24 g pro.

This recipe has been in the Test Kitchen files for decades and endures as a favorite way to dress up a can of soup. The easy add-ins make it taste fresh and homemade.

CHEESY CHICKEN-CORN CHOWDER

PREP:

20 minutes

COOK:

15 minutes

MAKES:

4 servings

8   ounces skinless, boneless chicken breast halves

1   cup water

¼   cup chopped onion

¼   cup chopped celery

1   10¾-ounce can condensed cream of chicken soup

1   cup frozen loose-pack whole kernel corn

½   cup milk

½   cup shredded American cheese or cheddar cheese (2 ounces)

2   tablespoons chopped pimiento

1 In a medium saucepan combine chicken breast halves, the water, onion, and celery. Bring to boiling; reduce heat. Simmer, covered, for 15 to 20 minutes or until chicken is no longer pink. Remove chicken, reserving cooking liquid.

2 When cool enough to handle, chop chicken. Return chicken to reserved cooking liquid in saucepan. Stir in cream of chicken soup, corn, milk, American cheese, and pimiento. Bring just to boiling, stirring until cheese melts.

Nutrition Facts per serving: 258 cal., 11 g total fat (5 g sat. fat), 55 mg chol., 825 mg sodium, 19 g carbo., 2 g fiber, 21 g pro.

If you think dumplings are something only your grandmother had the time and talent to make, think again! They stir together quickly and puff up magically in this easy soup your family will cherish.

CHICKEN-BROCCOLI SOUP WITH DUMPLINGS

2	10¾-ounce cans condensed cream of chicken soup
3	cups milk
1	9-ounce package frozen chopped, cooked chicken breast
1½	cups frozen loose-pack cut broccoli
½	cup coarsely shredded carrot
1	teaspoon Dijon-style mustard
¼	teaspoon dried thyme, crushed
1	recipe Dumplings
½	cup shredded cheddar cheese (2 ounces)

START TO FINISH:

30 minutes

MAKES:

4 or 5 servings

1 In a 4-quart Dutch oven stir together cream of chicken soup, milk, chicken, broccoli, carrot, mustard, and thyme. Bring to boiling over medium heat.

2 Meanwhile, prepare Dumplings. Spoon batter in 4 or 5 mounds onto bubbling soup. Reduce heat. Simmer, covered, for 10 to 12 minutes or until a toothpick inserted into a dumpling comes out clean. Sprinkle dumplings with cheese.

DUMPLINGS: In a small bowl combine ⅔ cup all-purpose flour and 1 teaspoon baking powder. Add ¼ cup milk and 2 tablespoons cooking oil. Stir just until moistened.

Nutrition Facts per serving: 535 cal., 26 g total fat (9 g sat. fat), 75 mg chol., 1,701 mg sodium, 42 g carbo., 3 g fiber, 23 g pro.

Cayenne pepper and green chile peppers add a spicy spark to this creamy soup.

CREAM OF CHILE-CHICKEN SOUP

START TO FINISH:

25 minutes

MAKES:

4 servings

8	ounces ground chicken or turkey
$\frac{1}{4}$	cup chopped onion
2	cloves garlic, minced
2	cups milk
1	$10\frac{3}{4}$-ounce can condensed cream of chicken soup
1	7-ounce can whole kernel corn with sweet peppers, drained
1	medium tomato, chopped
1	4-ounce can diced green chile peppers, drained
2	tablespoons snipped fresh cilantro or parsley
$\frac{1}{8}$	to $\frac{1}{4}$ teaspoon cayenne pepper
1	cup shredded Monterey Jack cheese (4 ounces)

1 In a large saucepan or Dutch oven cook ground chicken, onion, and garlic until chicken is no longer pink and onion is tender. Drain off fat, if necessary.

2 Stir in milk, cream of chicken soup, corn, chopped tomato, chile peppers, cilantro, and cayenne pepper. Bring to boiling; reduce heat. Simmer, uncovered, for 5 minutes, stirring occasionally.

3 Add Monterey Jack cheese. Cook and stir until cheese is melted.

Nutrition Facts per serving: 388 cal., 21 g total fat (9 g sat. fat), 41 mg chol., 1,062 mg sodium, 26 g carbo., 3 g fiber, 24 g pro.

A chicken-flavored pilaf mix contributes both rice and seasonings to this hearty soup.

CREAMY CHICKEN & RICE SOUP

1	tablespoon butter or margarine
½	cup chopped onion
½	cup sliced celery
½	cup sliced carrot or sliced fresh mushrooms
1	14-ounce can reduced-sodium chicken broth
1	10¾-ounce can reduced-fat and reduced-sodium condensed cream of chicken soup
1	cup water
1	6¼-ounce package chicken-flavored rice pilaf mix
⅛	teaspoon black pepper
2½	cups milk
2	cups chopped cooked chicken (about 10 ounces)
	Snipped fresh parsley (optional)

PREP:
35 minutes
COOK:
20 minutes
MAKES:
6 servings

1 In a large saucepan melt butter over medium heat. Add onion, celery, and carrot; cook until tender.

2 Add chicken broth, cream of chicken soup, and water. Stir in pilaf mix with the seasoning packet and the pepper. Bring to boiling; reduce heat. Simmer, covered, for 20 minutes or until rice is tender, stirring occasionally.

3 Stir in milk and cooked chicken; heat through. If desired, sprinkle servings with snipped parsley.

Nutrition Facts per serving: 303 cal., 9 g total fat (4 g sat. fat), 60 mg chol., 979 mg sodium, 34 g carbo., 1 g fiber, 22 g pro.

This hearty chowder lives up to its name. It's easy—only takes about 30 minutes to make—and with a cup of cheddar cheese, it's definitely cheesy!

EASY CHEESY VEGETABLE-CHICKEN CHOWDER

START TO FINISH:

30 minutes

MAKES:

4 servings

1   cup small broccoli florets

1   cup frozen loose-pack whole kernel corn

½   cup water

¼   cup chopped onion

½   teaspoon dried thyme, crushed

2   cups milk

1½   cups chopped cooked chicken (about 8 ounces)

1   10¾-ounce can condensed cream of potato soup

1   cup shredded cheddar cheese (4 ounces)

     Black pepper

1 In a large saucepan combine broccoli, corn, water, onion, and thyme. Bring to boiling; reduce heat. Simmer, covered, for 8 to 10 minutes or until vegetables are tender. Do not drain.

2 Stir milk, chicken, cream of potato soup, and cheese into vegetable mixture. Cook and stir over medium heat until cheese melts and mixture is heated through. Sprinkle servings with pepper.

Nutrition Facts per serving: 374 cal., 18 g total fat (9 g sat. fat), 92 mg chol., 858 mg sodium, 24 g carbo., 2 g fiber, 29 g pro.

This meal-in-a-bowl has all the classic hallmarks of a great clam chowder, plus chicken to make it extra filling!

CHICKEN & CLAM CHOWDER

2	slices bacon, cut up
1	cup chopped onion
2	6½-ounce cans minced clams
3	medium potatoes, peeled and cut into bite-size pieces (3 cups)
1	medium carrot, shredded
¼	teaspoon black pepper
3	cups milk
2	cups chopped cooked chicken (about 10 ounces)
1	10¾-ounce can condensed cream of potato soup

START TO FINISH:
45 minutes
MAKES:
6 servings

1 In a 4- to 6-quart Dutch oven cook bacon until crisp; remove bacon from Dutch oven, reserving drippings. Add onion to hot drippings in Dutch oven; cook and stir over medium heat until tender.

2 Drain clams, reserving liquid; if necessary, add enough water to reserved liquid to equal 1 cup. Set clams aside.

3 Add reserved clam liquid, potatoes, carrot, and pepper to onion in Dutch oven. Bring to boiling; reduce heat. Simmer, covered, for 12 minutes or until potatoes are tender.

4 Stir in clams, bacon, milk, chicken, and cream of potato soup. Heat through.

Nutrition Facts per serving: 387 cal., 12 g total fat (4 g sat. fat), 101 mg chol., 634 mg sodium, 32 g carbo., 2 g fiber, 37 g pro.

Traditional gumbos start with a roux—a mixture of flour and fat that's cooked and stirred and stirred ... and stirred. A can of soup lets you skip that step!

EASY CHICKEN GUMBO

1	cup chopped red or green sweet pepper
1	cup chopped onion
1	teaspoon bottled minced garlic (2 cloves)
1	tablespoon cooking oil
1	14-ounce can chicken broth
1	10¾-ounce can condensed tomato bisque soup
1	10-ounce package frozen cut okra
¼	cup uncooked instant white rice
1	to 2 teaspoons Cajun seasoning
¼	teaspoon black pepper
1	cup chopped cooked chicken (about 5 ounces)

1 In a large saucepan cook sweet pepper, onion, and garlic in hot oil until vegetables are tender. Stir in chicken broth, tomato bisque soup, okra, rice, Cajun seasoning, and black pepper.

2 Bring to boiling; reduce heat. Simmer, covered, for 6 to 10 minutes or until okra is tender. Stir in chicken; heat through.

Nutrition Facts per serving: 265 cal., 9 g total fat (2 g sat. fat), 33 mg chol., 1,093 mg sodium, 32 g carbo., 5 g fiber, 15 g pro.

While the avocado, cilantro, and lime wedges are optional, they're the little extras that make this soup especially memorable.

TORTILLA CHICKEN SOUP

START TO FINISH:

40 minutes

MAKES:

6 servings

2	14-ounce cans reduced-sodium chicken broth
1	10¾-ounce can condensed tomato soup
1	medium onion, chopped
½	cup chopped green sweet pepper
4	skinless, boneless chicken breast halves (about 1¼ pounds total), cut into bite-size pieces
1	cup frozen loose-pack whole kernel corn
1½	teaspoons chili powder
½	teaspoon ground cumin
⅛	teaspoon black pepper
3	cups tortilla chips, coarsely crushed
1	cup shredded Monterey Jack cheese (4 ounces)
1	avocado, pitted, peeled, and cut into chunks (optional)
	Snipped fresh cilantro (optional)
	Lime wedges (optional)

1 In a 4-quart Dutch oven combine chicken broth, tomato soup, onion, and sweet pepper. Bring to boiling. Add chicken. Return to boiling; reduce heat. Simmer, covered, for 10 minutes.

2 Add corn, chili powder, cumin, and black pepper. Return to boiling; reduce heat. Simmer, covered, for 10 minutes more.

3 To serve, top with tortilla chips and cheese. If desired, serve with avocado and cilantro. If desired, squeeze lime wedges over servings.

Nutrition Facts per serving: 318 cal., 11 g total fat (5 g sat. fat), 71 mg chol., 905 mg sodium, 24 g carbo., 3 g fiber, 31 g pro.

Doctor up a can of chicken with rice soup, and you can have a fresh-tasting Asian-inspired treat in much less time than it takes to get takeout.

QUICK ASIAN CHICKEN SOUP

2½   cups water

2   10½-ounce cans condensed chicken with rice soup

2   cups frozen loose-pack broccoli stir-fry vegetables (broccoli, carrots, onions, red peppers, celery, water chestnuts, and mushrooms)

1   tablespoon soy sauce

½   teaspoon ground ginger

2   cups chopped cooked chicken or turkey (about 10 ounces)

1   In a large saucepan combine water and chicken with rice soup. Bring to boiling.

2   Stir in frozen vegetables, soy sauce, and ginger. Return to boiling; reduce heat. Simmer, covered, for 3 to 5 minutes or until vegetables are tender. Stir in chicken; heat through.

Nutrition Facts per serving: 247 cal., 9 g total fat (3 g sat. fat), 72 mg chol., 1,479 mg sodium, 14 g carbo., 1 g fiber, 27 g pro.

Cheddar cheese soup is normally a side dish, but here it gets transformed into a hearty one-pot meal, thanks to smoked turkey sausage and asparagus.

TURKEY-ASPARAGUS SOUP

¼	cup chopped celery
¼	cup chopped onion
1	tablespoon butter or margarine
3	cups milk
1	10¾-ounce can condensed cheddar cheese soup
1	teaspoon dry mustard
½	teaspoon Worcestershire sauce
1	14- to 16-ounce package smoked turkey sausage or kielbasa, halved lengthwise and sliced
1	10-ounce package frozen cut asparagus

START TO FINISH:

25 minutes

MAKES:

5 or 6 servings

1 In a large saucepan cook celery and onion in hot butter until tender. Stir in milk, cheddar cheese soup, dry mustard, and Worcestershire sauce. Bring to boiling.

2 Stir in turkey sausage and asparagus. Return to boiling; reduce heat. Cook, uncovered, about 6 minutes more or until asparagus is tender, stirring occasionally.

Nutrition Facts per serving: 281 cal., 16 g total fat (7 g sat. fat), 79 mg chol., 1,294 mg sodium, 17 g carbo., 2 g fiber, 22 g pro.

Cooked smoked turkey sausage has a long shelf life when kept in the refrigerator. Keep some on hand, along with the other ingredients, and you can stir together this soup in a hurry. Refrigerated breadsticks and apple slices would make quick, easy serve-alongs.

TURKEY-BEAN SOUP

START TO FINISH:
30 minutes

MAKES:
4 servings

2   15-ounce cans Great Northern or white kidney (cannellini) beans, rinsed and drained

1   10¾-ounce can condensed cream of celery soup

8   ounces cooked smoked turkey sausage, halved lengthwise and sliced

1½   cups milk

1   teaspoon dried minced onion

½   teaspoon dried thyme, crushed

⅛   to ¼ teaspoon black pepper

1   teaspoon bottled minced garlic (2 cloves) or ¼ teaspoon garlic powder

1 In a large saucepan combine beans, cream of celery soup, and turkey sausage; stir in milk, dried minced onion, thyme, pepper, and garlic.

2 Bring to boiling over medium-high heat, stirring occasionally; reduce heat. Simmer, covered, for 10 minutes, stirring occasionally.

Nutrition Facts per serving: 434 cal., 11 g total fat (3 g sat. fat), 54 mg chol., 1,129 mg sodium, 57 g carbo., 11 g fiber, 29 g pro.

Kids will love this soup—especially when you make it with frankfurters. But wait—why should you make it at all? Hand the recipe over; it's easy enough for older kids to prepare.

SAUSAGE-CORN CHOWDER

12	ounces cooked smoked turkey sausage or frankfurters
1	10¾-ounce can condensed cream of potato soup
1⅓	cups milk
1	8¾-ounce can cream-style corn
3	slices American cheese, torn into pieces (3 ounces)

START TO FINISH:
20 minutes
MAKES:
4 servings

1 Halve the sausage lengthwise and slice ½ inch thick. Set aside.

2 In a 2-quart saucepan combine cream of potato soup, milk, and cream-style corn. Stir in sausage pieces and cheese. Cook and stir over medium heat until heated through.

Nutrition Facts per serving: 342 cal., 18 g total fat (8 g sat. fat), 85 mg chol., 1,836 mg sodium, 27 g carbo., 1 g fiber, 23 g pro.

Parmesan cheese tastes best when freshly grated, so keep a hunk on hand in the refrigerator (because it's a hard cheese, it keeps well) and grate some right over each serving.

TURKEY SAUSAGE & TORTELLINI SOUP

START TO FINISH:

40 minutes

MAKES:

6 servings

6   ounces cooked smoked turkey sausage, halved lengthwise and cut into $1/2$-inch slices

1   cup shredded carrots

1   cup frozen loose-pack cut green beans or Italian-style green beans

2   $14^1/2$-ounce cans diced tomatoes with basil, oregano, and garlic, undrained

3   cups water

1   $10^1/2$-ounce can condensed French onion soup

1   9-ounce package refrigerated cheese-filled tortellini

Grated Parmesan cheese

1 In a 4-quart Dutch oven combine sausage, shredded carrots, and green beans. Stir in tomatoes, water, and French onion soup. Bring to boiling; reduce heat. Simmer, covered, for 20 minutes.

2 Stir in tortellini. Return to boiling; reduce heat. Cook, uncovered, for 5 to 6 minutes more or until tortellini is tender. Sprinkle servings with Parmesan cheese.

Nutrition Facts per serving: 272 cal., 7 g total fat (2 g sat. fat), 40 mg chol., 1,527 mg sodium, 40 g carbo., 3 g fiber, 15 g pro.

This colorful chowder gets an extra dose of freshness from some snipped fresh basil. In a pinch, dried basil will do, though use just a teaspoon, and add it in the first step, when you're boiling the vegetables.

TURKEY-VEGETABLE CHOWDER

1	cup small broccoli florets
1	medium carrot, coarsely shredded, or $\frac{1}{2}$ cup purchased shredded carrot
$\frac{1}{2}$	cup diced peeled potato or $\frac{1}{2}$ cup frozen loose-pack diced hash brown potatoes
$\frac{1}{2}$	cup water
$\frac{1}{4}$	cup chopped onion
2	cups milk
$1\frac{1}{2}$	cups chopped cooked turkey or chicken (about 8 ounces)
1	$10\frac{3}{4}$-ounce can condensed cream of chicken or cream of mushroom soup
1	tablespoon snipped fresh basil
$\frac{1}{4}$	teaspoon salt
$\frac{1}{4}$	teaspoon black pepper
	Fresh basil leaves, slivered (optional)

START TO FINISH:

30 minutes

MAKES:

4 servings

1 In a medium saucepan combine broccoli, carrot, potato, water, and onion. Bring to boiling; reduce heat. Simmer, covered, about 6 minutes or until vegetables are tender. Do not drain.

2 Stir in milk, turkey, cream of chicken soup, snipped basil, salt, and pepper. Cook and stir over medium heat until heated through. If desired, top servings with slivered basil.

Nutrition Facts per serving: 272 cal., 10 g total fat (4 g sat. fat), 59 mg chol., 825 mg sodium, 20 g carbo., 2 g fiber, 24 g pro.

Busy week ahead? Stock these ingredients in your refrigerator and cupboards now, and you'll be less than half an hour away from an incredibly satisfying supper when you need it most.

TURKEY-BISCUIT PIE

PREP:

15 minutes

BAKE:

12 minutes

MAKES:

4 servings

1	10¾-ounce can condensed cream of chicken soup
½	cup milk
¼	cup dairy sour cream
6	ounces cooked turkey breast, cubed (about 1 cup)
1½	cups frozen loose-pack mixed vegetables
½	teaspoon dried basil, crushed
⅛	teaspoon black pepper
1	4.5-ounce package (5 or 6) refrigerated biscuits, quartered

1 In a medium saucepan stir together cream of chicken soup, milk, and sour cream. Stir in turkey, mixed vegetables, basil, and pepper. Cook and stir over medium heat until boiling.

2 Spoon turkey mixture into a lightly greased 1½-quart casserole. Top with quartered biscuits.

3 Bake, uncovered, in a 450°F oven for 12 to 15 minutes or until biscuits are brown.

Nutrition Facts per serving: 335 cal., 14 g total fat (5 g sat. fat), 49 mg chol., 1,049 mg sodium, 33 g carbo., 3 g fiber, 20 g pro.

Tailor the vegetables to your family's tastes. For this recipe, you can use just about any combination of mixed vegetables or simply use peas.

POTATO-TOPPED TURKEY PIE

1	pound ground turkey or chicken
½	cup chopped onion
1	10¾-ounce can condensed golden mushroom soup
1	10-ounce package frozen peas and carrots, thawed
¼	cup water
½	teaspoon salt
⅛	teaspoon black pepper
1	20-ounce package refrigerated mashed potatoes
1	cup shredded cheddar cheese (4 ounces)

PREP:
25 minutes
BAKE:
40 minutes
MAKES:
4 to 6 servings

1 In a large skillet cook ground turkey and onion until turkey is lightly browned and onion is tender. Stir in golden mushroom soup, peas and carrots, the water, salt, and pepper. Spoon mixture into an ungreased 1½-quart casserole.

2 In a medium bowl stir together mashed potatoes and ½ cup of the cheddar cheese. Drop potato mixture in mounds on top of turkey mixture. Sprinkle with remaining ½ cup cheddar cheese.

3 Bake, uncovered, in a 350°F oven for 40 to 45 minutes or until heated through.

Nutrition Facts per serving: 491 cal., 23 g total fat (9 g sat. fat), 123 mg chol., 1,406 mg sodium, 36 g carbo., 4 g fiber, 34 g pro.

For a buffet, use the large baking dish. For a sit-down dinner, the individual au gratin dishes are more elegant.

TURKEY-SPINACH CASSEROLE

PREP:

30 minutes

BAKE:

25 minutes

MAKES:

4 servings

1   10-ounce package frozen chopped spinach or chopped broccoli

1   10¾-ounce can reduced-fat and reduced-sodium condensed cream of celery soup

1   cup water

2   tablespoons butter or margarine

3   cups herb-seasoned stuffing mix

2   cups chopped cooked turkey or chicken (about 10 ounces)

⅓   cup milk

1   tablespoon grated Parmesan cheese

1 In a large saucepan combine spinach, half of the cream of celery soup, water, and butter. Bring to boiling. (If using spinach, separate it with a fork.) Simmer, covered, for 5 minutes.

2 Add stuffing mix to saucepan; stir to moisten. Spread mixture in an ungreased 2-quart square baking dish or divide mixture among four 10-ounce au gratin dishes; top with turkey.

3 In a small bowl stir milk into remaining cream of celery soup; pour over turkey. Sprinkle with Parmesan cheese.

4 Bake, uncovered, in a 350°F oven about 25 minutes or until heated through.

Nutrition Facts per serving: 375 cal., 12 g total fat (5 g sat. fat), 65 mg chol., 1,065 mg sodium, 44 g carbo., 5 g fiber, 23 g pro.

For this recipe, it's best to use leftover roast turkey or chicken, as deli turkey or chicken can bring an abundance of salty flavor to the dish.

TURKEY-STUFFING BAKE

2	cups herb-seasoned stuffing mix
$\frac{1}{3}$	cup butter or margarine, melted
$\frac{1}{4}$	cup water
$\frac{1}{2}$	cup milk
1	$10\frac{3}{4}$-ounce can condensed cream of chicken or cream of celery soup
$1\frac{1}{2}$	cups cubed cooked turkey or chicken (about 8 ounces)
1	cup frozen loose-pack peas
1	4-ounce can (drained weight) sliced mushrooms, drained
$\frac{1}{2}$	teaspoon dried sage, crushed, or poultry seasoning

1 In a medium bowl combine stuffing mix, melted butter, and water. Press stuffing mixture onto the bottom and almost all the way up the side of a greased $1\frac{1}{2}$-quart casserole.

2 In another medium bowl stir milk into cream of chicken soup. Stir in turkey, peas, mushrooms, and sage. Spoon mixture into stuffing-lined casserole.

3 Bake, covered, in a 375°F oven for 30 minutes. Uncover and bake for 15 to 20 minutes more or until heated through.

Nutrition Facts per serving: 478 cal., 26 g total fat (13 g sat. fat), 92 mg chol., 1,341 mg sodium, 37 g carbo., 5 g fiber, 24 g pro.

PREP:
20 minutes
BAKE:
30 minutes + 15 minutes
MAKES:
4 to 6 servings

Next time you're shopping for a holiday meal, pick up these ingredients when you pick up your turkey. That way, you'll have an "off-the-shelf" option for serving leftovers.

TURKEY-BROCCOLI CASSEROLE

PREP:

25 minutes

BAKE:

35 minutes

MAKES:

6 servings

4	ounces dried noodles (2 cups)
2	cups frozen loose-pack cut broccoli
1	$10\frac{3}{4}$-ounce can condensed cream of onion or cream of celery soup
1	8-ounce carton dairy sour cream
$\frac{1}{2}$	cup milk
2	cups chopped cooked turkey or chicken (about 10 ounces)
1	8-ounce can sliced water chestnuts, drained
$\frac{1}{2}$	cup shredded Swiss cheese (2 ounces)
$\frac{1}{3}$	cup fine dry bread crumbs
2	tablespoons butter or margarine, melted

1 Cook noodles according to package directions, adding the broccoli during the last 2 minutes of cooking; drain and set aside.

2 In a large bowl stir together cream of onion soup, sour cream, and milk. Stir in turkey, water chestnuts, Swiss cheese, and noodle mixture. Transfer to an ungreased 2-quart square baking dish.

3 In a small bowl stir together bread crumbs and melted butter. Sprinkle over noodle mixture.

4 Bake, uncovered, in a 350°F oven about 35 minutes or until heated through.

Nutrition Facts per serving: 441 cal., 23 g total fat (11 g sat. fat), 100 mg chol., 656 mg sodium, 38 g carbo., 3 g fiber, 24 g pro.

The original version of this famous casserole, which was created in honor of an Italian opera singer, calls for making a rich, mushroom–studded cream sauce. While that's not too tricky a task, the canned soup in this version makes the dish come together much more quickly.

QUICK TURKEY TETRAZZINI

Nonstick cooking spray

6   ounces dried spaghetti

1   18¾-ounce can ready-to-serve chunky creamy chicken with mushroom soup

6   ounces cooked turkey breast, chopped (about 1 cup)

½   cup finely shredded Parmesan cheese (2 ounces)

2   tablespoons sliced almonds

PREP:
20 minutes
BAKE:
12 minutes
MAKES:
4 servings

1 Lightly coat a 2-quart square baking dish with nonstick cooking spray; set aside.

2 Cook spaghetti according to package directions. Drain spaghetti; return to pan. Add creamy chicken with mushroom soup, turkey, and half of the Parmesan cheese to cooked spaghetti; heat through. Transfer spaghetti mixture to baking dish. Sprinkle with almonds and remaining Parmesan cheese.

3 Bake, uncovered, in a 425°F oven for 12 to 15 minutes or until top is golden.

Nutrition Facts per serving: 413 cal., 13 g total fat (5 g sat. fat), 59 mg chol., 752 mg sodium, 43 g carbo., 2 g fiber, 28 g pro.

This recipe is a great one to make ahead. Simply prepare as directed through step 4. Cover and chill for at least 4 hours or up to 24 hours. Bake, covered, in a 350° F oven for 1 hour or until heated through. Continue as directed.

TURKEY ENCHILADAS

PREP:

40 minutes

BAKE:

40 minutes + 5 minutes

MAKES:

12 enchiladas

$\frac{1}{2}$ cup chopped onion

$\frac{1}{2}$ of an 8-ounce package reduced-fat cream cheese (Neufchâtel), softened

1 teaspoon ground cumin

4 cups chopped cooked turkey or chicken breast (about 1$\frac{1}{4}$ pounds)

$\frac{1}{4}$ cup chopped pecans, toasted

Nonstick cooking spray

12 7- to 8-inch flour tortillas

1 10$\frac{3}{4}$-ounce can reduced-fat and reduced-sodium condensed cream of chicken soup

1 8-ounce carton light dairy sour cream

1 cup fat-free milk

2 to 4 tablespoons finely chopped, pickled jalapeño peppers*

$\frac{1}{2}$ cup shredded reduced-fat sharp cheddar cheese (2 ounces)

1 For filling, in a covered small saucepan cook onion in a small amount of boiling water until tender; drain. In a medium bowl stir together cream cheese, 1 tablespoon water, the cumin, $\frac{1}{4}$ teaspoon black pepper, and $\frac{1}{8}$ teaspoon salt. Stir in cooked onion, turkey, and pecans; set aside.

2 Wrap tortillas in foil. Heat in a 350°F oven about 10 minutes or until softened. Meanwhile, coat an ungreased 3-quart rectangular baking dish with nonstick cooking spray.

3 Spoon about $\frac{1}{4}$ cup of the filling onto 1 of the tortillas; roll up. Place tortilla, seam side down, in the prepared baking dish. Repeat with the remaining filling and tortillas.

4 For sauce, stir together cream of chicken soup, sour cream, milk, and jalapeño peppers. Pour sauce over enchiladas in baking dish.

5 Bake, covered, in the 350°F oven about 40 minutes or until heated through. Sprinkle with cheddar cheese. Bake, uncovered, about 5 minutes more or until cheese is melted. If desired, top with tomatoes, sweet pepper, and cilantro.

*NOTE: When working with chile peppers, wear plastic or rubber gloves. If your bare hands do touch the peppers, wash your hands and nails well with soap and warm water.**

Nutrition Facts per enchilada: 273 cal., 11 g total fat (4 g sat. fat), 55 mg chol., 417 mg sodium, 21 g carbo., 1 g fiber, 21 g pro.

Stash away some holiday turkey in the freezer so you'll have the meat on hand for this lively bake. Freeze cooked turkey meat in freezer containers for up to four months.

MEXICAN TURKEY CASSEROLE

1½ cups chopped cooked turkey or chicken (about 8 ounces)

1 10¾-ounce can condensed cream of chicken or cream of mushroom soup

½ cup dairy sour cream

1 4-ounce can diced green chile peppers, undrained

1 2¼-ounce can sliced pitted ripe olives, undrained

2 green onions, sliced

1½ cups coarsely crushed tortilla chips or corn chips

1½ cups shredded Monterey Jack cheese with jalapeño peppers or Monterey Jack cheese (6 ounces)

1 cup chopped tomatoes

PREP:
20 minutes

BAKE:
35 minutes

MAKES:
4 to 6 servings

1 In a large bowl combine turkey, cream of chicken soup, sour cream, chile peppers, olives, and green onions.

2 Sprinkle one-third of the chips over bottom of a greased 2-quart square baking dish. Spoon half of the turkey mixture over chips. Top with half of the cheese. Repeat layers, ending with a layer of chips.

3 Bake, uncovered, in a 375°F oven about 35 minutes or until heated through. Sprinkle with tomatoes just before serving.

Nutrition Facts per serving: 487 cal., 32 g total fat (15 g sat. fat), 87 mg chol., 1,413 mg sodium, 26 g carbo., 3 g fiber, 27 g pro.

Filled with wild rice, turkey, and dried fruit, these cabbage rolls will warm you up on cold, harsh winter nights.

TURKEY-STUFFED CABBAGE ROLLS

PREP:
1 hour

COOK:
20 minutes

MAKES:
4 servings

1	6-ounce package uncooked long grain and wild rice mix
1	medium onion, finely chopped
8	ounces ground turkey
$^1/_3$	cup dried cranberries or raisins, coarsely chopped
8	large green cabbage leaves
1	10$^3/_4$-ounce can condensed golden mushroom soup
$^1/_3$	cup plain low-fat yogurt

1 In a medium saucepan cook rice mix and onion according to package directions for the rice. Cool completely. Transfer to a large bowl; mix in ground turkey and cranberries.

2 Trim heavy center vein from each cabbage leaf. In a large saucepan cook cabbage leaves, uncovered, in a large amount of boiling water for 3 to 5 minutes or until tender. Drain well. Set aside.

3 Place about $^1/_2$ cup of the turkey mixture in the center of a cabbage leaf. Fold both sides over turkey mixture and roll up; secure with a toothpick, if necessary. Repeat with remaining cabbage leaves and turkey mixture.

4 In a 12-inch skillet stir together golden mushroom soup and yogurt. Arrange the cabbage rolls, seam sides down, in the yogurt mixture. Bring to boiling; reduce heat. Cover and cook over low heat for 20 to 25 minutes or until no pink remains in filling. Spoon sauce onto serving plates; top with cabbage rolls.

MAKE-AHEAD DIRECTIONS: **Prepare as directed through step 3. Place cabbage rolls in a storage container. Cover and chill for up to 24 hours. Continue as directed in step 4.**

Nutrition Facts per serving : 305 cal., 7 g total fat (2 g sat. fat), 23 mg chol., 1,208 mg sodium, 48 g carbo., 5 g fiber, 15 g pro.

After the holidays, store extra turkey in the fridge. The next day, transform the leftovers into these exotic meal-in-a-crust turnovers.

INDONESIAN-STYLE TURKEY TURNOVERS

1	15-ounce package folded refrigerated unbaked piecrust (2 crusts)
1	10¾-ounce can condensed cream of chicken soup
¼	cup plain low-fat yogurt
3	cups cubed cooked turkey (about 1 pound)
½	cup raisins or dried currants
¼	cup chopped peanuts
¼	cup shredded coconut
¼	cup chopped green onions
1	teaspoon curry powder
1	egg yolk
1	teaspoon water

PREP:
30 minutes

BAKE:
30 minutes

MAKES:
6 to 8 servings

1 Let piecrusts stand at room temperature and unfold according to package directions.

2 Meanwhile, in a large bowl stir together cream of mushroom soup and yogurt. Stir in turkey, raisins, peanuts, coconut, green onions, and curry powder; set aside.

3 Place the unfolded piecrusts on a foil-lined baking sheet. Divide turkey mixture among piecrusts, spooning it onto half of each circle and spreading it to within 1 inch of the edge. Fold each crust in half over the turkey mixture. Seal edges by pressing with tines of a fork. Using a sharp knife, cut slits in the top of each turnover. In a small bowl beat together egg yolk and water. Brush over the top of each turnover.

4 Bake in a 375°F oven for 30 to 35 minutes or until pastry is golden.

Nutrition Facts per serving: 601 cal., 31 g total fat (12 g sat. fat), 107 mg chol., 741 mg sodium, 52 g carbo., 2 g fiber, 27 g pro.

People who love chicken livers are going to really appreciate this dish!

SAUCY CHICKEN LIVERS

START TO FINISH:

20 minutes

MAKES:

6 to 8 servings

1½ pounds chicken livers, halved

¼ cup all-purpose flour

2 tablespoons cooking oil

1 10¾-ounce can condensed cream of chicken soup

1 4-ounce can (drained weight) sliced mushrooms, undrained

⅛ teaspoon black pepper

Hot cooked noodles

1 Place chicken livers in a plastic bag. Add flour; shake to coat. In a 10-inch skillet heat oil over medium heat. Add floured chicken livers; cook about 5 minutes or just until livers are no longer pink.

2 Stir in cream of chicken soup, mushrooms, and pepper. Simmer, covered, about 5 minutes or until heated through. Serve over hot cooked noodles.

Nutrition Facts per serving: 361 cal., 13 g total fat (3 g sat. fat), 528 mg chol., 575 mg sodium, 32 g carbo., 2 g fiber, 26 g pro.

FISH & SEAFOOD

4

Creamy, cheesy, and packed full of flavor—what more do you want from a casserole? By the way—it's easy too.

CHEESY MEXICALI TUNA BAKE

PREP:

25 minutes

BAKE:

30 minutes + 5 minutes

MAKES:

6 servings

2¼ cups dried medium noodles (about 5 ounces)

1 11-ounce can condensed nacho cheese soup

½ cup dairy sour cream

½ cup milk

1 4-ounce can diced green chile peppers, undrained

1 tablespoon dried minced onion

1 12-ounce can tuna (water pack), drained and flaked

½ cup shredded cheddar or Monterey Jack cheese (2 ounces)

1 cup coarsely broken nacho cheese-flavored tortilla chips or plain tortilla chips

Bottled salsa

Dairy sour cream

1 Cook noodles according to package directions. Drain well.

2 In a large bowl combine nacho cheese soup, the ½ cup sour cream, and the milk. Stir in chile peppers and onion. Fold in cooked noodles and tuna. Spoon into an ungreased 1½-quart baking dish or casserole.

3 Bake, covered, in a 375°F oven for 30 minutes. Uncover. Sprinkle with cheese; top with chips. Bake, uncovered, for 5 to 10 minutes more or until heated through. Serve with salsa and additional sour cream.

Nutrition Facts per serving: 375 cal., 17 g total fat (9 g sat. fat), 77 mg chol., 810 mg sodium, 30 g carbo., 2 g fiber, 24 g pro.

Tuna casserole transcends the ordinary with cheese, water chestnuts, red sweet peppers, and broccoli.

BAKED TUNA SUPREME

1	10-ounce package frozen chopped broccoli
1	9-ounce can tuna, drained and flaked
1	8-ounce can sliced water chestnuts, drained
½	of a 7-ounce jar roasted red sweet peppers, drained and cut into strips (½ cup)
1	10¾-ounce can condensed cream of mushroom soup
4	ounces sharp process American cheese slices, torn
¼	cup milk
1	cup soft bread crumbs
1	tablespoon butter or margarine, melted
¼	teaspoon dried dill

PREP:
25 minutes
BAKE:
20 minutes
MAKES:
6 servings

1 Cook broccoli according to package directions, except omit salt; drain. Arrange cooked broccoli in an ungreased 2-quart square baking dish. Top with tuna. Sprinkle evenly with water chestnuts and roasted red pepper strips.

2 In a medium saucepan combine cream of mushroom soup, cheese, and milk; heat until cheese is melted. Pour over tuna mixture. In a small bowl stir together bread crumbs, melted butter, and dill; sprinkle over tuna mixture.

3 Bake, uncovered, in a 350°F oven for 20 to 25 minutes or until heated through.

Nutrition Facts per serving: 287 cal., 16 g total fat (7 g sat. fat), 42 mg chol., 869 mg sodium, 22 g carbo., 2 g fiber, 18 g pro.

Here the classic tuna-rice casserole gets an update with broccoli cheese soup and roasted red sweet peppers. Squeeze lemon over the dish if you like—it will add a nice spark of flavor, especially if you choose the salmon option.

TUNA & RICE BAKE

PREP:

25 minutes

BAKE:

30 minutes

MAKES:

6 servings

1   10¾-ounce can condensed broccoli cheese soup

1   cup cooked rice

¼   cup chopped bottled roasted red sweet pepper

2   tablespoons snipped fresh parsley

4   beaten egg yolks

1   6-ounce can tuna or skinless, boneless salmon, drained and flaked

4   egg whites

     Lemon wedges (optional)

1 In a medium saucepan combine broccoli cheese soup, cooked rice, red sweet pepper, and parsley; cook and stir until heated through. Remove from heat. Gradually stir into egg yolks. Fold in tuna; set aside.

2 In a large bowl beat egg whites until stiff peaks form (tips stand straight). Fold about 1 cup of the beaten egg whites into tuna mixture. Fold in remaining beaten whites. Spoon into an ungreased 2-quart casserole.

3 Bake, uncovered, in a 350°F oven for 30 to 35 minutes or until a knife inserted near center comes out clean (wiggle knife slightly to pull through top). Serve immediately. If desired, pass lemon wedges to squeeze over servings.

Nutrition Facts per serving: 190 cal., 9 g total fat (3 g sat. fat), 151 mg chol., 507 mg sodium, 12 g carbo., 1 g fiber, 15 g pro.

Tuna and noodle casserole is often a favorite for weekend lunches. When you're in a hurry, fix this speedy, no-bake version that comes together in just one pan.

TUNA & NOODLES

1   12-ounce package dried egg noodles (6 cups)

1   10¾-ounce can condensed cream of celery soup

6   ounces American cheese, cubed, or process Swiss cheese slices, torn

½   cup milk

1   12-ounce can solid white tuna (water pack), drained and broken into chunks

1 In a 4-quart Dutch oven cook noodles according to package directions; drain. Set aside.

2 In the same Dutch oven combine cream of celery soup, cheese, and milk. Cook and stir over medium heat until bubbly. Stir tuna into soup mixture. Gently stir in cooked noodles; cook for 2 to 3 minutes more or until heated through.

Nutrition Facts per serving: 645 cal., 23 g total fat (11 g sat. fat), 162 mg chol., 1,476 mg sodium, 68 g carbo., 3 g fiber, 40 g pro.

START TO FINISH:

25 minutes

MAKES:

4 to 6 servings

A can of condensed clam chowder adds flavor (and means you don't have to peel any potatoes), while cream cheese adds richness. In short, this is no ordinary potpie!

TUNA POTPIE

PREP:
25 minutes

BAKE:
20 minutes

MAKES:
4 servings

½ of a 15-ounce package folded refrigerated unbaked piecrust (1 crust)

1 10¾-ounce can condensed New England clam chowder

1 cup milk

1 3-ounce package cream cheese, cut up

½ teaspoon dried dill

¼ teaspoon black pepper

1 12-ounce can tuna (water pack), drained

1 10-ounce package frozen mixed vegetables

½ cup uncooked instant rice

1 Let piecrust stand at room temperature and unfold according to package directions.

2 Meanwhile, in a large saucepan combine New England clam chowder, milk, cream cheese, dill, and pepper. Cook and stir over medium-high heat until cheese melts. Gently stir in tuna, vegetables, and rice. Bring to boiling.

3 Pour tuna mixture into an ungreased 1½-quart casserole. Top with piecrust. Trim crust to ½ inch beyond edge of the casserole dish. Fold under extra crust; crimp edge. Cut slits in crust to allow steam to escape. Bake in a 450°F oven about 20 minutes or until crust is golden.

Nutrition Facts per serving: 520 cal., 23 g total fat (8 g sat. fat), 67 mg chol., 1,219 mg sodium, 45 g carbo., 4 g fiber, 32 g pro.

You'll be amazed at how easy it is to turn a can of tuna into such a colorful and varied entrée. Serve alongside a tartly dressed green salad for a pleasing contrast.

DEEP-DISH TUNA PIE

½	of an 11-ounce package piecrust mix (1⅓ cups)
1	large onion, chopped
1	cup diced, peeled potato
1	10¾-ounce can condensed cream of mushroom soup
⅓	cup milk
⅓	cup grated Parmesan cheese
1	tablespoon lemon juice
¾	teaspoon dried dill
¼	teaspoon black pepper
1	16-ounce package frozen mixed vegetables
1	9-ounce can tuna (water pack), drained and broken into chunks

PREP:
25 minutes
BAKE:
40 minutes
MAKES:
6 servings

1 Prepare piecrust mix according to package directions, except do not roll out. Cover dough; set aside.

2 In a covered large skillet cook onion and potato in a small amount of boiling water about 7 minutes or until tender. Drain off liquid. Stir in cream of mushroom soup, milk, Parmesan cheese, lemon juice, dill, and pepper. Cook and stir until bubbly. Gently stir in vegetables and tuna. Spoon mixture into an ungreased 2-quart casserole.

3 On a lightly floured surface, roll piecrust dough into a circle 2 inches larger than the diameter of the top of the casserole and about ⅛ inch thick. Make several 1-inch slits near the center of the pastry. Center pastry over casserole, allowing pastry to hang over edge. Trim pastry ½ inch beyond edge of casserole. Turn pastry under; flute to the casserole edge, pressing gently.

4 Bake in a 400°F oven for 40 to 45 minutes or until crust is golden. Serve immediately.

Nutrition Facts per serving: 347 cal., 15 g total fat (5 g sat. fat), 23 mg chol., 834 mg sodium, 35 g carbo., 4 g fiber, 18 g pro.

This is not your mother's tuna and noodle casserole. Italian-style ingredients—artichoke hearts, dried tomatoes, olives, and mozzarella cheese—give it a worldly update.

MEDITERRANEAN TUNA CASSEROLE

PREP:

25 minutes

BAKE:

20 minutes + 20 minutes

STAND:

10 minutes

MAKES:

6 servings

4	ounces dried fettuccine, broken
1/4	cup chopped onion
1	tablespoon butter or margarine
1	10¾-ounce can condensed cream of chicken soup
1	9- to 12-ounce can solid white tuna (water pack), drained and broken into chunks
1	8- to 9-ounce package frozen artichoke hearts, thawed and cut up
2/3	cup milk
1/2	cup shredded mozzarella cheese (2 ounces)
3	tablespoons oil-packed dried tomatoes, drained and snipped
3	tablespoons sliced pitted ripe olives
1/2	teaspoon dried thyme, crushed
3	tablespoons grated Parmesan cheese

1 Cook fettuccine according to package directions; drain.

2 Meanwhile, in a large skillet cook onion in hot butter until tender. Remove from heat. Stir in cream of chicken soup, tuna, artichoke hearts, milk, mozzarella cheese, dried tomatoes, olives, and thyme. Stir in cooked fettuccine. Transfer to a lightly greased 2-quart rectangular baking dish. Sprinkle with Parmesan cheese.

3 Bake, covered, in a 350°F oven for 20 minutes. Uncover and bake about 20 minutes more or until casserole is bubbly. Let stand for 10 minutes before serving.

MAKE-AHEAD DIRECTIONS: Prepare as directed through step 2. Cover with plastic wrap and chill for up to 24 hours. Remove plastic wrap and cover with foil. Bake in a 350°F oven for 35 minutes. Uncover and bake about 15 minutes more or until casserole is bubbly. Let stand for 10 minutes before serving.

Nutrition Facts per serving: 280 cal., 11 g total fat (5 g sat. fat), 37 mg chol., 732 mg sodium, 25 g carbo., 4 g fiber, 19 g pro.

A creamy tuna mixture bubbles underneath a hot biscuit topping for a satisfying Saturday noon casserole.

TUNA WITH CHEESE BISCUITS

3	tablespoons butter or margarine
½	cup chopped onion
½	cup chopped green sweet pepper
1	10¾-ounce can condensed cream of chicken soup
1	cup milk
1	9-ounce can tuna, drained and flaked
2	teaspoons lemon juice
1	7¾-ounce package cheese-garlic or 3-cheese complete biscuit mix

PREP:
20 minutes
BAKE:
15 minutes + 15 minutes
MAKES:
4 to 6 servings

1 In a large saucepan melt butter over medium heat. Add onion and sweet pepper; cook until tender. Stir in cream of chicken soup and milk. Cook and stir until bubbly. Stir in tuna and lemon juice.

2 Turn into an ungreased 1½-quart casserole. Bake in a 425°F oven for 15 minutes.

3 Meanwhile, prepare biscuit mix according to package directions. Drop batter in 6 mounds onto hot tuna mixture. Bake for 15 to 20 minutes more or until biscuits are golden and a toothpick inserted in center of a biscuit comes out clean.

Nutrition Facts per serving: 564 cal., 31 g total fat (12 g sat. fat), 46 mg chol., 1,470 mg sodium, 45 g carbo., 1 g fiber, 26 g pro.

Is it Cajun or Creole? This dish has, at its base, the rich, flavorful mix of celery, onions, and green peppers that is a hallmark of both styles of cooking. If crawfish tails are not available use 2 pounds of the chunk-style imitation crabmeat.

BLEND OF THE BAYOU SEAFOOD CASSEROLE

PREP:
1 hour

BAKE:
30 minutes

MAKES:
10 servings

1	pound fresh or frozen small shrimp in shells
1	pound fresh or frozen peeled, cooked crawfish tails
½	cup butter or margarine
1	8-ounce package cream cheese
1	large onion, chopped
2	stalks celery, sliced
1	medium green sweet pepper, chopped
1	pound chunk-style imitation crabmeat, chopped
1	10¾-ounce can condensed cream of mushroom soup
1	4-ounce can (drained weight) mushroom stems and pieces, drained
½	to 1 teaspoon bottled hot pepper sauce
½	teaspoon dried thyme, crushed
½	teaspoon dried oregano, crushed
½	teaspoon dried basil, crushed
1	tablespoon bottled minced garlic (6 cloves)
3	cups hot cooked rice*
¾	cup shredded sharp cheddar cheese (3 ounces)
½	cup fine dry bread crumbs

1 Thaw shrimp and crawfish, if frozen. Peel and devein shrimp. Rinse shrimp; pat dry with paper towels. Set aside. Set aside 2 tablespoons of the butter. In a small saucepan combine the remaining 6 tablespoons butter and the cream cheese. Heat over low heat until butter is melted and cream cheese is softened, stirring occasionally. Set aside.

2 In a Dutch oven melt the reserved 2 tablespoons butter over medium heat. Add onion, celery, and sweet pepper; cook and stir for 5 minutes. Add shrimp; cook and stir for 4 to 5 minutes or until shrimp turn opaque. Stir in cream cheese mixture, crawfish, crabmeat, cream of mushroom soup, mushrooms, hot pepper sauce, thyme, oregano, basil, and garlic. Stir in rice.

3 Transfer mixture to a 3-quart rectangular baking dish. Sprinkle with cheese and bread crumbs. Bake in a 350°F oven for 30 minutes until heated through.

*NOTE: For cooked rice, bring 2 cups water to boiling. Add 1 cup long grain rice to boiling water. Return to boiling; reduce heat. Simmer, covered, about 15 minutes or until rice is tender. Let stand, covered, for 5 minutes.

Nutrition Facts per serving: 429 cal., 24 g total fat (14 g sat. fat), 178 mg chol., 1,077 mg sodium, 27 g carbo., 2 g fiber, 25 g pro.

Stop by your supermarket's fish department or deli counter to get the cooked shrimp.

SHRIMP BAKE

²/₃	cup uncooked long grain rice
1	10¾-ounce can condensed cream of celery soup
1	10-ounce package frozen cut asparagus, thawed
8	ounces cooked, peeled, and deveined shrimp
1	8-ounce can sliced water chestnuts, drained
½	cup milk
1	tablespoon sliced green onion
½	teaspoon salt
½	teaspoon dried dill

PREP:
25 minutes
BAKE:
40 minutes
STAND:
5 minutes
MAKES:
6 servings

1 Cook rice according to package directions. In a large bowl combine cooked rice, cream of celery soup, asparagus, shrimp, water chestnuts, milk, green onion, salt, and dill. Transfer to an ungreased 1½-quart casserole.

2 Bake, covered, in a 350°F oven for 40 to 45 minutes or until heated through. Let stand for 5 minutes before serving.

Nutrition Facts per serving: 232 cal., 6 g total fat (1 g sat. fat), 77 mg chol., 683 mg sodium, 34 g carbo., 2 g fiber, 13 g pro.

Sherry adds a distinct depth of flavor to this dish. Look for cooked, peeled, and deveined shrimp at the supermarket—either in the frozen food aisle or at the fish counter. If frozen, thaw in the refrigerator before using.

TRIPLE SEAFOOD BAKE

PREP:

25 minutes

BAKE:

40 minutes

MAKES:

5 or 6 servings

2½ cups half-and-half, light cream, or milk

1 10¾-ounce can condensed cream of mushroom with roasted garlic soup

⅓ cup dry sherry

1⅓ cups uncooked instant rice

1 6½-ounce can minced clams, drained

1 6-ounce can crabmeat, drained

6 ounces cooked, peeled, and deveined shrimp, halved lengthwise

1 4-ounce can (drained weight) sliced mushrooms, drained

¼ cup sliced almonds

Snipped fresh parsley (optional)

1 In a large saucepan stir together half-and-half, cream of mushroom with roasted garlic soup, and dry sherry. Bring to boiling. Stir in rice, clams, crabmeat, shrimp, and mushrooms. Turn into an ungreased 2-quart casserole. Sprinkle with almonds.

2 Bake, uncovered, in a 350°F oven about 40 minutes or until rice is tender. If desired, sprinkle with snipped parsley before serving.

Nutrition Facts per serving: 476 cal., 20 g total fat (9 g sat. fat), 168 mg chol., 780 mg sodium, 37 g carbo., 2 g fiber, 32 g pro.

Lively seasonings, a wonderfully creamy base, rice, and okra make this a classic Louisiana-style dish.

SHRIMP LOUISIANA

1	tablespoon butter or margarine
¾	cup chopped green sweet pepper
½	cup chopped onion
1	10-ounce package frozen cut okra
2	cups cooked rice
1	10¾-ounce can condensed cream of shrimp soup
8	ounces cooked, peeled, and deveined shrimp
½	cup milk
½	to 1 teaspoon Cajun seasoning
¾	cup soft bread crumbs (1 slice)
1	tablespoon butter or margarine, melted

PREP:
25 minutes
BAKE:
40 minutes
MAKES:
4 servings

1 In a large skillet melt 1 tablespoon butter over medium heat. Add sweet pepper and onion; cook until tender. Stir in okra; cook and stir until okra is nearly thawed. Stir in rice, cream of shrimp soup, shrimp, milk, and Cajun seasoning.

2 Turn into an ungreased 1½-quart casserole. In a small bowl combine bread crumbs and 1 tablespoon melted butter; sprinkle over shrimp mixture.

3 Bake, uncovered, in a 350°F oven about 40 minutes or until heated through and crumbs are golden.

Nutrition Facts per serving: 343 cal., 11 g total fat (6 g sat. fat), 140 mg chol., 897 mg sodium, 41 g carbo., 4 g fiber, 19 g pro.

Cooks "of a certain age" will fondly remember this dish—it's quintessential ladies' luncheon fare. More saucy and delicate than a typical casserole, it's best served with crusty bread for a contrast.

CRAB-MUSHROOM BAKE

PREP:

20 minutes

BAKE:

25 minutes

MAKES:

4 servings

½	cup finely chopped celery
1	tablespoon butter or margarine
1	10¾-ounce can condensed cream of shrimp soup
¾	cup soft bread crumbs (1 slice)
1	4-ounce can (drained weight) sliced mushrooms, drained
⅓	cup milk
2	tablespoons dry sherry
1	6½-ounce can pasteurized crabmeat, drained, or one 6½-ounce can crabmeat, drained, flaked, and cartilage removed
⅓	cup finely shredded Parmesan cheese
	Lemon wedges (optional)
	Crusty bread slices

1 In a medium saucepan cook celery in hot butter until tender. Stir in cream of shrimp soup, ½ cup of the bread crumbs, the mushrooms, milk, and sherry. Bring mixture just to boiling, stirring constantly. Stir in crabmeat. Spoon into an ungreased 9-inch pie plate.

2 In a small bowl combine remaining ¼ cup bread crumbs and the Parmesan cheese; sprinkle over crab mixture.

3 Bake, uncovered, in a 350°F oven about 25 minutes or until mixture is bubbly and crumbs are golden. If desired, serve with lemon wedges. Serve with crusty bread slices.

Nutrition Facts per serving: 276 cal., 10 g total fat (6 g sat. fat), 83 mg chol., 1,260 mg sodium, 26 g carbo., 2 g fiber, 17 g pro.

A main-dish stuffing bake is your ticket to stretching 12 ounces of shrimp into a satisfying meal for four.

SHRIMP & STUFFING BAKE

12	ounces fresh or frozen peeled and deveined medium shrimp
2	tablespoons butter or margarine
½	cup chopped celery
½	cup chopped onion
1	10¾-ounce can condensed cream of shrimp or cream of celery soup
¼	cup milk
½	teaspoon ground sage
¼	teaspoon dried thyme, crushed
	Dash black pepper
2	beaten eggs
4	cups dry French bread cubes*

PREP:
30 minutes

BAKE:
30 minutes + 15 minutes

STAND:
10 minutes

MAKES:
4 servings

1 Thaw shrimp, if frozen. Rinse shrimp; pat dry with paper towels. In a large saucepan cook shrimp in a large amount of boiling water for 1 to 3 minutes or just until shrimp turn opaque. Drain well; set aside.

2 In same saucepan melt butter over medium heat. Add celery and onion; cook until tender. Stir in cream of shrimp soup, milk, sage, thyme, and pepper. Add eggs; mix well. Fold in dry bread cubes and cooked shrimp. Turn into an ungreased 1½-quart casserole.

3 Bake, covered, in a 350°F oven for 30 minutes. Uncover; bake about 15 minutes more or until set in center. Let stand, covered, for 10 minutes before serving.

*NOTE: To dry the bread cubes, spread cubes in a 15×10×1-inch baking pan. Bake in a 300°F oven for 10 to 15 minutes or until bread cubes are dry, stirring twice. Cool. (Bread will continue to dry and crisp as it cools.) Or let bread stand, loosely covered, at room temperature for 8 to 12 hours.

Nutrition Facts per serving: 375 cal., 15 g total fat (7 g sat. fat), 263 mg chol., 1,099 mg sodium, 32 g carbo., 2 g fiber, 27 g pro.

Dried Italian seasoning is a real time-saver; by measuring just one ingredient, you get a windfall of herbs. Brands vary, but most include basil, oregano, thyme, and rosemary.

SHRIMP ITALIAN

PREP:

25 minutes

BAKE:

40 minutes

MAKES:

4 to 6 servings

8	ounces fresh or frozen cooked, peeled, and deveined medium shrimp
½	cup chopped onion
1	tablespoon butter or margarine
1	10¾-ounce can condensed cream of shrimp or cream of mushroom soup
⅔	cup half-and-half or light cream
1	4-ounce can (drained weight) sliced mushrooms, drained
⅓	cup grated Parmesan cheese
1	teaspoon dried Italian seasoning, crushed
4	ounces dried penne or gemelli pasta (about 1 cup), cooked and drained
3	tablespoons grated Parmesan cheese

1 Thaw shrimp, if frozen. In a medium saucepan cook onion in hot butter until tender. Stir in shrimp, cream of shrimp soup, half-and-half, mushrooms, the ⅓ cup Parmesan cheese, and the Italian seasoning. Stir in cooked pasta. Spoon into an ungreased 1½-quart casserole. Sprinkle with the 3 tablespoons Parmesan cheese.

2 Bake, uncovered, in a 350°F oven about 40 minutes or until heated through.

Nutrition Facts per serving: 365 cal., 16 g total fat (8 g sat. fat), 154 mg chol., 1,036 mg sodium, 32 g carbo., 3 g fiber, 23 g pro.

The dry white wine rounds out the flavor of the soup-based sauce.

SHRIMP WITH CREAMY ONION SAUCE

3 cups dried penne pasta (about 10 ounces)
1 10¾-ounce can condensed cream of onion soup
½ cup dairy sour cream
¼ cup dry white wine
2 tablespoons all-purpose flour
¼ teaspoon dried thyme or basil, crushed
   Dash black pepper
1 4-ounce can (drained weight) sliced mushrooms, drained
1 pound cooked, peeled, and deveined shrimp*
2 tablespoons snipped fresh parsley

START TO FINISH:
30 minutes
MAKES:
6 servings

1 Cook pasta according to package directions; drain and set aside.

2 Meanwhile, in a large saucepan stir together cream of onion soup, sour cream, white wine, flour, thyme, and pepper. Stir in mushrooms. Bring to boiling, stirring occasionally. Stir in shrimp and pasta; heat through.

3 Transfer to a serving bowl. Sprinkle with parsley.

*NOTE: **If shrimp have tails, remove them.**

Nutrition Facts per serving: 316 cal., 7 g total fat (3 g sat. fat), 163 mg chol., 647 mg sodium, 37 g carbo., 2 g fiber, 23 g pro.

Creamy rice is studded with shrimp, imbued with sherry, and sprinkled with almonds.
This is really one of those "what's not to like" sort of casseroles.

SHRIMP NEW ORLEANS

PREP:
30 minutes
BAKE:
30 minutes
MAKES:
6 servings

$\frac{1}{2}$	cup chopped onion
$\frac{1}{4}$	cup chopped green or red sweet pepper
2	tablespoons butter or margarine
12	ounces cooked, peeled, and deveined medium shrimp*
2	cups cooked long grain rice**
1	$10\frac{3}{4}$-ounce can condensed cream of shrimp soup
$\frac{1}{2}$	cup half-and-half or light cream
2	tablespoons dry sherry
1	teaspoon lemon juice
$\frac{1}{4}$	teaspoon salt
$\frac{1}{8}$	teaspoon cayenne pepper
3	tablespoons slivered almonds, toasted

1 In a medium saucepan cook onion and sweet pepper in hot butter about 4 minutes or until tender. Remove from heat.

2 Stir in shrimp, rice, cream of shrimp soup, half-and-half, dry sherry, lemon juice, salt, and cayenne pepper. Transfer to an ungreased 2-quart square baking dish.

3 Bake, uncovered, in a 350°F oven about 30 minutes or until heated through in the center. Sprinkle with almonds.

*NOTE: **If shrimp have tails, remove them.**

NOTE: **For 2 cups cooked rice, in a medium saucepan stir together 1$\frac{1}{3}$ cups water, $\frac{2}{3}$ cup uncooked long grain rice, and $\frac{1}{4}$ teaspoon salt (add 1 tablespoon butter, if desired). Bring to boiling; reduce heat. Simmer, covered, for 18 to 20 minutes or until rice is tender and liquid is absorbed.

Nutrition Facts per serving: 290 cal., 13 g total fat (5 g sat. fat), 141 mg chol., 624 mg sodium, 23 g carbo., 1 g fiber, 19 g pro.

If you want to cut some of the fat and calories, use reduced-fat cream of mushroom soup.

SHRIMP, CHEESE & WILD RICE BAKE

1	6-ounce uncooked package long grain and wild rice mix
1	cup chopped green sweet pepper
1	cup chopped celery
1	cup chopped onion
¼	cup butter or margarine
1	10¾-ounce can condensed cream of mushroom soup
1	cup shredded cheddar cheese (4 ounces)
1	cup shredded Swiss cheese (4 ounces)
1	to 1½ pounds cooked, peeled, and deveined shrimp
¼	teaspoon black pepper
2	lemons, thinly sliced

PREP:
25 minutes
BAKE:
40 minutes
STAND:
10 minutes
MAKES:
6 servings

1 Prepare rice mix according to package directions. Meanwhile, in a medium saucepan cook and stir sweet pepper, celery, and onion in hot butter about 5 minutes or just until tender.

2 In a large bowl combine cooked rice, cooked vegetable mixture, cream of mushroom soup, cheddar cheese, and Swiss cheese. Stir in cooked shrimp.

3 Spoon mixture into an ungreased 3-quart rectangular baking dish. Sprinkle with half of the black pepper. Arrange lemon slices over shrimp mixture. Sprinkle with remaining black pepper.

4 Bake, covered, in a 375°F oven about 40 minutes or until heated through. Let stand for 10 minutes before serving.

Nutrition Facts per serving: 488 cal., 26 g total fat (14 g sat. fat), 207 mg chol., 1,313 mg sodium, 33 g carbo., 2 g fiber, 31 g pro.

These days, it's easy to find shrimp that have already been peeled and deveined, both fresh and frozen. Take advantage of that convenience product!

ITALIAN-STYLE SHRIMP

START TO FINISH:

40 minutes

MAKES:

6 servings

1	pound fresh or frozen medium shrimp, peeled and deveined
2	tablespoons butter or margarine
2	cups sliced fresh mushrooms
½	cup chopped onion
½	cup chopped green sweet pepper
1	teaspoon bottled minced garlic (2 cloves)
1	10¾-ounce can condensed tomato bisque soup
⅔	cup water
½	teaspoon dried Italian seasoning, crushed
	Hot cooked penne or rotini pasta
	Shredded or grated Parmesan cheese (optional)

1 Thaw shrimp, if frozen. Rinse shrimp; pat dry with paper towels. Set aside.

2 In a large skillet melt butter over medium heat. Add mushrooms, onion, sweet pepper, and garlic; cook about 5 minutes or until tender. Stir in tomato bisque soup, water, and Italian seasoning. Bring to boiling; reduce heat. Simmer, covered, for 10 minutes.

3 Add shrimp to skillet; cook for 3 to 4 minutes or until shrimp turn opaque. Serve with hot cooked pasta. If desired, top servings with Parmesan cheese.

Nutrition Facts per serving: 269 cal., 7 g total fat (4 g sat. fat), 98 mg chol., 510 mg sodium, 34 g carbo., 2 g fiber, 17 g pro.

Skillet dinners aren't usually known for their elegance, but here, the already upscale title ingredients get tweaked with sherry and cream for a dish that travels well beyond the ordinary.

SHRIMP ARTICHOKE SKILLET

1	14-ounce can artichoke hearts, drained
1	small onion, chopped
1	tablespoon butter or margarine
1	10¾-ounce can condensed golden mushroom soup
¾	cup half-and-half or light cream
¼	cup dry sherry
½	cup finely shredded Parmesan cheese (2 ounces)
12	ounces cooked, peeled, and deveined shrimp*
	Hot cooked rice

START TO FINISH:
25 minutes
MAKES:
4 servings

1 Quarter artichoke hearts; set aside. In a large skillet cook onion in hot butter until tender. Add golden mushroom soup, half-and-half, and dry sherry, stirring until smooth. Add Parmesan cheese; heat and stir until melted.

2 Add artichoke hearts and shrimp; heat through. Serve over hot cooked rice.

*NOTE: **If shrimp have tails, remove them.**

Nutrition Facts per serving: 422 cal., 14 g total fat (8 g sat. fat), 202 mg chol., 1,349 mg sodium, 38 g carbo., 4 g fiber, 28 g pro.

Gumbo in 25 minutes? Yes! Purchased cooked bacon pieces, canned shrimp, canned soup, and quick-cooking instant rice make it happen.

EASY SEAFOOD GUMBO

START TO FINISH:

25 minutes

MAKES:

5 servings

8	ounces fresh or frozen white-fleshed fish fillets (such as orange roughy or cod)
1	14½-ounce can stewed tomatoes, undrained
1	10¾-ounce can condensed chicken gumbo soup
1	10-ounce package frozen cut okra
1	cup water
1	teaspoon dried thyme, crushed
¼	teaspoon bottled hot pepper sauce
1	6½-ounce can shrimp or two 4-ounce cans shrimp
¼	cup cooked bacon pieces
1	teaspoon filé powder (optional)
	Hot cooked rice

1 Thaw fish, if frozen. Rinse fish; pat dry with paper towels. Cut fish into 1-inch pieces; set aside.

2 In a large saucepan combine tomatoes, chicken gumbo soup, okra, the water, thyme, and hot pepper sauce. Bring to boiling; reduce heat. Simmer, covered, for 10 minutes. Add the fish pieces. Simmer, covered, about 5 minutes more or until fish flakes easily when tested with a fork.

3 Stir in undrained shrimp, cooked bacon pieces, and, if desired, filé powder; heat through. Serve over rice in bowls.

Nutrition Facts per serving: 283 cal., 4 g total fat (1 g sat. fat), 82 mg chol., 943 mg sodium, 37 g carbo., 4 g fiber, 22 g pro.

188 BIGGEST BOOK OF EASY CANNED SOUP RECIPES

Remember this flavor-packed soup next time you need to fix a meal in a jiffy.

BROCCOLI-CLAM CHOWDER

⅓	cup water
1	10-ounce package frozen chopped broccoli or spinach
1	small onion, chopped
½	teaspoon dried thyme, crushed
1½	cups milk
1	10¾-ounce can condensed cream of shrimp soup
1	teaspoon Worcestershire sauce
1	6½-ounce can minced clams, drained

START TO FINISH:

20 minutes

MAKES:

4 servings

1 In a medium saucepan bring the water to boiling; add frozen broccoli, onion, and thyme. Cover and cook about 8 minutes or just until broccoli is tender. Do not drain. Stir in milk, cream of shrimp soup, Worcestershire sauce, and clams. Heat through.

Nutrition Facts per serving: 181 cal., 7 g total fat (2 g sat. fat), 41 mg chol., 676 mg sodium, 16 g carbo., 3 g fiber, 15 g pro.

Expect this new, easy version of fish chowder to become an old favorite in no time.

FISH STEW WITH ASPARAGUS

20 minutes

4 servings

12 ounces fresh or frozen cod or other firm white-fleshed fish fillets

1 14-ounce can chicken broth

1 10¾-ounce can condensed cream of onion soup

1 10-ounce package frozen cut asparagus

1 cup water

½ teaspoon dried thyme, crushed

¼ cup grated Parmesan cheese (1 ounce)

1 Thaw fish, if frozen. Rinse fish; pat dry with paper towels.

2 Cut fish into ½-inch pieces; set aside. In a large saucepan stir together chicken broth, cream of onion soup, frozen asparagus, water, and thyme. Heat until bubbly, stirring occasionally.

3 Stir in fish. Simmer, covered, for 5 to 7 minutes or until fish flakes easily when tested with a fork. Sprinkle servings with Parmesan cheese.

Nutrition Facts per serving: 194 cal., 7 g total fat (2 g sat. fat), 53 mg chol., 1,129 mg sodium, 12 g carbo., 2 g fiber, 22 g pro.

Just a little bit of thyme and a sprinkling of cooked bacon add so much flavor to this soup!

TUNA CHOWDER

4	slices bacon
1	medium green sweet pepper, chopped
1	small onion, chopped
3	cups milk
2	10¾-ounce cans condensed cream of potato soup
½	teaspoon dried thyme, crushed
2	6-ounce cans tuna, drained and flaked

1 In a large skillet cook bacon until crisp. Drain, reserving drippings. Crumble bacon and set aside.

2 Add sweet pepper and onion to skillet and cook in reserved drippings until tender. Stir in milk, cream of potato soup, and thyme; bring just to boiling. Gently stir in tuna; heat through. Sprinkle servings with crumbled bacon.

Nutrition Facts per serving: 435 cal., 18 g total fat (7 g sat. fat), 49 mg chol., 1,651 mg sodium, 30 g carbo., 2 g fiber, 36 g pro.

START TO FINISH:

25 minutes

MAKES:

4 servings

Dry sherry subtly seasons this creamy soup. Serve it with a green salad for lunch or as the first course at a dinner party.

CRAB CHOWDER

1   cup chopped onion

½   cup chopped celery

¼   cup chopped red and/or green sweet pepper

3   tablespoons butter

1   10¾-ounce can condensed cream of celery or cream of potato soup

2   cups milk, half-and-half, or light cream

¼   cup dry sherry

1   6½-ounce can crabmeat, drained, flaked, and cartilage removed

    Freshly ground black pepper

1 In a medium saucepan cook onion, celery, and sweet pepper in hot butter about 5 minutes or until tender.

2 Stir in cream of celery soup and milk until smooth; add sherry. Cook and stir until heated through.

3 Stir in crabmeat; heat through. Sprinkle servings with freshly ground black pepper.

Nutrition Facts per main-dish serving: 298 cal., 17 g total fat (9 g sat. fat), 77 mg chol., 894 mg sodium, 17 g carbo., 2 g fiber, 16 g pro.

Serve this rich bisque as a sit-down starter to an intimate dinner party.
You needn't tell anyone that all the lusciousness started so simply with two cans of soup.

CRAB-TOMATO BISQUE

1 19-ounce can ready-to-serve tomato basil soup

1 10¾-ounce can condensed cream of shrimp soup

1 cup vegetable broth

1 cup half-and-half, light cream, or milk

1 tablespoon dried minced onion

1 teaspoon dried parsley, crushed

1 6½-ounce can crabmeat, drained, flaked,
   and cartilage removed

1 In a large saucepan combine tomato basil soup, cream of shrimp soup,
vegetable broth, half-and-half, dried minced onion, and parsley flakes.

2 Cook over medium heat until bubbly, stirring occasionally. Stir in crabmeat;
heat through.

Nutrition Facts per main-dish serving: 242 cal., 12 g total fat (6 g sat. fat), 73 mg chol.,
1,447 mg sodium, 20 g carbo., 1 g fiber, 15 g pro.

START TO FINISH:

15 minutes

MAKES:

4 main-dish or
8 appetizer servings

Consider this an "off the shelf" dinner on a busy weeknight. It calls on pantry staples and items with long storage lives in the fridge and freezer. Best of all, it can be ready in 30 minutes.

FISH STEW

START TO FINISH:

30 minutes

MAKES:

6 servings

1 pound fresh or frozen skinless, boneless sea bass, red snapper, and/or catfish fillets

1 medium onion, cut into wedges

1 tablespoon cooking oil

2 10¾-ounce cans condensed tomato soup

2 cups refrigerated diced red-skinned potatoes

1 14½-ounce can stewed tomatoes, undrained and cut up

1½ cups water

1 10-ounce package frozen mixed vegetables

½ teaspoon dried thyme, crushed

⅛ teaspoon black pepper

1 Thaw fish, if frozen. Cut fish into 1-inch cubes; set aside. In a 4-quart Dutch oven cook onion in hot oil until tender.

2 Stir tomato soup, potatoes, tomatoes, water, vegetables, thyme, and pepper into onion in Dutch oven. Bring to boiling. Stir in fish cubes; reduce heat. Simmer, covered, about 10 minutes or until fish flakes easily when tested with a fork and vegetables are tender.

Nutrition Facts per serving: 252 cal., 6 g total fat (1 g sat. fat), 31 mg chol., 847 mg sodium, 32 g carbo., 5 g fiber, 19 g pro.

How do you make 8 ounces of salmon serve six people? Take a tip from New England cooks and stir it into a rich chowder.

SALMON CHOWDER

1	tablespoon olive oil
½	cup thinly sliced celery
½	cup chopped onion
4	cups milk
1	10¾-ounce can condensed cream of celery soup
1	tablespoon snipped fresh dill or 1 teaspoon dried dill
¼	teaspoon caraway seeds
¼	teaspoon black pepper
⅛	teaspoon salt
1	large potato, peeled, if desired, and cut into ½-inch cubes (about 1⅓ cups)
1	8-ounce fresh or frozen skinless, boneless salmon fillet, cut into ¾-inch cubes

START TO FINISH:
35 minutes
MAKES:
6 servings

1 In a large saucepan heat oil over medium-high heat. Add celery and onion; cook and stir about 4 minutes or until tender. Carefully stir in milk, cream of celery soup, dill, caraway seeds, pepper, and salt. Stir in potato. Bring to boiling; reduce heat. Simmer, covered, for 10 to 15 minutes or until potato is tender.

2 Stir salmon into vegetable mixture in saucepan. Simmer, uncovered, for 2 to 3 minutes more or until salmon flakes easily when tested with a fork.

Nutrition Facts per serving: 215 cal., 9 g total fat (3 g sat. fat), 24 mg chol., 546 mg sodium, 21 g carbo., 1 g fiber, 13 g pro.

Flounder, haddock, and pollock would make good substitutes for the fish varieties called for in this intriguing Asian-inspired soup.

SHORTCUT ASIAN FISH SOUP

START TO FINISH:

25 minutes

MAKES:

6 servings

1	pound frozen or fresh monkfish, cusk, or cod fillets
2	$10\frac{3}{4}$-ounce cans condensed chicken with rice soup
3	cups water
$\frac{1}{4}$	cup reduced-sodium soy sauce
$\frac{1}{8}$	to $\frac{1}{4}$ teaspoon cayenne pepper
3	cups frozen loose-pack broccoli, red pepper, onions, and mushrooms
2	tablespoons lemon juice

1 Thaw fish, if frozen. Rinse fish; pat dry with paper towels. Cut into $\frac{1}{2}$-inch pieces; set aside.

2 In a large saucepan combine chicken with rice soup, water, soy sauce, and cayenne pepper. Bring to boiling. Stir in vegetables. Return to boiling; reduce heat. Simmer, covered, for 5 minutes.

3 Add fish pieces to saucepan. Cover and cook for 3 to 5 minutes more or until fish flakes easily when tested with a fork. Stir in lemon juice.

Nutrition Facts per serving: 139 cal., 3 g total fat (1 g sat. fat), 23 mg chol., 1,211 mg sodium, 11 g carbo., 1 g fiber, 15 g pro.

You're just 20 minutes to dinner with this recipe! Simply drape a quick, mushroom-studded tomato sauce over broiled whitefish fillets and top with a little Parmesan. Serve with pasta and your favorite frozen vegetable.

ITALIAN-STYLE FISH

1½	pounds fresh or frozen white-fleshed fish fillets, ½ to 1 inch thick
¼	teaspoon salt
⅛	teaspoon black pepper
2	cups sliced fresh mushrooms
1	tablespoon cooking oil
1	14½-ounce can Italian-style stewed tomatoes, undrained
1	10¾-ounce can condensed tomato bisque soup
⅛	teaspoon black pepper
⅓	cup finely shredded Parmesan cheese
	Hot cooked pasta

START TO FINISH:
20 minutes
MAKES:
6 servings

1 Thaw fish, if frozen. Rinse fish; pat dry with paper towels. If necessary, cut into 6 serving-size pieces. Measure thickness of fish. Place fish on greased unheated rack of a broiler pan. Turn any thin portions under to make uniform thickness. Sprinkle with salt and ⅛ teaspoon pepper.

2 Broil about 4 inches from heat until fish flakes easily when tested with a fork. Allow 4 to 6 minutes per ½-inch thickness of fish. (If fillets are 1 inch thick, turn once halfway through broiling.)

3 Meanwhile, for sauce, in a medium saucepan cook mushrooms in hot oil until tender. Stir in tomatoes, tomato bisque soup, and ⅛ teaspoon pepper. Cook and stir over medium heat until mixture is heated through.

4 Spoon hot sauce over fish fillets. Sprinkle with Parmesan cheese. Serve with hot cooked pasta.

Nutrition Facts per serving: 415 cal., 14 g total fat (6 g sat. fat), 71 mg chol., 1,218 mg sodium, 35 g carbo., 2 g fiber, 37 g pro.

Looking for a company-special entrée? This easy yet elegant fish dish fits the bill.

SAVORY FISH ROLL-UPS

PREP:

25 minutes

BAKE:

20 minutes + 25 minutes

MAKES:

4 servings

4	4-ounce fresh or frozen cod or sole fillets
1	10¾-ounce can condensed cream of asparagus or cream of mushroom soup
½	cup dairy sour cream
½	cup milk
½	teaspoon dry mustard
1	10-ounce package frozen chopped spinach, thawed and well drained
1	cup herb-seasoned stuffing mix
½	cup shredded carrot
¼	cup butter or margarine, melted
2	tablespoons sliced green onion

1 Thaw fish, if frozen. Rinse fish; pat dry with paper towels. Set aside. In a medium bowl combine cream of asparagus soup, sour cream, milk, and dry mustard; set aside.

2 In another medium bowl combine spinach, stuffing mix, carrot, melted butter, and green onion. Stir in ¼ cup of the soup mixture.

3 Place about 2 tablespoons of the stuffing mixture on a short side of each fish fillet; roll up fish around stuffing. Press remaining stuffing mixture evenly into an ungreased 2-quart square baking dish. Spoon 1 cup of the remaining soup mixture over the stuffing mixture. Arrange fish fillets, seam sides down, in baking dish; pour remaining soup mixture over all.

4 Bake, covered, in a 350°F oven for 20 minutes. Uncover and bake about 25 minutes more or until fish flakes easily when tested with a fork and stuffing is heated through.

Nutrition Facts per serving: 406 cal., 21 g total fat (12 g sat. fat), 97 mg chol., 1,063 mg sodium, 24 g carbo., 4 g fiber, 28 g pro.

Cod, sole, flounder, halibut, haddock, and orange roughy are good choices for the fish in this dish.

FISH WITH SHERRY-MUSHROOM SAUCE

1½   pounds fresh or frozen fish fillets, about 1 inch thick

     Salt

     Black pepper

1   10¾-ounce can condensed cream of shrimp soup

½   cup shredded Swiss cheese (2 ounces)

¼   cup milk

2   tablespoons dry sherry

½   teaspoon dried thyme, crushed

1   4-ounce can (drained weight) sliced mushrooms, drained

2   teaspoons sliced green onion tops

START TO FINISH:
25 minutes
MAKES:
6 servings

1. Thaw fish, if frozen. Rinse fish; pat dry with paper towels. If necessary, cut fish into 6 serving-size pieces. Measure thickness of fish. Place fish on greased unheated rack of a broiler pan. Turn any thin portions under to make uniform thickness. Sprinkle with salt and pepper.

2. Broil about 4 inches from heat until fish flakes easily when tested with a fork. Allow 4 to 6 minutes per ½-inch thickness of fish. (If fillets are 1 inch thick, turn once halfway through broiling.)

3. Meanwhile, in a small saucepan stir together cream of shrimp soup, Swiss cheese, milk, dry sherry, and thyme. Cook and stir over low heat until cheese is melted. Stir in mushrooms; heat through. Spoon sauce over fish. Sprinkle with sliced green onion tops.

Nutrition Facts per serving: 187 cal., 6 g total fat (3 g sat. fat), 66 mg chol., 584 mg sodium, 6 g carbo., 1 g fiber, 24 g pro.

Take your choice of sour cream or plain yogurt. Either one adds creaminess and a pleasant tang to the stir-together sauce.

FILLETS PARMESAN

PREP:

15 minutes

BAKE:

25 minutes

MAKES:

6 servings

1½	pounds fresh or frozen cod or tilapia fillets
1	10¾-ounce can condensed golden mushroom soup
½	cup dairy sour cream or plain yogurt
⅓	cup grated Parmesan cheese
½	teaspoon dried basil, crushed
½	teaspoon lemon juice
2	tablespoons grated Parmesan cheese
1	tablespoon snipped fresh parsley
	Hot cooked pasta

1 Thaw fish, if frozen. Rinse fish; pat dry with paper towels. Cut fish into 6 serving-size pieces. Place in an ungreased 2- or 3-quart rectangular baking dish; set aside.

2 In a medium bowl stir together golden mushroom soup, sour cream, the ⅓ cup Parmesan cheese, the basil, and lemon juice. Pour soup mixture over fish.

3 Bake, uncovered, in a 350°F oven for 25 to 30 minutes or until fish flakes easily when tested with a fork. Sprinkle with the 2 tablespoons Parmesan cheese and the parsley. Serve with hot cooked pasta.

Nutrition Facts per serving: 284 cal., 8 g total fat (4 g sat. fat), 63 mg chol., 565 mg sodium, 25 g carbo., 1 g fiber, 28 g pro.

Cheddar cheese soup makes an easy sauce for this quick pasta dish. To save on time and cleanup, the pasta and vegetables cook together in the same pan.

EASY SALMON PASTA

1½	cups dried penne, cut ziti, or gemelli pasta
2	cups frozen loose-pack broccoli florets
1	10¾-ounce can condensed cheddar cheese soup
½	cup milk
1	tablespoon Dijon-style mustard
½	teaspoon dried dill
⅛	teaspoon black pepper
2	6-ounce cans skinless, boneless salmon or tuna, drained
2	green onions, sliced
	Dried dill (optional)

START TO FINISH:
20 minutes
MAKES:
4 servings

1 In a large saucepan cook pasta according to package directions, adding broccoli for the last 3 minutes of cooking. Drain well; return to saucepan.

2 Stir cheddar cheese soup, milk, mustard, the ½ teaspoon dill, and the pepper into pasta mixture. Cook over low heat until heated through, stirring occasionally. Gently fold in salmon and green onions; heat through. If desired, garnish with additional dill.

Nutrition Facts per serving: 315 cal., 10 g total fat (3 g sat. fat), 58 mg chol., 1,049 mg sodium, 34 g carbo., 4 g fiber, 25 g pro.

Orange roughy is a wonderfully versatile fish from New Zealand. It has a moderately firm texture and a delicate flavor, making it a great choice for many styles of preparation. Serve this with cooked rice.

LEMONY ORANGE ROUGHY BAKE

PREP:

25 minutes

BAKE:

10 minutes + 5 minutes

MAKES:

4 servings

1	pound fresh or frozen orange roughy, cod, or catfish fillets
1	cup chopped onion
1	cup chopped red and/or green sweet pepper
2	teaspoons bottled minced garlic (4 cloves)
1	tablespoon cooking oil
1	10¾-ounce can condensed cream of shrimp or cream of mushroom soup
¾	cup half-and-half or light cream
1	teaspoon lemon juice
½	teaspoon lemon-pepper seasoning
¼	cup fine dry bread crumbs
¼	cup freshly grated Parmesan cheese (1 ounce)
	Hot cooked rice (optional)

1 Thaw fish, if frozen. Rinse fish; pat dry with paper towels. Cut fish fillets into 4 serving-size pieces, if necessary. Set aside.

2 In a large skillet cook onion, sweet pepper, and garlic in hot oil until vegetables are tender. Transfer vegetables to a greased 2-quart baking dish. Arrange fish on top of vegetables. Bake, uncovered, in a 400°F oven for 10 minutes.

3 Meanwhile, in the same skillet combine cream of shrimp soup, half-and-half, lemon juice, and lemon-pepper seasoning. Bring to boiling; reduce heat. Simmer, uncovered, for 5 minutes. Pour soup mixture over fish. In a small bowl combine bread crumbs and Parmesan cheese. Sprinkle over the soup mixture.

4 Bake, uncovered, for 5 to 10 minutes more or until bread crumbs are brown. If desired, serve with hot cooked rice.

Nutrition Facts per serving: 300 cal., 16 g total fat (6 g sat. fat), 55 mg chol., 1,001 mg sodium, 18 g carbo., 2 g fiber, 23 g pro.

MEATLESS MAIN DISHES

If you love hearty foods but want to cut some of the meat out of your diet, put Eggplant Parmesan Casserole in your repertoire. It's one of the most robust and filling vegetarian dishes around.

EGGPLANT PARMESAN CASSEROLE

PREP:

30 minutes

BAKE:

20 minutes

STAND:

10 minutes

MAKES:

6 servings

1   egg

½   cup milk

¾   cup all-purpose flour

¼   teaspoon salt

¼   teaspoon black pepper

1   large eggplant, peeled (if desired) and sliced ½ inch thick (1¼ to 1½ pounds)

2   tablespoons cooking oil

1   14½-ounce can diced tomatoes with green pepper and onion, undrained

1   10¾-ounce can condensed tomato soup

1   teaspoon dried Italian seasoning, crushed

¼   teaspoon black pepper

1   cup shredded mozzarella cheese (4 ounces)

¼   cup finely shredded Parmesan cheese (1 ounce)

1 In a shallow dish beat together egg and milk with a fork. In another shallow dish combine flour, salt, and ¼ teaspoon black pepper. Dip eggplant slices into egg mixture; coat with flour mixture.

2 In a large nonstick skillet cook eggplant slices, a few at a time, in hot oil for 4 to 6 minutes or until golden, turning once. (Add oil as necessary.) Drain on paper towels.

3 In a medium saucepan combine undrained tomatoes, tomato soup, Italian seasoning, and ¼ teaspoon black pepper. Bring to boiling over medium heat, stirring occasionally.

4 In a greased 2-quart rectangular baking dish layer half of the eggplant slices, cutting slices to fit. Spread with half of the tomato mixture; sprinkle with half of the mozzarella cheese. Repeat layers. Sprinkle with Parmesan cheese.

5 Bake, uncovered, in a 350°F oven about 20 minutes or until heated through. Let stand for 10 minutes before serving.

Nutrition Facts per serving: 342 cal., 17 g total fat (8 g sat. fat), 68 mg chol., 1,110 mg sodium, 31 g carbo., 4 g fiber, 18 g pro.

Bottled minced garlic is a step-saving ingredient that's easy to keep on hand in the refrigerator. Use one-half teaspoon bottled minced garlic for each clove of minced garlic called for in your recipe.

BROWN RICE & BEAN BAKE

Nonstick cooking spray
½   cup chopped onion
1   teaspoon bottled minced garlic (2 cloves)
1   tablespoon olive oil or cooking oil
2   teaspoons chili powder
1   teaspoon ground cumin
¼   teaspoon salt
1   15-ounce can pinto beans, rinsed and drained
1½ cups cooked brown rice*
1   10½-ounce can condensed vegetarian vegetable soup
1   cup shredded cheddar or Monterey Jack cheese (4 ounces)
2   slightly beaten eggs
½   cup crushed tortilla chips
Bottled salsa (optional)

1 Lightly coat a 9-inch pie plate or quiche dish with nonstick cooking spray; set aside. In a medium saucepan cook onion and garlic in hot oil until tender. Stir in chili powder, cumin, and salt. Cook for 1 minute more. Remove from heat.

2 Stir in beans, cooked rice, vegetarian vegetable soup, half of the cheese, and the eggs. Spoon mixture into prepared pie plate or quiche dish.

3 Bake, uncovered, in a 350°F oven for 35 minutes. Top with tortilla chips and remaining cheese. Bake about 5 minutes more or until set. Let stand for 5 minutes before serving. If desired, serve with salsa.

*NOTE: For 1½ cups cooked brown rice, in a medium saucepan stir together 1¼ cups water, ½ cup uncooked brown rice, and ⅛ teaspoon salt. Bring to boiling; reduce heat. Simmer, covered, about 40 minutes or until rice is tender and liquid is absorbed. Cool slightly before combining with bean mixture.

Nutrition Facts per serving: 455 cal., 20 g total fat (8 g sat. fat), 136 mg chol., 1,180 mg sodium, 51 g carbo., 9 g fiber, 20 g pro.

PREP:
20 minutes

BAKE:
35 minutes + 5 minutes

STAND:
5 minutes

MAKES:
4 servings

Use a gentle hand when browning the tofu. Stirring too vigorously will break up the cubes.

VEGETABLE COUSCOUS WITH TOFU

1 tablespoon olive oil

1 16-ounce package firm or extra-firm tub-style tofu (fresh bean curd), drained and cut into $\frac{1}{2}$-inch cubes

1 14-ounce can vegetable broth

1 $10\frac{3}{4}$-ounce can condensed tomato soup

1 medium zucchini, coarsely chopped ($1\frac{1}{4}$ cups)

2 tablespoons lemon juice

1 teaspoon dried basil, crushed

1 teaspoon bottled minced garlic (2 cloves)

$\frac{1}{4}$ teaspoon black pepper

1 cup quick-cooking couscous

$\frac{1}{2}$ cup crumbled feta cheese (2 ounces)

1 In a large saucepan heat oil over medium-high heat. Add tofu; cook for 8 to 10 minutes or until tofu is lightly browned, stirring gently and adding oil, if necessary. (If necessary, reduce heat to medium to prevent overbrowning.)

2 Stir in vegetable broth, tomato soup, zucchini, lemon juice, basil, garlic, and pepper. Bring to boiling. Stir in couscous. Remove from heat. Cover and let stand about 5 minutes or until liquid is absorbed.

3 Sprinkle servings with feta cheese.

Nutrition Facts per serving: 476 cal., 17 g total fat (4 g sat. fat), 12 mg chol., 1,080 mg sodium, 57 g carbo., 7 g fiber, 29 g pro.

Potatoes are a great way to meatlessly fill up an enchilada, without overdoing it on the cheese.

POTATO ENCHILADAS

2 pounds baking potatoes, peeled and quartered

3 tablespoons butter or margarine

½ teaspoon ground cumin

⅛ teaspoon cayenne pepper

4 to 6 tablespoons milk

1 4-ounce can diced green chile peppers

8 7- to 8-inch flour tortillas

1 10¾-ounce can condensed cream of celery soup

1 8-ounce carton dairy sour cream

¾ cup milk

1 cup shredded Colby and Montery Jack cheese or taco cheese (4 ounces)

Sliced pitted black olives (optional)

Sliced green onions (optional)

PREP:
30 minutes
BAKE:
30 minutes + 5 minutes
COOK:
20 minutes
MAKES:
8 enchiladas

1 In a covered medium saucepan cook potatoes in enough lightly salted boiling water to cover for 20 to 25 minutes or until tender; drain. Mash with a potato masher or beat with an electric mixer on low speed. Add butter, cumin, and cayenne pepper. Add enough of the 4 to 6 tablespoons milk to make potato mixture light and fluffy. Stir in chile peppers.

2 Meanwhile, wrap tortillas tightly in foil. Heat in a 350°F oven for 10 minutes to soften.

3 Divide potato mixture evenly among warmed tortillas; roll up tortillas. Arrange filled tortillas, seam sides down, in a greased 3-quart rectangular baking dish. In a medium bowl stir together cream of celery soup, sour cream, and the ¾ cup milk. Pour soup mixture over enchiladas in baking dish.

4 Bake, covered, in the 350°F oven for 30 minutes. Sprinkle with cheese. Bake, uncovered, for 5 to 10 minutes more or until heated through and cheese is melted. If desired, top with black olives and green onions.

Nutrition Facts per enchilada: 359 cal., 20 g total fat (11 g sat. fat), 44 mg chol., 643 mg sodium, 36 g carbo., 2 g fiber, 9 g pro.

This casserole is plenty spicy for most tastes, but if you like your flavors bold, pass a bottle of hot pepper sauce at the table.

CREAMY VEGETABLE ENCHILADAS

PREP:

30 minutes

BAKE:

18 minutes + 5 minutes

MAKES:

4 servings

8   6- or 7-inch corn or flour tortillas

2   tablespoons olive oil or cooking oil

2   medium carrots, thinly sliced

1   medium zucchini or yellow summer squash, quartered lengthwise and sliced (2 cups)

1   teaspoon chili powder or ½ teaspoon ground cumin

1   10¾-ounce can condensed cream of onion soup

1   cup shredded Monterey Jack cheese (4 ounces)

1   10-ounce can enchilada sauce or 1 cup bottled chunky salsa
    Dairy sour cream (optional)

1   Wrap tortillas tightly in foil. Heat in a 350°F oven for 10 minutes to soften.

2   Meanwhile, in a large skillet heat 1 tablespoon of the olive oil over medium-high heat. Add carrots; stir-fry for 2 minutes. Add zucchini and chili powder; stir-fry for 2 to 3 minutes more or until vegetables are crisp-tender. Remove skillet from heat. Stir in cream of onion soup and ¾ cup of the cheese.

3   Divide vegetable mixture evenly among warm tortillas; roll up tortillas. Arrange filled tortillas, seam sides down, in a lightly greased 2-quart rectangular baking dish. Lightly brush tops of tortillas with remaining 1 tablespoon olive oil.

4   Bake, uncovered, in the 350°F oven for 18 to 20 minutes or until mixture is heated through and tortillas are crisp.

5   Top with enchilada sauce and remaining cheese. Bake about 5 minutes more or until cheese is melted. If desired, serve with sour cream.

Nutrition Facts per serving: 431 cal., 22 g total fat (7 g sat. fat), 38 mg chol., 974 mg sodium, 47 g carbo., 5 g fiber, 13 g pro.

A strata is a layered dish that's usually made with eggs and bread. It's great for breakfasts and brunches, and also makes a wholesome and filling family supper.

VEGETABLE-CHEESE STRATA

3	cups cubed Italian bread
2	cups frozen loose-pack cut broccoli
1	4-ounce can (drained weight) sliced mushrooms, drained
1	cup shredded Swiss cheese (4 ounces)
3	eggs
1	10¾-ounce can condensed golden mushroom or cream of onion soup
¾	cup milk
½	teaspoon poultry seasoning
⅛	teaspoon black pepper

1 Arrange bread cubes in a greased 2-quart square baking dish. Top with broccoli and mushrooms. Sprinkle with Swiss cheese. In a medium bowl whisk together eggs, golden mushroom soup, milk, poultry seasoning, and pepper. Pour over mixture in baking dish.

2 Bake, covered, in a 325°F oven for 40 minutes. Uncover and bake about 20 minutes more or until center appears set. Let stand for 10 minutes before serving.

Nutrition Facts per serving: 229 cal., 10 g total fat (5 g sat. fat), 128 mg chol., 698 mg sodium, 20 g carbo., 3 g fiber, 14 g pro.

PREP:
20 minutes
BAKE:
40 minutes + 20 minutes
STAND:
10 minutes
MAKES:
6 servings

Easier than many egg casseroles but much dressier than scrambled eggs, this is a great way to serve eggs to a crowd.

CHEESE & MUSHROOM EGG CASSEROLE

PREP:
25 minutes

BAKE:
20 minutes

MAKES:
10 servings

16	eggs
1	cup milk
2	tablespoons butter or margarine
3	cups sliced fresh mushrooms
½	cup thinly sliced green onions
1	10¾-ounce can condensed cream of broccoli or cream of asparagus soup
¼	cup milk
1	cup shredded Monterey Jack cheese (4 ounces)
¼	cup grated Parmesan cheese (1 ounce)

1 In a large bowl beat together eggs and 1 cup milk with a rotary beater. In a 12-inch nonstick skillet melt 1 tablespoon of the butter over medium heat. Add half of the egg mixture. Cook over medium heat, without stirring, until mixture begins to set on the bottom and around the edge.

2 Using a large spoon, lift and fold the partially cooked egg mixture so the uncooked portion flows underneath. Continue cooking until egg mixture is cooked through but still glossy and moist. Remove from heat immediately.

3 Transfer scrambled eggs to a greased 3-quart rectangular baking dish. Scramble remaining eggs using remaining butter; remove from heat immediately. Transfer to the baking dish.

4 In the same nonstick skillet cook mushrooms and green onions until tender. Stir in cream of broccoli soup and ¼ cup milk. Stir in Monterey Jack and Parmesan cheeses. Spread mixture over eggs in baking dish.

5 Bake, covered, in a 350°F oven about 20 minutes or until heated through.

Nutrition Facts per serving: 239 cal., 17 g total fat (8 g sat. fat), 361 mg chol., 435 mg sodium, 6 g carbo., 1 g fiber, 16 g pro.

Sweet honeydew melon or cantaloupe wedges provide a perfect complement to this peppy dish.

HUEVOS CON FRIJOLES

4	eggs
1	15-ounce can red kidney beans, rinsed and drained
1	10¾-ounce can condensed cream of celery soup
1	4-ounce can diced green chile peppers, drained
2	green onions, sliced
2	tablespoons snipped fresh parsley
⅛	teaspoon black pepper
	Several dashes bottled hot pepper sauce
1½	cups shredded cheddar cheese (6 ounces)
	Bottled salsa (optional)
	Dairy sour cream (optional)

PREP:
20 minutes
BAKE:
30 minutes
STAND:
5 minutes
MAKES:
4 servings

1 In a large bowl beat eggs with a rotary beater. Stir in kidney beans, cream of celery soup, chile peppers, green onions, parsley, black pepper, and hot pepper sauce. Add cheese. Mix well. Pour mixture into a greased 2-quart square baking dish.

2 Bake, uncovered, in a 350°F oven for 30 to 35 minutes or until set in center. Let stand for 5 minutes before serving. If desired, top with salsa and sour cream.

Nutrition Facts per serving: 408 cal., 24 g total fat (12 g sat. fat), 259 mg chol., 1,154 mg sodium, 26 g carbo., 7 g fiber, 26 g pro.

A frittata is an Italian-style omelet. It's easier than a French omelet because it's served open-face—no tricky folding needed.

CHEESY VEGGIE FRITTATA

PREP:

25 minutes

STAND:

10 minutes

MAKES:

4 servings

6   eggs

1   teaspoon dried basil, crushed

1   10¾-ounce can condensed cream of celery soup

2   tablespoons olive oil or cooking oil

1   cup frozen loose-pack whole kernel corn

½   cup chopped zucchini

⅓   cup chopped red sweet pepper

½   cup shredded cheddar cheese (2 ounces)

1 Preheat broiler. In a medium bowl whisk together eggs and basil. Whisk in cream of celery soup; set aside. In a large ovenproof skillet heat oil over medium heat. Add corn, zucchini, and sweet pepper; cook about 5 minutes or until vegetables are crisp-tender, stirring occasionally.

2 Pour egg mixture over vegetables in skillet. Cook over medium heat. As mixture sets, run a spatula around edge of skillet, lifting egg mixture so uncooked portion flows underneath. Continue cooking and lifting edge for 3 to 5 minutes or until egg mixture is almost set (surface will be moist). Sprinkle with cheese.

3 Place skillet under broiler 4 to 5 inches from heat. Broil for 1 to 2 minutes or just until top is set and cheese is melted. Let stand for 10 minutes before serving.

Nutrition Facts per serving: 326 cal., 23 g total fat (7 g sat. fat), 342 mg chol., 761 mg sodium, 16 g carbo., 2 g fiber, 16 g pro.

This lovely, colorful quiche is a perfect brunch or luncheon entrée. You could use a refrigerated piecrust, but they contain lard and aren't appropriate if your guests are vegetarians.

TWO-CHEESE VEGETABLE QUICHE

1	recipe Pastry for a Single-Crust Pie
$\frac{1}{2}$	cup shredded Swiss cheese (2 ounces)
$\frac{1}{2}$	cup shredded cheddar cheese (2 ounces)
$\frac{1}{2}$	cup shredded carrot
$\frac{1}{3}$	cup sliced green onions
1	tablespoon all-purpose flour
4	eggs
1	10¾-ounce can condensed cream of broccoli soup
$\frac{1}{2}$	cup milk
$\frac{1}{8}$	teaspoon garlic powder
$\frac{1}{8}$	teaspoon black pepper

PREP:
35 minutes
BAKE:
45 minutes
STAND:
10 minutes
MAKES:
6 servings

1 Prepare Pastry for a Single-Crust Pie. Line the unpricked pastry shell with a double thickness of foil. Bake in a 450°F oven for 8 minutes. Remove foil. Bake for 4 to 5 minutes more or until pastry is set and dry. Remove from oven. Reduce oven temperature to 325°F.

2 Meanwhile, in a medium bowl combine Swiss cheese, cheddar cheese, carrot, green onions, and flour. Set aside.

3 In a large bowl beat eggs with a fork; stir in cream of broccoli soup, milk, garlic powder, and pepper. Stir in cheese mixture.

4 Pour egg-cheese mixture into the hot baked pastry shell. Bake in the 325°F oven for 45 to 50 minutes or until a knife inserted near the center comes out clean. If necessary, cover edge of pastry shell with foil to prevent overbrowning. Let stand for 10 minutes before serving.

PASTRY FOR A SINGLE-CRUST PIE: In a medium bowl stir together 1¼ cups all-purpose flour and ¼ teaspoon salt. Using a pastry blender, cut in ⅓ cup shortening until pieces are pea-size. Sprinkle 1 tablespoon cold water over part of the flour mixture; gently toss with a fork. Push moistened dough to side of bowl. Add additional cold water, 1 tablespoon at a time, until all is moistened (use 4 or 5 tablespoons cold water total). Form dough into a ball. On a lightly floured surface, roll dough from center to edge into a 12-inch circle. To transfer pastry, wrap it around the rolling pin. Unroll pastry into a 9-inch pie plate; ease pastry into pie plate, being careful not to stretch pastry. Trim pastry to ½ inch beyond edge of pie plate. Fold under extra pastry. Crimp edge as desired. Do not prick pastry.

Nutrition Facts per serving: 378 cal., 23 g total fat (9 g sat. fat), 163 mg chol., 563 mg sodium, 28 g carbo., 2 g fiber, 14 g pro.

If making this for friends, serve bowls of sour cream, salsa, and guacamole alongside the casserole. These extras will make it more interesting.

BLACK BEAN TORTILLA CASSEROLE

PREP:

20 minutes

BAKE:

25 minutes

STAND:

10 minutes

MAKES:

6 to 8 servings

10	6- to 7-inch corn tortillas
1	14½-ounce can diced tomatoes, undrained
2	medium green or red sweet peppers, seeded and chopped
1	large onion, chopped
¾	cup bottled chunky salsa or picante sauce
1	teaspoon ground cumin
1	15-ounce can black beans, rinsed and drained
1	11-ounce can condensed black bean soup
	Nonstick cooking spray
2	cups shredded Mexican cheese blend or Monterey Jack cheese (8 ounces)
	Dairy sour cream (optional)
	Bottled salsa (optional)
	Guacamole (optional)

1. Place the tortillas in a single layer on 2 baking sheets. Bake in a 350°F oven about 10 minutes or until crisp, turning once.

2. Meanwhile, in a large skillet combine undrained tomatoes, sweet peppers, onion, the ¾ cup salsa, and cumin. Bring to boiling; reduce heat. Simmer, uncovered, for 10 minutes. Stir in black beans and black bean soup.

3. Lightly coat a 2-quart rectangular baking dish with nonstick cooking spray. Spread one-third of the bean mixture over bottom of prepared baking dish. Top with half of the tortillas, overlapping as necessary, and half of the cheese. Add another one-third of the bean mixture; top with remaining tortillas and bean mixture.

4. Bake, covered, in the 350°F oven for 25 to 30 minutes or until heated through. Sprinkle with remaining cheese. Let stand for 10 minutes.

5. To serve, cut casserole into squares. If desired, serve with sour cream, additional salsa, and guacamole.

Nutrition Facts per serving: 399 cal., 14 g total fat (7 g sat. fat), 33 mg chol., 1,190 mg sodium, 52 g carbo., 10 g fiber, 19 g pro.

Summer is a good time to serve meatless entrées because appetites are light and the produce market brims with seasonal options. Also try this during the winter months. It's a hearty, filling dish that calls on broccoli, which is available year-round.

CREAMY BARLEY & BROCCOLI

1	14-ounce can vegetable broth
1	cup quick-cooking barley
2	cups broccoli florets
1	10¾-ounce can condensed cream of broccoli or cream of celery soup
½	cup milk
½	teaspoon dried basil, crushed
¼	teaspoon black pepper
1	cup shredded Swiss cheese (4 ounces)

START TO FINISH:

25 minutes

MAKES:

4 servings

1 In a medium saucepan bring vegetable broth to boiling. Stir in barley. Return to boiling; reduce heat. Simmer, covered, for 10 to 12 minutes or until barley is tender and most of the liquid is absorbed, adding broccoli during the last 5 minutes of cooking. Do not drain.

2 Stir in cream of broccoli soup, milk, basil, and pepper. Heat through. Add half of the cup of the Swiss cheese, stirring until melted.

3 Transfer to a serving dish. Sprinkle with the remaining Swiss cheese.

Nutrition Facts per serving: 331 cal., 13 g total fat (7 g sat. fat), 30 mg chol., 1,005 mg sodium, 40 g carbo., 6 g fiber, 16 g pro.

Canned beans make this dish a snap to prepare. Keep in mind that you can use any combination of beans that you like, so go ahead and clean out your pantry!

BEAN ENCHILADA CASSEROLE

PREP:
25 minutes

BAKE:
40 minutes

STAND:
5 minutes

MAKES:
4 to 6 servings

1   15-ounce can red kidney beans, pinto beans, or black beans, rinsed and drained

1   15-ounce can chickpeas (garbanzo beans), navy beans, and/or Great Northern beans, rinsed and drained

1   10¾-ounce can condensed cheddar cheese soup or one 11-ounce can condensed nacho cheese soup

1   10-ounce can enchilada sauce

1   8-ounce can tomato sauce

2   cups corn chips or tortilla chips, broken

3   ounces Monterey Jack cheese with jalapeño peppers or Monterey Jack cheese, shredded (¾ cup)

Toppers (sliced pitted ripe olives or green onions, chopped tomatoes or green sweet pepper, and/or shredded lettuce) (optional)

1 For filling, in a large bowl combine kidney beans, chickpeas, and cheddar cheese soup. In a medium bowl stir together enchilada sauce and tomato sauce. Spoon bean mixture into a greased 2-quart rectangular baking dish; pour sauce mixture over bean mixture. Top with chips.

2 Cover with lightly greased foil. Bake in a 350°F oven about 40 minutes or until heated through. Remove foil; sprinkle with cheese. Let stand about 5 minutes or until cheese melts. If desired, sprinkle with toppers.

Nutrition Facts per serving: 426 cal., 18 g total fat (7 g sat. fat), 28 mg chol., 2,037 mg sodium, 54 g carbo., 13 g fiber, 23 g pro.

Meatless, yes—but this casserole is by no means wimpy! With barley, bulgur, black beans, and a lentil soup base, this vegetable bake might paradoxically be described as meaty!

VEGETABLE TWO-GRAIN CASSEROLE

1	cup small fresh mushrooms, quartered
2	medium carrots, sliced
1	18.8-ounce can ready-to-serve lentil soup
1	15-ounce can black beans, rinsed and drained
1	cup frozen loose-pack whole kernel corn
1/2	cup pearl barley
1/3	cup bulgur
1/4	cup chopped onion
1/2	teaspoon black pepper
1/4	teaspoon salt
1/2	cup water
1/2	cup shredded cheddar cheese (2 ounces)

PREP:
15 minutes

BAKE:
1 1/4 hours

STAND:
5 minutes

MAKES:
4 servings

1 In an ungreased 2-quart casserole combine mushrooms, carrots, lentil soup, black beans, corn, pearl barley, bulgur, onion, pepper, and salt; stir in water.

2 Cover and bake in a 350°F oven about 1 1/4 hours or until barley and bulgur are tender, stirring twice. Stir again; sprinkle with cheese. Cover and let stand about 5 minutes or until cheese is melted.

Nutrition Facts per serving: 384 cal., 8 g total fat (3 g sat. fat), 15 mg chol., 929 mg sodium, 66 g carbo., 17 g fiber, 22 g pro.

With peas and vegetable soup—both kid-pleasing ingredients—this mild-tasting dish might be a good way to introduce little ones to lentils!

TOMATO & LENTIL MEDLEY

PREP:

25 minutes

COOK:

30 minutes

MAKES:

4 to 6 servings

1	large green sweet pepper, chopped
1	large yellow sweet pepper, chopped
1	cup sliced celery
1	cup chopped onion
2	teaspoons bottled minced garlic (4 cloves)
2	tablespoons olive oil or cooking oil
1½	cups water
1	10-ounce can condensed vegetarian vegetable soup
1	cup dry brown lentils, rinsed and drained
½	teaspoon salt
½	teaspoon ground turmeric
2	medium tomatoes, seeded and chopped
1	cup frozen loose-pack peas, thawed
¼	cup snipped fresh parsley (optional)
	Salt
	Black pepper

1 In a large saucepan cook sweet peppers, celery, onion, and garlic in hot oil until onion is tender. Stir in water, vegetarian vegetable soup, lentils, the ½ teaspoon salt, and the turmeric.

2 Bring to boiling; reduce heat. Simmer, covered, about 30 minutes or until lentils are tender and liquid is absorbed, stirring twice during cooking. Stir in tomatoes, peas, and, if desired, parsley. Heat through. Season to taste with additional salt and black pepper.

Nutrition Facts per serving: 353 cal., 8 g total fat (1 g sat. fat), 0 mg chol., 831 mg sodium, 56 g carbo., 21 g fiber, 19 g pro.

For an Italian-inspired serve-along, try refrigerated polenta. It's usually found in the produce department and is available in a variety of interesting flavor combinations.

ITALIAN RICE SKILLET

1   19-ounce can ready-to-serve hearty tomato soup

1   15- to 19-ounce can white kidney beans (cannellini beans), rinsed and drained

2   cups frozen loose-pack cut green beans

1   cup uncooked instant white rice

½   cup water

⅓   cup finely shredded Parmesan cheese

START TO FINISH:

20 minutes

MAKES:

4 servings

1 In a large skillet combine hearty tomato soup, white kidney beans, green beans, rice, and water. Bring to boiling; reduce heat. Simmer, covered, about 10 minutes or until rice and green beans are tender, stirring frequently.

2 Top servings with Parmesan cheese.

Nutrition Facts per serving: 271 cal., 4 g total fat (2 g sat. fat), 8 mg chol., 685 mg sodium, 51 g carbo., 9 g fiber, 14 g pro.

Lentils can be earthy and a little ho-hum by themselves. But when you pair them with the right seasonings and complements—such as the curry, soup, and spinach here—you'll get an inexpensive and flavorful meatless dish.

CURRIED LENTILS & SPINACH

PREP:

25 minutes

COOK:

30 minutes

MAKES:

6 servings

1	tablespoon butter or margarine
1	large red sweet pepper, chopped
1	large onion, chopped
1½	teaspoons bottled minced garlic (3 cloves)
2	14-ounce cans vegetable broth
1½	cups dry brown lentils, rinsed and drained
¼	cup water
2	teaspoons curry powder
¼	teaspoon black pepper
1	10¾-ounce can condensed tomato soup
1	6-ounce package prewashed baby spinach
	Hot cooked rice

1 In a large saucepan melt butter over medium heat. Add sweet pepper, onion, and garlic; cook for 3 to 4 minutes or just until vegetables are tender.

2 Stir in vegetable broth, lentils, water, curry powder, and black pepper. Bring to boiling; reduce heat. Simmer, covered, for 30 to 40 minutes or until lentils are tender and most of the liquid is absorbed, stirring occasionally.

3 Stir in tomato soup; heat through. Gradually stir in spinach until wilted. Serve with hot cooked rice.

Nutrition Facts per serving: 353 cal., 4 g total fat (2 g sat. fat), 5 mg chol., 895 mg sodium, 63 g carbo., 19 g fiber, 19 g pro.

Thai cuisine often melds an astonishing array of great flavor sensations, and this intriguing recipe is no exception.

GREEN CURRY TOFU & VEGETABLES

1   tablespoon cooking oil

1   cup sliced carrots

1   cup fresh pea pods, strings and tips removed

1   cup broccoli florets

1   cup sliced fresh mushrooms

1   13½-ounce can unsweetened coconut milk

1   10¾-ounce can condensed cream of celery soup

1   to 2 teaspoons green curry paste

1   16-ounce package firm or extra-firm tub-style tofu (fresh bean curd), drained and cut into ½-inch cubes

     Hot cooked rice

¼   cup coarsely chopped cashews

START TO FINISH:

25 minutes

MAKES:

4 servings

1 In a large skillet heat oil over medium heat. Add carrots, pea pods, broccoli, and mushrooms; cook until crisp-tender, stirring occasionally.

2 Meanwhile, in a medium bowl whisk together coconut milk, cream of celery soup, and green curry paste. Pour over vegetables in skillet. Bring just to boiling over medium heat. Stir in tofu; heat through.

3 Serve vegetable mixture over hot cooked rice. Sprinkle with cashews.

Nutrition Facts per serving: 531 cal., 34 g total fat (19 g sat. fat), 2 mg chol., 726 mg sodium, 43 g carbo., 3 g fiber, 17 g pro.

You can shred your own carrot or use packaged shredded carrot. Either way, it adds color to this hearty skillet.

BARLEY & BEAN SKILLET

START TO FINISH:

30 minutes

MAKES:

4 servings

1	14-ounce can vegetable broth
1/3	cup water
1 1/4	cups uncooked quick-cooking barley
2	cups frozen loose-pack cut green beans
1	10 3/4-ounce can condensed cream of onion soup
1/2	cup packaged shredded carrot
1/2	cup milk
1/2	teaspoon dried thyme, crushed
1	cup shredded sharp cheddar cheese (4 ounces)

1 In a large skillet bring vegetable broth and water to boiling. Stir in barley. Return to boiling; reduce heat. Simmer, covered, for 5 minutes.

2 Stir in green beans, cream of onion soup, carrot, milk, and thyme. Bring to boiling; reduce heat. Simmer, covered, for 12 to 15 minutes more or until barley is tender and most of the liquid is absorbed, stirring occasionally. Stir in half of the cheese.

3 Sprinkle with remaining cheese. Let stand for 2 to 3 minutes or until cheese is melted.

Nutrition Facts per serving: 394 cal., 15 g total fat (8 g sat. fat), 45 mg chol., 1,193 mg sodium, 52 g carbo., 8 g fiber, 16 g pro.

The vegetarians in your crowd will be grateful when you serve a meatless version of this ever-favorite casserole.

TOFU MANICOTTI

8   dried manicotti shells

     Nonstick cooking spray

1   cup chopped fresh mushrooms

½   cup chopped green onions

1   teaspoon dried Italian seasoning, crushed

1   12- to 16-ounce package soft tofu (fresh bean curd), drained

1   slightly beaten egg

¼   cup finely shredded Parmesan cheese (1 ounce)

1   11-ounce can condensed tomato bisque soup

1   14½-ounce can diced tomatoes with basil, oregano, and garlic, undrained

⅛   teaspoon black pepper

¾   cup shredded Italian blend cheese (3 ounces)

PREP:
40 minutes

BAKE:
30 minutes + 2 minutes

STAND:
10 minutes

MAKES:
4 servings

1 Cook manicotti shells according to package directions; drain. Rinse in cold water; drain.

2 Coat a medium skillet with nonstick cooking spray. Preheat skillet over medium heat. Add mushrooms and green onions; cook until tender. Stir in Italian seasoning; set aside.

3 In a medium bowl mash tofu. Stir in mushroom mixture, egg, and Parmesan cheese. Stuff each manicotti shell with about ¼ cup of the tofu mixture. Arrange stuffed shells in a single layer in an ungreased 3-quart rectangular baking dish.

4 In a medium bowl stir together tomato bisque soup, tomatoes, and pepper. Pour soup mixture over stuffed manicotti.

5 Bake, uncovered, in a 350°F oven about 30 minutes or until heated through. Sprinkle with Italian cheese. Bake, uncovered, about 2 minutes more or until cheese is melted. Let stand for 10 minutes before serving.

Nutrition Facts per serving: 411 cal., 13 g total fat (6 g sat. fat), 74 mg chol., 1,383 mg sodium, 53 g carbo., 4 g fiber, 21 g pro.

It's fun to go meatless now and then—especially with varied, flavor-packed recipes like this one. Six ounces may look like a lot of spinach at first, but it wilts pleasingly as you stir to the right amount.

ROASTED VEGETABLES & SPINACH WITH PASTA

PREP:

30 minutes

BAKE:

30 minutes + 10 minutes

MAKES:

6 servings

1 pound eggplant, peeled and cut into 1-inch chunks (about 6 cups)

1 large red onion, cut into thin wedges

2 yellow and/or green sweet peppers, coarsely chopped

1 tablespoon olive oil

½ teaspoon salt

1 teaspoon olive oil

½ teaspoon dried thyme, crushed

¼ teaspoon crushed red pepper

¼ teaspoon fennel seeds, crushed

¼ teaspoon black pepper

1 teaspoon bottled minced garlic (2 cloves)

1 18.7-ounce can ready-to-serve tomato soup

12 ounces dried cut ziti or rotini pasta (4 cups)

1 6-ounce bag prewashed baby spinach (about 8 cups)

1 cup shredded mozzarella cheese (4 ounces)

1 In a shallow roasting pan combine eggplant, red onion, sweet peppers, and the 1 tablespoon olive oil. Sprinkle with salt. Bake in a 400°F oven for 30 to 35 minutes or until vegetables begin to brown, stirring twice.

2 Meanwhile, in a small saucepan heat the 1 teaspoon olive oil over medium heat. Add thyme, crushed red pepper, fennel seeds, black pepper, and garlic. Cook and stir for 2 minutes. Stir in tomato soup. Bring to boiling; reduce heat. Simmer, uncovered, for 5 minutes, stirring occasionally.

3 Meanwhile, cook pasta according to package directions; drain well. Transfer to a large bowl. Add tomato soup mixture and roasted vegetables; toss to coat. Stir in baby spinach.

4 Spoon pasta mixture into a greased 3-quart rectangular baking dish. Sprinkle with cheese. Bake, uncovered, for 10 to 15 minutes or until heated through and cheese is melted.

Nutrition Facts per serving: 375 cal., 7 g total fat (2 g sat. fat), 12 mg chol., 617 mg sodium, 63 g carbo., 7 g fiber, 15 g pro.

In winter, when you crave hearty foods, it's easy to get into a meat, meat, and more meat rut! This meatless casserole provides the fullness and warmth you seek but offers a nice break from the usual. Serve a green salad topped with citrus slices and feta cheese to really perk things up.

CREAMY PENNE WITH VEGETABLES

8	ounces dried penne pasta
1	tablespoon butter or margarine
1	medium red sweet pepper, chopped
1	stalk celery, chopped
1	medium onion, chopped
½	teaspoon dried thyme, crushed
1	clove garlic, minced
1	10¾-ounce can condensed golden mushroom soup
½	cup dairy sour cream
½	cup milk

PREP:
25 minutes

BAKE:
30 minutes

MAKES:
4 servings

1 Cook pasta according to package directions; drain. Meanwhile, in a large saucepan melt butter over medium heat. Add sweet pepper, celery, onion, thyme, and garlic; cook and stir until tender. Remove saucepan from heat. Stir in golden mushroom soup, sour cream, and milk. Stir in cooked pasta.

2 Spoon pasta mixture into an ungreased 1½-quart casserole. Bake, covered, in a 350°F oven about 30 minutes or until heated through.

Nutrition Facts per serving: 376 cal., 12 g total fat (6 g sat. fat), 24 mg chol., 663 mg sodium, 56 g carbo., 3 g fiber, 11 g pro.

Onion, eggplant, red sweet pepper, and zucchini make this a wonderfully chunky vegetarian entrée.

EGGPLANT-TOMATO PASTA SAUCE

START TO FINISH:

45 minutes

MAKES:

4 servings

1	tablespoon olive oil or cooking oil
1	cup chopped onion
1	medium red sweet pepper, chopped
1	teaspoon dried Italian seasoning, crushed
1	large eggplant (about 1¼ pounds), peeled and cubed
1	medium zucchini, chopped (about 1¼ cups)
1	11-ounce can condensed tomato bisque soup
½	cup water
¼	teaspoon salt
	Hot cooked pasta
¼	cup grated Parmesan cheese (1 ounce)

1 In a large skillet heat oil over medium heat. Add onion, sweet pepper, and Italian seasoning; cook until tender. Add eggplant and zucchini; cook and stir about 10 minutes or until vegetables are tender and lightly browned.

2 In a small bowl combine tomato bisque soup, water, and salt. Stir soup mixture into vegetables in skillet. Cook, uncovered, until heated through, stirring occasionally.

3 Serve sauce over hot cooked pasta. Sprinkle servings with Parmesan cheese.

Nutrition Facts per serving: 405 cal., 8 g total fat (3 g sat. fat), 6 mg chol., 819 mg sodium, 71 g carbo., 7 g fiber, 13 g pro.

You'll be amazed at the richness just a half cup of Parmesan cheese brings to this creamy and colorful veggie-packed pasta.

CREAMY PASTA & VEGETABLE PRIMAVERA

1   pound fresh asparagus spears

8   ounces dried rotini pasta (about 2½ cups)

1   medium red or yellow sweet pepper, coarsely chopped

1   cup assorted fresh summer squash (such as halved sunburst squash and/or sliced zucchini or yellow summer squash)

2   cloves garlic, minced

2   teaspoons olive oil

1   10¾-ounce can condensed cream of broccoli soup

¾   cup milk

½   teaspoon dried basil, crushed

¼   teaspoon crushed red pepper

½   cup finely shredded Parmesan cheese (2 ounces)

    Black pepper

START TO FINISH:
35 minutes
MAKES:
4 servings

1   Snap off and discard woody bases from asparagus. Bias-slice asparagus into 1-inch pieces.

2   Cook pasta according to package directions, adding asparagus, sweet pepper, and squash to pasta for the last 3 minutes of cooking; drain. Return pasta and vegetables to hot pan.

3   Meanwhile, in a small saucepan cook and stir garlic in hot oil for 1 minute. Stir in cream of broccoli soup, milk, basil, and crushed red pepper. Cook and stir until mixture is bubbly. Pour over pasta and vegetables; toss gently to coat. Stir in Parmesan cheese. Season to taste with black pepper.

Nutrition Facts per serving: 399 cal., 11 g total fat (5 g sat. fat), 13 mg chol., 703 mg sodium, 58 g carbo., 5 g fiber, 17 g pro.

Cooks from countries bordering the Mediterranean know how to stretch the meat—or leave it out entirely—and still serve satisfying, full-flavored meals. This lively Greek-inspired casserole is proof positive!

GREEK PASTA CASSEROLE

PREP:

25 minutes

BAKE:

20 minutes

STAND:

10 minutes

MAKES:

6 servings

12 ounces dried rotini pasta (3½ cups)

1 15-ounce can tomato sauce

1 10¾-ounce can condensed tomato soup

1 15-ounce can white kidney beans (cannellini beans) or garbanzo beans (chickpeas), rinsed and drained

8 ounces feta cheese, crumbled (2 cups)

1 cup coarsely chopped pitted Greek black olives

½ cup seasoned fine dry bread crumbs

2 tablespoons butter or margarine, melted

2 tablespoons finely shredded or grated Parmesan cheese

1 Cook pasta according to package directions. Drain. In a large bowl combine cooked pasta, tomato sauce, and tomato soup; toss to coat. Stir in beans, feta cheese, and olives.

2 Spoon pasta mixture into a lightly greased 3-quart rectangular baking dish. In a small bowl stir together bread crumbs, melted butter, and Parmesan cheese; sprinkle over pasta mixture.

3 Bake, uncovered, in a 375°F oven for 20 to 25 minutes or until heated through and top is lightly browned. Let stand for 10 minutes before serving.

Nutrition Facts per serving: 553 cal., 19 g total fat (10 g sat. fat), 52 mg chol., 1,890 mg sodium, 74 g carbo., 7 g fiber, 24 g pro.

The roasted red sweet peppers add a lovely sweetness to the sauce, and the ricotta makes the entire dish creamy and luscious. It's hard to beat—and it's so easy to make.

VEGETABLE LASAGNA

1   7-ounce jar roasted red sweet peppers, drained

1   10¾-ounce can condensed tomato soup

1   teaspoon dried oregano, crushed

1   teaspoon bottled minced garlic (2 cloves)

    Nonstick cooking spray

1   tablespoon olive oil

2   cups coarsely chopped zucchini and/or yellow summer squash

2   cups sliced fresh mushrooms

1   medium onion, chopped

1   15-ounce carton ricotta cheese

¼   cup finely shredded or grated Parmesan cheese (1 ounce)

¼   teaspoon black pepper

6   no-boil lasagna noodles

1   cup shredded mozzarella cheese (4 ounces)

1 For sauce, in a blender container combine roasted sweet red peppers, tomato soup, oregano, and garlic. Cover and blend until nearly smooth; set aside. Coat a 2-quart square baking dish with nonstick cooking spray; set aside.

2 In a large skillet heat oil over medium heat. Add zucchini and/or squash, mushrooms, and onion; cook about 6 minutes or until zucchini is tender. Drain well. In a small bowl stir together ricotta cheese, Parmesan cheese, and black pepper.

3 To assemble, spoon about ¼ cup of the red pepper sauce in the bottom of the prepared dish. Top with 2 of the lasagna noodles. Top with one-third of the ricotta mixture, one-third of the vegetable mixture, one-third of the remaining red pepper sauce, and one-third of the mozzarella cheese. Repeat layers twice with remaining lasagna noodles, ricotta mixture, vegetable mixture, red pepper sauce, and mozzarella cheese.

4 Bake, covered, in a 375°F oven for 20 minutes. Uncover and bake for 15 to 20 minutes more or until heated through. Let stand for 15 minutes before serving.

Nutrition Facts per serving: 396 cal., 21 g total fat (12 g sat. fat), 63 mg chol., 837 mg sodium, 26 g carbo., 3 g fiber, 26 g pro.

PREP:

35 minutes

BAKE:

20 minutes + 15 minutes

STAND:

15 minutes

MAKES:

6 servings

A sprinkling of shredded cheddar cheese complements the savory barley stuffing.

BARLEY-STUFFED SWEET PEPPERS

PREP:
30 minutes
BAKE:
20 minutes
STAND:
5 minutes
MAKES:
4 servings

1	14-ounce can vegetable broth
½	cup shredded carrot
¼	cup chopped onion
½	teaspoon dried oregano, crushed
⅛	teaspoon salt
1	cup quick-cooking barley
2	large green and/or red sweet peppers
1	10¾-ounce can condensed cream of onion soup
½	cup shredded cheddar cheese (2 ounces)

1 In a medium saucepan combine vegetable broth, carrot, onion, oregano, and salt. Bring to boiling; reduce heat. Simmer, covered, for 5 minutes. Stir in barley; simmer, covered, for 2 minutes more. Remove from heat. Let stand, covered, about 15 minutes or until liquid is absorbed and barley is tender.

2 Meanwhile, halve the sweet peppers lengthwise; remove seeds and membranes. In a large saucepan cook pepper halves in a large amount of boiling water for 5 minutes. Drain on paper towels. Place peppers, cut sides up, in an ungreased 2-quart square baking dish.

3 Stir cream of onion soup into the barley mixture; spoon into pepper halves. Spoon any remaining barley mixture into the baking dish around the peppers.

4 Bake, uncovered, in a 350°F oven for 20 to 25 minutes or until peppers are crisp-tender and barley mixture is heated through. Sprinkle with cheese; let stand for 5 minutes before serving.

Nutrition Facts per serving: 288 cal., 10 g total fat (4 g sat. fat), 28 mg chol., 1,184 mg sodium, 44 g carbo., 6 g fiber, 10 g pro.

From scratch, split pea soup needs to boil more than an hour to soften the peas. By starting with canned soup and adding a few fresh stir-ins, you can have an almost-from-scratch alternative in much less time.

SPLIT PEA & VEGETABLE SOUP

2	tablespoons cooking oil
2	stalks celery, chopped
2	medium carrots, chopped
1	medium onion, chopped
1	clove garlic, minced
2	11¼-ounce cans condensed green pea soup
2	10-ounce cans condensed vegetarian vegetable soup
2	cups water
½	teaspoon dried thyme, crushed
⅛	teaspoon black pepper

START TO FINISH:
25 minutes
MAKES:
4 servings

1 In a large saucepan or 4-quart Dutch oven heat oil over medium heat. Add celery, carrots, onion, and garlic; cook about 5 minutes or until tender.

2 Stir in green pea soup, vegetarian vegetable soup, water, thyme, and pepper. Cook until heated through.

Nutrition Facts per serving: 403 cal., 11 g total fat (2 g sat. fat), 3 mg chol., 2,117 mg sodium, 62 g carbo., 11 g fiber, 15 g pro.

If you can't find udon noodles—Japanese noodles that are made from wheat or corn flour—angel hair pasta makes a good substitute, because it cooks in the same amount of time.

TOFU MUSHROOM NOODLE SOUP

1   16-ounce package extra-firm tofu (fresh bean curd), drained and cut into ½-inch cubes

1   tablespoon soy sauce

1   tablespoon toasted sesame oil

8   ounces fresh button mushrooms, sliced (3 cups)

1   clove garlic, minced

1   tablespoon cooking oil

2   14-ounce cans vegetable broth

1   10-ounce can condensed vegetarian vegetable soup

1   10-ounce package frozen chopped broccoli

2   ounces dried udon noodles or angel hair pasta, broken

1   to 2 tablespoons snipped fresh cilantro

1   In a medium bowl gently stir together tofu cubes, soy sauce, and sesame oil; set aside.

2   In a large saucepan cook mushrooms and garlic in hot oil for 4 minutes. Add vegetable broth, vegetarian vegetable soup, broccoli, and udon noodles. Bring to boiling; reduce heat. Simmer, covered, for 4 to 6 minutes or until vegetables and noodles are tender, stirring occasionally.

3   Gently stir in tofu mixture; heat through. Stir in cilantro.

Nutrition Facts per serving: 295 cal., 15 g total fat (2 g sat. fat), 0 mg chol., 1,545 mg sodium, 29 g carbo., 5 g fiber, 18 g pro.

Start with a can of soup, then add zucchini, carrot, and green beans for freshness and color, and barley for heartiness. Serve with crusty rolls and a cheese tray— and that's Sunday night's soup supper!

TOMATO BARLEY SOUP WITH GARDEN VEGETABLES

2	14-ounce cans vegetable broth
¾	cup quick-cooking barley
¾	cup thinly sliced carrot
1	teaspoon dried thyme, crushed
⅛	teaspoon black pepper
1	19-ounce can ready-to-serve tomato basil soup
2	cups coarsely chopped zucchini and/or yellow summer squash
1	cup frozen loose-pack cut green beans

1 In a large saucepan combine vegetable broth, barley, carrot, thyme, and pepper. Bring to boiling; reduce heat. Simmer, covered, for 10 minutes.

2 Stir in tomato basil soup, zucchini, and green beans. Return to boiling; reduce heat. Simmer, covered, for 8 to 10 minutes more or until vegetables and barley are tender.

Nutrition Facts per serving: 197 cal., 3 g total fat (0 g sat. fat), 0 mg chol., 1,265 mg sodium, 40 g carbo., 6 g fiber, 7 g pro.

START TO FINISH:
30 minutes
MAKES:
4 servings

Serve this thick, hearty soup with a loaf of crusty bread or sprinkle purchased croutons over the top.

TOMATO-LENTIL SOUP

PREP:

20 minutes

COOK:

45 minutes + 5 minutes

MAKES:

4 servings

1	tablespoon cooking oil
1	medium onion, chopped
2	teaspoons bottled minced garlic (4 cloves)
3	14-ounce cans vegetable broth
1	cup dry brown lentils, rinsed and drained
1	teaspoon dried oregano, crushed
$\frac{1}{2}$	teaspoon ground cumin
$\frac{1}{4}$	teaspoon black pepper
1	10¾-ounce can condensed tomato soup
1	10-ounce package frozen chopped spinach, thawed and well drained
1	tablespoon lemon juice

1 In a large saucepan heat oil over medium heat. Add onion and garlic; cook until tender. Stir in vegetable broth, lentils, oregano, cumin, and pepper. Bring to boiling; reduce heat. Simmer, covered, about 45 minutes or until lentils are tender.

2 Stir in tomato soup, spinach, and lemon juice. Cook, uncovered, for 5 minutes more.

Nutrition Facts per serving: 302 cal., 6 g total fat (1 g sat. fat), 0 mg chol., 1,767 mg sodium, 46 g carbo., 17 g fiber, 19 g pro.

A small amount of sour cream heightens the flavor of this main-dish soup. Spoon it onto individual servings just prior to serving.

CREAMY-STYLE LENTIL SOUP

¾ cup dry brown lentils, rinsed and drained
2   medium carrots, sliced
2   stalks celery, sliced
1   medium onion, chopped
3   cups water
1   10¾-ounce can condensed cream of mushroom soup
2   teaspoons instant beef bouillon granules
¼   cup snipped fresh parsley
     Dairy sour cream

1 In a 3½- or 4-quart slow cooker combine lentils, carrots, celery, and onion. Stir in water, cream of mushroom soup, and beef bouillon granules.

2 Cover and cook on low-heat setting for 6 to 8 hours or on high-heat setting for 3½ to 4½ hours. Stir in parsley. Top each serving with sour cream.

FOR 5- OR 6-QUART SLOW COOKER: **Prepare as directed, except double all ingredients. Makes 8 servings.**

Nutrition Facts per serving: 228 cal., 6 g total fat (2 g sat. fat), 1 mg chol., 999 mg sodium, 32 g carbo., 13 g fiber, 12 g pro.

PREP:
15 minutes

COOK:
6 to 8 hours (low-heat setting) or
3½ to 4½ hours (high-heat setting)

MAKES:
4 servings

What this chili lacks in meat, it makes up for—many times over—in variety!
It's a hearty soup that will please big appetites.

VEGETABLE CHILI

PREP:

40 minutes

COOK:

10 minutes + 10 minutes

MAKES:

6 to 8 servings

2   cups chopped onions

1   teaspoon bottled minced garlic (2 cloves)

1   tablespoon cooking oil

1   pound carrots, coarsely chopped (3 cups)

1   pound potatoes, cut into ¾-inch chunks (3 cups)

1   14-ounce can vegetable broth

2   teaspoons chili powder

1   teaspoon ground cumin

¼   teaspoon dried oregano, crushed

2   14½-ounce cans diced tomatoes, undrained

1   15-ounce can garbanzo beans (chickpeas), rinsed and drained

1   11-ounce can condensed black bean soup

1   tablespoon dried cilantro or ¼ cup snipped fresh cilantro

⅓   cup dairy sour cream or plain yogurt

1 In a 4- to 5-quart Dutch oven cook onion and garlic in hot oil until tender. Add carrots, potatoes, vegetable broth, chili powder, cumin, and oregano. Bring to boiling; reduce heat. Simmer, covered, for 10 minutes. Stir in tomatoes, garbanzo beans, and black bean soup. Return to boiling; reduce heat. Simmer, covered, for 10 to 15 minutes more or until vegetables are tender.

2 Stir in cilantro. Ladle chili into bowls. Top with sour cream.

Nutrition Facts per serving: 307 cal., 7 g total fat (2 g sat. fat), 5 mg chol., 1,273 mg sodium, 51 g carbo., 12 g fiber, 11 g pro.

SIDES

Served as a side to a Sunday roast, a holiday bird, or an everyday meat loaf, this versatile dish could easily become a family favorite.

SPINACH-CHEESE CASSEROLE

PREP:

20 minutes

BAKE:

30 minutes

STAND:

5 minutes

MAKES:

6 servings

1	tablespoon butter or margarine
½	cup chopped carrot
¼	cup chopped onion
1	10¾-ounce can condensed cream of onion soup
1	10-ounce package frozen chopped spinach, thawed and well drained
¾	cup uncooked instant white rice
½	cup milk
½	cup finely shredded Parmesan cheese (2 ounces)

1 In a 2-quart saucepan melt butter over medium heat. Add carrot and onion; cook until onion is tender. Remove from heat. Stir in cream of onion soup, spinach, rice, milk, and ¼ cup of the cheese. Spoon into an ungreased 1-quart casserole.

2 Bake, covered, in a 375°F oven about 30 minutes or until rice is tender. Sprinkle with remaining cheese. Let stand for 5 minutes before serving.

Nutrition Facts per serving: 175 cal., 7 g total fat (4 g sat. fat), 20 mg chol., 647 mg sodium, 19 g carbo., 2 g fiber, 8 g pro.

If you like the spinach dip that is always a hit at restaurants, chances are you'll like this side-dish version at home!

SPINACH & ARTICHOKE CASSEROLE

1   10¾-ounce can reduced-fat condensed cream of mushroom soup

1   8-ounce package reduced-fat cream cheese (Neufchâtel), cubed

2   10-ounce packages frozen chopped spinach, thawed and well drained

1   14-ounce can artichoke hearts, drained and coarsely chopped

1   2.8-ounce can french-fried onions, coarsely crushed

⅔   cup crushed crackers (such as rich round or saltine crackers)

2   tablespoons butter or margarine, melted

PREP:
15 minutes

BAKE:
40 minutes

MAKES:
8 servings

1 In a large saucepan combine cream of mushroom soup and cream cheese. Cook and stir over medium heat until cream cheese melts. Remove from heat. Stir in spinach, chopped artichokes, and french-fried onions. Spoon into a greased 2-quart casserole.

2 In a small bowl combine crushed crackers and melted butter. Sprinkle over top of spinach mixture.

3 Bake in a 350°F oven about 40 minutes or until heated through.

Nutrition Facts per serving: 247 cal., 17 g total fat (7 g sat. fat), 33 mg chol., 637 mg sodium, 17 g carbo., 4 g fiber, 7 g pro.

When you have a bumper crop of zucchini, serve this. Technically, it's a side dish, but in summer, it makes a satisfying light supper when served with a salad or a cup of cool gazpacho.

SUMMER SQUASH CASSEROLE

PREP:

25 minutes

BAKE:

25 minutes

MAKES:

8 to 10 servings

6   medium zucchini and/or yellow summer squash (about 2 pounds), halved lengthwise and cut into $3/8$-inch slices (about 7 cups)

¼   cup chopped onion

1    $10^3/4$-ounce can condensed cream of onion or cream of mushroom soup

1   8-ounce carton dairy sour cream

1   cup shredded carrot

2   cups herb-seasoned stuffing mix (about ½ of an 8-ounce package)

¼   cup butter or margarine, melted

1 In a large saucepan cook zucchini with onion in a small amount of boiling water for 3 to 5 minutes or until crisp-tender. Drain well. In a large bowl combine cream of onion soup and sour cream; stir in carrot. Fold in zucchini mixture. Set aside.

2 In a medium bowl toss together stuffing mix and melted butter. Sprinkle half of the stuffing mixture into an ungreased 2-quart rectangular baking dish. Top with vegetable mixture. Sprinkle with remaining stuffing mixture.

3 Bake in a 350°F oven for 25 to 30 minutes or until heated through.

Nutrition Facts per serving: 228 cal., 15 g total fat (8 g sat. fat), 35 mg chol., 574 mg sodium, 21 g carbo., 3 g fiber, 5 g pro.

Frozen vegetables are lifesavers in this quick-to-make side dish. It works well with any frozen vegetable mixture—choose the combination you like best.

SWISS VEGETABLE MEDLEY

1   16-ounce package frozen loose-pack broccoli, cauliflower, and carrots, thawed

1   10¾-ounce can condensed cream of mushroom soup

1   cup shredded Swiss cheese (4 ounces)

⅓   cup dairy sour cream

¼   teaspoon black pepper

1   2.8-ounce can french-fried onions

PREP:
15 minutes
BAKE:
30 minutes + 5 minutes
MAKES:
6 servings

1 In a large bowl combine vegetables, cream of mushroom soup, half of the Swiss cheese, the sour cream, and pepper. Stir in half of the french-fried onions. Spoon vegetable mixture into an ungreased 2-quart square baking dish.

2 Bake, covered, in a 350°F oven for 30 minutes. Uncover and sprinkle with remaining cheese and french-fried onions. Bake about 5 minutes more or until heated through.

Nutrition Facts per serving: 249 cal., 17 g total fat (6 g sat. fat), 22 mg chol., 589 mg sodium, 14 g carbo., 3 g fiber, 9 g pro.

The white wine Worcestershire sauce won't darken the dish the way regular Worcestershire sauce would.

CREAMY BROCCOLI BAKE

PREP:

15 minutes

BAKE:

25 minutes

MAKES:

6 to 8 servings

1½ pounds broccoli, cut up (6 cups)

1 10¾-ounce can condensed cream of broccoli or golden mushroom soup

½ cup shredded sharp cheddar cheese (2 ounces)

⅓ cup dairy sour cream

2 teaspoons white wine Worcestershire sauce

1 In a covered large saucepan cook broccoli in a small amount of boiling salted water for 2 minutes; drain well. Transfer to an ungreased 1½-quart casserole. In a medium bowl combine cream of broccoli soup, cheese, sour cream, and white wine Worcestershire sauce. Pour over broccoli.

2 Bake, covered, in a 350°F oven about 25 minutes or until broccoli is tender and sauce is heated through.

Nutrition Facts per serving: 129 cal., 8 g total fat (4 g sat. fat), 16 mg chol., 428 mg sodium, 9 g carbo., 3 g fiber, 6 g pro.

Here, a can of soup performs double duty. Half goes in the casserole to help bind the ingredients; the other half is heated later for a creamy sauce.

BROCCOLI BREAD BAKE

2	10-ounce packages frozen cut broccoli, thawed
1	slightly beaten egg
1	10¾-ounce can condensed cream of onion soup
¼	cup finely chopped celery
1	teaspoon dried parsley flakes, crushed
¼	teaspoon dried tarragon, crushed
	Dash black pepper
1	package (6 or 8) refrigerated dinner rolls
¼	cup milk

PREP:

15 minutes

BAKE:

20 minutes

MAKES:

6 servings

1 Spread broccoli in bottom of an ungreased 2-quart square baking dish; set aside. In a medium bowl combine egg, half of the cream of onion soup, the celery, parsley flakes, tarragon, and pepper. Spoon soup mixture over broccoli; set aside. Separate dinner rolls; snip each roll into quarters. Arrange roll quarters on top of broccoli mixture.

2 Bake, uncovered, in a 350°F oven for 20 to 25 minutes or until rolls are golden.

3 Meanwhile, for sauce, in a small saucepan combine remaining soup and milk; heat through. Serve sauce over baked casserole.

Nutrition Facts per serving: 200 cal., 5 g total fat (1 g sat. fat), 42 mg chol., 698 mg sodium, 28 g carbo., 3 g fiber, 9 g pro.

Take your pick—use fresh broccoli and cauliflower if you have time for a trip to the store. Or keep frozen vegetables on hand and make this without venturing out your door.

BROCCOLI-CAULIFLOWER BAKE

PREP:
20 minutes

BAKE:
15 minutes

MAKES:
10 servings

4 cups broccoli florets*

3 cups cauliflower florets*

1 10¾-ounce can condensed cream of mushroom soup or cream of chicken soup

3 ounces American cheese or process Swiss cheese slices, torn (¾ cup)

1 tablespoon dried minced onion

½ teaspoon dried basil, thyme, or marjoram, crushed

¾ cup soft bread crumbs (1 slice)

1 tablespoon butter or margarine, melted

1 In a covered large saucepan cook broccoli and cauliflower in a small amount of lightly salted boiling water for 6 to 8 minutes or until vegetables are almost crisp-tender. Drain well; remove from pan.

2 In the same saucepan combine cream of mushroom soup, cheese, dried minced onion, and basil. Cook and stir until bubbly. Stir in cooked broccoli and cauliflower. Transfer mixture to an ungreased 1½-quart casserole.

3 In a small bowl combine bread crumbs and melted butter; sprinkle over vegetable mixture. Bake in a 375°F oven about 15 minutes or until heated through.

*NOTE: **If you like, substitute 7 cups frozen loose-pack broccoli and cauliflower, thawed, for the fresh broccoli and cauliflower florets. Bake in a 375°F oven about 35 minutes or until heated through.**

Nutrition Facts per serving: 100 cal., 6 g total fat (3 g sat. fat), 12 mg chol., 376 mg sodium, 7 g carbo., 2 g fiber, 4 g pro.

The buttered bread crumb topping toasts as this creamy side dish bakes.

CARROTS AU GRATIN

1	pound carrots, cut into ½-inch slices (about 3 cups)
¼	cup fine dry bread crumbs
1	tablespoon butter or margarine, melted
1	10¾-ounce can condensed cream of celery soup or reduced-fat condensed cream of celery soup
1	cup shredded cheddar cheese (4 ounces)
1	tablespoon snipped fresh parsley
1	to 2 teaspoons snipped fresh rosemary

1 In a covered medium saucepan cook carrot slices in a small amount of boiling water for 10 to 12 minutes or just until tender. Drain well.

2 Meanwhile, in a small bowl stir together bread crumbs and melted butter; set aside.

3 In a medium bowl combine cooked carrots, cream of celery soup, cheese, parsley, and rosemary. Spoon into a greased 1-quart casserole. Sprinkle with bread crumb mixture.

4 Bake, uncovered, in a 350°F oven for 20 to 25 minutes or until heated through.

Nutrition Facts per serving: 177 cal., 11 g total fat (6 g sat. fat), 31 mg chol., 598 mg sodium, 14 g carbo., 3 g fiber, 7 g pro.

PREP:
15 minutes
BAKE:
20 minutes
MAKES:
6 servings

Brussels sprouts served in a creamy cheese sauce and topped with a golden-brown topping will make converts of those who are not yet fans of the vegetable.

BRUSSELS SPROUTS BAKE

PREP:

15 minutes

BAKE:

40 minutes

MAKES:

6 servings

1 ½   cups soft bread crumbs (2 slices bread)

1   10¾-ounce can condensed cream of mushroom soup

½   of an 8-ounce tub cream cheese with garlic and herb or ½ cup shredded American cheese (2 ounces)

½   cup finely chopped onion

Dash black pepper

2   8-ounce packages frozen Brussels sprouts, thawed

1   tablespoon butter or margarine, melted

❶ In a large bowl combine ½ cup of the bread crumbs, the cream of mushroom soup, cream cheese, onion, and pepper. Stir in thawed Brussels sprouts. Transfer to an ungreased 2-quart square baking dish. In a small bowl combine remaining bread crumbs and the melted butter; sprinkle over Brussels sprouts mixture.

❷ Bake, uncovered, in a 350°F oven for 40 to 45 minutes or until heated through.

Nutrition Facts per serving: 203 cal., 13 g total fat (6 g sat. fat), 23 mg chol., 547 mg sodium, 18 g carbo., 4 g fiber, 5 g pro.

Serve this rich, wonderful side dish with roast chicken. Refrigerated mashed potatoes round out the meal—no gravy needed, as the casserole is creamy enough!

SAUCY BAKED ASPARAGUS

1	10¾-ounce can condensed cream of asparagus or celery soup
½	cup dairy sour cream
¼	cup coarsely shredded carrot
1	teaspoon dried minced onion
⅛	teaspoon black pepper
2	10-ounce packages frozen cut asparagus, thawed
½	cup herb-seasoned stuffing mix
1	tablespoon butter or margarine, melted

PREP:

15 minutes

BAKE:

30 minutes + 5 minutes

MAKES:

6 servings

1 In a large bowl stir together cream of asparagus soup, sour cream, carrot, dried minced onion, and pepper. Fold in asparagus. Turn asparagus mixture into an ungreased 1½-quart casserole. In a small bowl toss together stuffing mix and melted butter; set aside.

2 Bake casserole, covered, in a 350°F oven for 30 minutes. Uncover casserole; stir. Sprinkle stuffing mix mixture around edge of asparagus mixture. Bake, uncovered, for 5 to 10 minutes more or until heated through.

Nutrition Facts per serving: 135 cal., 7 g total fat (4 g sat. fat), 15 mg chol., 469 mg sodium, 14 g carbo., 3 g fiber, 5 g pro.

This recipe is a little like the much-loved green bean casserole that has starred at holiday tables for years. Water chestnuts and chow mein noodles add a different type of crunch.

GOLDEN GREEN BEAN CRUNCH

PREP:

15 minutes

BAKE:

25 minutes + 5 minutes

MAKES:

4 to 6 servings

1   16-ounce package frozen French-cut green beans

1   10¾-ounce can condensed golden mushroom soup

1   8-ounce can sliced water chestnuts, drained (optional)

1   cup chow mein noodles or ½ of a 2.8-ounce can or ½ of a 2.8-ounce can French-fried onions (about ¾ cup)

1 Cook frozen beans according to package directions; drain well. In an ungreased 1½-quart casserole combine cooked beans, golden mushroom soup, and, if desired, water chestnuts.

2 Bake, uncovered, in a 350°F oven about 25 minutes or until bubbly around edges. Sprinkle with the chow mein noodles. Bake about 5 minutes more or until heated through.

Nutrition Facts per serving: 188 cal., 6 g total fat (1 g sat. fat), 3 mg chol., 719 mg sodium, 27 g carbo., 5 g fiber, 5 g pro.

Wax beans add an extra dimension of color to the mix, but if you prefer not to use them, just use another package or can of green beans.

HOME-STYLE GREEN BEAN BAKE

1	10¾-ounce can condensed cream of celery or cream of mushroom soup
½	cup shredded cheddar or American cheese (2 ounces)
1	2-ounce jar diced pimiento, drained (optional)
2	9-ounce packages frozen French-cut green beans, thawed and drained, or two 16-ounce cans French-cut green beans, drained
1	16-ounce can cut wax beans, drained
½	of a 2.8-ounce can French-fried onions (¾ cup)

PREP:
15 minutes
BAKE:
35 minutes + 5 minutes
MAKES:
6 servings

1 In a large bowl combine cream of celery soup, cheese, and, if desired, pimiento. Stir in green beans and wax beans. Transfer to an ungreased 1½-quart casserole.

2 Bake in a 350°F oven for 35 minutes. Remove from oven and stir; sprinkle with French-fried onions. Bake about 5 minutes more or until heated through.

Nutrition Facts per serving: 155 cal., 8 g total fat (3 g sat. fat), 15 mg chol., 686 mg sodium, 14 g carbo., 3 g fiber, 5 g pro.

This satisfying side dish has been in the Better Homes and Gardens *files for more than 50 years. Born in the days when canned-soup cooking was something new, it endures as a reason to get out the can opener.*

BARBECUED LIMAS

START TO FINISH:

25 minutes

MAKES:

6 servings

1   16-ounce package frozen baby lima beans

4   slices bacon, cut into ½-inch pieces

½   cup chopped onion

2   cloves garlic, minced

1   10¾-ounce can condensed tomato soup

2   tablespoons packed brown sugar

1   tablespoon white vinegar

1   tablespoon Worcestershire sauce

2   teaspoons yellow mustard

1   teaspoon chili powder

1 In a large saucepan cook lima beans according to package directions; drain and set aside.

2 Meanwhile, in the same large saucepan cook bacon, onion, and garlic over medium heat until bacon is brown and onion is tender. Stir in tomato soup, brown sugar, vinegar, Worcestershire sauce, mustard, and chili powder. Bring to boiling; reduce heat. Simmer, covered, for 5 minutes.

3 Stir cooked lima beans into tomato soup mixture; heat through.

Nutrition Facts per serving: 195 cal., 3 g total fat (1 g sat. fat), 5 mg chol., 487 mg sodium, 34 g carbo., 6 g fiber, 9 g pro.

This veggie-filled side-dish casserole is reminiscent of shepherd's pie, a mashed potato-topped meat casserole.

GARDENER'S PIE

1   16-ounce package frozen loose-pack vegetable medley (any combination), thawed

1   11-ounce can condensed cheddar cheese soup

½   teaspoon dried thyme, crushed

1   20-ounce package refrigerated mashed potatoes

1   cup shredded smoked cheddar cheese (4 ounces)

1   In an ungreased 1½-quart casserole combine vegetables, cheddar cheese soup, and thyme. Stir mashed potatoes to soften; spread carefully over vegetable mixture.

2   Bake, covered, in a 350°F oven for 30 minutes. Uncover and bake about 15 minutes more or until heated through, topping with cheese for the last 5 minutes of baking.

Nutrition Facts per serving: 239 cal., 11 g total fat (5 g sat. fat), 26 mg chol., 706 mg sodium, 28 g carbo., 4 g fiber, 11 g pro.

PREP:
15 minutes
BAKE:
30 minutes + 15 minutes
MAKES:
6 servings

With plenty of cheese and a creamy soup base, this dish might have just what it takes to get kids to eat their veggies.

CREAMY RICE & VEGETABLES

PREP:

20 minutes

COOK:

15 minutes

MAKES:

6 servings

¼ cup chopped onion

1 tablespoon butter or margarine

2 cups water

1 cup uncooked long grain rice

1 16-ounce package frozen loose-pack broccoli, cauliflower, and carrots

1 10¾-ounce can condensed cream of onion or cream of celery soup

⅛ teaspoon black pepper

1 cup shredded American cheese (4 ounces)

1 In a large saucepan cook onion in hot butter until tender. Add water and rice. Bring to boiling; reduce heat. Simmer, covered, for 5 minutes.

2 Add vegetables, cream of onion soup, and pepper. Return to boiling; reduce heat. Simmer, covered, for 15 to 20 minutes more or until rice is tender, stirring frequently. Stir in cheese until melted.

Nutrition Facts per serving: 274 cal., 11 g total fat (6 g sat. fat), 32 mg chol., 778 mg sodium, 35 g carbo., 3 g fiber, 9 g pro.

A little bit exotic, but still as comforting as a casserole can be, this recipe calls on curry powder and dried cherries to add a touch of intrigue.

CURRIED RICE-VEGETABLE BAKE

1	cup water
$^1\!/_2$	cup uncooked long grain rice
2	cups frozen loose-pack broccoli, cauliflower, and carrots
1	$10^3\!/_4$-ounce can condensed cream of celery soup
$^1\!/_2$	cup milk
1	3-ounce package cream cheese, cut up
1	to $1^1\!/_2$ teaspoons curry powder
1	teaspoon dried minced onion
$^1\!/_4$	cup snipped dried tart cherries or golden raisins
$^1\!/_3$	cup chopped peanuts

1 In a small saucepan bring water to boiling. Add rice. Return to boiling; reduce heat. Simmer, covered, about 15 minutes or until most of the water is absorbed and rice is tender. Let stand, covered, for 5 minutes. Cook vegetables according to package directions; drain.

2 Meanwhile, in an ungreased $1^1\!/_2$-quart casserole combine cream of celery soup, milk, cream cheese, curry powder, and minced onion. Stir in rice, drained vegetables, and cherries.

3 Bake, covered, in a 350°F oven for 25 minutes. Uncover and bake for 10 to 15 minutes more or until heated through. Sprinkle with peanuts.

Nutrition Facts per serving: 228 cal., 12 g total fat (5 g sat. fat), 23 mg chol., 546 mg sodium, 25 g carbo., 2 g fiber, 6 g pro.

PREP:
15 minutes
COOK:
15 minutes
BAKE:
25 minutes + 10 minutes
MAKES:
6 servings

Traditional risotto requires a lot of hands-on stirring duty. This one, which goes straight in the oven and is just stirred twice, was designed for people with better things to do!

EASY OVEN RISOTTO

PREP:

10 minutes

BAKE:

55 minutes

STAND:

10 minutes

MAKES:

6 servings

3¼   cups water

1   10¾-ounce can condensed cream of chicken and herbs, cream of chicken, or cream of celery soup

1¼   cups uncooked arborio or medium grain white rice

⅓   cup coarsely shredded carrot

¼   teaspoon salt

¼   teaspoon black pepper

½   cup frozen pea pods, thawed and bias-cut in half

½   cup finely shredded Parmesan cheese (2 ounces)

1 In an ungreased 2-quart casserole stir together water, cream of chicken and herbs soup, rice, carrot, salt, and pepper. Bake, covered, in a 375°F oven for 55 to 60 minutes or until rice is tender, stirring twice during baking.

2 Remove casserole from oven; gently stir in pea pods and Parmesan cheese. Let the risotto stand for 10 minutes before serving.

Nutrition Facts per serving: 137 cal., 4 g total fat (2 g sat. fat), 9 mg chol., 605 mg sodium, 21 g carbo., 1 g fiber, 6 g pro.

Here's a version of those great cheesy scalloped potatoes that everyone loves (including the cook, as they're easy as can be).

SHORTCUT POTATO SCALLOP

1   20-ounce package refrigerated diced potatoes with onion

1   4-ounce can (drained weight) sliced mushrooms, drained (optional)

1   10¾-ounce can condensed cheddar cheese soup

½   cup dairy sour cream

¼   teaspoon black pepper

1   cup cornflakes, finely crushed (½ cup)

1   tablespoon butter, melted

PREP:
15 minutes
BAKE:
25 minutes + 20 minutes
MAKES:
6 servings

1 In a large bowl stir together potatoes, mushrooms (if desired), cheddar cheese soup, sour cream, and pepper. Transfer to a greased 2-quart square baking dish. Bake, covered, in a 350°F oven for 25 minutes.

2 Meanwhile, in a small bowl combine crushed cornflakes and melted butter. Uncover potato mixture. Sprinkle with cornflake mixture. Bake, uncovered, about 20 minutes more or until hot in center.

Nutrition Facts per serving: 194 cal., 9 g total fat (5 g sat. fat), 19 mg chol., 649 mg sodium, 29 g carbo., 3 g fiber, 5 g pro.

For a meal that's kissed with a touch of the Irish, team these cheddary spuds with your favorite grilled or roasted meat or poultry.

POTATO-CABBAGE CASSEROLE

PREP:

25 minutes

BAKE:

30 minutes

MAKES:

6 servings

1	pound potatoes, sliced
2	tablespoons butter or margarine
⅓	cup chopped onion
8	cups shredded cabbage
1	10¾-ounce can condensed cream of mushroom soup
¾	cup milk
½	cup shredded cheddar cheese (2 ounces)
½	teaspoon black pepper
¼	teaspoon dried rosemary, crushed
⅛	teaspoon garlic salt
1	cup soft bread crumbs
2	tablespoons butter or margarine, melted

1 Place potatoes in a large saucepan; add enough water to cover. Bring to boiling; reduce heat. Simmer, covered, about 10 minutes or until tender. Drain; set aside.

2 Meanwhile, in a large saucepan or Dutch oven melt 2 tablespoons butter over medium heat. Add onion; cook until tender. Add cabbage; cover and cook about 5 minutes or just until cabbage is wilted. Stir in cream of mushroom soup, milk, cheese, pepper, rosemary, and garlic salt. Cook and stir until cheese is melted. Carefully stir in potatoes.

3 Spoon potato mixture into a lightly greased 2-quart square baking dish. In a small bowl stir together bread crumbs and 2 tablespoons melted butter; sprinkle over potato mixture.

4 Bake, uncovered, in a 350°F oven for 30 minutes.

Nutrition Facts per serving: 275 cal., 16 g total fat (5 g sat. fat), 13 mg chol., 594 mg sodium, 27 g carbo., 4 g fiber, 8 g pro.

Traditional scalloped potatoes—that ever-pleasing side dish—start with a white sauce, which takes a little more time than many cooks have today. A can of soup lets you skip that step!

CREAMY SCALLOPED POTATOES

1	tablespoon butter or margarine
½	cup chopped onion
½	cup chopped red and/or green sweet pepper
2	cloves garlic, minced
1	10¾-ounce can condensed cream of celery or cream of chicken soup
1	cup milk
⅛	teaspoon black pepper
4	cups sliced peeled potatoes (about 4 medium)
⅓	cup grated Parmesan cheese
½	cup soft bread crumbs
1	tablespoon butter or margarine, melted

PREP:
35 minutes
BAKE:
45 minutes + 20 minutes
STAND:
10 minutes
MAKES:
6 servings

1 In a medium saucepan melt 1 tablespoon butter over medium heat. Add onion, sweet pepper, and garlic; cook about 5 minutes or until tender, stirring occasionally. Stir in cream of celery soup, milk, and black pepper. Cook until bubbly, stirring occasionally.

2 Layer half of the potatoes in a lightly greased 2-quart rectangular baking dish. Cover with half (about 1⅓ cups) of the soup mixture. Sprinkle with 3 tablespoons of the Parmesan cheese. Layer with remaining potatoes and soup mixture. In a small bowl combine remaining Parmesan cheese, the bread crumbs, and melted butter; set aside.

3 Bake, covered, in a 350°F oven for 45 minutes. Uncover; sprinkle with bread crumb mixture. Bake about 20 minutes more or until potatoes are tender and crumbs are golden. Let stand 5 minutes before serving.

Nutrition Facts per serving: 202 cal., 9 g total fat (5 g sat. fat), 19 mg chol., 550 mg sodium, 24 g carbo., 2 g fiber, 6 g pro.

Use nacho cheese soup if you want a zestier dish. Either way, sprinkle these potatoes with chives or green onion for a little extra flavor and color.

CHEESY SCALLOPED POTATOES

PREP:

25 minutes

COOK:

20 minutes

BAKE:

25 minutes + 15 minutes

STAND:

10 minutes

MAKES:

6 servings

6 medium potatoes (2 pounds)

1 10¾-ounce can condensed cheddar cheese or nacho cheese soup

½ cup dairy sour cream

½ cup milk

¼ teaspoon salt

¼ teaspoon black pepper

1 to 2 tablespoons snipped fresh chives or sliced green onion

① In a covered large saucepan cook potatoes in a large amount of boiling salted water for 20 to 25 minutes or just until tender. Drain; cool slightly. Peel and slice potatoes. In a small bowl combine cheddar cheese cheese soup, sour cream, milk, salt, and pepper.

② Place half of the potato slices in an ungreased 2-quart square baking dish. Top with half of the soup mixture. Repeat with remaining potatoes and soup mixture.

③ Bake, covered, in a 375°F oven for 25 minutes. Uncover and bake about 15 minutes more or until heated through and potatoes are tender. Let stand for 10 minutes. Sprinkle with chives before serving.

Nutrition Facts per serving: 193 cal., 7 g total fat (4 g sat. fat), 15 mg chol., 522 mg sodium, 29 g carbo., 3 g fiber, 7 g pro.

Easy, cheesy, and incredibly lively, this super-simple dish is perfect to serve with roasted meats.

FIESTA POTATO BAKE

1   10¾-ounce can condensed cream of onion or cream of chicken soup

½   cup dairy sour cream

1   4-ounce can diced green chile peppers

4   cups frozen loose-pack diced hash brown potatoes with onion and peppers

1   cup shredded Colby and Monterey Jack cheese or taco cheese (4 ounces)

1 In a large bowl combine cream of onion soup, sour cream, and undrained chile peppers. Stir in potatoes and ½ cup of the cheese. Spoon potato mixture into an ungreased 2-quart square baking dish.

2 Bake, covered, in a 350°F oven for 40 minutes. Stir. Sprinkle with remaining cheese. Bake, uncovered, about 5 minutes more or until heated through.

Nutrition Facts per serving: 212 cal., 13 g total fat (7 g sat. fat), 32 mg chol., 583 mg sodium, 19 g carbo., 2 g fiber, 7 g pro.

PREP:
15 minutes

BAKE:
40 minutes + 5 minutes

MAKES:
6 servings

Creamy, cheesy potatoes are always a hit at family gatherings. Add a cornflake topper and they become downright irresistible.

CHEESY HASH BROWN POTATOES

PREP:

15 minutes

BAKE:

40 minutes + 10 minutes

STAND:

10 minutes

MAKES:

10 to 12 servings

1 30-ounce package frozen shredded hash brown potatoes, thawed

1 10¾-ounce can condensed cream of chicken soup

1 8-ounce carton dairy sour cream

8 ounces American cheese, shredded (2 cups)

¼ cup milk

¼ teaspoon garlic salt

2 cups cornflakes, crushed

¼ cup butter or margarine, melted

1 In a large bowl stir together potatoes, cream of chicken soup, sour cream, cheese, milk, and garlic salt. Transfer mixture to an ungreased 2-quart rectangular baking dish. In a small bowl stir together cornflakes and melted butter; set aside.

2 Bake potato mixture, covered, in a 350°F oven for 40 minutes. Uncover and stir. Sprinkle cornflake mixture over potato mixture. Bake about 10 minutes more or until heated through and topping is golden. Let stand for 10 minutes before serving.

Nutrition Facts per serving: 301 cal., 19 g total fat (11 g sat. fat), 47 mg chol., 702 mg sodium, 25 g carbo., 2 g fiber, 9 g pro.

This soup is based on knephla (dumpling) soup, a recipe that German immigrants brought to America.

POTATO DUMPLING SOUP

1⅓	cups all-purpose flour
½	teaspoon baking powder
¼	teaspoon salt
1	egg
⅔	cup milk
1	tablespoon butter
1	medium onion, chopped
2	medium potatoes, peeled and cubed
2	14-ounce cans reduced-sodium chicken broth
2	bay leaves
1⅓	cups whipping cream, half-and-half, or light cream
1	10¾-ounce can condensed cream of chicken soup
¼	teaspoon white pepper

PREP:
30 minutes

COOK:
15 minutes + 10 minutes + 5 minutes

MAKES:
6 servings

1 For dumpling dough, in a medium bowl stir together flour, baking powder, and salt. Make a well in center of flour mixture. In a small bowl whisk together egg and milk. Add egg mixture to flour mixture; mix well. Cover and set aside.

2 For soup, in a large saucepan melt butter over medium heat. Add onion. Cook and stir for 3 to 5 minutes or until onion is tender. Add potatoes, chicken broth, and bay leaves. Bring to boiling; reduce heat. Simmer, covered, for 15 minutes. Drop rounded teaspoons of the dumpling dough into potato mixture (don't worry if dumplings touch). Return to boiling; reduce heat. Simmer, uncovered, for 10 to 15 minutes or until potatoes are tender and dumplings float.

3 In a medium bowl stir together whipping cream, cream of chicken soup, and white pepper; add to potato mixture. Cook and stir about 5 minutes more or until heated through. Discard bay leaves.

Nutrition Facts per serving: 427 cal., 27 g total fat (15 g sat. fat), 120 mg chol., 936 mg sodium, 37 g carbo., 2 g fiber, 10 g pro.

If you're lucky enough to have fresh thyme growing in your garden or window box, use it! You'll need three times the amount of dried; stir it in toward the end of cooking time.

SQUASH-POTATO CHOWDER

1   tablespoon butter or margarine

1   cup sliced carrot

½   cup chopped onion

½   teaspoon bottled minced garlic (1 clove)

¾   teaspoon dried thyme, crushed

¼   teaspoon salt

⅛   to ¼ teaspoon black pepper

2   cups cubed yellow summer squash or zucchini

1   10¾-ounce can condensed cream of potato soup

2   cups milk

1 In a large saucepan melt butter over medium-low heat. Add carrot, onion, garlic, thyme, salt, and pepper. Cover and cook for 10 minutes, stirring occasionally. Stir in squash; cover and cook for 2 to 3 minutes more or until vegetables are crisp-tender.

2 Stir in cream of potato soup. Gradually stir in milk until combined; heat through.

Nutrition Facts per serving: 122 cal., 5 g total fat (3 g sat. fat), 16 mg chol., 543 mg sodium, 15 g carbo., 2 g fiber, 4 g pro.

Bacon adds a smoky angle to this luscious corn chowder, while a can of soup adds convenience.

CORN-BACON CHOWDER

5 slices bacon, chopped

1 medium onion, halved and thinly sliced

2 cups milk

2 cups frozen loose-pack corn

1 10¾-ounce can condensed cream of mushroom soup

1 cup diced cooked potato

¼ teaspoon black pepper

START TO FINISH:
25 minutes
MAKES:
4 to 6 servings

1 In a large saucepan cook bacon until crisp. Remove bacon with a slotted spoon, reserving 2 tablespoons of drippings in saucepan; drain bacon on paper towels.

2 Cook onion slices in reserved drippings over medium heat until tender. Stir in milk, corn, cream of mushroom soup, potato, and pepper.

3 Bring mixture to boiling; reduce heat. Simmer, uncovered, for 2 to 3 minutes. Remove from heat. Top servings with crumbled bacon.

Nutrition Facts per serving: 329 cal., 18 g total fat (7 g sat. fat), 24 mg chol., 750 mg sodium, 34 g carbo., 2 g fiber, 11 g pro.

Flag this recipe for a quick weekend lunch. Imagine how great it will taste with a simple ham sandwich.

BROCCOLI CHOWDER

START TO FINISH:

20 minutes

MAKES:

4 servings

½	cup water
1	10-ounce package frozen chopped broccoli
1	tablespoon dried minced onion
1	10¾-ounce can condensed cream of chicken soup
1	cup milk
1	cup shredded cheddar cheese (4 ounces)
⅛	teaspoon cayenne pepper
	Croutons (optional)

① In a medium saucepan bring water to boiling. Add broccoli and onion. Simmer, covered, about 5 minutes or until broccoli is crisp-tender. Do not drain. Stir in cream of chicken soup, milk, cheese, and cayenne pepper. Cook and stir about 4 minutes or until heated through. If desired, sprinkle servings with croutons.

Nutrition Facts per serving: 242 cal., 16 g total fat (8 g sat. fat), 40 mg chol., 824 mg sodium, 13 g carbo., 2 g fiber, 13 g pro.

Beer-cheese soups are a sports bar favorite. Bring the specialty home with this easy rendition and enjoy it with a deli-meat sandwich while cheering on your favorite team.

EASY BEER-CHEESE SOUP

2	cups frozen loose-pack cauliflower, broccoli, and carrots
½	cup beer
1	tablespoon dried minced onion
1	10¾-ounce can condensed cream of celery soup
1	cup milk
1½	cups shredded cheddar cheese (6 ounces)
	Croutons (optional)

START TO FINISH:
20 minutes
MAKES:
4 servings

1 In a 2-quart microwavable casserole combine vegetables, beer, and dried minced onion. Microwave, covered, on 100% power (high) for 3 to 4 minutes or until vegetables are nearly tender.

2 Stir in cream of celery soup and milk. Stir in cheese. Microwave, covered, on high for 6 to 8 minutes or until mixture is hot and bubbly. If desired, sprinkle servings with croutons.

Nutrition Facts per serving: 287 cal., 19 g total fat (11 g sat. fat), 58 mg chol., 936 mg sodium, 13 g carbo., 2 g fiber, 15 g pro.

RANGE-TOP METHOD: In a medium saucepan combine vegetables, beer, and dried minced onion. Bring to boiling; reduce heat. Simmer, covered, for 5 to 7 minutes or until vegetables are barely tender. Stir in cream of celery soup and milk. Heat through. Stir in cheese until melted. Serve as directed.

Looking to add a little zing to your holiday meal? Try this Southwest-inspired recipe. It's studded with chile peppers, sweet peppers, olives, and more for a colorful side dish your guests will remember.

SOUTHWESTERN CORN BREAD DRESSING

PREP:

25 minutes

BAKE:

20 minutes + 35 minutes + 5 minutes

COOL:

20 minutes

MAKES:

16 to 20 servings

1	cup all-purpose flour
1	cup cornmeal
3	tablespoons sugar
1	tablespoon baking powder
3	eggs
1	cup milk
¼	cup cooking oil
5	cups chopped yellow summer squash
1	cup chopped celery
¾	cup chopped green sweet pepper
½	cup chopped onion
⅓	cup butter or margarine
1	4-ounce can diced green chile peppers, undrained
½	cup sliced pitted ripe olives
1	10¾-ounce can condensed cream of mushroom soup
½	to ¾ cup milk
¾	cup shredded Monterey Jack cheese with jalapeño peppers

1 For corn bread, grease the bottom and ½ inch up the sides of a 9×9×2-inch baking pan; set aside. Stir together flour, cornmeal, sugar, baking powder, and ½ teaspoon salt. Make a well in flour mixture; set aside. In a small bowl beat 2 of the eggs with a fork; stir in the 1 cup milk and the cooking oil. Add egg mixture to flour mixture. Stir just until moistened (batter should be lumpy). Spread batter in prepared baking pan.

2 Bake in a 425°F oven about 20 minutes or until a toothpick comes out clean. Cool in pan on a wire rack. Remove corn bread from pan; coarsely crumble. Reduce oven temperature to 350°F. Meanwhile, grease a 3-quart rectangular baking dish. In a covered saucepan cook squash in boiling water about 5 minutes or just until tender. Drain; transfer to a large bowl.

3 In a large skillet cook celery, sweet pepper, and onion in hot butter until tender. Add to squash in bowl; stir in chile peppers and olives. Beat remaining egg; combine egg, cream of mushroom soup, and ½ cup milk. Add to squash mixture; mix well. Add corn bread; stir gently to combine. Add enough of the remaining milk to moisten. Transfer mixture to prepared baking dish. Bake, covered, for 35 minutes. Sprinkle with cheese. Bake about 5 minutes more or until cheese is melted.

Nutrition Facts per serving: 247 cal., 15 g total fat (9 g sat. fat), 75 mg chol., 517 mg sodium, 21 g carbo., 2 g fiber, 6 g pro.

Never underestimate the power of pancakes to stand in for supper on busy nights. Serve alongside cooked kielbasa and a dish of applesauce for a hearty dinner or a fresh fruit salad for a lighter meal.

POTATO & VEGETABLE PANCAKES

1   10¾-ounce can condensed cream of potato soup

½   cup all-purpose flour

3   slightly beaten eggs

2   tablespoons butter or margarine, melted

½   cup shredded carrot and/or finely chopped red sweet pepper

1   tablespoon finely chopped onion

2   slices bacon, crisp-cooked, drained, and crumbled, or 2 tablespoons cooked bacon pieces (optional)

   Dairy sour cream (optional)

START TO FINISH:

30 minutes

MAKES:

9 to 10 pancakes (4 to 5 servings)

1 In a medium bowl combine cream of potato soup and flour; stir in eggs and melted butter. Fold in carrot, onion, and, if desired, bacon.

2 Heat a lightly greased griddle or heavy skillet over medium heat until a few drops of water sprinkled on griddle dance across the surface. For each pancake, pour about ¼ cup batter onto the hot griddle. Spread batter into a circle about 4 inches in diameter.

3 Cook over medium heat until pancakes are golden, flipping to cook underside when pancake surfaces are bubbly and edges are slightly dry (1 to 2 minutes per side). Serve immediately or keep warm in a loosely covered ovenproof dish in a 300°F oven. If desired, serve with sour cream.

Nutrition Facts per pancake: 97 cal., 5 g total fat (3 g sat. fat), 80 mg chol., 321 mg sodium, 9 g carbo., 1 g fiber, 3 g pro.

Thanks to a can of potato soup, you can have a moist, light-textured potato bread without peeling, boiling, or mashing potatoes!

POTATO BREAD WITH SOUR CREAM & CHIVES

PREP:

30 minutes

RISE:

45 minutes + 30 minutes

BAKE:

20 minutes

MAKES:

2 loaves (24 servings)

6¼   to 6¾ cups all-purpose flour

2   packages active dry yeast

1½   cups milk

2   tablespoons sugar

2   tablespoons butter

2   teaspoons salt

1   10¾-ounce can condensed cream of potato soup

½   cup dairy sour cream

¼   cup snipped fresh chives

1   teaspoon dried tarragon, crushed, or 1 teaspoon dried dill

1 In large mixing bowl combine 2½ cups of the flour and the yeast. In a medium saucepan heat and stir milk, sugar, butter, and salt just until warm (120° to 130°F) and butter almost melts. Add milk mixture to flour mixture along with cream of potato soup, sour cream, chives, and tarragon. Beat with an electric mixer on low speed for 30 seconds, scraping side of bowl constantly. Beat on high speed for 3 minutes. Using a wooden spoon, stir in as much of the remaining flour as you can.

2 Turn out dough onto a lightly floured surface. Knead in enough of the remaining flour to make a moderately stiff dough that is smooth and elastic (6 to 8 minutes). Shape dough into a ball. Place in a lightly greased bowl, turning once to grease surface. Cover; let rise in a warm place until double in size (45 to 60 minutes).

3 Punch down dough. Cover; let rest for 10 minutes. Meanwhile, lightly grease two 9×5×3-inch loaf pans. Divide dough in half; shape into two loaves. Place into prepared pans. Cover and let rise in a warm place until nearly double in size (30 to 40 minutes).

4 Bake in a 400°F oven for 20 to 25 minutes or until bread sounds hollow when lightly tapped. Immediately remove bread from pans. Cool on wire racks.

Nutrition Facts per serving: 150 cal., 3 g total fat (2 g sat. fat), 7 mg chol., 309 mg sodium, 26 g carbo., 1 g fiber, 4 g pro.

SLOW COOKER FAVORITES

7

Ladle the wonderfully rich gravy—made simple with condensed cream of celery soup—over the tender steak and noodles for a real home-style main dish the family will love.

ROUND STEAK WITH HERBS

PREP:

15 minutes

COOK:

*10 to 12 hours
(low-heat setting) or*

*5 to 6 hours
(high-heat setting)*

MAKES:

6 servings

2 pounds beef round steak, cut ¾ inch thick

1 medium onion, sliced

1 10¾-ounce can condensed cream of celery soup

½ teaspoon dried oregano, crushed

¼ teaspoon dried thyme, crushed

¼ teaspoon black pepper

Hot cooked noodles

1 Trim fat from round steak. Cut meat into 6 serving-size pieces. Place onion in a 3½- or 4-quart slow cooker; place meat over onion. In a small bowl combine cream of celery soup, oregano, thyme, and pepper; pour over meat.

2 Cover and cook on low-heat setting for 10 to 12 hours or on high-heat setting for 5 to 6 hours. Serve over noodles.

Nutrition Facts per serving: 398 cal., 15 g total fat (5 g sat. fat), 120 mg chol., 456 mg sodium, 25 g carbo., 2 g fiber, 38 g pro.

Turn up the flavor a bit by adding salsa to this ever-pleasing saucy steak. It's still as family-pleasing (and easy) as ever.

SALSA SWISS STEAK

2 pounds boneless beef round steak, cut ¾ inch thick

1 large green sweet pepper, cut into bite-size strips

1 medium onion, sliced

1 10¾-ounce can condensed cream of mushroom soup

1 cup bottled salsa

2 tablespoons all-purpose flour

1 teaspoon dry mustard

Hot cooked rice

1 Trim fat from meat. Cut meat into 6 serving-size pieces. In a 3½- or 4-quart slow cooker place meat, sweet pepper, and onion.

2 In a medium bowl combine cream of mushroom soup, salsa, flour, and dry mustard. Pour over mixture in slow cooker.

3 Cover and cook on low-heat setting for 9 to 10 hours or on high-heat setting for 4½ to 5 hours. Serve over hot cooked rice.

Nutrition Facts per serving: 410 cal., 12 g total fat (4 g sat. fat), 66 mg chol., 533 mg sodium, 32 g carbo., 2 g fiber, 41 g pro.

PREP:

20 minutes

COOK:

9 to 10 hours (low-heat setting) or

4¹/₂ to 5 hours (high-heat setting)

MAKES:

6 servings

Paprikash (PAH-pree-kash) is a Hungarian dish that's often made with meat, onions, and—as its name suggests—paprika. This long-braising old-world stew is a shoo-in for the slow cooker.

EASY HUNGARIAN PAPRIKASH

PREP:

20 minutes

COOK:

8 to 10 hours (low) or
4 to 5 hours (high)

MAKES:

8 servings

2 pounds lean beef stew meat

2 medium onions, sliced

1 cup chopped red or green sweet pepper

1 4-ounce can (drained weight) sliced mushrooms, drained

1 14½-ounce can diced tomatoes, drained

1 10¾-ounce can condensed cream of mushroom soup

1 tablespoon paprika

1 teaspoon dried thyme, crushed

¼ teaspoon coarsely ground black pepper

8 cups hot cooked noodles

½ cup dairy sour cream

① Cut meat into 1-inch pieces. Set aside. In a 3½- or 4-quart slow cooker place onions and sweet pepper. Add meat and mushrooms.

② In a medium bowl stir together tomatoes, cream of mushroom soup, paprika, thyme, and black pepper. Pour over mixture in cooker.

③ Cover and cook on low-heat setting for 8 to 10 hours or on high-heat setting for 4 to 5 hours. Serve meat mixture over hot cooked noodles. Top servings with sour cream.

Nutrition Facts per serving: 452 cal., 12 g total fat (4 g sat. fat), 126 mg chol., 503 mg sodium, 50 g carbo., 4 g fiber, 34 g pro.

Doctor a can of minestrone soup, take advantage of your slow cooker, and you'll have a warming one-bowl supper you'll love coming home to on a wintry night.

HEARTY BEEF & BEAN MEDLEY

1½	pounds lean ground beef
2	10¾-ounce cans condensed minestrone soup
1	21-ounce can pork and beans in tomato sauce
1	12-ounce can tomato juice
1	cup sliced celery
1	cup chopped onion
1	cup water
2	teaspoons Worcestershire sauce
1	teaspoon dried oregano, crushed
¼	teaspoon black pepper
1	clove garlic, minced

PREP:
20 minutes

COOK:
*7 to 8 hours
(low-heat setting) or*
*3½ to 4 hours
(high-heat setting)*

MAKES:
8 servings

1 In a large skillet cook ground beef until meat is brown. Drain off fat.

2 Transfer meat to a 3½- or 4-quart slow cooker. Stir in minestrone soup, pork and beans, tomato juice, celery, onion, water, Worcestershire sauce, oregano, pepper, and garlic.

3 Cover and cook on low-heat setting for 7 to 8 hours or on high-heat setting for 3½ to 4 hours.

Nutrition Facts per serving: 287 cal., 10 g total fat (4 g sat. fat), 62 mg chol., 1,116 mg sodium, 28 g carbo., 7 g fiber, 22 g pro.

Stock up on frozen meatballs. For something off the beaten path, try them in this sumptuously saucy and super-easy presentation.

MEATBALLS IN DRIED TOMATO GRAVY

PREP:

15 minutes

COOK:

*5 to 6 hours
(low-heat setting) or*

*2¹/₂ to 3 hours
(high-heat setting)*

MAKES:

8 servings

1   10³/₄-ounce can condensed cream of mushroom with roasted garlic soup

1   cup water

1   4-ounce can (drained weight) sliced mushrooms, drained

¹/₂   cup snipped dried tomatoes (not oil packed)

¹/₂   cup chopped onion

¹/₂   teaspoon dried basil, crushed

¹/₂   teaspoon dried oregano, crushed

¹/₈   teaspoon black pepper

2   16-ounce packages frozen cooked Italian meatballs, thawed

1   recipe Polenta or 4 cups hot cooked noodles

1   In a 3¹/₂- or 4-quart slow cooker combine cream of mushroom soup, water, mushrooms, dried tomatoes, onion, basil, oregano, and pepper. Stir in thawed meatballs.

2   Cover and cook on low-heat setting for 5 to 6 hours or on high-heat setting for 2¹/₂ to 3 hours. Serve meatball mixture over Polenta.

POLENTA: In a large saucepan bring 3 cups milk just to simmering over medium heat. In a medium bowl stir together 1 cup cornmeal, 1 cup water, and 1 teaspoon salt. Stir cornmeal mixture slowly into hot milk. Cook and stir until mixture comes to boiling; reduce heat to low. Cook, uncovered, for 10 to 15 minutes or until mixture is thick, stirring occasionally. (If mixture is too thick, stir in additional milk.) Stir in 2 tablespoons butter or margarine until melted.

Nutrition Facts per serving: 525 cal., 33 g total fat (16 g sat. fat), 89 mg chol., 1,599 mg sodium, 31 g carbo., 7 g fiber, 25 g pro.

Taco flavors enliven this meat-and-potato bake. It's perfect for anyone who has a hearty appetite, from teens to tailgaters.

NACHO-STYLE CASSEROLE

1 pound lean ground beef

1 cup chopped onion

1 11-ounce can condensed nacho cheese soup

1 cup milk

1 4-ounce can diced green chile peppers

6 medium potatoes, cut into wedges (about 2 pounds)

¼ teaspoon garlic salt

Dairy sour cream (optional)

Bottled salsa (optional)

Sliced green onions (optional)

Shredded cheddar cheese (optional)

PREP:

20 minutes

COOK:

*7 to 8 hours
(low-heat setting) or*

*3½ to 4 hours
(high-heat setting)*

MAKES:

4 servings

1 In a large skillet cook ground beef and onion until meat is brown. Drain off fat. In a medium bowl stir together nacho cheese soup, milk, and chile peppers. Add beef mixture.

2 Place potato wedges in a 3½- or 4-quart slow cooker. Sprinkle with garlic salt. Spoon beef mixture over potatoes.

3 Cover and cook on low-heat setting for 7 to 8 hours or on high-heat setting for 3½ to 4 hours or until potatoes are tender.

4 Gently stir potato mixture just before serving. If desired, serve with sour cream, salsa, green onions, and/or shredded cheese.

Nutrition Facts per servings: 550 cal., 23 g total fat (10 g sat. fat), 90 mg chol., 809 mg sodium, 52 g carbo., 6 g fiber, 32 g pro.

A can of tomato soup brings just the right consistency and homey tomato flavor to these perfectly seasoned sloppy-joe-style sandwiches.

SAUCY CHEESEBURGER SANDWICHES

PREP:

20 minutes

COOK:

*6 to 8 hours
(low-heat setting) or*

*3 to 4 hours
(high-heat setting)*

*+ 5 to 10 minutes
(low-heat setting)*

MAKES:

12 to 15 servings

2½ pounds lean ground beef

1 10¾-ounce can condensed tomato soup

1 cup finely chopped onion

¼ cup water

2 tablespoons tomato paste

1 tablespoon Worcestershire sauce

1 tablespoon yellow mustard

2 teaspoons dried Italian seasoning, crushed

¼ teaspoon black pepper

2 cloves garlic, minced

6 ounces American cheese, cut into cubes

12 to 15 hamburger buns, split and toasted

1 In a 12-inch skillet cook ground beef until brown. Drain off fat. Transfer meat to a 3½- or 4-quart slow cooker. Stir in tomato soup, onion, water, tomato paste, Worcestershire sauce, mustard, Italian seasoning, pepper, and garlic.

2 Cover and cook on low-heat setting for 6 to 8 hours or on high-heat setting for 3 to 4 hours.

3 If using high-heat setting, turn to low-heat setting. Stir in American cheese. Cover and cook for 5 to 10 minutes more or until cheese is melted. Serve meat mixture on hamburger buns.

Nutrition Facts per serving: 357 cal., 16 g total fat (7 g sat. fat), 73 mg chol., 664 mg sodium, 28 g carbo., 2 g fiber, 25 g pro.

Come Saturday, get this family-pleasing meal together, then go about your day—from sports matches and piano recitals to shopping sprees. Then come home to a cheeseburger-flavored pie the kids will love digging into.

CHEESEBURGER PIE

1 20-ounce package refrigerated mashed potatoes (2⅔ cups)
1 teaspoon dried oregano, crushed
¼ teaspoon garlic salt
2 pounds lean ground beef
1 cup chopped onion
½ cup chopped green sweet pepper
2 cloves garlic, minced
2 14½-ounce cans Italian-style stewed tomatoes, undrained
1 10¾-ounce can condensed cheddar cheese soup
½ cup shredded cheddar cheese (2 ounces)

PREP:
25 minutes
COOK:
4½ to 5 hours (low-heat setting)
MAKES:
6 servings

1 In a medium bowl stir together mashed potatoes, oregano, and garlic salt; set aside.

2 In a large skillet cook ground beef, onion, sweet pepper, and garlic until meat is brown and vegetables are tender, stirring occasionally. Drain off fat. Stir in tomatoes and cheddar cheese soup.

3 Transfer meat mixture to a 3½- to 4½-quart slow cooker. Spoon mashed potato mixture into mounds on top of meat mixture.

4 Cover and cook on low-heat setting for 4½ to 5 hours. Sprinkle with cheddar cheese.

Nutrition Facts per serving: 467 cal., 23 g total fat (9 g sat. fat), 112 mg chol., 990 mg sodium, 30 g carbo., 3 g fiber, 35 g pro.

When the meat counter doesn't have three-fourths-inch-thick chops, ask a butcher to cut a bone-in pork top loin roast into three-fourths-inch-slices.

DIJON PORK CHOPS

PREP:

20 minutes

COOK:

*7 to 8 hours
(low-heat setting) or

3$\frac{1}{2}$ to 4 hours
(high-heat setting)*

MAKES:

4 servings

1	10¾-ounce can condensed cream of mushroom soup
¼	cup dry white wine or chicken broth
¼	cup Dijon-style mustard
1	teaspoon dried thyme, crushed
1	clove garlic, minced
¼	teaspoon black pepper
5	medium potatoes, cut into ¼-inch-thick slices (about 1⅔ pounds)
1	medium onion, sliced
4	pork loin chops, cut ¾ inch thick

1 In a large bowl combine cream of mushroom soup, wine, mustard, thyme, garlic, and pepper. Add potatoes and onion, stirring to coat. Transfer to a 4- to 5-quart slow cooker. Trim fat from chops. Place chops on potato mixture.

2 Cover and cook on low-heat setting for 7 to 8 hours or on high-heat setting for 3½ to 4 hours.

Nutrition Facts per serving: 385 cal., 12 g total fat (3 g sat. fat), 48 mg chol., 658 mg sodium, 39 g carbo., 4 g fiber, 26 g pro.

This might remind you of one of those filling skillet dinners served at popular chain restaurants. This recipe, adapted for the slow cooker, lets you bring the specialty home.

PORK CHOPS O'BRIEN

Nonstick cooking spray

5 cups frozen loose-pack diced hash brown potatoes with onion and peppers, thawed

1 10¾-ounce can reduced-fat and reduced-sodium condensed cream of mushroom soup

½ cup bottled roasted red sweet peppers, drained and chopped

½ cup dairy sour cream

½ cup shredded Colby and Monterey Jack cheese (2 ounces)

¼ teaspoon black pepper

4 pork loin chops, cut ¾ inch thick

1 tablespoon cooking oil

1 2.8-ounce can French-fried onions

1 Lightly coat a 3½- or 4-quart slow cooker with nonstick cooking spray; set aside. In a large bowl combine potatoes, cream of mushroom soup, roasted sweet peppers, sour cream, cheese, and black pepper. Transfer potato mixture to slow cooker.

2 Trim fat from chops. In a large skillet brown chops on both sides in hot oil. Drain off fat. Place chops on top of mixture in slow cooker.

3 Cover and cook on low-heat setting for 7 to 9 hours or on high-heat setting for 3½ to 4½ hours. Before serving, sprinkle with French-fried onions.

Nutrition Facts per serving: 670 cal., 29 g total fat (9 g sat. fat), 92 mg chol., 639 mg sodium, 64 g carbo., 4 g fiber, 37 g pro.

PREP:
20 minutes

COOK:
7 to 9 hours (low-heat setting) or
3½ to 4½ hours (high-heat setting)

MAKES:
4 servings

A splash of apple juice gives a fresh taste to this earthy comfort dish. For dessert, toss some sliced apples in the oven to bake while you eat; serve them warm over ice cream.

MUSHROOM-SAUCED PORK CHOPS

PREP:

20 minutes

COOK:

8 to 9 hours (low-heat setting) or

4 to 4$\frac{1}{2}$ hours (high-heat setting)

MAKES:

4 servings

4 pork loin chops, cut $\frac{3}{4}$ inch thick

1 tablespoon cooking oil

1 small onion, thinly sliced

2 tablespoons quick-cooking tapioca

1 10$\frac{3}{4}$-ounce can condensed cream of mushroom soup

$\frac{1}{2}$ cup apple juice

1 4-ounce can (drained weight) sliced mushrooms, drained

2 teaspoons Worcestershire sauce

$\frac{3}{4}$ teaspoon dried thyme, crushed

$\frac{1}{4}$ teaspoon garlic powder

Hot cooked rice or mashed potatoes

1 Trim fat from chops. In a skillet brown chops on both sides in hot oil. Drain off fat. In a 3$\frac{1}{2}$- or 4-quart slow cooker place onion; add chops. Grind tapioca with a mortar and pestle. In a medium bowl combine tapioca, cream of mushroom soup, apple juice, mushrooms, Worcestershire sauce, thyme, and garlic powder; pour over chops.

2 Cover and cook on low-heat setting for 8 to 9 hours or on high-heat setting for 4 to 4$\frac{1}{2}$ hours. Serve over rice.

Nutrition Facts per serving: 354 cal., 16 g total fat (5 g sat. fat), 77 mg chol., 740 mg sodium, 17 g carbo., 1 g fiber, 33 g pro.

FOR 5- TO 6-QUART SLOW COOKER: Use 6 pork loin chops, cut $\frac{3}{4}$ inch thick. Leave remaining ingredient amounts the same and prepare as directed. Makes 6 servings.

If you like, serve the coleslaw in the sandwich. It makes for a sloppy knife-and-fork treat, but some barbecue enthusiasts wouldn't have it any other way.

BBQ PORK SANDWICHES

2   large green sweet peppers, cut into strips
1   medium onion, thinly sliced and separated into rings
2   tablespoons quick-cooking tapioca
1   2½- to 3-pound pork shoulder roast
1   11-ounce can condensed tomato bisque soup
3   to 4 teaspoons chili powder
½   teaspoon ground cumin
¼   teaspoon salt
8   to 10 kaiser rolls, split and toasted
    Coleslaw, drained (optional)

PREP:

20 minutes

COOK:

*11 to 12 hours
(low-heat setting) or*

*5½ to 6 hours
(high-heat setting)*

*+ 15 to 30 minutes
(high-heat setting)*

MAKES:

8 to 10 servings

1 In a 3½- to 5-quart slow cooker combine sweet pepper strips and onion rings. Sprinkle tapioca over vegetables. Trim fat from roast. If necessary, cut roast to fit into slow cooker. Place roast over vegetables.

2 For sauce, in a small bowl combine tomato bisque soup, chili powder, cumin, and salt. Pour over roast.

3 Cover and cook on low-heat setting for 11 to 12 hours or on high-heat setting for 5½ to 6 hours.

4 Remove roast and sauce from slow cooker; thinly slice or shred the meat. Skim fat from sauce. Return meat to slow cooker; add enough sauce to moisten meat. Cover. If using low-heat setting, turn slow cooker to high-heat setting. Cook for 15 to 30 minutes more or until heated through.

5 Serve meat mixture on kaiser rolls. If desired, serve with coleslaw.

Nutrition Facts per serving: 450 cal., 14 g total fat (4 g sat. fat), 97 mg chol., 811 mg sodium, 44 g carbo., 3 g fiber, 35 g pro.

Diced ham simmers with the vegetables in this slow cooker dish, giving it a wonderfully rich flavor.

SIMPLE SUCCOTASH WITH HAM

PREP:

20 minutes

COOK:

*7 to 9 hours
(low-heat setting) or*

*3^1/$_2$ to 4^1/$_2$ hours
(high-heat setting)*

MAKES:

6 servings

1	16-ounce package frozen baby lima beans, thawed
1	16-ounce package frozen whole kernel corn, thawed
2^1/$_2$	cups diced cooked ham (about 13 ounces)
1	10^1/$_2$-ounce can condensed chicken white and wild rice soup
1	cup coarsely chopped red or green sweet pepper
^{1}/$_2$	cup chopped onion
^{1}/$_2$	cup chopped celery
^{1}/$_4$	teaspoon black pepper
2	cloves garlic, minced
^{1}/$_2$	cup chicken broth

1 In a 4- to 5-quart slow cooker combine lima beans, corn, ham, chicken white and wild rice soup, sweet pepper, onion, celery, black pepper, and garlic. Pour chicken broth over all.

2 Cover and cook on low-heat setting for 7 to 9 hours or on high-heat setting for 3^1/$_2$ to 4^1/$_2$ hours.

Nutrition Facts per serving: 288 cal., 5 g total fat (1 g sat. fat), 44 mg chol., 1,190 mg sodium, 42 g carbo., 8 g fiber, 20 g pro.

Did you know that stuffed baked potatoes are a popular pub food in England? Why not serve these—with glasses of English beer—next time you're having your "mates" over for an informal get-together?

HAM & BROCCOLI POTATOES

2	cups shredded smoked Gouda cheese (8 ounces)
1	10¾-ounce can condensed cream of celery or cream of chicken soup
1	10-ounce package frozen chopped broccoli, thawed
8	ounces diced cooked ham
6	medium potatoes, baked and split*
1	tablespoon snipped fresh chives

PREP:
15 minutes
COOK:
1½ to 2½ hours
MAKES:
6 servings

1 In a 1½-quart slow cooker combine Gouda cheese, cream of celery soup, frozen broccoli, and ham.

2 Cover and cook, on low-heat setting if available,** for 1½ to 2½ hours.

3 Stir before serving. Spoon ham mixture over baked potatoes. Sprinkle with chives.

*NOTE: Bake the potatoes while the ham and broccoli mixture cooks. To bake potatoes, scrub potatoes and pat dry. Prick potatoes with a fork. (If desired, for soft skins, rub potatoes with shortening or wrap each potato in foil.) Bake potatoes in a 425°F oven for 40 to 60 minutes or until tender. Roll each potato gently under your hand. Using a knife, cut an X in top of each potato. Press in and up on ends of each potato.

**NOTE: Some 1½-quart slow cookers include variable heat setting; others offer only one standard (low) setting. The 1½-quart slow cooker recipes in this book were only tested on the low-heat setting, if one was present.

TEST KITCHEN TIP: For a 3½- or 4-quart slow cooker, double the recipe. Cover and cook on low-heat setting for 3½ to 4 hours.

Nutrition Facts per serving: 352 cal., 16 g total fat (9 g sat. fat), 53 mg chol., 1,487 mg sodium, 34 g carbo., 4 g fiber, 19 g pro.

If you're going to a "bring-a-dish" gathering with people you don't know, take a sure thing. This chicken and stuffing dish is a perennial pleaser.

CHICKEN & STUFFING CASSEROLE

PREP:

30 minutes

COOK:

*4¹/₂ to 5 hours
(low-heat setting)*

MAKES:

16 to 20 servings

¹/₂	cup butter or margarine
1	cup thinly sliced celery
³/₄	cup chopped onion
	Nonstick cooking spray
1	6-ounce package long grain and wild rice mix
1	14-ounce package uncooked herb-seasoned stuffing croutons
4	cups cubed cooked chicken (about 1¹/₄ pounds)
1	8-ounce can sliced mushrooms, drained
¹/₄	cup snipped fresh parsley
1¹/₂	teaspoons poultry seasoning
¹/₄	teaspoon black pepper
2	eggs
2	14-ounce cans reduced-sodium chicken broth
1	10³/₄-ounce can reduced-fat and reduced-sodium condensed cream of chicken or cream of mushroom soup

1 In a large skillet heat butter over medium heat until melted. Add celery and onion; cook about 5 minutes or until vegetables are tender. Set aside.

2 Lightly coat a 5¹/₂- or 6-quart slow cooker with nonstick cooking spray. Add rice mix (reserve seasoning packet). Using a slotted spoon, transfer vegetables to slow cooker, reserving butter. Stir to combine.

3 Place croutons in a large bowl. Stir in reserved butter, chicken, mushrooms, parsley, poultry seasoning, pepper, and seasoning packet from rice mix.

4 In a large bowl beat eggs with a fork; stir in chicken broth and cream of chicken soup. Pour over crouton mixture, tossing gently to moisten. Transfer mixture to slow cooker.

5 Cover and cook on low-heat setting for 4¹/₂ to 5 hours. Stir gently before serving.

Nutrition Facts per serving: 287 cal., 11 g total fat (5 g sat. fat), 76 mg chol., 903 mg sodium, 31 g carbo., 3 g fiber, 16 g pro.

Mashed potatoes—with all that peeling, boiling, and mashing—didn't used to qualify as hassle-free fare. Now they do! Refrigerated mashed potatoes make a satisfying topper for this casserole-style dish.

CREAMY POTATO-TOPPED CHICKEN & VEGETABLES

1	16-ounce package peeled baby carrots
1	medium onion, cut into wedges
2	pounds skinless, boneless chicken thighs
1	10¾-ounce can condensed cream of chicken or cream of mushroom soup
1	teaspoon dried basil, crushed
¼	teaspoon black pepper
1	20-ounce package refrigerated mashed potatoes
½	cup shredded cheddar cheese (2 ounces)
4	cloves garlic, minced

PREP:

20 minutes

COOK:

7 to 8 hours
(low-heat setting) or

3½ to 4 hours
(high-heat setting)

+ 30 minutes
(low-heat setting)

MAKES:

6 servings

1 In a 3½- to 4½-quart slow cooker combine carrots and onion. Add chicken thighs. In a medium bowl combine cream of chicken soup, basil, and pepper. Spoon over mixture in cooker.

2 Cover and cook on low-heat setting for 7 to 8 hours or on high-heat setting for 3½ to 4 hours.

3 If using high-heat setting, turn to low-heat setting. In a large bowl stir together mashed potatoes, cheese, and garlic. Spoon over chicken mixture. Cover and cook about 30 minutes more or until potatoes are heated through. (Do not overcook or potatoes will become too soft.)

Nutrition Facts per serving: 393 cal., 14 g total fat (5 g sat. fat), 135 mg chol., 707 mg sodium, 27 g carbo., 4 g fiber, 37 g pro.

There's no need to cook the rice separately. Simply stir it into the chicken mixture and cook in the sauce for a convenient one-dish dinner.

EASY CHICKEN & RICE

PREP:

20 minutes

COOK:

*5 to 6 hours
(low-heat setting) or*

*2½ to 3 hours
(high-heat setting)*

*+ 10 minutes
(high-heat setting)*

MAKES:

4 servings

2	cups sliced fresh mushrooms
1	cup sliced celery
½	cup chopped onion
1½	teaspoons dried dill
¼	teaspoon black pepper
2	pounds chicken thighs, skinned and fat removed
1	10¾-ounce can condensed cream of mushroom or cream of chicken soup
¾	cup chicken broth
1½	cups uncooked instant white rice

1 In a 3½- or 4-quart slow cooker combine mushrooms, celery, onion, dill, and pepper. Place chicken on top of mushroom mixture. In a small bowl combine cream of mushroom soup and chicken broth; pour over the chicken.

2 Cover and cook on low-heat setting for 5 to 6 hours or on high-heat setting for 2½ to 3 hours.

3 If using low-heat setting, turn slow cooker to high-heat setting. Stir rice into the mushroom mixture. Cover and cook for 10 minutes more.

Nutrition Facts per serving: 516 cal., 12 g total fat (3 g sat. fat), 108 mg chol., 840 mg sodium, 66 g carbo., 3 g fiber, 34 g pro.

When there's no leftover chicken, thaw a package of frozen diced cooked chicken or cut up a deli-roasted chicken to make this family-pleasing meal.

HOME-STYLE CHICKEN & STUFFING

1   10¾-ounce can reduced-fat and reduced-sodium condensed cream of chicken or cream of mushroom soup

¼   cup butter or margarine, melted

¼   cup water

2½   cups cubed cooked chicken (about 13 ounces)

1   16-ounce package frozen loose-pack broccoli, corn, and red peppers

1   8-ounce package corn bread stuffing mix

PREP:

15 minutes

COOK:

*5 to 6 hours
(low-heat setting) or*

*2½ to 3 hours
(high-heat setting)*

MAKES:

6 servings

1 In a large bowl stir together cream of chicken soup, melted butter, and water. Add chicken, vegetables, and stuffing mix; stir until combined. Transfer mixture to a 3½- or 4-quart slow cooker.

2 Cover and cook on low-heat setting for 5 to 6 hours or on high-heat setting for 2½ to 3 hours.

Nutrition Facts per serving: 387 cal., 14 g total fat (5 g sat. fat), 76 mg chol., 795 mg sodium, 41 g carbo., 2 g fiber, 23 g pro.

The slow cooker version of this popular casserole makes it possible to serve family-pleasing supper any day of the week.

CHICKEN & NOODLES WITH VEGETABLES

PREP:

25 minutes

COOK:

*8 to 9 hours
(low-heat setting) or*

*4 to 4 1/2 hours
(high-heat setting)*

MAKES:

6 servings

2	cups sliced carrots
1 1/2	cups chopped onion
1	cup sliced celery
2	tablespoons snipped fresh parsley
1	bay leaf
3	medium chicken legs (drumstick-thigh portion) (about 2 pounds total), skinned
2	10 3/4-ounce cans reduced-fat and reduced-sodium condensed cream of chicken soup
1/2	cup water
1	teaspoon dried thyme, crushed
1/4	teaspoon black pepper
10	ounces dried wide noodles (about 5 cups)
1	cup frozen loose-pack peas
	Salt (optional)
	Black pepper (optional)

1 In a 3 1/2- or 4-quart slow cooker place carrots, onion, celery, parsley, and bay leaf. Place chicken on top of vegetables. In a large bowl stir together cream of chicken soup, the water, thyme, and the 1/4 teaspoon pepper. Pour over chicken and vegetables.

2 Cover and cook on low-heat setting for 8 to 9 hours or on high-heat setting for 4 to 4 1/2 hours. Remove chicken from slow cooker; cool slightly. Discard bay leaf.

3 Cook noodles according to package directions; drain. Meanwhile, stir frozen peas into mixture in slow cooker. Remove chicken from bones; discard bones. Cut meat into bite-size pieces; stir into mixture in slow cooker.

4 To serve, pour chicken mixture over noodles; toss gently to combine. If desired, season to taste with salt and additional pepper.

Nutrition Facts per serving: 406 cal., 7 g total fat (2 g sat. fat), 122 mg chol., 532 mg sodium, 56 g carbo., 5 g fiber, 28 g pro.

This dish is patterned after an ever-favorite oven casserole with the same ingredients. By tweaking it a bit, the recipe adapted to a slow cooker for fix-and-forget ease.

ONE-DISH CHICKEN, BROCCOLI & RICE

2	pounds skinless, boneless chicken breast halves and/or thighs, cut into bite-size pieces
¾	cup chopped onion
2	10¾-ounce cans condensed cream of mushroom soup
1	14-ounce can chicken broth
1	8-ounce package shredded process cheese food
½	teaspoon black pepper
1	16-ounce package frozen cut broccoli, thawed and well drained
2¼	cups uncooked instant white rice

PREP:

20 minutes

COOK:

*4 to 5 hours
(low-heat setting) or*

*2 to 2½ hours
(high-heat setting)*

*+ 30 minutes
(high-heat setting)*

MAKES:

8 servings

1 In a 4- to 5-quart slow cooker combine chicken and onion. In a medium bowl stir together cream of mushroom soup, chicken broth, cheese food, and pepper. Pour over mixture in slow cooker.

2 Cover and cook on low-heat setting for 4 to 5 hours or on high-heat setting for 2 to 2½ hours.

3 If using low-heat setting, turn to high-heat setting. Stir in thawed broccoli and uncooked rice. Cover and cook for 30 minutes more.

Nutrition Facts per serving: 428 cal., 15 g total fat (7 g sat. fat), 85 mg chol., 1,149 mg sodium, 34 g carbo., 3 g fiber, 37 g pro.

The wild and brown rice add nuttiness and satisfaction to this slow cooker casserole.

TURKEY & WILD RICE AMANDINE

PREP:

15 minutes

COOK:

*6 to 7 hours
(low-heat setting) or*

*3 to 3 1/2 hours
(high-heat setting)*

MAKES:

10 servings

1	15-ounce jar (drained weight) whole straw mushrooms, drained
1	10¾-ounce can condensed cream of mushroom with roasted garlic soup
1	8-ounce can sliced water chestnuts, drained
1	cup uncooked wild rice, rinsed and drained
1	cup uncooked brown rice
½	cup chopped onion
¼	teaspoon black pepper
3	14-ounce cans reduced-sodium chicken broth
½	cup water
3	cups chopped cooked turkey or chicken (about 1 pound)
½	cup dairy sour cream
½	cup sliced almonds, toasted

1 In a 4- to 5-quart slow cooker combine mushrooms, cream of mushroom soup, water chestnuts, wild rice, brown rice, onion, and pepper. Stir in chicken broth and water.

2 Cover and cook on low-heat setting for 6 to 7 hours or on high-heat setting for 3 to 3½ hours. Stir in turkey and sour cream. Sprinkle with toasted almonds.

Nutrition Facts per serving: 316 cal., 11 g total fat (3 g sat. fat), 36 mg chol., 721 mg sodium, 34 g carbo., 4 g fiber, 22 g pro.

Super-simple is right! It's hard to believe that so few ingredients add up to such a satisfying one-dish winner!

SUPER-SIMPLE BEEF STEW

12	ounces small red potatoes, quartered (about 2 cups)
4	medium carrots, cut into ½-inch pieces
1	small red onion, cut into wedges
1	pound beef stew meat
1	10¾-ounce can condensed cream of mushroom or cream of celery soup
1	cup beef broth
½	teaspoon dried marjoram or thyme, crushed
1	9-ounce package frozen cut green beans, thawed

PREP:

15 minutes

COOK:

8 to 9 hours (low-heat setting) or

4 to 4½ hours (high-heat setting)

+ 10 minutes (high-heat setting)

MAKES:

4 servings

1 In a 3½- or 4-quart slow cooker place potatoes, carrots, onion, stew meat, cream of mushroom soup, beef broth, and marjoram. Stir to combine.

2 Cover and cook on low-heat setting for 8 to 9 hours or on high-heat setting for 4 to 4½ hours.

3 If using low-heat setting, turn to high-heat setting. Stir in thawed green beans. Cover and cook for 10 to 15 minutes more or until green beans are tender.

Nutrition Facts per serving: 316 cal., 11 g total fat (3 g sat. fat), 38 mg chol., 766 mg sodium, 31 g carbo., 6 g fiber, 24 g pro.

This full-flavored soup calls for surprisingly few ingredients. If desired, you could substitute ground turkey for the ground beef.

VEGETABLE-BEEF SOUP

PREP:

15 minutes

COOK:

*7 to 8 hours
(low-heat setting) or*

*3 1/2 to 4 hours
(high-heat setting)*

MAKES:

4 to 6 servings

1   pound ground beef

1   14-ounce can beef broth

1 1/4   cups water

1   14 1/2-ounce can tomatoes, undrained, cut up

1   10 3/4-ounce can condensed tomato soup

1   10-ounce package frozen mixed vegetables

1   tablespoon dried minced onion

1   teaspoon dried Italian seasoning, crushed

1/4   teaspoon garlic powder

1 In a large skillet cook beef until brown. Drain off fat.

2 Transfer meat to a 3 1/2- or 4-quart slow cooker. Add beef broth, water, tomatoes, tomato soup, vegetables, onion, Italian seasoning, and garlic powder.

3 Cover and cook on low-heat setting for 7 to 8 hours or on high-heat setting for 3 1/2 to 4 hours.

Nutrition Facts per serving: 314 cal., 12 g total fat (4 g sat. fat), 71 mg chol., 1,011 mg sodium, 26 g carbo., 5 g fiber, 27 g pro.

Potatoes, sauerkraut, smoked sausage, and vinegar are essential flavorings in this soup. The other ingredients (aside from the base of broth and soup) can vary according to what you have on hand.

VEGETABLE-SAUERKRAUT SOUP

4	cups chicken broth
1	14- to 16-ounce can sauerkraut, rinsed and drained
12	ounces cooked Polish sausage, cubed
1	10¾-ounce can condensed cream of mushroom soup
8	ounces fresh mushrooms, sliced
2	medium carrots, chopped
2	medium stalks celery, chopped
1	medium potato, peeled, cut into small cubes
1	medium onion, chopped
½	cup chopped cooked chicken (about 3 ounces)
2	tablespoons vinegar
2	teaspoons dried dill
½	teaspoon black pepper
2	slices bacon, crisp-cooked, drained, and crumbled (optional)
2	hard-cooked eggs, chopped (optional)

PREP:

25 minutes

COOK:

10 to 12 hours (low-heat setting) or

4½ to 6 hours (high-heat setting)

MAKES:

8 servings

1 In a 3½- or 4-quart slow cooker stir together chicken broth, sauerkraut, Polish sausage, cream of mushroom soup, mushrooms, carrots, celery, potato, onion, chicken, vinegar, dill, and pepper.

2 Cover and cook on low-heat setting for 10 to 12 hours or on high-heat setting for 4½ to 6 hours. If necessary, skim off fat before serving. If desired, sprinkle servings with bacon and chopped eggs.

Nutrition Facts per serving: 250 cal., 17 g total fat (6 g sat. fat), 39 mg chol., 1,364 mg sodium, 13 g carbo., 3 g fiber, 14 g pro.

For an extra touch of freshness, sprinkle each serving with snipped fresh chives.

GOLDEN-SAUCED CHICKEN

PREP:

15 minutes

COOK:

*4 to 5 hours
(low-heat setting)*

MAKES:

6 servings

6   skinless, boneless chicken breast halves
    (about 2 pounds total)

¼   cup butter

1   0.7-ounce package dry Italian salad dressing mix

1   10¾-ounce can condensed golden mushroom soup

½   cup dry white wine or chicken broth

½   of an 8-ounce tub cream cheese with chives and onion
    Hot cooked fettuccine or angel hair pasta
    Snipped fresh chives (optional)

1 Place chicken in a 3½- or 4-quart slow cooker. In a medium saucepan melt the butter. Stir in the dry Italian salad dressing mix. Stir in golden mushroom soup, white wine, and cream cheese until combined. Pour over the chicken. Cover and cook on low-heat setting for 4 to 5 hours.

2 Serve chicken and sauce over hot cooked pasta. If desired, sprinkle with chives.

Nutrition Facts per serving: 457 cal., 18 g total fat (10 g sat. fat), 130 mg chol., 1,062 mg sodium, 27 g carbo., 2 g fiber, 40 g pro.

Cream of chicken soup adds velvety lusciousness to this creamy soup. Top with bacon for a final touch.

CREAMED CHICKEN & CORN SOUP

12	ounces skinless, boneless chicken thighs
1	26-ounce can condensed cream of chicken soup
1	14³/₄-ounce can cream-style corn
1	14-ounce can reduced-sodium chicken broth
1	cup chopped carrots
1	cup finely chopped onion
1	cup frozen loose-pack whole kernel corn
¹/₂	cup chopped celery
¹/₂	cup water
2	slices bacon, crisp-cooked, drained, and crumbled

PREP:
20 minutes

COOK:
*5 to 6 hours
(low-heat setting) or*

*2¹/₂ to 3 hours
(high-heat setting)*

MAKES:
4 to 6 servings

1 In a 3¹/₂- or 4-quart slow cooker combine chicken, cream of chicken soup, corn, chicken broth, carrots, onion, corn, celery, and water.

2 Cover and cook on low-heat setting for 5 to 6 hours or on high-heat setting for 2¹/₂ to 3 hours. Remove chicken from slow cooker; cool slightly. Chop chicken; stir into mixture in slow cooker.

3 Sprinkle servings with bacon.

Nutrition Facts per serving: 469 cal., 19 g total fat (6 g sat. fat), 87 mg chol., 2,063 mg sodium, 50 g carbo., 5 g fiber, 28 g pro.

Watching your sodium intake? Try reduced-sodium versions of the soups and broths called for in this recipe—the Mexican flavors will be just as lively!

CREAMY CHICKEN CHOWDER

PREP:

20 minutes

COOK:

*4 to 6 hours
(low-heat setting) or*

*2 to 3 hours
(high-heat setting)*

STAND:

5 minutes

MAKES:

6 servings

1   pound skinless, boneless chicken breast halves,
cut into $\frac{1}{2}$-inch pieces

1   11-ounce can whole kernel corn with sweet peppers, drained

1   10$\frac{3}{4}$-ounce can condensed cream of potato soup

1   4-ounce can diced green chile peppers

2   tablespoons snipped fresh cilantro

1   1$\frac{1}{4}$-ounce envelope taco seasoning mix

3   cups chicken broth

1   8-ounce carton dairy sour cream

$\frac{1}{2}$ of an 8-ounce package cheese spread with
jalapeño peppers, cubed

1 In a 3$\frac{1}{2}$- or 4-quart slow cooker combine chicken, corn, cream of potato soup, chile peppers, cilantro, and taco seasoning mix. Stir in chicken broth. Cover and cook on low-heat setting for 4 to 6 hours or on high-heat setting for 2 to 3 hours.

2 Stir about 1 cup of the hot soup into the sour cream. Stir sour cream mixture and cheese into the mixture in slow cooker; cover and let stand for 5 minutes. Whisk until combined.

Nutrition Facts per serving: 327 cal., 15 g total fat (8 g sat. fat), 74 mg chol., 1,906 mg sodium, 23 g carbo., 2 g fiber, 25 g pro.

Mushrooms, wild and brown rice, plus leeks and rosemary add fragrant, earthy tones to this classic fare.

CHICKEN & RICE STEW GONE WILD

3	cups quartered button mushrooms (8 ounces)
2	medium carrots, sliced
2	medium leeks, sliced (²⁄₃ cup)
½	cup uncooked brown rice
½	cup uncooked wild rice, rinsed and drained
12	ounces skinless, boneless chicken breast halves, cut into ¾-inch pieces
1	teaspoon dried thyme, crushed
½	teaspoon dried rosemary, crushed
¼	teaspoon coarsely ground black pepper
3	14-ounce cans reduced-sodium chicken broth (5¼ cups)
1	10¾-ounce can condensed cream of mushroom soup

PREP:

20 minutes

COOK:

7 to 8 hours
(low-heat setting) or

3¹⁄₂ to 4 hours
(high-heat setting)

MAKES:

6 servings

1 In a 3½- to 6-quart slow cooker place mushrooms, carrots, leeks, brown rice, and wild rice. Place chicken on vegetables and rice. Top with thyme, rosemary, and pepper. Pour chicken broth over all.

2 Cover and cook on low-heat setting for 7 to 8 hours or on high-heat setting for 3½ to 4 hours. Stir in cream of mushroom soup.

Nutrition Facts per serving: 264 cal., 6 g total fat (2 g sat. fat), 33 mg chol., 908 mg sodium, 32 g carbo., 3 g fiber, 22 g pro.

To round out the meal, bake a can of refrigerated biscuits and serve a crisp green salad topped with citrus slices and your favorite vinaigrette.

SPINACH, CHICKEN & WILD RICE SOUP

PREP:

15 minutes

COOK:

*7 to 8 hours
(low-heat setting) or*

*3½ to 4 hours
(high-heat setting)*

MAKES:

6 servings

3   cups water

1   14-ounce can chicken broth

1   10¾-ounce can condensed cream of chicken soup

⅔   cup uncooked wild rice, rinsed and drained

½   teaspoon dried thyme, crushed

¼   teaspoon black pepper

3   cups chopped cooked chicken or turkey (about 1 pound)

2   cups shredded fresh spinach

1 In a 3½- or 4-quart slow cooker combine water, chicken broth, cream of chicken soup, wild rice, thyme, and pepper.

2 Cover and cook on low-heat setting for 7 to 8 hours or on high-heat setting for 3½ to 4 hours. Just before serving, stir in chicken and spinach.

Nutrition Facts per serving: 263 cal., 9 g total fat (3 g sat. fat), 66 mg chol., 741 mg sodium, 19 g carbo., 2 g fiber, 25 g pro.

Yellow split peas add an autumnal hue. During cooking, the peas soften and begin to fall apart, which helps bring a pleasing—but not overly thick—consistency to the cozy soup.

GOLDEN TURKEY-SPLIT PEA SOUP

2	cups dry yellow split peas
2	14-ounce cans reduced-sodium chicken broth
2	cups water
2	cups frozen loose-pack whole kernel corn
3	medium carrots, sliced
1	10¾-ounce can condensed cream of chicken soup
8	ounces cooked smoked turkey sausage, halved lengthwise and sliced
½	cup sliced green onions
½	cup chopped red sweet pepper
2	teaspoons dried thyme, crushed

PREP:

20 minutes

COOK:

9 to 10 hours (low-heat setting) or

4½ to 5 hours (high-heat setting)

MAKES:

6 servings

1 Rinse and drain split peas. In a 4½- or 5-quart slow cooker combine split peas, chicken broth, water, corn, carrots, cream of chicken soup, turkey sausage, green onions, sweet pepper, and thyme.

2 Cover and cook on low-heat setting for 9 to 10 hours or on high-heat setting for 4½ to 5 hours.

Nutrition Facts per serving: 409 cal., 8 g total fat (2 g sat. fat), 30 mg chol., 1,076 mg sodium, 60 g carbo., 19 g fiber, 27 g pro.

Thick and chunky, this chowder measures up to a full-meal deal. Halibut or haddock are fine substitutes for the cod.

HEARTY FISH CHOWDER

PREP:

20 minutes

COOK:

*6 to 7 hours
(low-heat setting) or*

*3 to 3¹/₂ hours
(high-heat setting)*

*+ 1 hour
(high-heat setting)*

MAKES:

6 servings

2   medium potatoes, finely chopped

1   cup chopped onion

2   cloves garlic, minced

1   10³/₄-ounce can condensed cream of celery soup

1   10-ounce package frozen whole kernel corn

1   10-ounce package frozen baby lima beans or
     2 cups frozen loose-pack baby lima beans

1¹/₂ cups chicken broth

¹/₃   cup dry white wine or chicken broth

1   teaspoon lemon-pepper seasoning

1   pound fresh or frozen cod or other white fish fillets
     (thawed, if frozen)

1   14¹/₂-ounce can stewed tomatoes, undrained

¹/₃   cup nonfat dry milk powder

1 In a 3¹/₂- or 4-quart slow cooker combine potatoes, onion, and garlic. Stir in cream of celery soup, corn, lima beans, chicken broth, white wine, and lemon-pepper seasoning.

2 Cover and cook on low-heat setting for 6 to 7 hours or on high-heat setting for 3 to 3¹/₂ hours.

3 Place fish on the soup mixture in slow cooker. If using low-heat setting, turn slow cooker to high-heat setting. Cover and cook for 1 hour more.

4 Add tomatoes and dry milk powder to slow cooker, stirring gently to break up the fish.

Nutrition Facts per serving: 295 cal., 4 g total fat (1 g sat. fat), 39 mg chol., 955 mg sodium, 40 g carbo., 6 g fiber, 23 g pro.

Need a new party stew? This one's festive and great for a group. Set the chowder on a buffet table next to bowls, spoons, and toppings. Round out the meal with cold Mexican beer.

CHEESE ENCHILADA CHOWDER

1	15-ounce can black beans, rinsed and drained
1	14½-ounce can diced tomatoes, drained
1	10-ounce package frozen whole kernel corn
½	cup chopped onion
½	cup chopped yellow, green, or red sweet pepper
1	small fresh jalapeño chile pepper (seeded, if desired), finely chopped*
1	19-ounce can enchilada sauce
1	10¾-ounce can condensed cream of chicken soup
2	cups milk
1	cup shredded Monterey Jack cheese (4 ounces)
1	cup shredded cheddar cheese (4 ounces)
	Dairy sour cream (optional)
	Guacamole (optional)
	Tortilla chips, coarsely broken (optional)

PREP:

20 minutes

COOK:

*6 to 8 hours
(low-heat setting) or*

*3 to 4 hours
(high-heat setting)*

MAKES:

6 servings

1 In a 3½- to 5-quart slow cooker combine black beans, tomatoes, corn, onion, sweet pepper, and jalapeño pepper. In a large bowl whisk together enchilada sauce and cream of chicken soup. Gradually whisk in milk until smooth. Pour sauce mixture over bean mixture in slow cooker.

2 Cover and cook on low-heat setting for 6 to 8 hours or on high-heat setting for 3 to 4 hours.

3 Stir in Monterey Jack cheese and cheddar cheese until melted. If desired, top servings with sour cream, guacamole, and tortilla chips.

*NOTE: **Because chile peppers contain volatile oils that can burn your skin and eyes, avoid direct contact with them as much as possible. When working with chile peppers, wear plastic or rubber gloves. If your bare hands do touch the peppers, wash your hands and nails well with soap and warm water.**

Nutrition Facts per serving: 374 cal., 18 g total fat (10 g sat. fat), 47 mg chol., 1,536 mg sodium, 37 g carbo., 6 g fiber, 21 g pro.

Egg-sausage casseroles dominate the brunch buffet. Do the vegetarians in your circle of friends a favor. Serve this satisfying meatless alternative.

POTATO-VEGETABLE BRUNCH CASSEROLE

PREP:

20 minutes

COOK:

*5 to 6 hours
(low-heat setting) or*

*2¹/₂ to 3 hours
(high-heat setting)*

STAND:

15 minutes

MAKES:

6 to 8 servings

Nonstick cooking spray

1 8- to 10-ounce package meatless breakfast links

1 10³/₄-ounce can condensed cream of potato soup

²/₃ cup milk

2 teaspoons Worcestershire sauce or bottled steak sauce

¹/₄ teaspoon freshly ground black pepper

1 28-ounce package frozen loose-pack diced hash brown potatoes with onion and peppers, thawed

1 10-ounce package frozen broccoli, cauliflower, and carrots in cheese sauce, thawed

¹/₂ cup shredded cheddar cheese (2 ounces)

1 Lightly coat a 3¹/₂- or 4-quart slow cooker with nonstick cooking spray. Brown breakfast links according to package directions; cool slightly. Slice links into ¹/₂-inch-thick pieces.

2 In prepared slow cooker combine cream of potato soup, milk, Worcestershire sauce, and black pepper. Stir in potatoes, vegetables with cheese sauce, and breakfast link pieces.

3 Cover and cook on low-heat setting for 5 to 6 hours or on high-heat setting for 2¹/₂ to 3 hours. Turn off slow cooker. Sprinkle mixture with cheese. Cover and let stand for 15 minutes before serving.

Nutrition Facts per serving: 290 cal., 8 g total fat (3 g sat. fat), 15 mg chol., 1,075 mg sodium, 40 g carbo., 6 g fiber, 18 g pro.

Kidney and black beans elevate scalloped potatoes from a supporting side-dish role to the main-dish attraction. To cut down on prep time, leave the potatoes unpeeled.

SCALLOPED POTATOES WITH BEANS

1   15-ounce can red kidney beans, rinsed and drained

1   15-ounce can black beans, rinsed and drained

1   cup chopped onion

1   cup sliced celery

1   cup frozen loose-pack peas

1   cup chopped green sweet pepper

1   10¾-ounce can condensed cheddar cheese, cream of potato, or cream of mushroom soup

1   teaspoon dried thyme, crushed

¼   teaspoon black pepper

4   cloves garlic, minced

3   medium potatoes, cut into ¼-inch-thick slices

1   cup shredded cheddar cheese (4 ounces) (optional)

PREP:
20 minutes

COOK:
8 to 10 hours (low-heat setting) or

4 to 5 hours (high-heat setting)

MAKES:
5 servings

1   In a large bowl combine kidney beans, black beans, onion, celery, peas, sweet pepper, cheddar cheese soup, thyme, pepper, and garlic.

2   Spoon half of the bean mixture into a 3½- or 4-quart slow cooker. Top with potatoes and remaining bean mixture.

3   Cover and cook on low-heat setting for 8 to 10 hours or on high-heat setting for 4 to 5 hours. If desired, sprinkle servings with cheddar cheese.

Nutrition Facts per serving: 315 cal., 6 g total fat (3 g sat. fat), 14 mg chol., 851 mg sodium, 55 g carbo., 14 g fiber, 19 g pro.

If you like creamy potatoes, but don't particularly enjoy making a cream sauce (or peeling potatoes), this recipe is for you! Because it makes eight servings, it's a great choice to serve with the holiday bird.

CREAMY HERBED POTATOES

PREP:

10 minutes

COOK:

*5 to 6 hours
(low-heat setting)*

MAKES:

8 side-dish servings

Nonstick cooking spray

1   28-ounce package frozen loose-pack diced hash brown potatoes with onion and peppers, thawed

1   10³⁄₄-ounce can condensed cream of chicken soup

1   8-ounce package cream cheese, cut into cubes

2   teaspoons dried Italian seasoning, crushed

¹⁄₄   teaspoon salt

¹⁄₄   teaspoon black pepper

1 Lightly coat a 3¹⁄₂- or 4-quart slow cooker with nonstick cooking spray; set aside. In a large bowl stir together potatoes, cream of chicken soup, cream cheese, Italian seasoning, salt, and pepper. Spoon into prepared slow cooker.

2 Cover and cook on low-heat setting for 5 to 6 hours. Stir before serving.

Nutrition Facts per serving: 213 cal., 13 g total fat (7 g sat. fat), 34 mg chol., 490 mg sodium, 21 g carbo., 2 g fiber, 5 g pro.

It's hard to believe that just four ingredients add up to a rich, tasty side dish.
Serve this at your next get-together and you can count on ending up with an empty cooker.

CREAMY RANCH POTATOES

2½   pounds small red potatoes, quartered

1   10¾-ounce can condensed cream of mushroom soup

1   8-ounce carton dairy sour cream

1   0.4-ounce package buttermilk ranch salad dressing mix

1 Place potatoes in a 3½- or 4-quart slow cooker. In a small bowl combine cream of mushroom soup, sour cream, and dry salad dressing mix. Spoon soup mixture over potatoes; stir.

2 Cover and cook on low-heat setting for 7 to 8 hours or on high-heat setting for 3½ to 4 hours. Stir gently before serving.

Nutrition Facts per serving: 245 cal., 12 g total fat (6 g sat. fat), 17 mg chol., 517 mg sodium, 30 g carbo., 2 g fiber, 5 g pro.

PREP:

15 minutes

COOK:

7 to 8 hours
(low-heat setting) or

3½ to 4 hours
(high-heat setting)

MAKES:

6 side-dish servings

Chopped prosciutto, leeks, smoked Gouda, and provolone add a gourmet angle to potatoes. Because it cooks in the slow cooker, this recipe is a great way to save oven and range top space when cooking for a crowd.

CHEESY POTATOES

PREP:

20 minutes

COOK:

*5 to 6 hours
(low-heat setting)*

MAKES:

12 side-dish servings

1	28-ounce package frozen loose-pack diced hash brown potatoes with onion and peppers, thawed
1	10¾-ounce can condensed cream of chicken and herbs soup
1	cup finely shredded smoked Gouda cheese (4 ounces)
1	cup finely shredded provolone cheese (4 ounces)
1	8-ounce package cream cheese, cut into cubes
¾	cup milk
¼	cup finely chopped leek or thinly sliced green onions
¼	cup chopped prosciutto or 4 slices bacon, crisp-cooked and crumbled
½	teaspoon black pepper
2	tablespoons snipped fresh chives

1 In a 3½- or 4-quart slow cooker combine potatoes, cream of chicken and herbs soup, Gouda cheese, provolone cheese, cream cheese, milk, leek, prosciutto (if using), and pepper.

2 Cover and cook on low-heat setting for 5 to 6 hours. Before serving, gently stir in bacon (if using) and chives.

Nutrition Facts per serving: 216 cal., 14 g total fat (8 g sat. fat), 39 mg chol., 534 mg sodium, 16 g carbo., 2 g fiber, 8 g pro.

This recipe is a sure-fire potluck pleaser, but remember it at the holidays, too, when you're short on stove and oven space. It's a great way to serve potatoes, and no one will miss the gravy (especially the cook, who has better things to do at the last minute!).

COMPANY-SPECIAL SCALLOPED POTATOES

	Nonstick cooking spray
1½	pounds Yukon gold potatoes
1½	pounds sweet potatoes
1	7-ounce round smoked Gouda cheese, shredded, or 2 cups shredded American cheese (8 ounces)
1	10¾-ounce can condensed cream of celery soup
1	8-ounce carton dairy sour cream
½	cup chicken broth
1	large onion, sliced

Lightly coat a 4½- or 5-quart slow cooker with nonstick cooking spray; set aside.

2 Thinly slice Yukon gold potatoes (do not peel). Peel and cut sweet potatoes into ¼-inch-thick slices. Set aside.

3 In a medium bowl combine cheese, cream of celery soup, sour cream, and chicken broth. In prepared slow cooker layer half of the potatoes and half of the onion. Top with half of the soup mixture. Repeat layers.

4 Cover and cook on low-heat setting for 6 to 8 hours or on high-heat setting for 3 to 4 hours.

Nutrition Facts per serving: 265 cal., 12 g total fat (7 g sat. fat), 26 mg chol., 612 mg sodium, 33 g carbo., 4 g fiber, 8 g pro.

PREP:
25 minutes

COOK:
6 to 8 hours (low-heat setting) or

3 to 4 hours (high-heat setting)

MAKES:
10 side-dish servings

Bits of dried apricot are sun-flavored jewels in this pretty side dish. Pair it with roast chicken or broiled salmon and steamed broccoli for an easy and colorful meal.

CREAMY WILD RICE PILAF

PREP:

25 minutes

COOK:

*7 to 8 hours
(low-heat setting) or*

*3¹/₂ to 4 hours
(high-heat setting)*

MAKES:

12 side-dish servings

1	cup uncooked wild rice, rinsed and drained
1	cup uncooked brown rice
1	cup shredded carrot
1	cup sliced fresh mushrooms
¹/₂	cup thinly sliced celery
¹/₃	cup chopped onion
¹/₄	cup snipped dried apricots
1	teaspoon dried thyme, crushed
1	teaspoon poultry seasoning
³/₄	teaspoon salt
¹/₂	teaspoon black pepper
5¹/₂	cups water
1	10³/₄-ounce can condensed cream of mushroom with roasted garlic or golden mushroom soup
¹/₂	cup dairy sour cream

1 In a 3¹/₂- or 4-quart slow cooker combine wild rice, brown rice, carrot, mushrooms, celery, onion, apricots, thyme, poultry seasoning, salt, and pepper. Stir in water and cream of mushroom with roasted garlic soup.

2 Cover and cook on low-heat setting for 7 to 8 hours or on high-heat setting for 3¹/₂ to 4 hours. Stir in sour cream.

Nutrition Facts per serving: 165 cal., 4 g total fat (2 g sat. fat), 4 mg chol., 339 mg sodium, 28 g carbo., 2 g fiber, 4 g pro.

As if cheesy cauliflower wasn't already wonderful enough, this classic is made even better with corn, green onions, and a bonus of crisp bacon.

CHEESY CAULIFLOWER & CORN

4   cups cauliflower florets

2   cups frozen loose-pack whole kernel corn

6   ounces American cheese, cut into cubes

1   10¾-ounce can reduced-fat and reduced-sodium condensed cream of celery soup

½   cup sliced green onions

¼   teaspoon black pepper

4   slices bacon, crisp-cooked, drained, and crumbled

PREP:

15 minutes

COOK:

*6 to 7 hours
(low-heat setting) or*

*3 to 3½ hours
(high-heat setting)*

MAKES:

8 to 10 side-dish servings

1 In a 3½- or 4-quart slow cooker combine cauliflower, corn, American cheese, cream of celery soup, green onions, and pepper.

2 Cover and cook on low-heat setting for 6 to 7 hours or on high-heat setting for 3 to 3½ hours. Before serving, stir in crumbled bacon.

Nutrition Facts per serving: 156 cal., 8 g total fat (5 g sat. fat), 23 mg chol., 559 mg sodium, 14 g carbo., 2 g fiber, 9 g pro.

You'll find it's more convenient to stir the ingredients in a large bowl before placing them in a cooker. The saucy side dish is best served in small bowls.

CREAMY CORN & BROCCOLI

PREP:

10 minutes

COOK:

*5 to 6 hours
(low-heat setting) or*

*2$\frac{1}{2}$ to 3 hours
(high-heat setting)*

MAKES:

8 to 10 side-dish servings

Nonstick cooking spray

1   16-ounce bag frozen cut broccoli

1   16-ounce bag frozen whole kernel corn

1   10$\frac{3}{4}$-ounce can condensed cream of chicken soup

1   cup shredded American cheese (4 ounces)

$\frac{1}{2}$ cup shredded cheddar cheese (2 ounces)

$\frac{1}{4}$ cup milk

① Lightly coat the inside of a 4- to 5-quart slow cooker with nonstick cooking spray. In a large bowl combine broccoli, corn, cream of chicken soup, American cheese, cheddar cheese, and milk. Spoon broccoli mixture into slow cooker.

② Cover and cook on low-heat setting for 5 to 6 hours or on high-heat setting for 2$\frac{1}{2}$ to 3 hours.

Nutrition Facts per serving: 191 cal., 10 g total fat (5 g sat. fat), 25 mg chol., 548 mg sodium, 19 g carbo., 3 g fiber, 9 g pro.

A classic comfort food sparked with cream cheese and chives, this vegetable side dish serves a crowd and will be a hit at any gathering.

CREAMED CORN

2   16-ounce packages frozen whole kernel corn

2   cups coarsely chopped red or green sweet pepper

1   cup chopped onion

$\frac{1}{4}$ teaspoon black pepper

1   10$\frac{3}{4}$-ounce can condensed cream of celery soup

1   8-ounce tub cream cheese with chive and onion or cream cheese with garden vegetables

$\frac{1}{4}$ cup milk

1 In a 3$\frac{1}{2}$- or 4-quart slow cooker combine corn, sweet pepper, onion, and black pepper. In a large bowl combine cream of celery soup, cream cheese, and milk; whisk to combine. Add soup mixture to slow cooker.

2 Cover and cook on low-heat setting for 8 to 10 hours or on high-heat setting for 4 to 5 hours.

Nutrition Facts per serving: 166 cal., 8 g total fat (5 g sat. fat), 21 mg chol., 280 mg sodium, 22 g carbo., 2 g fiber, 4 g pro.

PREP:

15 minutes

COOK:

8 to 10 hours (low-heat setting) or

4 to 5 hours (high-heat setting)

MAKES:

12 side-dish servings

Kids don't often get excited about vegetables, but they love cheese! This creamy, cheesy offering is a great way to nudge little ones to give green beans a try.

GREEN BEANS IN CHEESE-BACON SAUCE

PREP:

15 minutes

COOK:

*5 to 6 hours
(low-heat setting) or*

*2 1/2 to 3 hours
(high-heat setting)*

MAKES:

8 to 10 servings

2   16-ounce packages frozen cut green beans

1   4-ounce can (drained weight) sliced mushrooms, drained

1   4-ounce can sliced pimiento, drained

1/2   cup finely chopped onion

1 1/2 cups shredded cheddar cheese (6 ounces)

1   10 3/4-ounce can condensed cream of mushroom soup

1/4   teaspoon black pepper

6   slices bacon, crisp-cooked, drained, and crumbled

1 In a 3 1/2- or 4-quart slow cooker combine green beans, mushrooms, pimiento, and onion. Add cheddar cheese, cream of mushroom soup, and pepper. Sprinkle with bacon.

2 Cover and cook on low-heat setting for 5 to 6 hours or on high-heat setting for 2 1/2 to 3 hours. Stir before serving.

Nutrition Facts per serving: 199 cal., 13 g total fat (6 g sat. fat), 27 mg chol., 536 mg sodium, 14 g carbo., 4 g fiber, 10 g pro.

PERFECT FOR POTLUCKS

8

A poultry-rice bake is a handy way to use leftover chicken or turkey. This recipe adds a few flavor flourishes with artichokes and crisp crumbled bacon.

ARTICHOKE-TURKEY CASSEROLE

PREP:

30 minutes

BAKE:

20 minutes + 20 minutes

STAND:

10 minutes

MAKES:

6 servings

½	cup chopped carrot
½	cup chopped red sweet pepper
¼	cup sliced green onions
1	tablespoon butter or margarine
1	10¾-ounce can condensed cream of chicken soup
1	8- to 9-ounce package frozen artichoke hearts, thawed and cut up
1½	cups chopped cooked turkey or chicken (about 8 ounces)
1	cup cooked long grain rice or wild rice
⅔	cup milk
½	cup shredded mozzarella cheese (2 ounces)
2	slices bacon, crisp-cooked, drained, and crumbled
½	teaspoon dried thyme, crushed
3	tablespoons grated Parmesan cheese

1 In a large skillet cook carrot, sweet pepper, and green onions in hot butter until carrot is crisp-tender. Remove from heat. Stir in cream of chicken soup, artichoke hearts, turkey, rice, milk, mozzarella cheese, bacon, and thyme. Transfer turkey mixture to an ungreased 2-quart rectangular baking dish. Sprinkle with Parmesan cheese.

2 Bake, covered, in a 350°F oven for 20 minutes. Uncover and bake about 20 minutes more or until bubbly. Let stand for 10 minutes before serving.

MAKE-AHEAD DIRECTIONS: Prepare as directed, except after assembling, cover and refrigerate for up to 24 hours. Bake, covered, in a 350°F oven for 30 minutes. Uncover and bake about 20 minutes more or until bubbly.

TO TOTE: Do not let stand after baking. Cover tightly. Transport in an insulated carrier.

Nutrition Facts per serving: 248 cal., 11 g total fat (5 g sat. fat), 47 mg chol., 611 mg sodium, 18 g carbo., 3 g fiber, 18 g pro.

Your slow cooker adds fix-and-forget ease to this recipe. The long, slow, moist-heat cooking also perfectly tenderizes the bottom round steak, which is a less-expensive cut than top round steak.

HERBED STEAK & MUSHROOMS

2	pounds beef round steak, cut ¾ inch thick
1	medium onion, sliced
2	cups sliced fresh mushrooms or two 4-ounce cans (drained weight) sliced mushrooms, drained
1	10¾-ounce can condensed cream of mushroom soup
¼	cup dry white wine or beef broth
½	teaspoon dried basil, crushed
¼	teaspoon dried marjoram, crushed
¼	teaspoon black pepper
	Hot cooked noodles

PREP:

20 minutes

COOK:

*8 to 10 hours
(low-heat setting) or*

*4 to 5 hours
(high-heat setting)*

MAKES:

6 servings

1 Trim fat from meat. Cut meat into serving-size portions. Place onion slices and mushrooms in a 3½- or 4-quart slow cooker. Place meat on top of vegetables.

2 In a small bowl combine cream of mushroom soup, wine, basil, marjoram, and pepper; pour over meat.

3 Cover and cook on low-heat setting for 8 to 10 hours or on high-heat setting for 4 to 5 hours. Serve meat and sauce over hot cooked noodles.

TO TOTE: Cover tightly after cooking. Place cooked noodles in a tightly covered container; transport in an insulated carrier.

Nutrition Facts per serving: 332 cal., 7 g total fat (2 g sat. fat), 87 mg chol., 442 mg sodium, 26 g carbo., 2 g fiber, 38 g pro.

A No. 16 scoop makes quick work of shaping these meatballs. If you don't have a scoop, use a one-fourth cup measure and then roll the meat mixture between the palms of your hands to shape into balls.

NORWEGIAN MEATBALLS

PREP:
25 minutes
BAKE:
30 minutes
MAKES:
5 or 6 servings

2 eggs

½ cup milk

⅔ cup crushed saltine crackers (about 18 crackers)

⅓ cup finely chopped onion

½ teaspoon celery salt

½ teaspoon ground nutmeg

½ teaspoon black pepper

2 pounds lean ground beef

1 10¾-ounce can condensed cream of mushroom soup

¾ cup milk

1 In a large bowl beat eggs with a fork; stir in the ½ cup milk. Stir in crushed crackers, onion, celery salt, ¼ teaspoon of the nutmeg, and the pepper. Add ground beef; mix well. Shape mixture into 20 meatballs. Arrange meatballs in a greased 3-quart rectangular baking dish. Bake in a 350°F oven about 30 minutes or until done (160°F).*

2 For sauce, in a medium saucepan combine cream of mushroom soup, the ¾ cup milk, and the remaining ¼ teaspoon nutmeg. Cook and stir over medium heat until heated through.

3 To serve, transfer meatballs to a serving bowl. Spoon sauce over meatballs.

*NOTE: The internal color of a meatball is not a reliable doneness indicator. A beef meatball cooked to 160°F is safe, regardless of color. To measure the doneness of a meatball, insert an instant-read thermometer into the center of the meatball.

TO TOTE: Cover tightly. Transport in an insulated carrier.

Nutrition Facts per serving: 469 cal., 26 g total fat (10 g sat. fat), 204 mg chol., 842 mg sodium, 17 g carbo., 1 g fiber, 39 g pro.

A saucy, meaty dish like this demands something green as a side. Green beans with almonds, peas with pearl onions, and sparkling fresh sauteed spinach make good pairings.

SAUCY STEAK

1½	pounds tenderized beef round steak
2	tablespoons cooking oil
1	10¾-ounce can condensed golden mushroom soup
1	4-ounce can (drained weight) sliced mushrooms, drained
½	cup water
1	teaspoon dried basil, crushed, or 1 tablespoon snipped fresh basil
1	8-ounce carton dairy sour cream
2	tablespoons all-purpose flour
	Hot cooked noodles or rice
1	tablespoon snipped fresh parsley

PREP:

30 minutes

COOK:

45 minutes

MAKES:

6 servings

1 Cut meat into 6 serving-size pieces. In a large skillet brown meat, half at a time, on both sides in hot oil. Drain off fat. Return all meat to skillet.

2 Meanwhile, in a medium bowl stir together golden mushroom soup, mushrooms, water, and, if using, dried basil. Pour over meat in skillet. Bring to boiling; reduce heat. Simmer, covered, for 45 to 60 minutes or until meat is tender. Transfer meat to a serving platter, reserving mushroom mixture in skillet. Cover meat to keep warm.

3 For sauce, in a small bowl stir together sour cream and flour. Stir sour cream mixture into mushroom mixture. Cook and stir until thickened and bubbly. Cook and stir for 1 minute more. If using, stir in fresh basil.

4 Serve sauce and meat over hot cooked noodles or rice. Sprinkle with parsley.

TO TOTE: **Transfer meat to a baking dish; spoon sauce over meat. Cover tightly. Cover noodles or rice tightly. Transport in an insulated carrier. Transport parsley in an insulated cooler with ice packs.**

Nutrition Facts per serving: 419 cal., 19 g total fat (8 g sat. fat), 111 mg chol., 567 mg sodium, 29 g carbo., 2 g fiber, 31 g pro.

The tomato soup gives a pleasant sweetness to this dish, and the mixture of two cheeses makes it extra luscious.

BAKED BEEF RAVIOLI

PREP:
15 minutes

BAKE:
20 minutes

MAKES:
8 to 10 servings

2	9-ounce packages refrigerated 4-cheese ravioli
1½	pounds ground beef
1	large onion, chopped
1	tablespoon bottled minced garlic (6 cloves)
1	14-ounce can diced tomatoes, undrained
1	10¾-ounce can condensed tomato soup
1	teaspoon dried basil, crushed
1	teaspoon dried oregano, crushed
1½	cups shredded mozzarella cheese (6 ounces)
½	cup finely shredded Parmesan cheese (2 ounces)

1. Cook pasta according to package directions; drain and keep warm.

2. Meanwhile, in a large skillet cook ground beef, onion, and garlic until meat is brown and onion is tender. Drain off fat. Stir tomatoes, tomato soup, basil, and oregano into meat mixture in skillet. Gently stir in cooked pasta. Spread mixture into an ungreased 3-quart rectangular baking dish. Sprinkle with mozzarella and Parmesan cheeses.

3. Bake, uncovered, in a 375°F oven about 20 minutes or until heated through.

Nutrition Facts per serving: 503 cal., 20 g total fat (9 g sat. fat), 113 mg chol., 854 mg sodium, 40 g carbo., 3 g fiber, 40 g pro.

TO TOTE: Cover tightly. Transport in an insulated carrier.

These could be called Beef Fun-Burgers because they're a great choice for informal get-togethers. Serve with an array of chips, dips, deli salads, and bar cookies, and you'll have an instant party.

BEEF BUNBURGERS

1½	pounds ground beef
½	cup chopped onion
⅓	cup chopped green sweet pepper
1	10¾-ounce can condensed tomato soup
1	tablespoon vinegar
1	teaspoon dry mustard
1	teaspoon poultry seasoning
½	teaspoon dried thyme, crushed
¼	teaspoon salt
8	hamburger buns, split and toasted

1 In a large skillet cook ground beef, onion, and sweet pepper until beef is brown and onion is tender. Drain well. Stir in tomato soup, vinegar, dry mustard, poultry seasoning, thyme, and salt.

2 Bring to boiling; reduce heat. Simmer, uncovered, about 15 minutes or until desired consistency. Serve on toasted hamburger buns.

TO TOTE: **Cover meat mixture tightly; tightly wrap buns. Transport in an insulated carrier.**

Nutrition Facts per serving: 364 cal., 19 g total fat (7 g sat. fat), 62 mg chol., 584 mg sodium, 28 g carbo., 2 g fiber, 20 g pro.

PREP:
15 minutes
COOK:
15 minutes
MAKES:
8 servings

A can of black beans stretches a pound and a half of pork into a dish that serves eight. The cream of chicken soup makes it extra satisfying.

PORK & GREEN CHILE CASSEROLE

PREP:

20 minutes

BAKE:

30 minutes

STAND:

10 minutes

MAKES:

8 servings

1½	pounds boneless pork
1	tablespoon cooking oil
1	15-ounce can black beans, rinsed and drained
1	14½-ounce can diced tomatoes, undrained
1	10¾-ounce can condensed cream of chicken soup
2	4-ounce cans diced green chile peppers, undrained
1	cup uncooked instant brown rice
¼	cup water
2	to 3 tablespoons bottled salsa
½	cup shredded cheddar cheese (2 ounces)

1 Trim fat from pork. Cut pork into ½-inch pieces. In a large skillet brown pork, half at a time, in hot oil. Drain off fat. Return pork to skillet.

2 Stir in black beans, tomatoes, cream of chicken soup, chile peppers, brown rice, water, and salsa. Bring to boiling. Carefully pour into an ungreased 2-quart square baking dish.

3 Bake, uncovered, in a 350°F oven for 30 minutes. Sprinkle with cheese. Let stand for 10 minutes before serving.

TO TOTE: **Do not let stand after sprinkling with cheese. Cover tightly. Transport in an insulated carrier.**

Nutrition Facts per serving: 271 cal., 13 g total fat (4 g sat. fat), 49 mg chol., 717 mg sodium, 22 g carbo., 4 g fiber, 20 g pro.

Combine canned soup—long a staple for making casseroles easier—with refrigerated diced potatoes, and you have the easiest version of this comfort food classic in history!

SCALLOPED POTATOES & HAM

1	10¾-ounce can condensed cream of onion or cream of celery soup
½	cup milk
⅛	teaspoon black pepper
1	pound cooked ham, cubed
1	20-ounce package refrigerated diced potatoes with onion
¾	cup shredded Swiss or cheddar cheese (3 ounces)

PREP:
15 minutes
BAKE:
40 minutes + 5 minutes
STAND:
10 minutes
MAKES:
6 to 8 servings

1 In a large bowl stir together cream of onion soup, milk, and pepper. Stir in ham and potatoes. Transfer to an ungreased 2-quart rectangular baking dish.

2 Bake, covered, in a 350°F oven for 40 minutes. Stir mixture. Sprinkle with cheese. Bake, uncovered, for 5 to 10 minutes more or until heated through and cheese is melted. Let stand for 10 minutes before serving.

TO TOTE: **Do not let stand after baking. Cover tightly. Transport in an insulated carrier.**

Nutrition Facts per serving: 332 cal., 14 g total fat (6 g sat. fat), 64 mg chol., 1,613 mg sodium, 29 g carbo., 2 g fiber, 21 g pro.

Longstanding partners ham and eggs—hard-cooked this time—star in this flavorful casserole.

HAM & EGG SUPPER

PREP:

25 minutes

BAKE:

25 minutes

MAKES:

6 servings

½ cup chopped onion

½ cup chopped yellow or green sweet pepper

¼ cup butter or margarine

⅓ cup all-purpose flour

½ teaspoon dried thyme, crushed

2 10½-ounce cans condensed chicken with rice soup

1 cup milk

3 cups cubed cooked ham (about 1 pound)

6 hard-cooked eggs, sliced

1½ cups soft bread crumbs

2 tablespoons butter or margarine, melted

1 In a large saucepan cook onion and sweet pepper in the ¼ cup hot butter until tender. Stir in flour and thyme; stir in chicken with rice soup and milk. Cook and stir over medium heat until thickened and bubbly. Fold in ham and hard-cooked eggs. Turn mixture into an ungreased 2-quart rectangular baking dish.

2 In a medium bowl toss bread crumbs with the 2 tablespoons melted butter. Sprinkle over ham mixture in baking dish.

3 Bake, uncovered, in a 350°F oven for 25 minutes.

TO TOTE: Cover tightly. Transport in an insulated carrier.

Nutrition Facts per serving: 451 cal., 28 g total fat (13 g sat. fat), 291 mg chol., 1,934 mg sodium, 25 g carbo., 1 g fiber, 24 g pro.

Think ahead! You can freeze leftover cooked holiday ham for up to three months. Why not freeze some in 3-cup portions so you can have the meat measured and ready to thaw for this yummy bake?

HAM & BROCCOLI BAKE

1	medium onion, chopped
2	tablespoons butter or margarine
2	10¾-ounce cans condensed cream of mushroom soup and/or cream of celery soup
1¼	cups milk
1	cup shredded cheddar or Swiss cheese (4 ounces)
1	teaspoon Worcestershire sauce
3	cups cubed cooked ham (about 1 pound)
2	cups uncooked instant white rice
1	16-ounce package frozen cut broccoli, thawed

PREP:
25 minutes
BAKE:
50 minutes + 10 minutes
MAKES:
6 to 8 servings

1 In a small saucepan cook onion in hot butter until tender.

2 In a large bowl stir together cream of mushroom soup, milk, cheese, and Worcestershire sauce. Stir in cooked onion, ham, rice, and broccoli. Transfer mixture to an ungreased 2-quart rectangular baking dish.

3 Bake, covered, in a 350°F oven for 50 minutes. Uncover; bake about 10 minutes more or until rice is and mixture is hot in center.

TO TOTE: Cover tightly. Transport in an insulated carrier.

Nutrition Facts per serving: 516 cal., 25 g total fat (12 g sat. fat), 80 mg chol., 1,947 mg sodium, 44 g carbo., 3 g fiber, 26 g pro.

This is it: that creamy, potato-chip-topped casserole that has been popular for years at bridge parties and luncheons. As always, it's a pleasing choice when serving a crowd.

HOT CHICKEN SALAD

PREP:
25 minutes
BAKE:
30 minutes
STAND:
10 minutes
MAKES:
12 servings

1	cup coarsely crushed potato chips
2/3	cup finely chopped almonds
6	cups cubed cooked chicken (about 2 pounds)
3	cups chopped celery
2	cups shredded mozzarella cheese (8 ounces)
2	8-ounce cartons dairy sour cream or plain yogurt
1	10¾-ounce can condensed cream of chicken soup
¼	cup chopped onion
1	teaspoon dried thyme or basil, crushed
4	hard-cooked eggs, chopped

1 In a small bowl combine potato chips and almonds; set aside. In a large bowl combine chicken, celery, cheese, sour cream, cream of chicken soup, onion, and thyme. Gently fold in hard-cooked eggs. Transfer to an ungreased 3-quart rectangular baking dish. Sprinkle with potato chip mixture.

2 Bake, uncovered, in a 400°F oven for 30 to 35 minutes or until heated through. Let stand for 10 minutes before serving.

TO TOTE: Do not let stand after baking. Cover tightly. Transport in an insulated carrier.

Nutrition Facts per serving: 398 cal., 25 g total fat (10 g sat. fat), 168 mg chol., 437 mg sodium, 9 g carbo., 2 g fiber, 33 g pro.

At a loss for what to take to the next bring-a-dish gathering? You just can't go wrong with a chicken-and-stuffing concoction. Tote this one—and watch it disappear!

BUFFET CHICKEN SCALLOP

1	large onion, chopped
¾	cup chopped green sweet pepper
2	tablespoons butter or margarine
3	cups herb-seasoned stuffing mix
1	cup chicken broth
3	slightly beaten eggs
1	10¾-ounce can condensed cream of celery soup
4	cups chopped cooked chicken or turkey (about 1¼ pounds)
1½	cups cooked rice*
1	10¾-ounce can condensed cream of chicken soup
½	cup dairy sour cream
¼	cup milk

PREP:
25 minutes
BAKE:
25 minutes
STAND:
10 minutes
MAKES:
12 servings

1 In a large skillet cook onion and sweet pepper in hot butter over medium heat until tender.

2 In a large bowl combine stuffing mix and chicken broth; stir in eggs and cream of celery soup. Stir in onion mixture, chicken, and rice. Spread in a lightly greased 3-quart rectangular baking dish.

3 Bake, uncovered, in a 350°F oven for 25 to 30 minutes or until an instant-read thermometer inserted in the center registers 160°F. Let stand for 10 minutes.

4 Meanwhile, for sauce, in a small saucepan combine cream of chicken soup, sour cream, and milk; heat and stir until smooth and heated through. Serve sauce with baked chicken mixture.

*NOTE: **For 1½ cups cooked rice, in a medium saucepan combine 1 cup water and ½ cup uncooked long grain rice. Bring to boiling; reduce heat. Simmer, covered, for 15 to 18 minutes or until rice is tender.**

TO TOTE: **Do not let stand after baking. Cover baking dish tightly; cover sauce tightly. Transport in an insulated carrier.**

Nutrition Facts per serving: 286 cal., 12 g total fat (5 g sat. fat), 106 mg chol., 758 mg sodium, 23 g carbo., 2 g fiber, 19 g pro.

Who doesn't love Chicken à la King? It's the sort of dish that has been starring at luncheons for decades. This serve-a-crowd version, easily totable in your slow cooker, is a great way to let everyone in on this ever-pleasing classic.

CHICKEN À LA KING

PREP:

25 minutes

COOK:

*6 to 7 hours
(low-heat setting) or*

*3 to 3 1/2 hours
(high-heat setting)*

STAND:

10 minutes

MAKES:

8 to 10 servings

4 cups chopped cooked chicken or turkey (about 1 1/4 pounds)

2 10 3/4-ounce cans condensed cream of chicken soup

2 4 1/2-ounce jars (drained weight) sliced mushrooms, drained

3/4 cup chopped green sweet pepper

3/4 cup chopped celery

1 5-ounce can (2/3 cup) evaporated milk

1/2 cup bottled roasted red sweet peppers, drained and coarsely chopped

1/2 cup chopped onion

3 tablespoons dry sherry or dry white wine

1 teaspoon dried basil, crushed

1/2 teaspoon black pepper

1 10-ounce package frozen peas

4 or 5 English muffins, split and toasted; 8 to 10 baked potatoes; or 4 to 5 cups hot cooked rice

1 In a 4- to 5-quart slow cooker combine cooked chicken, cream of chicken soup, mushrooms, sweet pepper, celery, evaporated milk, roasted sweet peppers, onion, sherry, basil, and black pepper.

2 Cover and cook on low-heat setting for 6 to 7 hours or on high-heat setting for 3 to 3 1/2 hours. Turn off cooker. Stir in peas. Cover and let stand for 10 minutes.

3 Serve chicken mixture over English muffin halves.

TO TOTE: Do not let stand after stirring in frozen peas. Cover tightly. Transport English muffin halves in an insulated carrier.

Nutrition Facts per serving: 357 cal., 12 g total fat (4 g sat. fat), 74 mg chol., 940 mg sodium, 31 g carbo., 5 g fiber, 28 g pro.

This dish scores well among people who enjoy Asian foods but prefer them mildly spiced. For a lower-sodium version, use reduced-fat and reduced-sodium condensed cream of chicken soup.

CHICKEN CHOW MEIN CASSEROLE

4 cups chopped cooked chicken (about 1¼ pounds)

2 cups chopped celery

1 cup shredded carrots

1 cup chopped green sweet pepper

2 4-ounce cans (drained weight) sliced mushrooms, drained

⅔ cup sliced or slivered almonds, toasted

2 tablespoons diced pimiento, drained

2 10¾-ounce cans condensed cream of chicken soup

2 cups chow mein noodles

1 In a large bowl stir together chicken, celery, carrots, sweet pepper, mushrooms, almonds, and pimiento. Stir in cream of chicken soup. Transfer chicken mixture to an ungreased 3-quart rectangular baking dish.

2 Bake, covered, in a 350°F oven for 45 minutes. Uncover and top with chow mein noodles. Bake, uncovered, for 5 to 10 minutes more or until heated through.

TO TOTE: Cover tightly. Transport in an insulated carrier.

Nutrition Facts per serving: 366 cal., 19 g total fat (4 g sat. fat), 68 mg chol., 921 mg sodium, 21 g carbo., 4 g fiber, 27 g pro.

PREP:

25 minutes

BAKE:

45 minutes + 5 minutes

MAKES:

8 servings

Pesto—made from garlic, basil, nuts, olive oil, and Parmesan cheese—is traditionally a sauce for pasta. However it's also used to add flavor and freshness to many recipes.

CHICKEN-ASPARAGUS CASSEROLE

PREP:

25 minutes

BAKE:

25 minutes + 10 minutes

STAND:

10 minutes

MAKES:

6 servings

2	10-ounce packages frozen cut asparagus
1	10¾-ounce can condensed cream of chicken soup
⅓	cup grated Parmesan cheese
¼	cup purchased pesto sauce
¼	cup half-and-half, light cream, or milk
2	cups chopped cooked chicken (about 10 ounces)
2	tablespoons grated Parmesan cheese

1 Cook asparagus according to package directions, except cook for only half of the time called for on package; drain. Set aside.

2 In a large bowl stir together cream of chicken soup, the ⅓ cup Parmesan cheese, the pesto, and half-and-half. Stir in asparagus and chicken. Spoon mixture into an ungreased 2-quart rectangular baking dish.

3 Bake, uncovered, in a 350°F oven about 25 minutes or until heated through. Sprinkle with the 2 tablespoons Parmesan cheese. Bake for 10 to 15 minutes more or until topping is golden. Let stand for 10 minutes before serving.

TO TOTE: Do not let stand after baking. Cover baking dish tightly. Transport in an insulated carrier.

Nutrition Facts per serving: 259 cal., 15 g total fat (5 g sat. fat), 56 mg chol., 613 mg sodium, 10 g carbo., 3 g fiber, 22 g pro.

There are two secrets to success when making dumplings. First, be sure the stew is bubbling hot before dropping in the dough. Second, don't peek in the slow cooker until the minimum cooking time because the dumplings may deflate.

CHICKEN & DUMPLINGS

2	cups chopped carrots
2	cups chopped potatoes
1½	cups chopped parsnips
2	bay leaves
1	teaspoon dried sage, crushed
1	clove garlic, minced
2	pounds boneless, skinless chicken thighs, cut into 1-inch pieces
1	14-ounce can chicken broth
1	10¾-ounce can condensed cream of chicken soup
1	tablespoon cornstarch
½	cup all-purpose flour
½	cup shredded cheddar cheese (2 ounces)
⅓	cup cornmeal
1	teaspoon baking powder
¼	teaspoon salt
1	egg
2	tablespoons milk
2	tablespoons butter, melted

PREP:

25 minutes

COOK:

8 to 10 hours (low-heat setting) or

4 to 5 hours (high-heat setting)

+ 25 minutes (high-heat setting)

MAKES:

8 servings

1 For stew, in a 4- or 5-quart slow cooker combine carrots, potatoes, parsnips, bay leaves, sage, ½ teaspoon salt, ¼ teaspoon black pepper, and garlic. Place chicken on top of vegetables. In a bowl gradually whisk chicken broth into cream of chicken soup; pour over chicken. Cover and cook on low-heat setting for 8 to 10 hours or on high-heat setting for 4 to 5 hours.

3 If using low-heat setting, turn slow cooker to high-heat setting. With a wooden spoon, stir stew. Discard bay leaves. In a small bowl combine 2 tablespoons cold water and cornstarch; stir into stew until combined.

4 For dumplings, in a bowl combine flour, cheese, cornmeal, baking powder, and the ¼ teaspoon salt. Whisk together egg, milk, and melted butter. Add egg mixture to flour mixture. Stir until moistened. Drop dough from a tablespoon into 8 mounds on top of bubbling stew. Cover and cook for 25 to 30 minutes more or until a toothpick inserted into a dumpling comes out clean. (Do not lift cover during cooking.)

TO TOTE: Cover tightly. Transport in an insulated carrier.

Nutrition Facts per serving: 361 cal., 14 g total fat (6 g sat. fat), 140 mg chol., 948 mg sodium, 29 g carbo., 4 g fiber, 29 g pro.

This old-fashioned, family-friendly dish is quintessential "Sunday afternoon with the folks" fare. Why not rekindle the tradition and ask some relatives over to enjoy lunch this weekend?

CHICKEN SUPREME CASSEROLE

PREP:

25 minutes

BAKE:

30 minutes

STAND:

10 minutes

MAKES:

6 to 8 servings

8   ounces dried rotini pasta

1   16-ounce package frozen stir-fry vegetables
     (broccoli, carrots, onions, red peppers, celery,
     water chestnuts, and mushrooms)

2   10¾-ounce cans condensed cream of chicken soup

2   cups milk

¼   cup mayonnaise or salad dressing

¼   teaspoon black pepper

2   cups chopped cooked chicken (about 10 ounces)

2   cups cubed French bread

2   tablespoons butter or margarine, melted

¼   teaspoon garlic powder

1   tablespoon snipped fresh parsley

1 Cook rotini according to package directions, except add the stir-fry vegetables for the last 5 minutes of cooking; drain well.

2 Meanwhile, in a large bowl stir together cream of chicken soup, milk, mayonnaise, and pepper. Stir in cooked pasta mixture and chicken.

3 Transfer to an ungreased 3-quart rectangular baking dish. In a medium bowl toss bread cubes with melted butter and garlic powder; sprinkle over pasta mixture.

4 Bake, uncovered, in a 350°F oven for 30 to 35 minutes or until heated through and bread cubes are golden. Let stand for 10 minutes. Sprinkle with parsley before serving.

TO TOTE: **Do not let stand after baking. Cover tightly. Transport in an insulated carrier. Transport snipped parsley in an insulated cooler with ice packs.**

Nutrition Facts per serving: 584 cal., 25 g total fat (8 g sat. fat), 71 mg chol., 1,123 mg sodium, 60 g carbo., 4 g fiber, 28 g pro.

The golden topper starts with a package of corn muffin mix.

CORN BREAD-TOPPED CHICKEN PIE

1   8½-ounce package corn muffin mix

1   pound skinless, boneless chicken breasts or thighs, cut into 1-inch pieces

⅓   cup chopped onion

⅓   cup chopped green sweet pepper

1   tablespoon olive oil or cooking oil

1   10¾-ounce can condensed cream of mushroom soup

¼   cup all-purpose flour

1   teaspoon dried sage, crushed

1   cup chicken broth

1   10-ounce package frozen peas and carrots

PREP:
20 minutes
BAKE:
18 minutes
MAKES:
6 servings

1 Prepare corn muffin mix according to package directions but do not bake; set aside.

2 In a large skillet cook chicken, onion, and sweet pepper in hot oil until chicken is brown and vegetables are tender. In a medium bowl stir together cream of mushroom soup, flour, and sage; stir into chicken mixture. Stir in chicken broth and peas and carrots. Cook and stir until thickened and bubbly.

3 Pour bubbling chicken mixture into an ungreased 2-quart square baking dish. Spoon corn muffin batter over casserole.

4 Bake, uncovered, in a 425°F oven for 18 to 20 minutes or until toothpick inserted in corn bread comes out clean.

TO TOTE: **Cover tightly. Transport in an insulated carrier.**

Nutrition Facts per serving: 399 cal., 15 g total fat (2 g sat. fat), 71 mg chol., 927 mg sodium, 44 g carbo., 2 g fiber, 25 g pro.

Serving chicken in chunks rather than whole breasts makes it easy for diners to take just a spoonful of a dish at a potluck table. Don't be surprised, however, if they come back for more.

CHICKEN, WILD RICE & VEGETABLE CASSEROLE

PREP:

35 minutes

BAKE:

30 minutes + 5 minutes

MAKES:

8 servings

1 6-ounce package long grain and wild rice mix

3 cups chopped cooked chicken (about 1 pound)

1 14½-ounce can French-cut green beans, drained

1 10¾-ounce can condensed cream of celery soup

1 8-ounce can sliced water chestnuts, drained

½ cup mayonnaise or salad dressing

½ cup chopped onion

3 tablespoons sliced almonds

1 2-ounce jar sliced pimientos, drained

1 teaspoon lemon juice

1 cup shredded cheddar cheese (4 ounces)

1 Prepare rice mix according to package directions. Meanwhile, in a large bowl combine chicken, green beans, cream of celery soup, water chestnuts, mayonnaise, onion, almonds, pimientos, and lemon juice. Stir in cooked rice. Spoon mixture into an ungreased 3-quart rectangular baking dish.

2 Bake, covered, in a 350°F oven for 30 minutes. Uncover and sprinkle with cheese. Bake about 5 minutes more or until heated through and cheese is melted.

MAKE-AHEAD DIRECTIONS: Prepare as directed through step 1. Cover and chill for up to 24 hours. Bake casserole, covered, in a 350°F oven for 45 minutes. Uncover and sprinkle with cheese. Bake about 5 minutes more or until heated through and cheese is melted.

TO TOTE: Cover tightly. Transport in an insulated carrier.

Nutrition Facts per serving: 431 cal., 25 g total fat (6 g sat. fat), 67 mg chol., 872 mg sodium, 30 g carbo., 2 g fiber, 23 g pro.

Layered with tortilla strips, a tomato sauce, chicken, and cheddar cheese, this casserole will tickle the fancy of Mexican food fans.

MEXICAN-STYLE CHICKEN

2	10¾-ounce cans condensed cream of chicken soup
1	10-ounce can diced tomatoes with green chile peppers, undrained
¾	cup chopped green sweet pepper
½	cup chopped onion
1½	teaspoons chili powder
¼	teaspoon black pepper
12	6- or 7-inch corn tortillas, cut into thin bite-size strips
3	cups cubed cooked chicken (about 1 pound)
1	8-ounce package shredded cheddar cheese (2 cups)
	Tomato slices (optional)
	Sliced green onions (optional)

PREP:
20 minutes
BAKE:
45 minutes
STAND:
10 minutes
MAKES:
8 servings

1 In a medium bowl combine cream of chicken soup, tomatoes with chile peppers, sweet pepper, onion, chili powder, and black pepper; set aside.

2 To assemble, sprinkle about one-third of the tortilla strips over the bottom of an ungreased 3-quart rectangular baking dish. Layer half of the chicken over tortilla strips; spoon half of the soup mixture on top. Sprinkle half of the cheese and another one-third of the tortilla strips over the soup mixture. Layer with remaining chicken, soup mixture, and tortilla strips.

3 Bake, uncovered, in a 350°F oven about 45 minutes or until bubbly around edges and center is hot. Remove from oven; sprinkle with remaining cheese. Let stand for 10 minutes before serving. If desired, top with sliced tomatoes and green onions.

TO TOTE: **Do not let stand after sprinkling with cheese. Cover tightly. Transport in an insulated carrier. If desired, transport tomatoes and green onions in an insulated cooler with ice packs.**

Nutrition Facts per serving: 407 cal., 20 g total fat (8 g sat. fat), 82 mg chol., 916 mg sodium, 31 g carbo., 3 g fiber, 27 g pro.

Water chestnuts and almonds lend a contrasting crunch to this creamy bake.

CREAMY CHICKEN CASSEROLE

PREP:

25 minutes

BAKE:

45 minutes

STAND:

5 minutes

MAKES:

6 servings

3½ ounces dried elbow macaroni (about 1 cup)

¾ cup milk

1 10¾-ounce can condensed cream of chicken soup

2 cups chopped cooked chicken (about 10 ounces)

1 cup shredded American cheese (4 ounces)

1 8-ounce can sliced water chestnuts, drained

1 4-ounce can (drained weight) sliced mushrooms, drained

¼ cup chopped bottled roasted red sweet pepper

1 teaspoon dried thyme, crushed

3 tablespoons sliced almonds, toasted (optional)

1 Cook macaroni according to package directions; drain. In a large bowl stir milk into cream of chicken soup. Stir in chicken, half of the the American cheese, the water chestnuts, mushrooms, roasted sweet red pepper, thyme, and cooked macaroni. Spoon mixture into an ungreased 2-quart casserole.

2 Bake, covered, in a 350°F oven for 45 to 50 minutes or until heated through. Top with remaining American cheese. Let stand about 5 minutes or until cheese is melted. If desired, sprinkle with toasted almonds.

TO TOTE: **Do not let stand after sprinkling with cheese. Cover tightly. Transport in an insulated carrier.**

Nutrition Facts per serving: 311 cal., 14 g total fat (6 g sat. fat), 66 mg chol., 776 mg sodium, 22 g carbo., 2 g fiber, 23 g pro.

Stratas can hardly be beat for entertaining! You can get them oven-ready up to 24 hours in advance, easing the last-minute time crunch when you're serving a crowd.

CHICKEN MUSHROOM STRATA

2	5½-ounce packages large croutons (about 6 cups)
2½	cups chopped cooked chicken or turkey (about 12 ounces)
1	4-ounce can (drained weight) sliced mushrooms, drained
½	cup sliced green onions
1½	cups shredded Colby and Monterey Jack cheese or cheddar cheese (6 ounces)
5	eggs
1	10¾-ounce can condensed cream of chicken or cream of mushroom soup
1½	cups milk
1	tablespoon Dijon-style mustard
¼	teaspoon black pepper

1 Place croutons in a greased 3-quart rectangular baking dish. Layer chicken, mushrooms, and green onions over croutons; sprinkle with cheese.

2 In a large bowl whisk together eggs, cream of chicken soup, milk, mustard, and pepper. Carefully pour over layers in dish. Cover and chill for at least 2 hours or up to 24 hours.

3 Bake, uncovered, in a 325°F oven about 45 minutes or until set in center (180°F). Let stand for 10 minutes before serving.

TO TOTE: **Do not let stand after baking. Cover tightly. Transport in an insulated carrier.**

Nutrition Facts per serving: 355 cal., 15 g total fat (7 g sat. fat), 158 mg chol., 722 mg sodium, 29 g carbo., 2 g fiber, 23 g pro.

PREP:
25 minutes
BAKE:
45 minutes
STAND:
10 minutes
CHILL:
2 to 24 hours
MAKES:
10 to 12 servings

While most casseroles are variations on the same theme—a combination of meat, vegetables, a starchy ingredient, and a creamy sauce—the concept leaves lots of room for invention. Here's yet another creative take on that much-loved formula.

CHICKEN-SPAGHETTI CASSEROLE

PREP:

25 minutes

BAKE:

45 minutes

MAKES:

6 servings

4 ounces dried spaghetti

3 slices bacon, chopped

½ cup chopped onion

1 clove garlic, minced

3 tablespoons all-purpose flour

1 14½-ounce can diced tomatoes, undrained

1 10¾-ounce can condensed golden mushroom soup

½ cup milk

1 cup shredded Swiss cheese (4 ounces)

2 cups cubed cooked chicken (about 10 ounces)

½ of a 16-ounce package frozen loose-pack cauliflower, broccoli, and carrots, thawed

❶ Break spaghetti pieces in half. Cook according to package directions. Drain; set aside.

❷ Meanwhile, in a large saucepan cook bacon, onion, and garlic until bacon is crisp; stir in flour. Add tomatoes, golden mushroom soup, and milk. Cook and stir until thickened and bubbly. Add Swiss cheese; stir until melted. Stir in cooked spaghetti, chicken, and vegetables. Turn into an ungreased 2½-quart casserole.

❸ Bake, uncovered, in a 350°F oven about 45 minutes or until heated through.

TO TOTE: **Cover tightly. Transport in an insulated carrier.**

Nutrition Facts per serving: 366 cal., 15 g total fat (7 g sat. fat), 68 mg chol., 701 mg sodium, 29 g carbo., 3 g fiber, 26 g pro.

The tried-and-true chicken-broccoli bake is reinvented as an easy slow-cooker supper. It's also a good choice to tote to potlucks.

CREAMY CHICKEN-BROCCOLI BAKE

Nonstick cooking spray

6	ounces dried medium noodles
12	ounces skinless, boneless chicken breast halves, cut into bite-size pieces
1½	cups sliced fresh mushrooms
4	green onions, sliced
½	of a medium red sweet pepper, chopped
1	tablespoon cooking oil (optional)
1	10¾-ounce can condensed cream of broccoli soup
1	8-ounce carton dairy sour cream
¼	cup chicken broth
1	teaspoon dry mustard
⅛	teaspoon black pepper
1	10-ounce package frozen chopped broccoli, thawed and drained
¼	cup fine dry bread crumbs
1	tablespoon butter or margarine, melted

PREP:
30 minutes
BAKE:
30 minutes + 15 minutes
MAKES:
6 servings

1 Coat a 2-quart square baking dish with nonstick cooking spray; set dish aside. Cook noodles according to package directions; drain. Rinse with cold water; drain again.

2 Meanwhile, coat a large skillet with nonstick cooking spray. Preheat over medium heat. Add chicken to skillet. Cook and stir about 3 minutes or until chicken is no longer pink. Transfer chicken to a large bowl.

3 Add mushrooms, green onions, and sweet pepper to skillet. Cook and stir until vegetables are tender. If necessary, add cooking oil to skillet.

4 Transfer vegetables to bowl with chicken. Stir in cream of broccoli soup, sour cream, chicken broth, mustard, and black pepper. Gently stir in cooked noodles and broccoli.

5 Spoon chicken mixture into prepared baking dish. In a small bowl combine bread crumbs and melted butter; sprinkle over chicken mixture.

6 Bake, covered, in a 350°F oven for 30 minutes. Uncover and bake about 15 minutes more or until heated through.

TO TOTE: Cover tightly. Transport in an insulated carrier.

Nutrition Facts per serving: 354 cal., 16 g total fat (8 g sat. fat), 83 mg chol., 545 mg sodium, 33 g carbo., 3 g fiber, 22 g pro.

To keep the sauce warm while toting, pack it in a wide-mouthed insulated vacuum bottle.

TURKEY STUFFING BAKE

PREP:

35 minutes

BAKE:

35 minutes

STAND:

5 minutes

MAKES:

8 servings

1	cup water
1	cup chopped red sweet pepper
$\frac{1}{2}$	cup uncooked long grain rice
1	medium onion, chopped
1	8-ounce package herb-seasoned stuffing mix
2	cups water
4	cups diced cooked turkey or chicken (about 1¼ pounds)
3	beaten eggs
1	10¾-ounce can condensed cream of chicken soup
$\frac{1}{2}$	cup dairy sour cream
$\frac{1}{4}$	cup milk
2	teaspoons dry sherry or chicken broth

1 In a medium saucepan bring the 1 cup water to boiling. Stir in sweet pepper, rice, and onion. Reduce heat to low. Cover and cook about 20 minutes or until rice and vegetables are tender and water is absorbed.

2 In a large bowl combine stuffing mix and 2 cups water. Stir in turkey, eggs, and half of the cream of chicken soup. Stir in cooked rice mixture. Spread in a greased 3-quart rectangular baking dish.

3 Bake, uncovered, in a 350°F oven for 35 to 40 minutes or until heated through.

4 Meanwhile, for sauce, in a small saucepan combine remaining cream of chicken soup, sour cream, and milk. Cook over low heat until heated through. Stir in dry sherry.

5 Let casserole stand for 5 minutes before serving. Cut casserole into squares to serve. Spoon sauce over servings.

TO TOTE: **Do not let casserole stand after baking. Cover casserole tightly; cover sauce tightly. Transport in an insulated carrier.**

Nutrition Facts per serving: 383 cal., 12 g total fat (4 g sat. fat), 142 mg chol., 765 mg sodium, 38 g carbo., 3 g fiber, 29 g pro.

Two cheeses, a packaged rice mix, and cream of chicken soup transform leftover roasted turkey into a rich, oven meal.

TURKEY-WILD RICE BAKE

1	6-ounce package uncooked long grain and wild rice mix
1	large onion, chopped
3	cloves garlic, minced
1	tablespoon butter
1	10¾-ounce can condensed cream of chicken soup
1	cup milk
1½	teaspoons dried basil, crushed
2	cups shredded Swiss cheese (8 ounces)
1	4-ounce can (drained weight) sliced mushrooms, drained
3	cups chopped cooked turkey
½	cup shredded Parmesan cheese (2 ounces)
⅓	cup sliced almonds, toasted

1 Prepare long grain and wild rice mix according to package directions, discarding the seasoning packet; set aside.

2 In a 12-inch skillet cook onion and garlic in hot butter over medium heat until onion is tender. Stir in cream of chicken soup, milk, and basil. Heat through. Slowly add Swiss cheese to skillet, stirring until cheese melts. Stir in mushrooms, turkey, and rice.

3 Transfer to a 3-quart rectangular baking dish. Top with Parmesan. Bake, uncovered, in a 350°F oven for 15 to 20 minutes or until heated through. Top with almonds before serving.

TO TOTE: **Cover tightly. Transport in an insulated carrier.**

Nutrition Facts per serving: 700 cal., 36 g total fat (19g sat. fat), 132 mg chol., 1,400 mg sodium, 37 g carbo., 4 g fiber, 76 g pro.

PREP:
35 minutes
BAKE:
15 minutes
MAKES:
6 servings

How do you improve on Mom's cooking? In this case, you don't. Her tuna casserole tastes as good today as it did 30 years ago.

MOM'S TUNA-NOODLE CASSEROLE

PREP:
20 minutes

BAKE:
30 minutes

MAKES:
6 servings

4	ounces dried medium egg noodles (2 cups)
1	cup frozen loose-pack peas or peas and carrots
1	medium onion, finely chopped
½	cup finely chopped celery
2	tablespoons butter or margarine
1	10¾-ounce can condensed cream of mushroom or cream of celery soup
¾	cup milk
1	9-ounce can tuna, drained and flaked
¼	cup chopped red sweet pepper
⅛	teaspoon black pepper
¼	cup grated Parmesan cheese (1 ounce)

1 Cook noodles according to package directions, adding peas for the last 3 minutes of cooking. Drain and set aside.

2 Meanwhile, in a medium saucepan cook onion and celery in hot butter until tender. Stir in cream of mushroom soup and milk. Gently stir in tuna, sweet pepper, and black pepper. Add tuna mixture to noodle mixture; toss gently to coat. Turn into an ungreased 2-quart casserole. Sprinkle with cheese.

3 Bake, uncovered, in a 375°F oven for 30 to 35 minutes or until heated through.

TO TOTE: **Cover tightly. Transport in an insulated carrier.**

Nutrition Facts per serving: 267 cal., 11 g total fat (5 g sat. fat), 47 mg chol., 652 mg sodium, 24 g carbo., 2 g fiber, 18 g pro.

Mushrooms, green beans, and Swiss cheese bring extra panache to the good-old standby.

TUNA-NOODLE CASSEROLE

4	ounces dried medium noodles
1	10-ounce package frozen whole or cut green beans
1/4	cup fine dry bread crumbs
1	tablespoon butter or margarine, melted
1	tablespoon butter or margarine
1	cup sliced fresh mushrooms
3/4	cup chopped red or green sweet pepper
1/2	cup chopped onion
1/2	cup sliced celery
1	clove garlic, minced
1	10¾-ounce can condensed cream of mushroom or cream of celery soup
1/2	cup milk
1/2	cup shredded process Swiss or American cheese (2 ounces)
1	9-ounce can tuna, drained and flaked

PREP:
30 minutes
BAKE:
30 minutes
MAKES:
6 servings

1 Cook noodles according to package directions, adding the green beans for the last 3 minutes of cooking. Drain and set aside. Meanwhile, toss the bread crumbs with the 1 tablespoon melted butter; set aside.

2 In a 12-inch skillet melt 1 tablespoon butter over medium heat. Add mushrooms, sweet pepper, onion, celery, and garlic. Cook and stir until vegetables are tender. Add cream of mushroom soup, milk, and cheese, stirring until cheese is melted. Stir in tuna and cooked noodles and green beans.

3 Spoon tuna mixture into an ungreased 2-quart casserole. Sprinkle bread crumb mixture around outside edge of casserole.

4 Bake, uncovered, in a 350°F oven for 30 to 35 minutes or until heated through and bread crumbs are golden.

TO TOTE: **Cover tightly. Transport in an insulated carrier.**

Nutrition Facts per serving: 301 cal., 13 g total fat (6 g sat. fat), 53 mg chol., 682 mg sodium, 27 g carbo., 3 g fiber, 20 g pro.

This casserole transcends ho-hum with added richness from mayonnaise, flavorful and colorful roasted red sweet pepper, and an irresistible buttery crumb topping.

TUNA-MACARONI CASSEROLE

PREP:

25 minutes

BAKE:

40 minutes

MAKES:

4 servings

4   ounces dried small shell macaroni (1 cup)

1   10¾-ounce can condensed cream of onion soup

⅓   cup milk

¼   cup mayonnaise or salad dressing

½   teaspoon dry mustard

1   6-ounce can tuna, drained and flaked

1   cup shredded American or cheddar cheese (4 ounces)

½   cup chopped roasted red sweet pepper

¼   cup fine dry bread crumbs

1   tablespoon butter or margarine, melted

½   teaspoon paprika

Snipped fresh parsley (optional)

1 Cook macaroni according to package directions; drain. In a large bowl stir together cream of onion soup, milk, mayonnaise, and mustard. Stir in tuna, cheese, and roasted red pepper. Gently fold in cooked macaroni. Spoon into an ungreased 1½-quart casserole.

2 In a small bowl combine bread crumbs, melted butter, and paprika; sprinkle evenly over casserole.

3 Bake, uncovered, in a 350°F oven for 40 to 45 minutes or until hot in center. If desired, sprinkle with parsley.

TO TOTE: **Cover casserole tightly. Transport in an insulated carrier. If desired, transport parsley in an insulated cooler with ice packs.**

Nutrition Facts per serving: 498 cal., 29 g total fat (11 g sat. fat), 72 mg chol., 1,394 mg sodium, 36 g carbo., 2 g fiber, 23 g pro.

Many old favorites make top-notch potluck dishes. Here a double dose of cheese adds a flavorful twist to a beloved comfort food.

CHEESY TUNA-NOODLE CASSEROLE

8	ounces dried medium noodles (4 cups)
1/3	cup chopped onion
2	tablespoons butter or margarine
2	tablespoons all-purpose flour
1	10¾-ounce can condensed cheddar cheese soup
¾	cup milk
1	10-ounce package frozen chopped broccoli
1	9-ounce can tuna, drained and flaked
1	2¼-ounce can sliced pitted ripe olives, drained
½	cup shredded cheddar cheese (2 ounces)

1 Cook noodles according to package directions; drain. Return noodles to saucepan.

2 Meanwhile, in a medium saucepan cook onion in hot butter until tender. Stir in flour; stir in cheddar cheese soup. Gradually stir in milk. Cook and stir until thickened and bubbly. Gently stir in broccoli, tuna, and olives. Add tuna mixture to noodles; toss gently to coat.

3 Turn mixture into a 2-quart casserole. Bake, covered, in a 375°F oven for 25 minutes. Top with shredded cheddar cheese; bake, uncovered, about 5 minutes more or until cheese is melted and mixture is heated through.

TO TOTE: **Cover tightly. Transport in an insulated carrier.**

Nutrition Facts per serving: 358 cal., 14 g total fat (7 g sat. fat), 79 mg chol., 769 mg sodium, 38 g carbo., 3 g fiber, 23 g pro.

PREP:
25 minutes
BAKE:
25 minutes + 5 minutes
MAKES:
6 servings

Use an instant-read thermometer to test the doneness of the strata. If you don't have one, bake the strata until almost set in center. Although the dish may seem soupy at first, it will set up as it stands.

SALMON STRATA

PREP:

25 minutes

CHILL:

1 to 3 hours

BAKE:

55 minutes

STAND:

10 minutes

MAKES:

6 servings

5   cups dry bread cubes*

2   6-ounce cans skinless, boneless salmon, drained and flaked

¼   cup chopped green sweet pepper

2   tablespoons finely chopped onion

4   eggs

1   10¾-ounce can condensed cream of asparagus or cream of celery soup

1   cup milk

¼   teaspoon dried dill

2   tablespoons butter or margarine, melted

1 Place 2 cups of the bread cubes in a greased 2-quart square baking dish. Sprinkle salmon, sweet pepper, and onion over bread cubes. Top with another 2 cups of the bread cubes.

2 In a medium bowl whisk together eggs, cream of asparagus soup, milk, and dill. Pour evenly over bread cubes. Cover and chill for at least 1 hour or up to 3 hours.

3 Toss remaining 1 cup bread cubes with melted butter; sprinkle over casserole.

4 Bake, uncovered, in a 325°F oven for 55 to 60 minutes or until an instant-read thermometer inserted in the center registers 170°F. Let stand for 10 minutes before serving. (Center will continue to set up during standing.)

*TEST KITCHEN TIP: To dry bread cubes, cut about 8 slices bread into ½-inch cubes. Spread cubes in a 15×10×1-inch baking pan. Bake in a 300°F oven for 10 to 15 minutes or until dry, stirring once or twice. (Bread will continue to dry and crisp as it cools.)

TO TOTE: Do not let stand after baking. Cover tightly. Transport in an insulated carrier.

Nutrition Facts per serving: 307 cal., 14 g total fat (5 g sat. fat), 189 mg chol., 939 mg sodium, 25 g carbo., 1 g fiber, 19 g pro.

Newburg-style dishes are usually made of shellfish in an elaborate, sherry-enhanced cream sauce. While a "Newburg" is usually served over toast points, the concept adapts deliciously well to a noodle casserole.

CRAB NOODLE NEWBURG

1   10¾-ounce can condensed cream of celery soup

⅔   cup milk

½   cup shredded cheddar cheese (2 ounces)

⅓   cup dairy sour cream

¼   cup dry sherry

4   ounces medium dried noodles, cooked and drained

1   cup finely chopped celery

¼   cup chopped red sweet pepper

2   6-ounce cans crabmeat, drained, flaked, and cartilage removed, or two 6-ounce cans tuna (water pack), drained and flaked

PREP:
25 minutes
BAKE:
45 minutes
MAKES:
4 servings

1 In an ungreased 1½-quart casserole whisk together cream of celery soup, milk, cheese, and sour cream. Stir in dry sherry. Stir in noodles, celery, and sweet pepper. Gently fold in crabmeat.

2 Bake, covered, in a 350°F oven about 45 minutes or until heated through.

TO TOTE: Cover tightly. Transport in an insulated carrier.

Nutrition Facts per serving: 403 cal., 16 g total fat (8 g sat. fat), 130 mg chol., 1,001 mg sodium, 32 g carbo., 2 g fiber, 28 g pro.

This irresistibly oozy lasagna is a relatively inexpensive way to treat diners to a luscious dinner starring seafood.

SEAFOOD LASAGNA

8 dried lasagna noodles

1 cup chopped onion

2 tablespoons butter or margarine

1 3-ounce package cream cheese, softened and cut up

1 12-ounce carton cream-style cottage cheese

1 beaten egg

2 teaspoons dried basil, crushed

¼ teaspoon salt

⅛ teaspoon black pepper

2 10¾-ounce cans condensed cream of mushroom soup

⅓ cup milk

12 ounces cooked, peeled, and deveined shrimp, halved lengthwise

1 6-ounce can crabmeat, drained, flaked, and cartilage removed

¼ cup finely shredded Parmesan cheese (1 ounce)

1 Cook lasagna noodles according to package directions; drain. Arrange 4 of the noodles in the bottom of a greased 3-quart rectangular baking dish. Set aside.

2 In a medium skillet cook onion in hot butter until tender. Remove from heat. Add cream cheese and stir until melted. Stir in cottage cheese, egg, basil, salt, and pepper. Spread half of the cheese mixture over the noodles.

3 In a large bowl combine cream of mushroom soup and milk; stir in shrimp and crabmeat. Spread half of the shrimp mixture over cheese layer. Repeat layers. Sprinkle with Parmesan cheese.

4 Bake, uncovered, in a 350°F oven about 45 minutes or until an instant-read thermometer inserted in center registers 170°F. Let stand for 10 to 15 minutes before serving.

TO TOTE: **Do not let stand after baking. Cover tightly. Transport in an insulated carrier.**

Nutrition Facts per serving: 243 cal., 11 g total fat (5 g sat. fat), 112 mg chol., 720 mg sodium, 18 g carbo., 1 g fiber, 17 g pro.

Hearty enough to be a main dish but fine as a side, this dish is great to take when you don't know what else will be on the potluck table when you arrive.

BROCCOLI-CHEESE CASSEROLE

8	ounces dried macaroni (2 cups)
2	cups broccoli florets
1	10¾-ounce can condensed tomato soup
1	10¾-ounce can condensed cream of broccoli soup
1½	cups shredded cheddar cheese (6 ounces)
½	cup milk
1	medium tomato, chopped

PREP:
25 minutes
BAKE:
30 minutes
STAND:
5 minutes
MAKES:
6 to 8 servings

1 Cook macaroni according to package directions, except add broccoli for the last 2 minutes of cooking; drain. In a large bowl stir together tomato soup, cream of broccoli soup, 1 cup of the cheese, and the milk. Stir in cooked macaroni mixture.

2 Turn mixture into an ungreased 2-quart rectangular baking dish. Sprinkle with remaining ½ cup cheese.

3 Bake, uncovered, in a 350°F oven for 30 minutes. Sprinkle with tomato. Let stand for 5 minutes before serving.

TO TOTE: **Cover tightly after baking. Transport in an insulated carrier. Transport tomato in an insulated cooler with ice packs.**

Nutrition Facts per serving: 353 cal., 13 g total fat (7 g sat. fat), 32 mg chol., 832 mg sodium, 43 g carbo., 3 g fiber, 15 g pro.

The flavors of steak Diane, a classic French dish, translate well to this hearty stew that cooks perfectly in the slow cooker.

MUSHROOM STEAK DIANE STEW

PREP:

20 minutes

COOK:

8 to 10 hours (low-heat setting) or

4 to 5 hours (high-heat setting)

MAKES:

6 servings

1½ pounds boneless beef round steak

2 medium onions, cut into thin wedges

3 cups sliced fresh mushrooms (8 ounces)

1 10¾-ounce can condensed golden mushroom soup

¼ cup tomato paste

2 teaspoons Worcestershire sauce

1 teaspoon dry mustard

½ teaspoon cracked black pepper

Hot cooked noodles

① Trim fat from meat. Cut meat into 1-inch pieces. Set aside. Place onion wedges in a 3½- or 4-quart slow cooker; top with mushrooms. Add meat. In a medium bowl stir together golden mushroom soup, tomato paste, Worcestershire sauce, dry mustard, and pepper. Pour over meat mixture in slow cooker.

② Cover and cook on low-heat setting for 8 to 10 hours or on high-heat setting for 4 to 5 hours. Serve over hot cooked noodles.

TO TOTE: Cover meat mixture tightly. Cover hot cooked noodles tightly; transport in an insulated carrier.

Nutrition Facts per serving: 314 cal., 7 g total fat (2 g sat. fat), 92 mg chol., 569 mg sodium, 30 g carbo., 3 g fiber, 33 g pro.

Diced hash brown potatoes bring rib-sticking goodness to this filling stew—with no peeling or slicing involved. The taste panel also appreciated the nice, smoky flavor the sausage brought to the mix.

EASY SAUSAGE & CHICKEN STEW

1	pound cooked smoked turkey sausage, halved lengthwise and sliced
2	cups packaged peeled baby carrots
1	14-ounce can reduced-sodium chicken broth
1½	cups frozen loose-pack diced hash brown potatoes
1	10¾-ounce can condensed cream of chicken soup
1	teaspoon dried oregano, crushed
2	cups chopped cooked chicken or turkey (about 10 ounces)
1	9-ounce package frozen cut green beans, thawed

1 In a 3½- or 4-quart slow cooker combine turkey sausage, carrots, chicken broth, potatoes, cream of chicken soup, and oregano.

2 Cover and cook on low-heat setting for 8 to 10 hours or on high-heat setting for 4 to 5 hours.

3 If using low-heat setting, turn slow cooker to high-heat setting. Stir in cooked chicken and green beans. Cover and cook for 30 minutes more.

TO TOTE: Cover tightly. Transport in an insulated carrier.

Nutrition Facts per serving: 477 cal., 30 g total fat (13 g sat. fat), 79 mg chol., 1,238 mg sodium, 25 g carbo., 4 g fiber, 27 g pro.

PREP:
10 minutes

COOK:
8 to 10 hours
(low-heat setting) or

4 to 5 hours
(high-heat setting)

+ 30 minutes
(high-heat setting)

MAKES:
6 to 8 servings

Turn a can of tomato soup into a full-meal deal with some hearty stir-ins, including that ever-favorite comfort food: smoked sausage.

TURKEY SAUSAGE & SWEET PEPPER STEW

PREP:

25 minutes

COOK:

15 minutes

MAKES:

6 servings

1   pound smoked turkey sausage or cooked turkey kielbasa

4   medium red, yellow, and/or green sweet peppers, cut into 1-inch pieces

2   stalks celery, cut into $\frac{1}{2}$-inch pieces

1   large onion, chopped

1    $10\frac{3}{4}$-ounce can condensed tomato soup

1    $14\frac{1}{2}$-ounce can diced tomatoes, undrained

1   15-ounce can Great Northern or navy beans, rinsed and drained

1   cup water

1 Cut sausage in half lengthwise; cut into $\frac{1}{2}$-inch slices. Set aside.

2 In a Dutch oven combine sausage pieces, sweet peppers, celery, and onion. Add tomato soup, tomatoes, beans, and water. Bring to boiling; reduce heat. Simmer, covered, for 15 to 20 minutes or until vegetables are tender.

TO TOTE: **Cover tightly. Transport in an insulated carrier.**

Nutrition Facts per serving: 258 cal., 7 g total fat (2 g sat. fat), 51 mg chol., 1,275 mg sodium, 31 g carbo., 7 g fiber, 18 g pro.

Who would have thought such an elegant soup could be so simple?

CRAB BISQUE

1   10¾-ounce can condensed cream of asparagus soup

1   10¾-ounce can condensed cream of mushroom soup

2¾   cups milk

1   cup half-and-half or light cream

1   6-ounce can crabmeat, drained, flaked, and cartilage removed

3   tablespoons dry sherry or milk

1 In a large saucepan combine cream of asparagus soup, cream of mushroom soup, milk, and half-and-half. Bring to boiling over medium heat, stirring frequently.

2 Stir in crabmeat and dry sherry; heat through.

TO TOTE: Cover tightly. Transport in an insulated carrier.

Nutrition Facts per serving: 227 cal., 12 g total fat (6 g sat. fat), 63 mg chol., 921 mg sodium, 16 g carbo., 1 g fiber, 12 g pro.

START TO FINISH:

20 minutes

MAKES:

6 servings

Refrigerated tortellini ranks with canned soup as an all-time-great convenience product. When you pair them, as in this recipe, it's no surprise you can get a satisfying soup ready in twenty minutes.

TUNA TORTELLINI SOUP

START TO FINISH:

20 minutes

MAKES:

6 servings

3 cups milk

2 10¾-ounce cans condensed cream of potato soup

1 cup frozen loose-pack peas

1 teaspoon dried basil, crushed

1 9-ounce package refrigerated cheese tortellini

1 12-ounce can tuna (water pack), drained and flaked

⅓ cup dry white wine

1 In a large saucepan combine milk, cream of potato soup, peas, and basil; bring just to boiling. Add tortellini. Simmer, uncovered, for 6 to 8 minutes or until tortellini is tender, stirring frequently to prevent sticking. Stir in tuna and wine. Heat through.

TO TOTE: **Cover tightly. Transport in an insulated carrier.**

Nutrition Facts per serving: 351 cal., 9 g total fat (4 g sat. fat), 59 mg chol., 1,267 mg sodium, 38 g carbo., 2 g fiber, 27 g pro.

For something a little different, substitute four ounces of cooked bulk pork sausage for the bacon.

POTATO SOUP WITH BACON

6   slices bacon, halved crosswise (about 4 ounces)

½   cup chopped onion

½   cup chopped celery

2   large potatoes, peeled and coarsely chopped

1   cup water

1   teaspoon mustard seeds or Dijon-style mustard

1½   cups half-and-half, light cream, or milk

1   10¾-ounce can condensed cream of chicken or golden mushroom soup

Snipped fresh parsley (optional)

PREP:
30 minutes
COOK:
15 minutes
MAKES:
6 servings

1 In a large saucepan cook bacon over medium heat until crisp. Remove bacon, reserving 1 tablespoon drippings in saucepan. Drain bacon on paper towels. Crumble bacon and set aside; if desired, reserve several bacon pieces for garnish.

2 Add onion and celery to hot drippings in saucepan; cook until tender. Stir in potatoes, water, and mustard seeds. Bring to boiling; reduce heat. Simmer, covered, about 15 minutes or just until potatoes are tender.

3 Stir in half-and-half and cream of chicken soup. Heat through but do not boil. Stir in crumbled bacon. If desired, garnish with parsley and reserved bacon.

TO TOTE: Cover soup tightly. Transport in an insulated carrier. If desired, transport parsley and reserved bacon in an insulated cooler with ice packs.

Nutrition Facts per serving: 317 cal., 22 g total fat (9 g sat. fat), 44 mg chol., 728 mg sodium, 20 g carbo., 2 g fiber, 11 g pro.

Chili is a sure-fire crowd-pleaser, so when you have some vegetarians on the invite list, serve this hearty veggie version alongside your meaty favorite. You might be surprised to find the meat-eaters greedily dipping into it too!

THREE BEAN CHILI

PREP:

25 minutes

COOK:

30 minutes + 10 minutes

MAKES:

8 servings

2   15-ounce cans pinto beans, rinsed and drained

1   28-ounce can crushed tomatoes

1   18.8-ounce can ready-to-serve lentil soup

1   15-ounce can garbanzo beans (chickpeas), rinsed and drained

1   15-ounce can black beans, rinsed and drained

1   4-ounce can diced green chile peppers, undrained

2   medium onions, chopped

1   cup water

1   tablespoon chili powder

2   medium zucchini, halved lengthwise and sliced (about 2½ cups)

1   cup shredded Monterey Jack cheese with jalapeño peppers (4 ounces)

Dairy sour cream (optional)

Snipped fresh cilantro (optional)

1   In a 4- to 5-quart Dutch oven combine pinto beans, tomatoes, lentil soup, garbanzo beans, black beans, chile peppers, onion, water, and chili powder. Bring to boiling; reduce heat. Simmer, covered, for 30 minutes, stirring occasionally.

2   Stir in zucchini. Cover and cook for 10 minutes more. Remove from heat. Sprinkle servings with cheese. If desired, serve with sour cream and garnish with cilantro.

TO TOTE: Cover tightly. Transport in an insulated carrier. Transport cheese and, if desired, sour cream and cilantro, in an insulated cooler with ice packs.

Nutrition Facts per serving: 319 cal., 7 g total fat (3 g sat. fat), 15 mg chol., 1,173 mg sodium, 48 g carbo., 15 g fiber, 18 g pro.

This side dish is definitely potluck-worthy. At home, consider serving it with a tossed green salad when you're aiming for a simple meatless supper.

CALIFORNIA VEGETABLE CASSEROLE

1   16-ounce package frozen loose-pack California-blend vegetables (cauliflower, broccoli, and carrots)

1   10¾-ounce can condensed cream of mushroom soup

1   cup uncooked instant white rice

½   of a 15-ounce jar (about 1 cup) process cheese dip

⅔   cup milk

⅓   cup chopped onion

¼   cup water

2   tablespoons butter or margarine, cut up

1 Place vegetables in a 3½ or 4-quart slow cooker. In a small bowl combine cream of mushroom soup, rice, cheese dip, milk, onion, water, and butter. Pour over vegetables.

2 Cover and cook on low-heat setting for 4½ to 5½ hours or until vegetables and rice are tender. Stir before serving.

TO TOTE: **Cover tightly. Transport in an insulated carrier.**

Nutrition Facts per serving: 292 cal., 17 g total fat (10 g sat. fat), 36 mg chol., 1,124 mg sodium, 26 g carbo., 3 g fiber, 9 g pro.

PREP:
15 minutes

COOK:
4½ to 5½ hours (low-heat setting)

MAKES:
6 side-dish servings

No peeling or chopping the vegetables! An easy-to-use bag of frozen vegetables goes gourmet with a buttery walnut topping.

VEGETABLE MEDLEY AU GRATIN

PREP:

15 minutes

BAKE:

50 minutes + 15 minutes

MAKES:

10 side-dish servings

1	10¾-ounce can condensed cream of chicken and mushroom soup
½	cup dairy sour cream
½	teaspoon dried dill
2	16-ounce packages frozen loose-pack broccoli, cauliflower, and carrots, thawed
⅔	cup crushed stone-ground wheat crackers (about 15 crackers)
⅓	cup finely chopped walnuts
¼	cup finely shredded Parmesan cheese
2	tablespoons butter or margarine, melted

1 In a large bowl combine cream of chicken and mushroom soup, sour cream, and dill; stir in vegetables. Transfer to an ungreased 2-quart rectangular baking dish. Cover with foil. Bake in a 300°F oven for 50 minutes.

2 In a small bowl combine crackers, walnuts, Parmesan cheese, and melted butter. Uncover baking dish; sprinkle vegetable mixture with crumb mixture.

3 Increase oven temperature to 375°F. Bake, uncovered, about 15 minutes more or until topping is brown.

TO TOTE: Cover tightly. Transport in an insulated carrier.

Nutrition Facts per serving: 157 cal., 10 g total fat (4 g sat. fat), 16 mg chol., 452 mg sodium, 11 g carbo., 3 g fiber, 5 g pro.

Every potluck needs a good vegetable side dish, so consider taking this to your next gathering.

CREAMY BROCCOLI & CAULIFLOWER

1	10¾-ounce can condensed cream of chicken soup
1	8-ounce tub cream cheese with chive and onion
½	cup milk
1	teaspoon finely shredded lemon peel
1	16-ounce package frozen cauliflower, thawed
1	16-ounce package frozen cut broccoli, thawed
1	cup crushed rich round crackers
2	tablespoons butter or margarine, melted

PREP:
15 minutes

BAKE:
30 minutes + 10 minutes

MAKES:
10 side-dish servings

1 In a large bowl combine cream of chicken soup, cream cheese, milk, and lemon peel. Cut up any large pieces of vegetables. Add vegetables to soup mixture, stirring to coat. Spoon into an ungreased 2-quart rectangular baking dish. In a small bowl combine crushed crackers and melted butter; set aside.

2 Bake, uncovered, in a 375°F oven for 30 minutes. Carefully stir vegetable mixture; sprinkle with cracker mixture. Bake about 10 minutes more or until heated through.

TO TOTE: Cover tightly. Transport in an insulated carrier.

Nutrition Facts per serving: 192 cal., 14 g total fat (8 g sat. fat), 32 mg chol., 425 mg sodium, 13 g carbo., 3 g fiber, 4 g pro.

When you're looking for an any-occasion side dish that you know will please a crowd, turn to this recipe. It's a keeper!

CREAMY POTLUCK POTATOES

PREP:

25 minutes

BAKE:

25 minutes

STAND:

5 minutes

MAKES:

10 side-dish servings

3   pounds potatoes, peeled and cut up (about 6 cups)

1   10¾-ounce can condensed cream of chicken soup

½   cup dairy sour cream

1   3-ounce package cream cheese, softened

2   tablespoons butter or margarine, melted

¾   cup shredded cheddar cheese (3 ounces)

¼   cup sliced green onions

¼   cup milk

¼   teaspoon garlic salt

¼   teaspoon black pepper

1 In a covered large saucepan cook potatoes in enough boiling salted water to cover for 10 to 12 minutes or just until tender. Drain; rinse with cold water. Drain again.

2 Meanwhile, in a large bowl stir together cream of chicken soup, sour cream, cream cheese, and butter. Stir in ¼ cup of the shredded cheese, 3 tablespoons of the green onions, the milk, garlic salt, and pepper. Stir in the cooked potatoes. Transfer mixture to an ungreased 2-quart rectangular baking dish.

3 Bake, uncovered, in a 350°F oven for 25 to 30 minutes or until heated through. Sprinkle with the remaining ½ cup shredded cheese. Let stand about 5 minutes or until cheese melts. Sprinkle with the remaining 1 tablespoon green onion.

TO TOTE: Do not let stand after sprinkling with cheese. Cover tightly. Transport in an insulated carrier. Transport remaining 1 tablespoon green onion in an insulated cooler with ice packs.

Nutrition Facts per serving: 224 cal., 12 g total fat (7 g sat. fat), 32 mg chol., 367 mg sodium, 22 g carbo., 2 g fiber, 6 g pro.

BONUS
CHAPTER

9

This version of the ever-favorite spinach and vegetable dip calls on jicama, a crisp, mild-tasting root vegetable, to add a delicate crunch and "wow, what is it?" appeal to the classic.

CREAMY SPINACH DIP

2 8-ounce cartons plain low-fat yogurt

1 8-ounce carton light dairy sour cream

1 1.4-ounce envelope dry vegetable soup mix

1 10-ounce package frozen chopped spinach, thawed

½ cup finely chopped jicama or ½ cup sliced water chestnuts, drained and finely chopped

¼ cup finely chopped onion

Dash cayenne pepper

Assorted cut-up vegetables and/or assorted crackers

1 In a large bowl stir together yogurt, sour cream, and vegetable soup mix. Squeeze excess liquid from spinach. Finely chop spinach. Stir spinach, jicama, onion, and cayenne pepper into yogurt mixture.

2 Cover and chill for at least 2 hours or up to 24 hours. Serve with vegetables.

Nutrition Facts per ¼ cup dip: 50 cal., 2 g total fat (1 g sat. fat), 6 mg chol., 220 mg sodium, 6 g carbo., 1 g fiber, 3 g pro.

This might just be the most well-known of the 1950s-style dips—and it endures as a favorite today. It combines sour cream with a new product of that time—dry onion soup mix. This version is updated with a little crumbled blue cheese.

CREAMY ONION DIP

1½ cups dairy sour cream

2 tablespoons dry onion soup mix

½ cup crumbled blue cheese (2 ounces)

¼ cup crumbled blue cheese (1 ounce) (optional)

Snipped fresh parsley (optional)

Assorted cut-up vegetables and/or crackers

① In a medium bowl stir together sour cream and onion soup mix. Stir in the ½ cup blue cheese. Cover and chill for at least 2 hours or up to 48 hours.

② If desired, sprinkle with the ¼ cup blue cheese and/or snipped parsley. Serve with vegetables.

Nutrition Facts per ¼ cup dip: 128 cal., 11 g total fat (7 g sat. fat), 25 mg chol., 308 mg sodium, 3 g carbo., 0 g fiber, 3 g pro.

PREP:
10 minutes

CHILL:
2 to 48 hours

MAKES:
1¾ cups
(7 appetizer servings)

Top peppered steak with colorful and crisp stir-fried peppers. If you're lucky enough to have leftovers, spoon them into hoagie rolls for sandwiches or toss them in a green salad.

PEPPER OF A STEAK

PREP:

15 minutes

BROIL:

12 minutes

MAKES:

8 servings

Cracked black pepper

4   12-ounce beef top loin steaks, cut 1 inch thick

½   of a medium red sweet pepper, cut into thin strips

½   of a medium yellow sweet pepper, cut into thin strips

½   of a medium green sweet pepper, cut into thin strips

2   tablespoons butter or cooking oil

1   0.6-ounce envelope dry au jus gravy mix

1 Press cracked black pepper into one side of each steak, using about ½ teaspoon pepper per steak.

2 Place steaks on the unheated rack of a broiler pan. Broil 3 to 4 inches from the heat to desired doneness, turning once. Allow 12 to 14 minutes for medium-rare doneness (145°F) or 15 to 18 minutes for medium doneness (160°F).

3 Meanwhile, in a medium skillet cook sweet pepper strips in hot butter until tender. Prepare gravy mix according to package directions. To serve, top steaks with sweet pepper strips and gravy.

Nutrition Facts per serving: 352 cal., 24 g total fat (11 g sat. fat), 110 mg chol., 181 mg sodium, 2 g carbo., 1 g fiber, 32 g pro.

If you like, stir a couple of tablespoons of dry red wine into the beef mixture just before serving to add even more depth of flavor to this dish.

MUSHROOM & ONION-SAUCED ROUND STEAK

2   pounds boneless beef round steak, cut ¾ inch thick

1   tablespoon cooking oil

2   medium onions, sliced

3   cups sliced fresh mushrooms

1   12-ounce jar beef gravy

1   1.1-ounce envelope dry mushroom gravy mix

Hot cooked noodles (optional)

1   Trim fat from meat. Cut meat into 8 serving-size pieces. In a large skillet brown meat, half at a time, in hot oil. Drain off fat. Set aside.

2   Place onions in a 3½- or 4-quart slow cooker. Add meat and mushrooms. In a small bowl stir together beef gravy and mushroom gravy mix. Pour over meat mixture in slow cooker.

3   Cover and cook on low-heat setting for 8 to 10 hours or on high-heat setting for 4 to 5 hours. If desired, serve over hot cooked noodles.

Nutrition Facts per serving: 194 cal., 7 g total fat (2 g sat. fat), 57 mg chol., 479 mg sodium, 7 g carbo., 1 g fiber, 24 g pro.

PREP:
20 minutes

COOK:
8 to 10 hours (low-heat setting) or
4 to 5 hours (high-heat setting)

MAKES:
8 servings

Put ingredients into the slow cooker, then forget about them until dinner. Weeknight cooking doesn't get much easier than this!

BEEF IN RED WINE GRAVY

PREP:

15 minutes

COOK:

10 to 12 hours (low-heat setting) or

5 to 6 hours (high-heat setting)

MAKES:

6 servings

1½   pounds beef stew meat, cut into 1-inch cubes

2   medium onions, cut up

1   envelope (½ of a 2-ounce package) dry onion soup mix

3   tablespoons cornstarch

Salt

Black pepper

1½   cups dry red wine

Hot cooked noodles (optional)

1 Place the beef and onions in a 3½- or 4-quart slow cooker. Add onion soup mix. Sprinkle with cornstarch, salt, and pepper. Pour red wine over all.

2 Cover and cook on low-heat setting for 10 to 12 hours or on high-heat setting for 5 to 6 hours. If desired, serve over hot cooked noodles.

Nutrition Facts per serving: 248 cal., 6 g total fat (2 g sat. fat), 54 mg chol., 590 mg sodium, 10 g carbo., 1 g fiber, 26 g pro.

Bordelaise means "from Bordeaux" and generally signifies that a dish will be served with a brown sauce flavored with the region's famous red wine. This wine-laced sauce gets a head start with brown gravy mix.

BORDELAISE PEPPERY STEAK

1¼ cups water

1 cup sliced fresh mushrooms

½ cup finely chopped onion

¼ cup dry red wine

1 0.87- to 1.2-ounce package dry brown gravy mix

4 6-ounce beef ribeye, top loin, or tenderloin steaks, cut ¾ inch thick

2 teaspoons garlic-pepper seasoning

2 tablespoons olive oil

START TO FINISH:

30 minutes

MAKES:

4 servings

1 For sauce, in a medium saucepan bring water to boiling. Add mushrooms and onion; reduce heat. Cover and cook for 3 minutes. Stir in red wine and gravy mix. Cook, uncovered, about 3 minutes more or until thickened, stirring occasionally. Cover and keep warm.

2 Meanwhile, trim fat from steaks. Sprinkle both sides of each steak evenly with garlic-pepper seasoning; rub in with your fingers.

3 In a large, heavy skillet heat olive oil over medium-high heat. Add steaks; reduce heat to medium. Cook to desired doneness, turning once. Allow 5 to 7 minutes for medium-rare doneness (145°F) or 7 to 9 minutes for medium doneness (160°F). Serve steaks with sauce.

Nutrition Facts per serving: 366 cal., 18 g total fat (5 g sat. fat), 81 mg chol., 954 mg sodium, 7 g carbo., 1 g fiber, 39 g pro.

This dish goes well with a simply prepared green vegetable, such as lightly sauteed fresh spinach or steamed green beans.

BEEF BRISKET WITH VEGETABLES

PREP:

15 minutes

BAKE:

2 hours + 1 ¹/₂ hours

MAKES:

8 to 10 servings

1   4- to 4¹/₄-pound fresh beef brisket

1   18-ounce bottle barbecue sauce

1   cup ginger ale

1   envelope (¹/₂ of a 2-ounce package) dry onion soup mix

¹/₂   teaspoon black pepper

2   cloves garlic, minced

6   inches stick cinnamon

2   pounds potatoes, quartered (6 medium)

1   pound carrots, cut into 2-inch pieces (6 medium)

2   medium onions, cut into wedges

2   tablespoons snipped fresh parsley

1 Trim excess fat from meat. Place meat in a large shallow roasting pan. For sauce, in a medium bowl stir together barbecue sauce, ginger ale, onion soup mix, pepper, and garlic. Pour over meat. Arrange stick cinnamon around meat. Cover pan with foil.

2 Bake in a 325°F oven for 2 hours, turning meat once. Arrange potatoes, carrots, and onions around meat. Bake meat and vegetables, covered, about 1¹/₂ hours more or until tender.

3 Transfer meat and vegetables to a large serving platter. Discard stick cinnamon. Thinly slice meat. Pour some of the sauce over the meat and vegetables. Sprinkle with parsley. Pass remaining sauce.

Nutrition Facts per serving: 436 cal., 10 g total fat (3 g sat. fat), 96 mg chol., 1,257 mg sodium, 48 g carbo., 4 g fiber, 37 g pro.

This hearty recipe makes 10 to 12 servings, so why not tap into the "cook once, eat twice" plan? Freeze half, and you can have another supper ready in minutes after a crazy day.

BEEF BRISKET WITH SPICY GRAVY

1 3¹/₂- to 4-pound fresh beef brisket

2 cups water

¹/₄ cup catsup

1 envelope (¹/₂ of a 2-ounce package) dry onion soup mix

2 tablespoons Worcestershire sauce

¹/₂ teaspoon ground cinnamon

¹/₂ teaspoon bottled minced garlic (1 clove)

¹/₄ teaspoon black pepper

¹/₄ cup cold water

3 tablespoons all-purpose flour

PREP:

15 minutes

COOK:

10 to 11 hours (low-heat setting) or

5 to 5¹/₂ hours (high-heat setting)

MAKES:

10 to 12 servings

1 Place beef brisket in a 3¹/₂-or 4-quart slow cooker, cutting to fit if necessary.

2 In a medium bowl combine the 2 cups water, the catsup, onion soup mix, Worcestershire sauce, cinnamon, garlic, and pepper. Pour over brisket. Cover and cook on low-heat setting for 10 to 11 hours or on high-heat setting for 5 to 5¹/₂ hours.

3 Remove beef; keep warm. For gravy, pour slow cooker liquid into a glass measuring cup. Skim off fat. Measure 1¹/₂ cups cooking liquid; set aside (discard remaining liquid). For gravy, in a small saucepan stir the ¹/₄ cup cold water into the flour. Stir in the 1¹/₂ cups cooking liquid. Cook and stir until thickened and bubbly. Cook and stir for 1 minute more.

4 Thinly slice beef across the grain. Serve sliced beef with hot gravy.

Nutrition Facts per serving: 185 cal., 7 g total fat (2 g sat. fat), 67 mg chol., 425 mg sodium, 6 g carbo., 0 g fiber, 24 g pro.

Here's a lazy-day dinner if there ever was one! It's a great way to serve cheesy pasta sauce and meatballs—without even having to cook spaghetti.

MEATBALL OVEN DINNER

PREP:

10 minutes

BAKE:

20 minutes + 25 minutes

MAKES:

8 servings

16 frozen Italian-style meatballs (1 ounce each), thawed

2 cups purchased Parmesan-Romano pasta sauce

8 frozen cheddar garlic biscuits or one 10-ounce package (10) refrigerated flaky buttermilk biscuits

1 Cut the meatballs in half and place in the bottom of an ungreased 2-quart rectangular baking dish. Pour pasta sauce over meatballs.

2 Bake, covered, in a 375°F oven for 20 to 25 minutes or until sauce is bubbly. Top meatball mixture with biscuits. Bake, uncovered, about 25 minutes more for frozen biscuits or about 20 minutes more for refrigerated biscuits or until biscuits are golden.

Nutrition Facts per serving: 402 cal., 24 g total fat (12 g sat. fat), 49 mg chol., 1,424 mg sodium, 29 g carbo., 4 g fiber, 18 g pro.

With this recipe, you can make six individual meat loaves—some to enjoy now, others to freeze and enjoy later.

TWO-MEAT MEAT LOAVES

1   beaten egg
1   cup soft bread crumbs (about 1½ slices)
1   cup purchased spaghetti sauce or pasta sauce
½   to 1 teaspoon bottled minced garlic (1 or 2 cloves)
½   teaspoon dried rosemary, crushed
1   pound lean ground beef
8   ounces bulk Italian or pork sausage or lean ground beef
6   2½×½×½-inch sticks provolone or mozzarella cheese
6   tablespoons shredded provolone or mozzarella cheese

PREP:
20 minutes
BAKE:
30 minutes + 5 minutes
STAND:
5 minutes
MAKES:
6 servings

1 In a large bowl combine egg, bread crumbs, ½ cup of the spaghetti sauce, the garlic, and rosemary. Add ground beef and sausage; mix well.

2 Divide meat mixture into 6 equal portions; form each portion into a 3½×2-inch loaf. Press a stick of cheese lengthwise into the center of each loaf, shaping so that meat completely covers the cheese. Place loaves in an ungreased 13×9×2-inch baking pan.

3 Bake, uncovered, in a 350°F oven for 30 minutes. Spoon remaining ½ cup spaghetti sauce over the meat loaves; sprinkle each with 1 tablespoon of the shredded cheese. Bake about 5 minutes more or until an instant-read thermometer inserted in the thickest part of each loaf registers 160°F.

4 Let stand for 5 minutes before serving.

MAKE-AHEAD DIRECTIONS: **Prepare meat loaves as directed through step 2. Cover and freeze until firm. Wrap each meat loaf in moisture- and vapor-proof freezer wrap or heavy foil. Label and freeze for up to 3 months. To serve, place desired number of frozen meat loaves in a shallow baking pan. Bake in a 325°F oven, covered loosely with foil, for 1 hour. Uncover and bake for 10 minutes more. Spoon remaining ½ cup spaghetti sauce over the loaves and sprinkle each with 1 tablespoon of the shredded cheese. Bake about 5 minutes more or until an instant-read thermometer inserted in the thickest part of each loaf registers 160°F. Let stand for 5 minutes before serving.**

Nutrition Facts per serving: 369 cal., 26 g total fat (10 g sat. fat), 124 mg chol., 715 mg sodium, 8 g carbo., 2 g fiber, 26 g pro.

Think you don't have time to bake a meat loaf tonight? Think again. Mini loaves cut cooking time remarkably. Speaking of remarkable, you'll love the loaves' oozy (and easy) mozzarella and prosciutto filling.

INDIVIDUAL SICILIAN MEAT LOAVES

PREP:

15 minutes

BAKE:

20 minutes

MAKES:

4 servings

1	beaten egg
1	14-ounce jar garlic and onion pasta sauce (1¾ cups)
¼	cup seasoned fine dry bread crumbs
¼	teaspoon salt
¼	teaspoon black pepper
12	ounces ground beef
2	ounces mozzarella cheese
4	thin slices proscuitto or cooked ham (about 2 ounces)
1	9-ounce package refrigerated plain or spinach fettuccine
	Finely shredded Parmesan cheese (optional)

1 In a medium bowl combine egg, ¼ cup of the pasta sauce, the fine dry bread crumbs, salt, and pepper. Add ground beef; mix well.

2 Cut mozzarella cheese into four logs, each measuring approximately 2¼×¾×½ inches. Wrap a slice of proscuitto around each cheese log. Shape one-fourth of the ground beef mixture around each cheese log to form a loaf. Flatten each meat loaf to 1½ inches thick and place in a shallow baking pan.

3 Bake loaves, uncovered, in a 400°F oven about 20 minutes or until meat is done (160°F).*

4 Meanwhile, cook pasta according to package directions. In a small saucepan heat remaining pasta sauce over medium heat until bubbly.

5 Arrange meat loaves over hot cooked pasta. Spoon sauce over top. If desired, sprinkle with Parmesan cheese.

*NOTE: The internal color of a meat loaf is not a reliable doneness indicator. A beef meat loaf cooked to 160°F is safe, regardless of color. To measure the doneness of the meat loaf, insert an instant-read thermometer through the side of the meat loaf, making sure bulb is in meat, not cheese.

Nutrition Facts per serving: 631 cal., 31 g total fat (12 g sat. fat), 173 mg chol., 1,132 mg sodium, 55 g carbo., 3 g fiber, 31 g pro.

Crescent rolls pinch-hit for the crust of this casserole, cutting the time spent in the kitchen. Use your favorite brand of spaghetti or pasta sauce (including chunky vegetable, if you like) to tailor the dish to your taste.

ITALIAN CRESCENT CASSEROLE

1	pound lean ground beef
¼	cup chopped onion
1	cup purchased spaghetti or pasta sauce
1½	cups shredded mozzarella or Monterey Jack cheese (6 ounces)
½	cup dairy sour cream
1	4-ounce package (4) refrigerated crescent rolls
1	tablespoon butter or margarine, melted
¼	cup grated Parmesan cheese (1 ounce)

PREP:
25 minutes
BAKE:
20 minutes
MAKES:
6 servings

1 In a large skillet cook ground beef and onion until meat is brown and onion is tender. Drain off fat. Stir in spaghetti sauce; heat through. Spread meat mixture in an ungreased 2-quart casserole.

2 Meanwhile, combine mozzarella cheese and sour cream; spoon over meat mixture in casserole.

3 Unroll crescent rolls; separate into triangles. Arrange dough triangles on top of cheese layer. Brush with melted butter and sprinkle with Parmesan cheese. Bake, uncovered, in a 375°F oven for 20 to 25 minutes or until top is deep golden brown.

Nutrition Facts per serving: 360 cal., 23 g total fat (11 g sat. fat), 81 mg chol., 593 mg sodium, 14 g carbo., 0 g fiber, 25 g pro.

Garden-fresh vegetables—zucchini and tomato in this case—brighten this tasty ground beef and rice casserole. All you need to round out the menu is some crusty bread..

BEEF & RICE BAKE

PREP:
20 minutes

BAKE:
30 minutes

MAKES:
4 servings

1	pound lean ground beef
½	cup chopped onion
½	cup chopped celery
1½	cups cooked rice*
1	medium zucchini, halved lengthwise and sliced (about 1¼ cups)
1	medium tomato, seeded and chopped
1	cup milk
1	4-ounce can (drained weight) sliced mushrooms, drained
1	envelope (½ of a 2.4-ounce package) dry herb with garlic soup mix
⅛	teaspoon black pepper
½	cup shredded cheddar cheese (2 ounces)

1 In a large skillet cook ground beef, onion, and celery until meat is brown and onion is tender. Drain off fat. Stir in cooked rice, zucchini, tomato, milk, mushrooms, herb with garlic soup mix, and pepper. Transfer to an ungreased 2-quart square baking dish.

2 Bake, covered, in 375°F oven for 30 to 35 minutes or until heated through. Stir. Sprinkle with cheese.

*NOTE: For 1½ cups cooked rice, in a medium saucepan combine 1 cup water and ½ cup uncooked long grain rice. Bring to boiling; reduce heat. Simmer, covered, for 15 to 18 minutes or until rice is tender.

Nutrition Facts per serving: 578 cal., 17 g total fat (8 g sat. fat), 91 mg chol., 983 mg sodium, 71 g carbo., 3 g fiber, 32 g pro.

Mafalda are curly-edged noodles that look a little like a slim lasagna noodle. They come in long ribbons or short pieces. If you purchase the longer variety, break the pasta before cooking.

ITALIAN-STYLE MEATBALLS & PASTA

1½	cups dried mafalda pasta* (about 4 ounces)
1	14½-ounce can Italian-style stewed tomatoes, undrained
1	8-ounce can tomato sauce
¼	cup dry red wine
2	tablespoons dry onion soup mix
½	teaspoon dried oregano, crushed
	Dash black pepper
16	frozen Italian-style cooked meatballs (½ ounce each)
½	cup shredded mozzarella cheese (2 ounces)

① Cook mafalda according to package directions; drain. In a large saucepan combine tomatoes, tomato sauce, red wine, onion soup mix, oregano, and pepper. Stir in meatballs. Bring mixture to boiling over medium heat. Stir in cooked mafalda.

② Spoon mixture into an ungreased 1½-quart casserole. Bake, covered, in a 350°F oven for 20 minutes. Sprinkle with cheese. Bake, uncovered, about 5 minutes more or until cheese is melted.

*TEST KITCHEN TIP: **If you purchase the longer mafalda pasta, break into 1- to 1½-inch pieces before measuring.**

Nutrition Facts per serving: 389 cal., 16 g total fat (7 g sat. fat), 45 mg chol., 1,308 mg sodium, 39 g carbo., 4 g fiber, 18 g pro.

PREP:
25 minutes

BAKE:
20 minutes + 5 minutes

MAKES:
4 servings

A bottle of beer transforms brown gravy mix into a tasty complement for mushrooms and beef.

BISTRO BEEF WITH MUSHROOM SAUCE

START TO FINISH:

30 minutes

MAKES:

4 servings

1	medium onion, cut in half
1¼	pounds ground beef
¾	teaspoon salt
8	ounces sliced assorted fresh mushrooms (such as oyster, crimini, and shiitake) (about 3 cups)
1½	cups beer (preferably honey lager) or nonalcoholic beer (12 ounces)
1	0.75- to 0.88-ounce envelope dry brown gravy mix
2	teaspoons snipped fresh thyme or ½ teaspoon dried thyme, crushed

1 Finely shred half of the onion. Thinly slice remaining onion; set aside.

2 In a large bowl combine shredded onion, ground beef, and salt, mixing lightly but thoroughly. Lightly shape into four ½-inch-thick oval patties.

3 Heat a large nonstick skillet over medium heat until hot. Place patties in skillet; cook for 10 to 12 minutes or until done,* turning once. Remove from skillet; keep warm.

4 Add sliced onion, mushrooms, and ¼ cup of the beer to same skillet; cook over medium-high heat about 5 minutes or until vegetables are tender, stirring occasionally. In a small bowl combine gravy mix with remaining 1¼ cups beer, mixing until smooth; stir into mushroom mixture in skillet. Add half of the thyme; simmer about 1 minute or until thickened, stirring frequently. Spoon sauce over patties; sprinkle with remaining thyme.

*NOTE: **The internal color of a burger is not a reliable doneness indicator. A beef patty cooked to 160°F is safe, regardless of color. To measure the doneness of a patty, insert an instant-read thermometer through the side of the patty to a depth of 2 to 3 inches.**

Nutrition Facts per serving: 351 cal., 18 g total fat (7 g sat. fat), 89 mg chol., 732 mg sodium, 12 g carbo., 1 g fiber, 29 g pro.

If you like the combination of corn bread and chili, you'll love the idea of a polenta topper! And it's easy using refrigerated cooked polenta, which is usually found in tubes in the produce aisle.

CHILI WITH POLENTA

12   ounces ground beef

½   cup chopped onion

1   15-ounce can hot-style chili beans with chili gravy, undrained

1   15-ounce can black beans, rinsed and drained

1   8-ounce can tomato sauce

½   teaspoon ground cumin

1   16-ounce tube refrigerated cooked polenta, crumbled

½   cup shredded taco cheese (2 ounces)

     Sliced green onion (optional)

     Dairy sour cream (optional)

START TO FINISH:

25 minutes

MAKES:

4 servings

1 In a large skillet cook ground beef and onion until beef is brown. Drain off fat. Stir chili beans, black beans, tomato sauce, and cumin into ground beef mixture in skillet. Bring to boiling.

2 Sprinkle the crumbled polenta over the ground beef-bean mixture. Simmer, covered, about 5 minutes or until heated through. Sprinkle with cheese. If desired, sprinkle with green onion and serve with sour cream.

Nutrition Facts per serving: 497 cal., 15 g total fat (7 g sat. fat), 65 mg chol., 1,464 mg sodium, 58 g carbo., 14 g fiber, 34 g pro.

American cheese replaces mozzarella, and chili replaces marinara for a Tex-Mex take on the traditional Italian baked manicotti casserole.

CHILI MANICOTTI

PREP:

25 minutes

BAKE:

35 minutes

STAND:

10 minutes

MAKES:

4 servings

8	dried manicotti shells
¼	cup chopped onion
1	clove garlic, minced
1	tablespoon cooking oil
1	11¼-ounce can condensed chili beef soup
½	cup water
1¼	cups cream-style cottage cheese, drained
1	cup shredded sharp American cheese (4 ounces)
1	4-ounce can diced green chile peppers, undrained
2	slightly beaten eggs

1 Cook manicotti according to package directions; drain and set aside. In a large skillet cook onion and garlic in hot oil until tender; stir in chili beef soup and water.

2 In a medium bowl stir together cottage cheese, half of the American cheese, chile peppers, and eggs. Spoon cheese mixture into the cooked manicotti shells.

3 Pour half of the soup mixture into an ungreased 2-quart rectangular baking dish. Top with stuffed manicotti. Top with remaining soup mixture, making sure all manicotti are coated. Cover and bake in a 350°F oven for 35 to 40 minutes or until heated through. Uncover; sprinkle with remaining American cheese. Let stand for 10 minutes before serving.

Nutrition Facts per serving: 485 cal., 22 g total fat (10 g sat. fat), 153 mg chol., 1,387 mg sodium, 44 g carbo., 4 g fiber, 27 g pro.

Brimming with all the flavors and fixings of a traditional stir-fry, this ever-so-easy beef and veggie combo is draped in a sauce that begins with an envelope of gravy mix.

GINGER BEEF WITH BROCCOLI

6   medium carrots, cut into 1-inch pieces

2   medium onions, cut into wedges

1½   pounds beef round steak, cut into ½-inch-thick bias-sliced strips

1   tablespoon minced fresh ginger

2   cloves garlic, minced

½   cup water

2   tablespoons reduced-sodium soy sauce

1   0.75- to 0.88-ounce envelope dry brown gravy mix

4   cups broccoli florets

     Hot cooked rice

PREP:

20 minutes

COOK:

*8 to 10 hours
(low-heat setting) or*

*4 to 5 hours
(high-heat setting)*

*+ 15 minutes
(high-heat setting)*

MAKES:

6 servings

1 In a 3½- or 4-quart slow cooker place carrots, onions, beef strips, ginger, and garlic. In a small bowl stir together water, soy sauce, and brown gravy mix. Pour over meat and vegetables in slow cooker.

2 Cover and cook on low-heat setting for 8 to 10 hours or on high-heat setting for 4 to 5 hours.

3 If using low-heat setting, turn slow cooker to high-heat setting. Stir in broccoli. Cover and cook about 15 minutes more or until broccoli is crisp-tender. Serve over hot cooked rice.

Nutrition Facts per serving: 327 cal., 6 g total fat (2 g sat. fat), 54 mg chol., 476 mg sodium, 37 g carbo., 4 g fiber, 31 g pro.

This meal-in-a-bun features ricotta and mozzarella cheeses layered with a saucy ground beef mixture.

LASAGNA IN A BUN

PREP:

35 minutes

BAKE:

20 minutes

MAKES:

6 to 8 servings

12	ounces lean ground beef
1	8-ounce can tomato sauce
1	tablespoon dry onion soup mix
¼	teaspoon dried oregano, crushed
¼	teaspoon dried basil, crushed
6	to 8 large hard rolls*
¾	cup drained ricotta cheese or cream-style cottage cheese
½	cup shredded mozzarella cheese (2 ounces)
1	beaten egg

1 In a large skillet cook ground beef until brown. Drain off fat. Stir in the tomato sauce, onion soup mix, oregano, and basil. Bring mixture to boiling; reduce heat. Simmer, covered, for 15 minutes to blend flavors.

2 Meanwhile, cut a thin slice from the top of each roll; set tops of rolls aside. Scoop out insides of rolls, leaving ½-inch-thick shells. Set shells aside. Reserve scooped-out bread for another use.

3 In a small bowl combine ricotta cheese, mozzarella cheese, and beaten egg; set aside.

4 Spoon half of the meat mixture evenly into the bread shells. Spread cheese mixture evenly over meat mixture. Top with remaining meat mixture and tops of rolls. Wrap each roll in foil. Place on a large baking sheet. Bake in a 400°F oven about 20 minutes or until hot in centers.

***TEST KITCHEN TIP:** You'll need hard rolls that are at least 4 inches in diameter to hold all of the meat and cheese fillings.

Nutrition Facts per serving: 379 cal., 16 g total fat (7 g sat. fat), 91 mg chol., 705 mg sodium, 34 g carbo., 2 g fiber, 23 g pro.

Taco salads are popular fare on restaurant menus. The same concept adapts well to a north-of-the-border favorite, the cheeseburger.

CHEESEBURGER SALAD

1   pound ground beef

1   envelope (½ of a 2-ounce package) dry onion soup mix

¾   cup water

6   cups shredded leaf or iceberg lettuce

1   cup cherry tomatoes, halved or quartered

1   medium green, red, or yellow sweet pepper,
      cut into bite-size strips

½   of a small red onion, thinly sliced and separated into rings

1½   cups shredded sharp cheddar, Swiss, American,
      or Colby cheese (6 ounces)

1   recipe French Pickle Dressing
      Crumbled crisp-cooked bacon (optional)

PREP:
40 minutes
CHILL:
30 minutes to 3 days
(dressing)
MAKES:
6 servings

1 In a large skillet cook ground beef until brown. Drain off fat. Sprinkle onion soup mix over beef; stir in water. Bring to boiling; reduce heat to medium. Cook, uncovered, about 4 minutes or until no water remains.

2 Meanwhile, in a large bowl combine lettuce, cherry tomatoes, sweet pepper, and red onion. To serve, divide lettuce mixture among salad plates. Top servings with some of the warm beef mixture. Sprinkle with cheese. Serve with French Pickle Dressing. If desired, sprinkle with crisp-cooked bacon.

FRENCH PICKLE DRESSING: In a small bowl stir together 1 cup bottled creamy French salad dressing and ⅓ cup mustard-style hot dog relish, sweet pickle relish, or dill pickle relish. Cover; chill for at least 30 minutes or up to 3 days.

Nutrition Facts per serving: 489 cal., 36 g total fat (14 g sat. fat), 77 mg chol., 1,292 mg sodium, 20 g carbo., 2 g fiber, 23 g pro.

Every great summer gathering needs a delicious batch of baked beans. Studded with pineapple tidbits, this version brings something unique to the table.

HAWAIIAN PINEAPPLE BAKED BEANS

PREP:

20 minutes

BAKE:

1 hour

MAKES:

8 to 10 side-dish servings

1	pound ground beef
$^1/_2$	cup chopped onion
$^1/_2$	cup catsup
$^1/_2$	cup bottled hot-style barbecue sauce
2	tablespoons packed brown sugar
1	15- or 16-ounce can pork and beans in tomato sauce
1	15-ounce can chili beans with chili gravy, undrained
1	8-ounce can pineapple tidbits (juice pack), drained

1 In a large skillet cook ground beef and onion until meat is brown and onion is tender. Drain off fat. Stir in catsup, barbecue sauce, and brown sugar. Stir in pork and beans, chili beans, and pineapple.

2 Transfer to an ungreased 2-quart casserole. Bake, uncovered, in a 350°F oven about 1 hour or until heated through.

Nutrition Facts per serving: 322 cal., 14 g total fat (5 g sat. fat), 41 mg chol., 833 mg sodium, 35 g carbo., 6 g fiber, 15 g pro.

SLOW COOKER DIRECTIONS: Cook ground beef and onion as directed. Drain off fat. In a $3^1/_2$- or 4-quart slow cooker combine ground beef mixture, catsup, barbecue sauce, brown sugar, pork and beans, chili beans, and pineapple. Cover and cook on low-heat setting for 5 to 6 hours or on high-heat setting for $2^1/_2$ to 3 hours.

If the thawed bread dough is difficult to roll, let it rest 10 minutes before continuing. It will relax and roll more easily.

HAM CALZONES

Boiling water

4 cups torn fresh spinach, stems removed

1 16-ounce loaf frozen white bread dough, thawed

1½ teaspoons bottled minced garlic (3 cloves)

1 teaspoon dried Italian seasoning, crushed

1 cup ricotta cheese or cottage cheese, well drained

4 ounces thinly sliced cooked ham, chopped (1 cup)

4 ounces thinly sliced Swiss cheese

1 cup purchased tomato and herb pasta sauce, heated

PREP:
25 minutes
BAKE:
20 minutes
MAKES:
4 calzones

1 In a large bowl pour enough boiling water over spinach to cover. Let stand for 5 minutes. Drain well, squeezing out excess liquid; set aside.

2 Divide bread dough into 4 equal portions. On a lightly floured surface, roll each portion of dough into a 7-inch circle. Brush circles with minced garlic; sprinkle with Italian seasoning. Divide ricotta cheese evenly among circles, spreading only on one-half of each crust and to within ½ inch of edges. Layer spinach, ham, and Swiss cheese over ricotta cheese.

3 Moisten edges of dough with water. Fold dough in half over filling. Seal edges with the tines of a fork. Prick tops 3 or 4 times with the tines of the fork. Place calzones on a lightly greased baking sheet.

4 Bake in a 375°F oven about 20 minutes or until golden. Serve with warm pasta sauce.

MAKE-AHEAD DIRECTIONS: Prepare and bake calzones as directed. Cool on a wire rack. Cover and chill overnight. To serve, place calzones on a baking sheet. Bake, uncovered, in a 375°F oven for 12 to 15 minutes or until heated through. Serve with warm pasta sauce.

Nutrition Facts per calzone: 564 cal., 19 g total fat (11 g sat. fat), 73 mg chol., 696 mg sodium, 59 g carbo., 3 g fiber, 30 g pro.

Lasagna—ready for the oven in 25 minutes? Yes, thanks to no-boil lasagna noodles, a jar of pasta sauce, and smoked chicken sausage, which doesn't require precooking.

SMOKED SAUSAGE LASAGNA

PREP:

25 minutes

BAKE:

50 minutes

STAND:

20 minutes

MAKES:

6 servings

Nonstick cooking spray

2 cups purchased tomato-basil pasta sauce

½ cup pitted kalamata olives, halved

6 no-boil lasagna noodles

½ of a 15-ounce container ricotta cheese

6 ounces Monterey Jack cheese with jalapeño peppers, shredded (1½ cups)

¼ cup finely shredded Parmesan cheese (1 ounce)

8 ounces smoked chicken sausage with apple, halved lengthwise and sliced

1 medium fennel bulb, trimmed, halved lengthwise, and thinly sliced

1 Lightly coat a 2-quart square baking dish with nonstick cooking spray; set aside. In a medium bowl stir together pasta sauce and olives. Spoon ⅓ cup of the sauce mixture in the prepared dish. Top with 2 of the lasagna noodles.

2 In a small bowl stir together the ricotta cheese and 1 cup of the Monterey Jack cheese. Spoon half of the ricotta mixture over the noodles in the dish. Sprinkle with half of the Parmesan cheese. Top with half of the sausage and half of the fennel. Spoon half of the remaining sauce mixture over the sausage layer.

3 Top with 2 more noodles, the remaining ricotta mixture, and the remaining sausage and fennel. Add the remaining noodles and the remaining sauce. Sprinkle top with remaining Monterey Jack and Parmesan cheeses.

4 Cover with foil. Bake in a 350°F oven for 50 minutes. Let stand, covered, on a wire rack for 20 minutes before serving.

Nutrition Facts per serving: 541 cal., 33 g total fat (16 g sat. fat), 85 mg chol., 1,357 mg sodium, 29 g carbo., 8 g fiber, 32 g pro.

This homey casserole contains many popular pizza ingredients—marinara sauce, mushrooms, onion, green sweet pepper, pepperoni, and lots of cheese.

ITALIAN PENNE BAKE

Nonstick cooking spray

1½ cups dried penne pasta

1 medium green or red sweet pepper, cut into thin, bite-size strips

3 ounces sliced pepperoni or Canadian-style bacon, cut up

½ cup sliced fresh mushrooms

½ cup quartered, thinly sliced onion

1½ teaspoons bottled minced garlic (3 cloves)

1½ teaspoons olive oil or cooking oil

1½ cups purchased marinara pasta sauce

⅔ cup shredded Italian blend cheese

PREP:
25 minutes

BAKE:
25 minutes + 5 minutes

MAKES:
4 servings

1 Lightly coat a 2-quart square baking dish with nonstick cooking spray; set dish aside. Cook pasta according to package directions; drain well. Return pasta to saucepan. Meanwhile, in a medium skillet cook sweet pepper, pepperoni, mushrooms, onion, and garlic in hot oil for 3 minutes. Add vegetable mixture and marinara sauce to pasta; toss to coat. Spread pasta mixture evenly in prepared baking dish.

2 Bake, covered, in a 350°F oven about 25 minutes or until heated through. Uncover and sprinkle with cheese. Bake, uncovered, about 5 minutes more or until cheese is melted.

Nutrition Facts per serving: 390 cal., 19 g total fat (7 g sat. fat), 31 mg chol., 848 mg sodium, 41 g carbo., 3 g fiber, 15 g pro.

Just a couple decades ago, only a few brands of marinara sauce were available nationwide. These days, there are dozens of options to please all tastes. Choose your favorite for this boldly flavored take on stuffed peppers.

STUFFED PIZZA PEPPERS

PREP:

40 minutes

BAKE:

40 minutes + 5 minutes

MAKES:

4 to 6 servings

4	medium red and/or yellow sweet peppers (6 to 8 ounces each)
8	ounces bulk Italian sausage or sweet Italian sausage
1	cup chopped fresh mushrooms
1	cup purchased marinara pasta sauce
$1/3$	cup sliced pitted ripe or kalamata olives
$1/4$	teaspoon black pepper
1	cup soft bread crumbs*
$1/4$	cup shredded mozzarella cheese (1 ounce)
$1/4$	cup shredded Parmesan cheese (1 ounce)
3	tablespoons pine nuts

1 Cut tops from sweet peppers; remove seeds. Chop sweet pepper tops; set aside. Halve sweet peppers lengthwise. Set the sweet pepper halves, cut sides up, in a greased 3-quart rectangular baking dish.

2 In a large skillet cook sausage until brown. Drain off fat. Stir in chopped sweet pepper and mushrooms; cook and stir until vegetables are tender. Stir in marinara sauce, olives, and black pepper; heat through. Remove from heat. Stir in bread crumbs. Spoon about $1/3$ cup of the sausage mixture into each sweet pepper half.

3 Bake stuffed sweet peppers, covered, in a 350°F oven for 40 to 45 minutes or until sweet peppers are tender. Uncover and sprinkle with mozzarella cheese, Parmesan cheese, and pine nuts. Bake, uncovered, about 5 minutes more or until cheese is melted.

*NOTE: **To make soft bread crumbs, tear 1$1/2$ slices white bread into large chunks and place in a food processor bowl or blender container. Cover and process or blend to make crumbs.**

Nutrition Facts per serving: 365 cal., 23 g total fat (8 g sat. fat), 49 mg chol., 837 mg sodium, 22 g carbo., 4 g fiber, 18 g pro.

Next time your menu features grilled or broiled chicken breasts, cook a couple extra and make this hearty dish the next day.

DIJON-CHICKEN POTPIE

1½	cups frozen loose-pack broccoli, cauliflower, and carrots
1	11½-ounce package (8) refrigerated corn bread twists
1	1.8-ounce envelope dry white sauce mix
10	ounces cooked chicken breast, chopped (about 2 cups)
2	tablespoons Dijon-style mustard
1	teaspoon instant chicken bouillon granules

① Place vegetables in a colander. Run hot water over vegetables just until thawed. Drain well. Cut up any large pieces.

② Meanwhile, unroll corn bread dough. Separate into 16 sticks. Set aside.

③ In a medium saucepan prepare white sauce mix according to package directions, except after mixture starts to boil, stir in vegetables, chicken, mustard, and chicken bouillon granules. Return to boiling; reduce heat. Cook and stir for 1 minute more.

④ Transfer chicken mixture to an ungreased 2-quart rectangular baking dish. Arrange corn bread sticks in a single layer on top of the chicken mixture.

⑤ Bake, uncovered, in a 375°F oven for 15 to 20 minutes or until corn bread sticks are golden.

Nutrition Facts per serving: 496 cal., 18 g total fat (6 g sat. fat), 50 mg chol., 1,875 mg sodium, 51 g carbo., 1 g fiber, 29 g pro.

PREP:
25 minutes
BAKE:
15 minutes
MAKES:
4 servings

Feel free to experiment with variations on this theme! Substitute other colorful vegetables for the broccoli or use leftover cooked vegetables.

BROCCOLI & CHICKEN FETTUCCINE ALFREDO

START TO FINISH:

15 minutes

MAKES:

4 servings

1   9-ounce package refrigerated fettuccine

1   10-ounce package frozen cut broccoli

1   10-ounce container refrigerated Alfredo pasta sauce

6   ounces smoked chicken or turkey breast, chopped

1   teaspoon dried basil, crushed

Finely shredded Parmesan or Romano cheese (optional)

1 In a large saucepan cook fettuccine and broccoli in a large amount of boiling water for 3 minutes. Drain pasta and broccoli; return to saucepan. Cover and keep warm.

2 Meanwhile, in a medium saucepan combine Alfredo sauce, chicken, and basil. Cook and stir just until heated through (do not boil).

3 Add chicken mixture to cooked pasta mixture; toss gently to coat. If desired, sprinkle each serving with cheese.

Nutrition Facts per serving: 480 cal., 25 g total fat (13 g sat. fat), 133 mg chol., 781 mg sodium, 43 g carbo., 4 g fiber, 22 g pro.

Paella is a Spanish specialty that usually marries meat and seafood in a saffron-infused rice. This easy version gets its flavor from a soup mix.

LAZY PAELLA

Nonstick cooking spray

2½   to 3 pounds chicken thighs, skinned

2   tablespoons cooking oil

1   14-ounce can chicken broth

1   cup uncooked long grain rice

1   cup frozen loose-pack peas, thawed

1   cup cooked, peeled, and deveined shrimp

1   4-ounce can (drained weight) sliced mushrooms, drained

2   tablespoons dry onion soup mix

Salt

Black pepper

Paprika

1 Lightly coat a 3-quart rectangular baking dish with nonstick cooking spray; set aside. In a large skillet brown chicken thighs in hot oil, turning to brown evenly. In a large bowl combine broth, rice, peas, shrimp, mushrooms, and onion soup mix. Spread in prepared baking dish. Arrange chicken thighs on rice mixture. Sprinkle chicken lightly with salt, pepper, and paprika.

2 Cover dish tightly with foil. Bake in a 350°F oven about 45 minutes or until chicken is tender and no longer pink (180°F). Let stand, covered, for 10 minutes before serving.

Nutrition Facts per serving: 500 cal., 12 g total fat (2 g sat. fat), 212 mg chol., 1,101 mg sodium, 47 g carbo., 3 g fiber, 49 g pro.

PREP:
25 minutes

BAKE:
45 minutes

STAND:
10 minutes

MAKES:
4 to 6 servings

The minute you get home after a busy day, pop this zesty dish in the oven—it will take just a few minutes of hands-on prep. That gives you plenty of time to relax before readying dinner's final touches, such as rice and a quick-fixing frozen vegetable mix.

GLAZED CRANBERRY CHICKEN

PREP:

15 minutes

BAKE:

1¹/₂ hours

MAKES:

4 to 6 servings

1   16-ounce can whole cranberry sauce

1   cup bottled Russian salad dressing or French salad dressing

1   envelope (¹/₂ of a 2-ounce package) dry onion soup mix

2¹/₂   to 3 pounds meaty chicken pieces
(breast halves, thighs, and drumsticks)

Hot cooked rice (optional)

① In a medium bowl stir together cranberry sauce, Russian salad dressing, and onion soup mix. If desired, skin chicken. Arrange chicken pieces, meaty sides down, in an ungreased 3-quart rectangular baking dish. Pour cranberry mixture over chicken pieces.

② Bake, uncovered, in a 325°F oven about 1¹/₂ hours or until the chicken is no longer pink (170°F for breasts; 180°F for thighs and drumsticks), stirring cranberry mixture and spooning over chicken once or twice. If desired, serve over hot cooked rice.

Nutrition Facts per serving: 803 cal., 47 g total fat (9 g sat. fat), 141 mg chol., 919 mg sodium, 53 g carbo., 1 g fiber, 43 g pro.

None of the flavors of this chunky casserole are particularly bold. Instead, they meld into a satisfying dish that will please many tastes.

TURKEY-VEGETABLE GOULASH

1 pound ground turkey

1 14½-ounce can diced tomatoes with basil, oregano, and garlic, undrained

1½ cups water

1 10-ounce package frozen mixed vegetables

1 8-ounce can tomato sauce

2 stalks celery, sliced

1 small onion, chopped

1 0.9-ounce envelope dry turkey gravy mix

1 cup dried fine egg noodles

⅓ cup shredded sharp cheddar, Monterey Jack, or Parmesan cheese

PREP:
20 minutes
COOK:
6 to 8 hours (low-heat setting) or
3 to 4 hours (high-heat setting)
+ 20 to 30 minutes (high-heat setting)
MAKES:
6 servings

1 In a large skillet cook ground turkey until brown. Drain off fat. Transfer turkey to a 3½- or 4-quart slow cooker. Stir in tomatoes, water, vegetables, tomato sauce, celery, onion, and turkey gravy mix.

2 Cover and cook on low-heat setting for 6 to 8 hours or on high-heat setting for 3 to 4 hours.

3 If using low-heat setting, turn slow cooker to high-heat setting. Stir in uncooked noodles. Cover and cook for 20 to 30 minutes more or until noodles are tender. Sprinkle with shredded cheese.

Nutrition Facts per serving: 251 cal., 9 g total fat (3 g sat. fat), 73 mg chol., 918 mg sodium, 22 g carbo., 3 g fiber, 19 g pro.

Your family will enjoy this turkey-and-vegetable one-dish meal. Because it's quick to put together, you will too. It only takes 25 minutes to prepare and about 25 minutes to bake.

TURKEY TAMALE CASSEROLE

PREP:

25 minutes

BAKE:

25 minutes + 2 minutes

STAND:

5 minutes

MAKES:

6 to 8 servings

1	pound ground turkey
2	cloves garlic, minced
1	15- to 17-ounce can cream-style corn
1	10½-ounce can chili without beans
2	teaspoons dried oregano, crushed
½	teaspoon ground cumin
¼	teaspoon salt
8	6-inch corn tortillas
1	cup chicken broth or water
1	2¼-ounce can sliced pitted ripe olives, drained
1	cup shredded cheddar cheese (4 ounces)
	Dairy sour cream (optional)
	Thinly sliced green onion (optional)

1 In a large skillet cook turkey and garlic over medium heat until turkey is no longer pink. Drain off fat. Stir in corn, chili, oregano, cumin, and salt. Bring to boiling; reduce heat. Simmer, covered, for 5 minutes. Remove from heat. Set aside.

2 Stack the tortillas; cut into 6 wedges. Place the wedges in a medium bowl; add broth. Let stand for 1 minute. Drain, reserving ¼ cup of the liquid. Stir reserved liquid and olives into turkey mixture. In an ungreased 2-quart rectangular baking dish layer 2 cups of the turkey mixture and half of the tortilla wedges; repeat layers. Top with remaining turkey mixture, spreading to cover tortilla wedges.

3 Bake, uncovered, in a 350°F oven about 25 minutes or until heated through. Sprinkle with cheese; bake for 2 minutes more. Let stand for 5 minutes before serving. If desired, top servings with sour cream and green onion.

Nutrition Facts per serving: 416 cal., 21 g total fat (7 g sat. fat), 64 mg chol., 988 mg sodium, 37 g carbo., 2 g fiber, 24 g pro.

Pesto has come a long way in the convenience category! The Italian sauce used to be handmade with a mortar and pestle; today, ready-made versions are widely available, and they add an instant windfall of fresh flavor to everything they touch.

EASY TURKEY-PESTO POTPIE

1   18-ounce jar turkey gravy
¼   cup purchased basil or dried tomato pesto
3   cups cubed cooked turkey (about 1 pound)
1   16-ounce package frozen loose-pack peas and carrots
1   7-ounce package (6) refrigerated breadsticks

1 In a large saucepan combine turkey gravy and pesto; stir in turkey and vegetables. Bring to boiling, stirring frequently. Divide mixture evenly among six 8-ounce au gratin dishes. Unroll and separate breadsticks. Arrange a breadstick on top of each au gratin dish.

2 Bake in a 375°F oven about 15 minutes or until breadsticks are golden.

Nutrition Facts per serving: 372 cal., 14 g total fat (2 g sat. fat), 59 mg chol., 988 mg sodium, 30 g carbo., 3 g fiber, 30 g pro.

PREP:
15 minutes
BAKE:
15 minutes
MAKES:
6 servings

Pan-fried whitefish is a specialty of Michigan's Upper Peninsula. Here's how you can bring the specialty home.

FRIED WHITEFISH

1	cup all-purpose breading mix (about $\frac{1}{2}$ of a 10-ounce package)
1	cup packaged biscuit mix
$\frac{1}{3}$	cup grated Parmesan cheese
1	tablespoon dry onion soup mix
$1\frac{1}{2}$	teaspoons paprika
$1\frac{1}{2}$	teaspoons dried Italian seasoning, crushed
$1\frac{1}{2}$	teaspoons dried parsley, crushed
$\frac{1}{2}$	teaspoon garlic powder
1	to $1\frac{1}{4}$ pounds fresh or frozen whitefish, haddock, or other firm-textured fish fillets
	Shortening or cooking oil

1 In a medium bowl stir together breading mix, biscuit mix, Parmesan cheese, onion soup mix, paprika, Italian seasoning, parsley, and garlic powder. Place half of the mixture in a shallow dish. (Place remaining mixture in a jar or self-sealing plastic bag. Cover or seal. Store in the refrigerator for up to 3 weeks. Stir or shake mixture before using.)

2 Thaw fish, if frozen. Rinse fish; pat dry with paper towels. Cut fish into 4 pieces. Measure thickness of fish. Dip fish pieces into breading mixture, turning to coat both sides.

3 In a large skillet heat $\frac{1}{4}$ inch melted shortening or cooking oil over medium heat. Add fish pieces in a single layer. (If fish pieces have skin, fry skin side last.) Fry on one side until golden brown. Allow 3 to 4 minutes per side for $\frac{1}{2}$-inch-thick fillets or 5 to 6 minutes per side for 1-inch-thick fillets. Turn carefully. Fry until fish flakes easily when tested with a fork. Drain on paper towels. Keep warm in a 300°F oven while frying remaining fish.

Nutrition Facts per serving: 352 cal., 17 g total fat (4 g sat. fat), 69 mg chol., 795 mg sodium, 21 g carbo., 0 g fiber, 25 g pro.

Mmmm! You'll love the way refrigerated Alfredo sauce adds a creamy fullness to this so-easy casserole.

TUNA ALFREDO CASSEROLE

PREP:
20 minutes
BAKE:
10 minutes
MAKES:
6 servings

3　cups dried rigatoni or penne pasta

2　tablespoons purchased dried-tomato pesto

1　10-ounce container refrigerated Alfredo or four-cheese pasta sauce or 1¼ cups purchased Alfredo or four-cheese pasta sauce

3　tablespoons milk

1　12-ounce can solid white tuna (water pack), drained and broken into chunks

¼　cup finely shredded Parmesan cheese (1 ounce)

1 Cook pasta according to package directions. Drain; return pasta to pan. Meanwhile, for sauce, in a medium bowl combine pesto, Alfredo sauce, and milk. Add sauce to pasta, stirring gently to coat. Gently fold in tuna.

2 Transfer pasta mixture to an ungreased 2-quart baking dish. Sprinkle with cheese. Bake in a 425°F oven for 10 to 15 minutes or until heated through and cheese is melted.

Nutrition Facts per serving: 453 cal., 24 g total fat (4 g sat. fat), 53 mg chol., 587 mg sodium, 35 g carbo., 2 g fiber, 24 g pro.

Instant brown rice, canned chili beans, shredded cheese, and a package of mixed salad greens make easy work of these tostadas.

RICE 'N' BEAN TOSTADAS

PREP:

20 minutes

BAKE:

10 minutes

MAKES:

4 servings

1½   cups water

1½   cups uncooked instant brown rice

1   medium onion, chopped

1   15-ounce can chili beans with chili gravy, undrained

1   8-ounce can whole kernel corn, drained

4   9- to 10-inch flour tortillas

3   cups torn mixed salad greens

½   cup shredded cheddar cheese (2 ounces)

¼   cup dairy sour cream

1   medium tomato, chopped

1 In a large saucepan bring water to boiling. Stir in rice and onion. Return to boiling; reduce heat. Simmer, covered, for 5 minutes. Remove from heat. Stir. Cover and let stand for 5 minutes. Stir chili beans and corn into rice mixture. Heat through.

2 Meanwhile, place tortillas on a large baking sheet, overlapping as necessary. Bake in a 400°F oven about 10 minutes or until tortillas begin to brown around the edges.

3 Place tortillas on dinner plates. Top tortillas with salad greens and the rice-bean mixture. Sprinkle with cheddar cheese. Serve with sour cream and chopped tomato.

Nutrition Facts per serving: 512 cal., 14 g total fat (6 g sat. fat), 21 mg chol., 735 mg sodium, 81 g carbo., 9 g fiber, 19 g pro.

Count on these mini quiches to add unmistakable elegance to an appetizer buffet. And count on the make-ahead directions to ease the day-of-party time crunch.

PETITE QUICHES

1   cup butter, softened

2   3-ounce packages cream cheese, softened

2   cups all-purpose flour

1   cup milk

½   of a 1.8-ounce package (4 tablespoons) dry leek soup mix or 1 envelope (½ of a 2-ounce package) dry onion soup mix

½   cup half-and-half or light cream

4   ounces Swiss cheese, finely shredded (1 cup)

2   slightly beaten eggs

½   teaspoon dry mustard

⅛   teaspoon black pepper

    Snipped fresh chives (optional)

PREP:

40 minutes

BAKE:

18 minutes

MAKES:

48 mini quiches

1 For pastry, in a large bowl stir together butter and cream cheese until smooth. Stir in flour until combined (if necessary, knead mixture with your hands). Press a 1-inch ball of the pastry dough evenly into bottom and up side of each of 48 ungreased 1¾-inch muffin cups.* Set aside.

2 For filling, in a small saucepan combine milk and leek soup mix; cook over medium heat until boiling. Remove from heat; cool for 5 minutes. Stir in half-and-half. Stir in cheese, eggs, mustard, and pepper. Spoon a scant tablespoon of filling into each pastry-lined muffin cup.

3 Bake in a 375°F oven for 18 to 20 minutes or until filling is puffed and pastry and filling are golden. Remove from muffin cups; serve warm. If desired, sprinkle with chives.

*NOTE: Use the pestle from your mortar and pestle to press the ball of dough evenly into bottoms and up the sides of the muffin cups, dipping the pestle in flour each time.

MAKE-AHEAD DIRECTIONS: Prepare and bake as directed. Remove from muffin cups; cool on wire racks. Wrap cooled quiches in foil. Label and freeze for up to 1 month. Bake the foil-wrapped frozen quiches in a 350°F oven about 25 minutes or until heated through.

Nutrition Facts per mini quiche: 87 cal., 7 g total fat (4 g sat. fat), 27 mg chol., 89 mg sodium, 5 g carbo., 0 g fiber, 2 g pro.

Trim the time needed to prepare this luscious lasagna by using purchased pasta sauce and no-boil lasagna noodles. All brands of the no-boil lasagna noodles are not the same size, so use enough noodles to have three single layers.

LASAGNA WITH ZUCCHINI AND WALNUTS

PREP:

35 minutes

BAKE:

20 minutes + 20 minutes

STAND:

15 minutes

MAKES:

6 servings

2	medium zucchini
4	teaspoons olive oil
2	large carrots, finely chopped
2	cups finely chopped onion
4	cloves garlic, minced
1	25- to 26-ounce jar chunky tomato pasta sauce (about 2½ cups)
1	tablespoon snipped fresh basil or 1 teaspoon dried basil, crushed
⅛	teaspoon black pepper
1	cup shredded mozzarella cheese (4 ounces)
⅓	cup finely shredded Parmesan cheese
6	no-boil lasagna noodles
¼	cup chopped walnuts

1 Trim ends off zucchini. Thinly slice zucchini lengthwise. (You should have a total of 9 long slices, each about ¼ inch thick.) Place in a single layer on a lightly greased baking sheet; brush lightly with 1 teaspoon of the oil. Broil 3 to 4 inches from heat about 5 minutes or until crisp-tender, turning once. Let cool before handling.

2 In a large saucepan heat the remaining oil over medium-high heat. Add carrots, onion, and garlic; cook and stir about 5 minutes or until tender. Add pasta sauce, basil, and pepper. Bring to boiling; reduce heat. Simmer, covered, for 10 minutes, stirring occasionally. In a small bowl toss together the mozzarella and Parmesan cheeses; set aside.

3 Arrange 2 of the lasagna noodles in a greased 2-quart square baking dish. Spread with one-third of the pasta sauce. Sprinkle with one-third of the nuts. Top with one-third of the zucchini; sprinkle with one-third of the cheese mixture. Repeat layering, alternating direction of the zucchini in each layer and finishing with the zucchini; set remaining cheese mixture aside.

4 Bake, covered, in a 375°F oven for 20 minutes. Uncover; sprinkle with remaining cheese mixture. Bake, uncovered, about 20 minutes more or until heated through. Let stand for 15 minutes before serving.

Nutrition Facts per serving: 272 cal., 12 g total fat (4 g sat. fat), 16 mg chol., 470 mg sodium, 33 g carbo., 3 g fiber, 13 g pro.

Onion soup mix and chili powder add a little kick to beef stew. Serve with crusty French bread.

BEEF & BEAN STEW

⅓ cup all-purpose flour

1 envelope (½ of a 2-ounce package) dry onion soup mix

1 tablespoon chili powder

¼ teaspoon black pepper

1½ pounds beef stew meat, cut into 1-inch cubes

2 tablespoons cooking oil

1 14-ounce can beef broth

3 medium carrots, sliced into ½-inch pieces

3 medium potatoes, peeled and cut into 1-inch cubes

1 large green sweet pepper, chopped

1 stalk celery, sliced into ½-inch pieces

1 15- to 16-ounce can golden hominy, drained

1 15- to 16-ounce can Great Northern or red kidney beans, rinsed and drained

Shredded American or cheddar cheese (optional)

1 In a plastic bag combine flour, onion soup mix, chili powder, and black pepper. Add beef cubes. Shake to coat. In a large skillet brown meat, half at a time, in hot oil. Drain off fat. Place beef cubes in an ungreased 3-quart casserole.

2 Gradually stir in beef broth; add carrots, potatoes, sweet pepper, and celery. Bake, covered, in a 350°F oven for 1½ hours.

3 Stir in hominy and beans. Bake, covered, for 20 to 30 minutes more or until beef is tender. If desired, sprinkle with cheese.

Nutrition Facts per serving: 424 cal., 10 g total fat (3 g sat. fat), 54 mg chol., 639 mg sodium, 47 g carbo., 8 g fiber, 35 g pro.

PREP:
35 minutes
BAKE:
1½ hours + 20 minutes
MAKES:
6 servings

It's amazing how much time a soup mix can shave off your dinnertime preparation. Amazing, too, is the windfall of fresh flavor a sprinkling of snipped basil brings to a stew. Convenience from the soup mix and freshness from the fresh herb? Talk about the best of both worlds!

BASIL BEEF STEW

PREP:

20 minutes

COOK:

1 1/2 hours

MAKES:

6 to 8 servings

1	2-pound boneless beef chuck roast
1/4	cup all-purpose flour
1/2	teaspoon seasoned salt
2	tablespoons butter or margarine
1	pound tiny new potatoes, quartered
2	cups whole fresh mushrooms, halved
1 1/2	cups packaged, peeled baby carrots
1	2.4-ounce package dry tomato-basil soup mix
2	cups water
1	large tomato, chopped
2	tablespoons snipped fresh basil

1 Trim fat from beef. Cut beef into 1 1/2-inch pieces. In a plastic bag combine flour and seasoned salt. Add beef pieces, a few at a time; shake to coat. In a 4-quart Dutch oven melt butter over medium-high heat. Brown beef, half at a time, in hot butter. Drain off fat. Return all of the beef to Dutch oven.

2 Add potatoes, mushrooms, and carrots. Sprinkle with tomato-basil soup mix; stir in water. Bring to boiling; reduce heat. Simmer, covered, about 1 1/2 hours or until beef and vegetables are tender.

3 Stir in chopped tomato and snipped basil; heat through.

MAKE-AHEAD DIRECTIONS: Prepare as directed through step 2. Transfer to a bowl. Cool quickly; cover and chill for up to 24 hours. To serve, return to Dutch oven; bring to boiling, stirring occasionally. Stir in chopped tomato and snipped basil; heat through.

Nutrition Facts per serving: 444 cal., 16 g total fat (7 g sat. fat), 120 mg chol., 716 mg sodium, 33 g carbo., 3 g fiber, 40 g pro.

Be prepared! Stock frozen meatballs and mixed vegetables in the freezer and cans of diced tomatoes and jars of mushroom gravy in the pantry, and you'll be ready to start this hearty stew at a moment's notice.

MEATBALL & VEGETABLE STEW

32	to 36 frozen cooked meatballs (½ ounce each)
½	of a 16-ounce package (about 2 cups) frozen mixed vegetables
1	14½-ounce can diced tomatoes with onion and garlic or stewed tomatoes, undrained
1	12-ounce jar mushroom gravy
⅓	cup water
1½	teaspoons dried basil, crushed

1 In a 3½- or 4-quart slow cooker layer meatballs and vegetables. In a medium bowl stir together tomatoes, mushroom gravy, water, and basil; pour over meatballs and vegetables.

2 Cover and cook on low-heat setting for 6 to 8 hours or on high-heat setting for 3 to 4 hours.

FOR A 5- TO 6-QUART SLOW COOKER: Double the recipe.

Nutrition Facts per serving: 458 cal., 32 g total fat (14 g sat. fat), 87 mg chol., 2,003 mg sodium, 23 g carbo., 5 g fiber, 21 g pro.

PREP:

10 minutes

COOK:

*6 to 8 hours
(low-heat setting) or*

*3 to 4 hours
(high-heat setting)*

MAKES:

4 servings

Put this beefy soup in the slow cooker before you leave for work. On the way home, pick up a fresh loaf of bread from an artisan baker, some intriguing cheeses, and a few in-season fruits for a terrific spread to savor when you get home.

BEEF & POTATO SOUP

PREP:

25 minutes

COOK:

8 to 10 hours (low-heat setting) or

4 to 5 hours (high-heat setting)

MAKES:

6 servings

1   pound lean boneless beef chuck pot roast, cut into ¾-inch pieces

1   tablespoon cooking oil

4   cups water

1   14½-ounce can diced tomatoes, undrained

2   cups frozen loose-pack mixed vegetables

2   cups frozen loose-pack hash brown potatoes or 2 medium potatoes, peeled and chopped

1   envelope (½ of a 2-ounce package) dry onion soup mix

1   teaspoon instant beef bouillon granules

⅛   teaspoon black pepper

1   clove garlic, minced, or ⅛ teaspoon garlic powder

1 In a large skillet brown beef pieces, half at a time, in hot oil. Drain off fat. In a 3½- or 4-quart slow cooker combine beef, water, tomatoes, vegetables, potatoes, onion soup mix, beef bouillon granules, pepper, and garlic.

2 Cover and cook on low-heat setting for 8 to 10 hours or on high-heat setting for 4 to 5 hours.

Nutrition Facts per serving: 289 cal., 12 g total fat (4 g sat. fat), 48 mg chol., 519 mg sodium, 26 g carbo., 3 g fiber, 19 g pro.

Put away your measuring spoons—prespiced chili beans with spicy chili gravy is your shortcut ticket to this simple, four-ingredient chili. Bake some refrigerated corn bread sticks for an easy accompaniment.

CHUNKY CHICKEN CHILI

Nonstick cooking spray

12 ounces skinless, boneless chicken thighs, cut into 1-inch pieces

2 15-ounce cans chili beans with spicy chili gravy, undrained

1½ cups frozen pepper stir-fry vegetables (yellow, green, and red peppers and onion)

¾ cup bottled salsa

1 Coat a large saucepan with nonstick cooking spray. Preheat over medium-high heat. Add chicken; cook and stir until brown. Stir in chili beans, vegetables, and salsa.

2 Bring to boiling; reduce heat. Simmer, uncovered, about 7 minutes or until chicken is no longer pink.

Nutrition Facts per serving: 320 cal., 5 g total fat (1 g sat. fat), 70 mg chol., 930 mg sodium, 39 g carbo., 12 g fiber, 29 g pro.

Gravy mix adds a down-home flavor to this soup, while sour cream brings irresistible creaminess and a mild tang.

CREAMY CHICKEN & VEGETABLE STEW

PREP:

30 minutes

COOK:

8 to 9 hours (low-heat setting) or

4 to 4¹/₂ hours (high-heat setting)

MAKES:

6 servings

1¹/₂   pounds skinless, boneless chicken thighs, cut into 1-inch pieces

1   tablespoon cooking oil

1   pound potatoes, peeled and cut into 1-inch pieces

2   cups packaged, peeled baby carrots

2   cups frozen loose-pack cut green beans

1   medium onion, chopped

1   teaspoon dried thyme, crushed

¹/₂   teaspoon salt

¹/₂   teaspoon poultry seasoning

2   cups water

2   0.87-ounce envelopes dry chicken gravy mix

1   8-ounce carton dairy sour cream

1   In a large skillet brown chicken, half at a time, in hot oil. Drain off fat.

2   Transfer chicken to a 3¹/₂- or 4-quart slow cooker. Stir in potatoes, carrots, green beans, onion, thyme, salt, and poultry seasoning. In a small bowl stir together water and chicken gravy mix; stir into mixture in slow cooker.

3   Cover and cook on low-heat setting for 8 to 9 hours or on high-heat setting for 4 to 4¹/₂ hours.

4   In a medium bowl gradually stir about 1 cup of the hot chicken mixture into the sour cream. Add sour cream mixture to cooker, stirring gently until combined.

Nutrition Facts per serving: 344 cal., 14 g total fat (6 g sat. fat), 107 mg chol., 769 mg sodium, 26 g carbo., 4 g fiber, 26 g pro.

Think you're all thumbs when it comes to making dumplings? Biscuit mix makes them a snap!

CHICKEN STEW WITH CORNMEAL DUMPLINGS

$1\frac{1}{2}$ cups water

1   envelope ($\frac{1}{2}$ of a 1.8-ounce package)
dry onion-mushroom soup mix

$1\frac{1}{2}$ pounds skinless, boneless chicken breasts or thighs,
cut into bite-size pieces

3   medium potatoes, peeled and cubed

3   medium carrots, sliced

1   teaspoon dried sage, crushed

$\frac{1}{8}$ teaspoon black pepper

1     $7\frac{3}{4}$-ounce package cheese-garlic or 3-cheese
complete biscuit mix

$\frac{1}{4}$ cup cornmeal

PREP:
20 minutes
COOK:
10 minutes + 15 minutes
MAKES:
6 servings

1   In a 4-quart Dutch oven stir together water and onion-mushroom soup mix. Add chicken, potatoes, carrots, dried sage, and pepper. Bring to boiling; reduce heat. Simmer, covered, for 10 to 15 minutes or until vegetables are almost tender.

2   Meanwhile, prepare biscuit mix according to package directions, except stir cornmeal into dry biscuit mix and increase water to $\frac{3}{4}$ cup. Drop batter in 6 mounds onto simmering chicken mixture. Simmer, covered, for 15 to 20 minutes more or until a toothpick inserted in center of a dumpling comes out clean.

Nutrition Facts per serving: 379 cal., 9 g total fat (3 g sat. fat), 66 mg chol., 651 mg sodium, 42 g carbo., 3 g fiber, 30 g pro.

What's the twist? It's the tasty flavor combination that comes from spicy sausage, lime-sparked salsa, and the colorful bonus of hominy.

TURKEY CHILI WITH A TWIST

12   ounces uncooked bulk turkey Italian sausage or ground turkey

2   15-ounce cans chili beans with chili gravy, undrained

1   15-ounce can golden hominy, drained

1   cup bottled salsa with lime

²/₃   cup water

¹/₃   cup sliced green onions

1 In a large saucepan cook turkey sausage until brown. Stir in chili beans, hominy, salsa, and water. Heat through. Sprinkle with green onions.

Nutrition Facts per serving: 470 cal., 11 g total fat (3 g sat. fat), 45 mg chol., 1,897 mg sodium, 64 g carbo., 16 g fiber, 28 g pro.

This slow-simmering soup tickles your taste buds with the robust flavors of Tex-Mex cooking—jalapeño peppers, black beans, cilantro, and chili powder.

VEGGIE SOUTHWEST SOUP

4	14½-ounce cans stewed tomatoes, undrained
2	15-ounce cans black beans, rinsed and drained
2	cups chopped celery
2	cups water
1	15¼-ounce can whole kernel corn, drained
1	large green sweet pepper, chopped
1	large onion, chopped
1	1.4-ounce package dry vegetable soup mix
1	fresh jalapeño chile pepper, seeded and finely chopped*
1	teaspoon dried cilantro, crushed
1	teaspoon garlic powder
1	teaspoon black pepper
½	teaspoon dried basil, crushed
½	teaspoon chili powder

PREP:
20 minutes
COOK:
2 hours
MAKES:
8 to 10 servings

1 In a 4- to 5-quart Dutch oven combine tomatoes, black beans, celery, water, corn, sweet pepper, onion, vegetable soup mix, jalapeño pepper, cilantro, garlic powder, black pepper, basil, and chili powder.

2 Bring to boiling; reduce heat. Simmer, covered, for 2 hours.

*NOTE: Because chile peppers, such as jalapeños, contain volatile oils that can burn your skin and eyes, avoid direct contact with them as much as possible. When working with chile peppers, cover your hands with plastic bags or wear plastic or rubber gloves. If your bare hands do touch the chile peppers, wash your hands well with soap and warm water.

SLOW COOKER DIRECTIONS: Halve all ingredients, except use one 8-ounce can whole kernel corn and ¼ cup dry vegetable soup mix. In a 3½- or 4-quart slow cooker combine all ingredients. Cover and cook on low-heat setting for 7 to 8 hours or on high-heat setting for 3½ to 4 hours.

Nutrition Facts per serving: 209 cal., 2 g total fat (0 g sat. fat), 0 mg chol., 1,288 mg sodium, 44 g carbo., 7 g fiber, 11 g pro.

INDEX

METRIC INFORMATION

The charts on this page provide a guide for converting measurements from the U.S. customary system, which is used throughout this book, to the metric system.

Product Differences

Most of the ingredients called for in the recipes in this book are available in most countries. However, some are known by different names. Here are some common American ingredients and their possible counterparts:

- Sugar (white) is granulated, fine granulated, or castor sugar.
- Powdered sugar is icing sugar.
- All-purpose flour is enriched, bleached or unbleached white household flour. When self-rising flour is used in place of all-purpose flour in a recipe that calls for leavening, omit the leavening agent (baking soda or baking powder) and salt.
- Light-colored corn syrup is golden syrup.
- Cornstarch is cornflour.
- Baking soda is bicarbonate of soda.
- Vanilla or vanilla extract is vanilla essence.
- Green, red, or yellow sweet peppers are capsicums or bell peppers.
- Golden raisins are sultanas.

Volume and Weight

The United States traditionally uses cup measures for liquid and solid ingredients. The chart below shows the approximate imperial and metric equivalents. If you are accustomed to weighing solid ingredients, the following approximate equivalents will be helpful.

- 1 cup butter, castor sugar, or rice = 8 ounces = 1/2 pound = 250 grams
- 1 cup flour = 4 ounces = 1/4 pound = 125 grams
- 1 cup icing sugar = 5 ounces = 150 grams

Canadian and U.S. volume for a cup measure is 8 fluid ounces (237 ml), but the standard metric equivalent is 250 ml.

1 British imperial cup is 10 fluid ounces.

In Australia, 1 tablespoon equals 20 ml, and there are 4 teaspoons in the Australian tablespoon.

Spoon measures are used for smaller amounts of ingredients. Although the size of the tablespoon varies slightly in different countries, for practical purposes and for recipes in this book, a straight substitution is all that's necessary. Measurements made using cups or spoons always should be level unless stated otherwise.

Common Weight Range Replacements

Imperial / U.S.	Metric
1/2 ounce	15 g
1 ounce	25 g or 30 g
4 ounces (1/4 pound)	115 g or 125 g
8 ounces (1/2 pound)	225 g or 250 g
16 ounces (1 pound)	450 g or 500 g
1 1/4 pounds	625 g
1 1/2 pounds	750 g
2 pounds or 2 1/4 pounds	1,000 g or 1 Kg

Oven Temperature Equivalents

Fahrenheit Setting	Celsius Setting*	Gas Setting
300°F	150°C	Gas Mark 2 (very low)
325°F	160°C	Gas Mark 3 (low)
350°F	180°C	Gas Mark 4 (moderate)
375°F	190°C	Gas Mark 5 (moderate)
400°F	200°C	Gas Mark 6 (hot)
425°F	220°C	Gas Mark 7 (hot)
450°F	230°C	Gas Mark 8 (very hot)
475°F	240°C	Gas Mark 9 (very hot)
500°F	260°C	Gas Mark 10 (extremely hot)
Broil	Broil	Grill

*Electric and gas ovens may be calibrated using celsius. However, for an electric oven, increase celsius setting 10 to 20 degrees when cooking above 160°C. For convection or forced air ovens (gas or electric) lower the temperature setting 25°F/10°C when cooking at all heat levels.

Baking Pan Sizes

Imperial / U.S.	Metric
9×1 1/2-inch round cake pan	22- or 23×4-cm (1.5 L)
9×1 1/2-inch pie plate	22- or 23×4-cm (1 L)
8×8×2-inch square cake pan	20×5-cm (2 L)
9×9×2-inch square cake pan	22- or 23×4.5-cm (2.5 L)
11×7×1 1/2-inch baking pan	28×17×4-cm (2 L)
2-quart rectangular baking pan	30×19×4.5-cm (3 L)
13×9×2-inch baking pan	34×22×4.5-cm (3.5 L)
15×10×1-inch jelly roll pan	40×25×2-cm
9×5×3-inch loaf pan	23×13×8-cm (2 L)
2-quart casserole	2 L

U.S. / Standard Metric Equivalents

1/8 teaspoon = 0.5 ml	
1/4 teaspoon = 1 ml	
1/2 teaspoon = 2 ml	
1 teaspoon = 5 ml	
1 tablespoon = 15 ml	
2 tablespoons = 25 ml	
1/4 cup = 2 fluid ounces = 50 ml	
1/3 cup = 3 fluid ounces = 75 ml	
1/2 cup = 4 fluid ounces = 125 ml	
2/3 cup = 5 fluid ounces = 150 ml	
3/4 cup = 6 fluid ounces = 175 ml	
1 cup = 8 fluid ounces = 250 ml	
2 cups = 1 pint = 500 ml	
1 quart = 1 litre	